Table of Contents

Great Antitrust Enforcers
Lessons from Regulators

Editor
William E. Kovacic

Forewords
Andreas Mundt
Alberto Heimler

106 West 32nd Street, Suite 144, New York, NY 10001, USA
www.concurrences.com
books@concurrences.com

First Printing, September 2023
978-1-954750-04-3 (Paperback)
Library of Congress Control Number: 2023947061

Cover: Yves Buliard, www.yvesbuliard.fr
Book design and layout implementation: Nord Compo

Concurrences Books

Tributes

Eleanor M. Fox – Antitrust Ambassador to the World, *2021*

Herbert Hovenkamp – The Dean of American Antitrust Law, *2021*

Frédéric Jenny – Standing Up for Convergence and Relevance in Antitrust, (Vol. I & II), *2019 & 2021*

Albert Foer – A Consumer Voice in the Antitrust Arena, *2020*

Richard Whish – Taking Competition Law Outside the Box, *2020*

Douglas H. Ginsburg – An Antitrust Professor on the Bench (Vol. I & II), *2018 & 2020*

Wang Xiaoye – The Pioneer of Competition Law in China, *A. Emch, W. Ng (eds.), 2019*

Ian S. Forrester – A Scot without Borders (Vol. I & II), *A. Komninos (eds.), 2015*

William E. Kovacic – An Antitrust Tribute (Vol. I & II), *2013 & 2014*

Practical Books

Global Dictionary of Competition Law, *D. Healey, W. Kovacic, P. Trevisan, R. Whish, 2023*

Antitrust in Life Sciences, *M. Cowie, G. Gordon M. Thill-Tayara, 2023*

Antitrust and the Digital Economy, *Y. Katsoulacos (ed.), 2023 (in collaboration with Competition & Regulation European Summer School and Conference)*

State Aid & the Energy Transition, *D. Buschle, L. Hancher, M.-T. Richter-Kuhnert (eds.), 2023 (in collaboration with the Energy Community)*

State Aid & National Enforcement, *J. Derenne, D. Jouve, C. Lemaire, F. Martucci (eds.), 2023*

Competition Law Treatment of Joint Ventures, *B. Bleicher, N. Campbell, A. Hamilton, N. Hukkinen, A. Khan, A. Mordaunt (eds.), 2022 (in collaboration with the IBA)*

Information Exchange & Related Risks, *Z. Marosi, M. Soares (eds.), 2022 (in collaboration with the IBA)*

Rulemaking Authority of the US Federal Trade Commission, *D. Crane (ed.), 2022*

The International Competition Network at Twenty, *D. Anderson & P. Lugard (eds.), 2022*

Competition Case Law Digest – 5th Edition, *F. Jenny, N. Charbit (eds.), 2022*

Competition Inspections in 21 Jurisdictions – A Practitioner's Guide, *N. Jalabert-Doury (ed.), 2022*

Perspectives on Antitrust Compliance, *A. Riley, A. Stephan, A. Tubbs (eds.), 2022 (in collaboration with the ICC)*

Turkish Competition Law, *G. Gürkaynak, 2021*

Competition Law – Climate Change & Environmental Sustainability, *S. Holmes, D. Middelschulte, M. Snoep (eds.), 2021*

Merger Control in Latin America – A Jurisdictional Guide, *P. Burnier da Silveira, P. Sittenfeld (eds.), 2020*

Competition Inspections under EU Law – A Practitioner's Guide, *N. Jalabert-Doury, 2020*

Gun Jumping in Merger Control – A Jurisdictional Guide, *C. Hatton, Y. Comtois, A. Hamilton (eds.), 2019 (in collaboration with the IBA)*

Choice – A New Standard for Competition Analysis? *P. Nihoul (ed.), 2016*

PhD Theses

Reform of Chinese State-Owned Enterprises, *X. Bai, 2023*

Bargaining Power, Competition and Innovation, *M. Guignard, 2023*

Competition & Regulation in Network Industries – Essays in Industrial Organization, *J-M. Zogheib, 2021*

The Role of Media Pluralism in the Enforcement of EU Competition Law, *K. Bania, 2019*

Buyer Power, *I. Herrera Anchustegui, 2017*

General Interest

Women and Antitrust – Voices from the Field (Vol I & II), *E. Kurgonaite & K. Nordlander, 2020*

Conference Proceedings

Antitrust in Emerging and Developing Countries – (Vol I & II), *E. Fox, H. First, 2015 & 2016*

Global Antitrust Law – Current Issues in Antitrust Law and Economics, *D. Ginsburg, J. Wright, (eds.) 2015*

Competition Law on the Global Stage – David Gerber's Global Competition Law in Perspective, *D. Gerber, 2014*

Foreword

Andreas Mundt

President, Bundeskartellamt
Chair, ICN Steering Group
Member of the Bureau, OECD Competition Committee

I remember very well sitting with Bill Kovacic in Cartagena, Colombia, talking about what it is like leading an agency, remembering how it was when starting the job and what would have been helpful to know at that time. On the one hand, you cannot really try it out, simulate it; the day you start, the job will be very different to any other position in the agency. On the other hand, as always in life, preparation is key for success. An athlete cannot simulate the atmosphere and pressure at a tournament, but being well trained and well advised, ideally by a person that has been in the same situation before and can share first-hand experience, will not just help, it is generally acknowledged practice. This book is a wonderful project – I am pretty sure that I would have read all the interviews before my first day in office, and even today they are a valuable inspiration.

We conducted the interview in Cartagena because that is where the 2019 ICN Annual Conference took place, bringing together agency representatives and non-governmental advisors from around the globe. Traditionally, the event attracts many agency heads, and each ICN Annual Conference features at least one head of agencies-only session. For me, exchanging ideas with colleagues is an important element of my work because of two reasons. First, as the head of a competition agency I can confirm that when you are in the front line, it is a great advantage having allies. Second, I firmly believe that good relationships, deeper insight and mutual trust at the leadership level facilitate cooperation at the working level enormously.

My special thanks go to Bill and Concurrences for initiating and conducting this project which provides a rare, and also personal, look behind the scenes and reminds veterans and aspiring colleagues that it is worth talking and listening to each other. However, the ultimate goal is not to create a feel-good atmosphere for agency leaders. As competition law enforcers we have an important task, a social responsibility. This is not only true for the leaders of an authority, but for every single member of staff. If we can learn from each other and strengthen each other to do successful work, everyone benefits.

Foreword

Alberto Heimler
Professor, Scuola Nazionale dell'Amministrazione

When Bill interviewed me[1], I very much appreciated the way he approached us, not forgetting the human element of antitrust enforcement. Indeed, there is always something very special and unique that leads us into our profession. Many years ago, in one of the bureau dinners that accompany our OECD competition committee meetings in Paris, our host, an ambassador, led the discussion asking everybody around the table what had brought each of us into antitrust. The answers were so interesting and diverse that I was astonished and enlightened. Sometimes it is just an occasion that made us what we are, sometimes it is a certain determination. But, in any case, nothing happens without attitude and passion. Yes, in order to succeed in what we do, capacity and knowledge are important, but even more essential is the passion we bring in. And indeed, the passion and love which each of us puts in our profession and in our public life characterize the interviews in this book. The merit is mainly of Bill, who was able to extract all this from us, but of course also thanks to the publisher.

As for my own experience, I became involved in antitrust by chance (I became one of the directors of the newly created Italian antitrust authority in early 1991). I was

1 One of the very minor side effects of the Covid pandemic and the subsequent lockdowns was the fact that my interview with Bill disappeared from the computer it was stored in. I will very briefly summarize here what I had said.

really attracted by the unique blend of antitrust and its analytical rigor associated to public policy. The economic approach to antitrust enforcement that the OECD was promoting in those early years fascinated me; and my main contribution was trying to transfer the same approach into public policy. I proposed the creation of the OECD working party on competition and regulation and have been chairing it since the start. I contributed with the experience gained in Italy with competition advocacy and the important, very simple insight that first market failures have to be identified, and second the least restrictive public interventions to overcome them have to be found. The OECD competition assessment toolkit (which was developed in the early 2000) follows this approach and is indeed very effective and helpful both for developed and developing countries.

This brings me to my second point. In public policy there is a political and a technical dimension. The political approach is mainly driven by our heart, the technical dimension by our brain. Public policy needs both heart and brain but with the right balance. The economic approach to regulation tries to identify that balance, which is why I believe that it is so important. It allows technical discussions on the approach to take, where pros and cons are easily identified and weighted, without the animosity that characterizes the political debate. At best, this leads to better and more appropriate public interventions.

Altogether, the choice of a leader for an antitrust authority is very challenging. Capacity and knowledge are important but not essential. What we need are visionary people who are down to earth at the same time. Having met many chairs of competition authorities in the course of the years this blend is difficult to identify ex ante. What is important for a good leader is to be able to make decisions, but also to be an attentive listener. Listening (which also means reading) enriches us and makes us evolve. Lastly, we must be able to act. These personal characteristics matter the most for being an effective leader. They are difficult but not impossible to identify when you are still a candidate. Reading the interviews in this book will certainly help.

Contributors

Skaidrīte Ābrama

Tembinkosi Bonakele

Terry Calvani

Andrea Coscelli

Carles Esteva Mosso

Allan Fels

John Fingleton

Peter Freeman

Douglas Ginsburg

Antonio Gomes

Michal Halperin

Frédéric Jenny

Francis Kariuki

Bruno Lasserre

Norman Manoim

Andreas Mundt

Maureen Ohlhausen

John Pecman

Eduardo Pérez Motta

James Rill

Barbara Rosenberg

Sheridan Scott

Jacques Steenbergen

Mariana Tavares de Araujo

Han Li Toh

Leading a Competition Agency

William E. Kovacic*

Introduction

Commentary on competition policy is long on advice to agency leaders about what policies to adopt, but short on how to carry them out. Getting from a policy aspiration to its actual accomplishment is a hard journey. As a university undergraduate, I worked part time for a newspaper, and I had many occasions to see the gap between theory and practice. I once covered a college tennis match in which the home team's first singles player was taking a beating. Between sets the player asked the team's coach how to stem the onslaught. The coach furrowed his brow and said, "Hit winners."

The coach's conceptually sound advice said nothing about *how* to hit winners; he sidestepped the crucial matter of implementation. We can pose a similar question for competition policy: how does a competition agency leader hit policy winners? What techniques improve the likelihood of good policy results? Senior leaders usually acquire useful implementation knowhow on the job. Sometimes this learning is captured in accessible written form – for

* Global Competition Professor of Law and Policy, George Washington University Law School; Visiting Professor, King's College London.

example, in books,[1] journal articles,[2] oral histories,[3] or interviews.[4] In many (perhaps most) other instances, the knowhow is transmitted, if at all, as an evanescent, unwritten oral tradition that fades away as the original actors and their acquaintances leave public life. Hard won lessons from experience, the good and the bad, gradually disappear, only to be relearned by new generations of leaders.

The motivation for this volume, and the project that supported it, is to preserve a larger amount of the knowhow that agency leaders acquire in doing the job. In the first group of what we anticipate to be a longer series of interviews, we asked 25 current and former agency leaders from around the world to reflect on fundamental questions about leading a competition agency – in particular, to consider what they have learned in the course of leading an agency that they wished they had known on the first day in the senior leadership role. The interviews yielded an abundance of helpful observations about how to lead a competition agency, as well as fascinating portraits of the paths that the interviewees took to reach the pinnacle of their institutions. We asked the interviewees to reflect upon what their successors ought to know about agency leadership, and they responded magnificently. We are extremely grateful to all of the enforcers for their generous participation. Edited transcripts of the interviews appear below, and videos of the interviews are available on the *Concurrences* web page.

---

1 Among the most informative accounts are two volumes on the career of Allan Fels, who chaired the Australia Competition and Consumer Commission from 1995 to 2003. Allan Fels, Tough Customer: Chasing a better deal for battlers (2019); Fred Benchley, Allan Fels: A Portrait of Power (2004). Another outstanding example is Michael Pertschuk's account of his tenure as a member of the Federal Trade Commission from 1977 to 1984 and his time as chair from 1977 to 1981. Michael Pertschuk, Revolt Against Regulation: The Rise and Pause of the Consumer Movement (1982).

2 For example, during and after his term as chair of the FTC from 2001 to 2004, Timothy Muris published several papers dealing with an agency's definition of priorities and its determination of priorities for realizing its stated goals. Timothy J. Muris, Principles for a Successful Competition Agency, 72 University of Chicago Law Review 165 (2005); Timothy J. Muris, Looking Forward: The Federal Trade Commission and the Future Development of Competition Policy, 2003 Columbia Business Law Review 359 (2003).

3 The oral history project of the American Bar Association's Antitrust Law Section includes interviews of numerous former heads of competition agencies. Some individual agency leaders have prepared oral histories that have been preserved by university research libraries or professional societies. Examples include oral histories prepared by former FTC board members Rand Dixon (John F. Kennedy Library), Phillip Elman (Columbia University Center for Oral History), Robert Pitofsky (Historical Society of the D.C. Circuit).

4 In a conversation published by the Antitrust Law Journal in 2005, former FTC chairs Timothy Muris and Robert Pitofsky devoted extensive attention to policy implementation issues at the Commission. More than Law Enforcement: The FTC's Many Tools – A Conversation with Tim Muris and Bob Pitofsky, 72 Antitrust Law Journal 773 (2004). In 2009, the FTC published a report that presented policy implementation suggestions provided in roundtable discussions with, among other participants, current and former competition agency heads around the world. The Commission also placed the roundtable transcripts on the agency's website. William E. Kovacic, Chair, Federal Trade Commission, The Federal Trade Commission at 100: Into Our Second Century (2009).

Our primary intended audience for the interviews consists of current and future competition agency leaders. The interviews offer important general observations and practical advice about how to address challenges that immediately confront a new agency head and demand attention throughout the leader's tenure. The officials interviewed for this volume provided guidance that cannot be easily obtained, or gathered at all, from the written sources mentioned above.

We are confident that the volume will be especially valuable for prospective or new appointees. It will give them a clearer idea of what is coming at them and reveal how demanding the leadership role can be. I served one year as chair of the U.S. Federal Trade Commission (FTC), from March 2008 to March 2009. My earlier experiences at the FTC (as a junior attorney, general counsel, and a commissisoner) and as a researcher had given me an idea of what the role of chair required. When I became the agency's chair, the experience was still overwhelming. Nonetheless, it was invaluable to me to understand in advance what the position required, and to have the advice of many who had performed the role before.

Our intended audience extends beyond those who lead, or are about to lead, competition authorities. A secondary aim in describing the characteristics of good competition agency leadership is to guide those responsible for nominating and confirming candidates for high office. This volume identifies the types of professional experience and personality traits that help predict success in an agency leader. In setting out these characteristics, we also seek to encourage the competition policy community of academics, advocacy groups, practitioners, and government officials to urge political leadership to nominate the best possible candidates.

The remainder of this introduction distills some of the principal insights from the interviews. It is not a comprehensive summary, but the main themes of the interviews appear here. The discussion proceeds in three parts. The first section describes a self-assessment exercise that prospective nominees should perform to prepare for leadership positions. The self-assessment involves benchmarking the new appointee by reference to desirable characteristics for a competition agency leader. The second section identifies specific suggestions for how the appointee should perform the leadership role. The final section discusses the need to make the observations of this volume and related work accessible to new appointees and to those who recently have assumed leadership roles.

Desiderata in Competition Agency Leaders: Capabilities and Experiences

Taken as a group, the interviews for this volume identified capabilities and experiences that best prepare a candidate for the leadership role. The section lays out the desiderata and then sketches how a candidate can compensate for limitations in experience, knowledge, or personality. No individual candidate for appointment to high office scores perfectly on all criteria. Successful leaders honestly take stock of their strengths and weaknesses and seek, through various means, to correct for weaknesses and take the best possible advantage of strengths.

Desiderata for a Competition Agency Leader

The following is a roster of desirable characteristics for a competition agency leader.

Knowledge of the economy. An appointee should have broad knowledge of the jurisdiction's economy and the forces that shape commerce. This is an indispensable foundation for effective leadership of a competition agency. The appointee can gain this knowledge from various sources, including academic study and previous employment experience in the private sector or public service. To some degree, an appointee can acquire the requisite knowledge of the economy on the job at the competition agency, but it is a terrible disadvantage to enter a leadership role without it.

Awareness of the Enabling Environment. Successful agency leaders resemble astute midfielders in the global sport of football. They see the entire pitch in depth, they comprehend the flow of the match, and they grasp how the interaction of all players (on one's own side and on the opponent's team) create opportunities to be exploited and vulnerabilities to shore up.

Well-prepared appointees understand the roles of all of the institutions outside the walls of the agency; these include the legislature, government ministers, other regulators, courts, academic hubs, the media, advocacy groups, professional societies, and the business community. To a large degree, the appointee must apply the perspective of a political scientist who recognizes how the agency's success depends on how skillfully it interacts with these external institutions and players. The broader the experience an appointee has had in working with all of these institutions, the better prepared the appointee will be to lead a competition agency.

Communications Skills. The head of a competition agency is the main face of the agency to external bodies and to the public at large. A vital role of the leader is to communicate the agency's program to external bodies and to respond to interventions about the agency's program. This role places a premium on deftness in dealing with media organizations, with legislators, and with other government bodies.

External communication is integral to the use of competition policy instruments other than the litigation of cases and promulgation of substantive rules. Publicity can be a powerful means of policymaking, and the agency leader stands on center stage as the institution's chief spokesperson. Other agency personnel can and should participate in media interviews and other forms of outreach, but the leader is the main face of the agency. Moreover, an important function of many competition agencies is to serve as an advocate for the adoption of procompetitive policies across the government. The agency leader ordinarily is the foremost voice in advocacy initiatives. The capacity for effective communications also is necessary for the leader to inform the agency's own staff and to motivate them to pursue the leader's suggested program.

Not all appointees relish these responsibilities. Some individuals thrive in the role, and others perform it with reluctance. Individuals who could be described as introverts might be predisposed to avoid the types of encounters the communications role entails. Whether the role seems appealing or appalling, the appointee must be prepared to do it, and do it well.

A Vision for the Agency: Having the Job Versus Doing Something the Job. An infinite distance separates appointees who want the job for the prestige it confers and those who want the job because they aspire to carry out a program. If the leader finds value chiefly in the perquisites amd trappings of the role (e.g., invitations to elegant public gatherings, the sound of being called "chair" or "the honorable"), the agency will sag. If the government has a habit of using leadership appointments to reward loyal political operatives, mercenaries with limited interest in the agency's substantive mission will appear with unfortunate frequency.

Effective leaders come to the agency with a vision for its future – a perspective informed by an awareness of the aims that inspired the agency's creation and an understanding of the types of programs that will fulfill the agency's mandate. Appointees who come to the job with extensive familiarity with the agency's work and knowledge of the jurisdiction's economy are best situated to devise a successful positive agenda. An ideal agenda preserves good work and practices that already are in place and adds new initiatives regarding the agency's substantive programs, organization, and processes.

Long-term Orientation. Successful agencies require continuing investments (e.g., in research, facilities, and administrative infrastructure) that improve performance over time but may not yield observable events for which incumbent agency leaders can claim credit while in office. Good leadership requires sound judgments about allocating resources, respectively, to "consumption" in the form of launching new cases or rules versus "investment" in building agency capability to initiate better rules and cases in the future.[5] Effective leaders fully understand that ongoing investments in capability are necessary even though the good results from these investments may not emerge until well after an incumbent leader has departed.

A fascination with short-term credit-claiming can lead an agency to commence projects that at first attract acclaim but ultimately fail because the agency lacked the capacity to execute them successfully. Ambition is a powerful motivation for individual behavior and, often, a necessary spur to beneficial accomplishments. The ambition fueled by the desire for individual recognition must be disciplined by fidelity to the agency's longer-term needs. The larger surrounding community should press the leader to make necessary investments in capability and applaud leaders who make them. If the agency performs well, there will be glory enough to go around for all.

Accept Blame and Deflect Credit. In public presentations, good leaders accept responsibility for agency failures, and they generously give credit to agency personnel for successful agency initiatives. Inside the house, good leaders examine failures for the purpose of doing better the next time and not to seek scapegoats. The leader's self-effacing attitude also is instrumental in creating positive internal moral and demonstrating the leader's commitment to the long-term success of the institution.

Timely and Decisive Decision Making. Effective leaders have the capacity to make timely and decisive decisions about agency matters. This applies to issues involving the agency's substantive program (e.g., whether to give a green light to a proposed project) or to administrative issues (e.g., whom to appoint

5 William E. Kovacic & David A. Hyman, Consume or Invest: What Do (and Should) Agency Leaders Maximize?, 91 University of Washington Law Review 295 (2016).

to an agency post where two or more capable internal candidates are seeking the job). An individual who, by personality or habit, is inclined to postpone decisions repeatedly is akin to an air traffic controller who tells arriving aircraft to continue to circle the field. This demoralizes agency staff and slows the agency's production line to a crawl.

Previous Management Experience. The leadership roles in most competition agencies come with significant management duties. Many agency leaders also are the chief operating officers of their institutions. This role includes responsibility not only for the substantive program (e.g., agenda setting) but also for important administrative decisions involving personnel, budget, and facilities. Even when many of these management tasks are delegated to another senior official (e.g., a director general), the agency leader remains deeply involved in management duties regarding the establishment of policy strategy and priorities, the appointment of key personnel, and the development of relationships with important external constitutencies.

Appointees to top leadership posts are likely to perform these management duties more effectively if they have previous significant management experience – best of all, experience in a managing another regulatory body or a substantial division of another regulatory authority. As suggested above, a continuous stream of substantive and administrative matters requires the agency leader to make many decisions each day. The ability to make these decisions in a timely and effective manner generally increases as the leader's knowledge and base of management experience expands. Knowledge and experience combine to form intuition that guides the leader toward better decisions. It is a serious disadvantage to be thrust into a top leadership role that entails important management duties if the candidate has never managed another organization or a major unit of another body.

Openness to Criticism (Especially in Internal Agency Deliberations). Constructive debate and hearing out contrarian views are valuable means for an agency to make sound decisions. Organizations that demand obeisance to the leader's views and stifle debate invite peril. Agency leaders must embrace this disciple as a general principle of agency operations and in their own behavior. In many areas of life, the heads of institutions are trained to tell subordinates to speak their minds and not merely parrot the leader's stated views. In practice, a number of leaders who espouse this precept shun or berate subordinates who contradict the leader.

Openness to criticism does not oblige the leader to agree with dissenters. It requires the leader to listen and explain why their recommendations have or have not been accepted.

Emotional, Mental, and Physical Resilience. The leadership of a competition agency can be stressful and grueling. As suggested above, the formulation of the agency's substantive program, the communication of the agency's program to external bodies (e.g., legislative committees), and the fulfillment of various management duties place agency leaders on a high-speed treadmill that never lets up. Th leader's execution of these responsibilities does not always attract praise from outside or inside the agency. Criticism can be severe and, in the era of uninhibited expression on social media, caustic and savagely personal. Emotional, mental, and physical resilience is necessary to carry on effectively. Otherwise, the job can devour the occupant.

For Members of a Multimember Board, Collegiality. A substantial majority of the world's 140 or so competition agencies are governed by multimember boards.[6] A basic degree of collegiality is essential if the board is to function effectively. The multimember framework does not require unanimity of thought. The expression of competing views can serve crucial quality control functions. At the same time, courtesy and respect in relating disagreements is necessary to preserve trust without which boards founder..

The chair of a multimember board must exert special effort to engage non-chair colleagues and promote a constructive environment in board deliberations. The chair must understand that many or all of the non-chair members believe they would be better chairs than the incumbent chair. The desire to escape the shadow of the chair can inspire non-chair members to engage in "look at me" behavior that degrades the agency's brand. The chair can subdue centrifugal impulses by lavishing praise on colleagues, consulting them regularly, and taking the "accept blame and deflect credit" precept, mentioned above, to heart in dealing with other colleagues.

Historical Awareness. Knowledge of the history of the agency is a valuable asset for a competition agency leader. Among other contributions, historical awareness provides insights into what an agency can do to increase its prospects for success and to avoid serious errors. It identifies conditions in the external environment that facilitate effective policy making, and it reveals

6 William E. Kovacic & Marianela Lopez-Galdos, Lifecycles of Competition Systems: Explaining Variation in the Implementation Regimes, 79 Journal of Law & Contemporary Problems 85 (2016).

processes the agency can adopt to improve project selection and execution. Learning an agency's origins and evolution should be a high priority for an appointee who is unfamiliar with the agency.

Understanding of Competition Policy. In my earlier days as an academic, I considered deep substantive expertise in competition policy to be an indispensable prerequisite to appointment to the leadership of a competition agency. From my own experience and in light of the interviews for this project, I have modified my views. Deep knowledge of the technical features of competition law is less important for an appointee who has broad knowledge of the economy and a related understanding of the competitive environment. Such a nominee can acquire a suitable understanding of competition policy by studying the technical elements of competition law on the job. For example, for agency leadership roles, I would prefer to appoint a person with deep economic knowledge, strong awareness of the enabling environment, good communications capability, and demonstrated management skills rather than a candidate with profound understanding of competition policy but few of the other characteristics mentioned here.

Personal Self-Assessment: Compensating for Limitations

The criteria set out above provide a baseline for prospective appointees to assess their suitability for leadership. An honest self-assessment takes stock of strengths and weaknesses with respect to substantive knowledge, experience, and personality. There are no perfect candidates. A person's weaknesses need not be disabling if the candidate takes steps to compensate for them. There is no shame in lacking certain personal traits, capabilities, or professional background. The shame for an appointee (or an existing leader) comes from failing to recognize limitations and take steos to mitigate them.

The most important means to compensate for an appointee's limitations is for the appointee to assemble a team that offsets the leader's weaknesses. A supporting team with strong knowledge of disciplines relevant to the agency's substantive mandate can help guide a leader who comes to the agency with limited knowledge in these fields. A strong-minded chief of staff can help a leader overcome a tendency to delay decisions by pressing the leader to act. A seasoned team of senior managers can help the leader bear the burden of administrative management duties for which the leader's experience has provided no preparation.

An honest self-diagnosis grounded in the desiderata set out above can show the path to accumulating the expertise that will help the leader overcome weaknesses. This works for some weaknesses (e.g., gaps in management experience or substantive knowledge in competition policy). There may be no antidote for an appointee's deeply engrained compulsion for self-aggrandizement, myopic attention on short-term credit-claiming activities, and disregard for investments needed to ensure good policy making over the longer term. Indeed, an unrepentant mercenary is unlikely to carry out an honest self-assessment in the first place. It is the duty of political leadership to screen out such candidates in the first place.

Good Leadership Practices

Our interviews identified a number of specific steps that agency leaders can take to improve their effectiveness. The discussion above has highlighted one such step: building a management team and personal staff that complements the leader's own strengths and compensates for gaps in the leader's background. Presented below are additional measures that leaders can take to perform their roles better.

Pre-Appointment Preparation. There are a number of resources that a leadership appointee can draw upon to prepare for the new assignment. One of the most important is the community of those who have led the agency in the past or who have similar positions in agencies outside the appointee's jurisdiction. Predecessors can identify the challenges facing the agency and offer suggestions for addressing them. Predecessors can convey knowhow about the customs and norms that shape behavior within the agency and offer views about the capabilities of existing personnel.

A second valuable source of information is the agency's senior managers and professional staff. For new appointees, the staff ordinarily prepares a comprehensive briefing of existing projects and key administrative matters such as the existing allocation of resources within the agency's budget. The appointee should study this material carefully and discuss it with senior managers before the term of office begins. It is most helpful to develop an accurate sense of the agency's programmatic assets and liabilities, especially in the form of hard problems that previous management sidestepped.

In the run up to the senior leadership post, the appointee should obtain a clear view of the timetable for the inventory of matters in progress and those proposed for approval. It is helpful to have staff identify matters that will require attention in the first two weeks, the first few months, and in the first year. Special care is required for important matters that require a decision in the short term. The appointee should form an independent assessment of the merits of inherited pending matters and not to assume automatically that they warrant approval or require no amendment. The failure to bear down on such matters can result in the mechanical approval of significant initiatives that ought to have been vetted more rigorously and can become a burden upon the agency (and a millstone around the leader's neck).

A third useful form of preparation consists of courses and readings that deal with the art of public administration. One of the most promising instructional offerings is a short course on agency management offered in the summer by CRESSE and the Competition Committee of the Organization for Economic Cooperation and Development. A helpful list of readings on agency leadership would include works such as Malcolm Sparrow's *The Regulatory Craft*[7] and Richard Neustadt's and Ernest May's *Thinking in Time*.[8] Even appointees with previous experience in regulatory agency management will learn a lot from these volumes.

Choosing Advisors and the Senior Management Team. The capabilities and character of the leader's personal staff are major determinants of the leader's success. One requirement, described above, is that the leader's inner circle complements the leader's own skills and compensates for weaknesses. No person is more important than the leader's chief of staff who, in effect, is the leader's alter ego in dealing with internal and external constituencies. The chief of staff should have good personal sensibilities, be familiar with the agency, and be well-suited to cope with the frantic demands associated with being the leader's gatekeeper.

It is probably best that the remainder of the leader's cabinet consist of some agency insiders and some advisors brought in from outside the agency. The insiders can explain the existing state of the agency and illuminate significant institutional features that do not show up on the formal organization chart or handbook of agency procedures. Well-informed outsiders bring a perspective that may reflect more accurately the perceptions of the agency by important external

7 Malcolm K. Sparrow, The Regulatory Craft (2000).

8 Richard E. Neustadt & Ernest A. May, Thinking in Time (1987).

observers, such as courts and legislators. In all of these choices, the leader should actively control the hiring process and not simply inherit the professional staff that has served a soon-to-be-departed agency leader.

A further important set of personnel decisions involves the agency's senior management team, including heads of key operating units. In some jurisdictions, the leadership appointee controls the selection of senior managements. In other countries, personnel rules and agency customs severely limit the replacement of incumbent managers. To the greatest extent possible, the appointee should seek to obtain senior managers who share the appointee's vision of the agency. Their attitude and capabilities are important because the leadership appointee must delegate significant tasks to them. (The willingness to delegate, to one's immediate staff and to senior managers is essential if the agency leader is to function effectively.)

The best leaders encourage subordinates to express their views candidly whether or not they agree with the leader. This is especially important for the leader's personal staff. Their special access to the leader gives the inner circle greater opportunities to give advice that helps correct deficiencies, avoid errors, and make policy and operational choices that improve agency performance.

Being the Center of Attention. An appointee needs to be aware that the spotlight always shines on the leader, inside and outside the agency. The leader always stands at center stage. Comments or behavior that would be unremarkable or invisible for a junior case handler or a mid-level manager assumes outsized significance when the actor is the agency leader. No move is unnoticed.[9] Everything is magnified. Thus, a comment that is spoken at an intended volume of two to a journalist is reported at a volume of nine or ten. The fact of ubiquitous observation by external observers and by the agency's staff requires anticipation about how different audiences will respond to specific forms of behavior. The leader should assume in all instances that a flamboyant comment or reckless act will be reported widely and swiftly.

One dimension of the ubiquitous observation consists of public access to records statutes. A variety of laws give outsiders (e.g., journalists) access to a wide array of agency records, including the leader's calendar of appointments, emails, text

9 This extends to mundane matters such as the choice of clothing. If the leader wears the same necktie, scarf, or suit with some regularity, you can be sure that some agency employees are keeping score.

messages, internet posts, and social network communications. Agency leaders should assume that third parties beyond their control will see the content of these communications and related records.[10]

Defining Goals and Settting Priorities. The leader's chief substantive responsibility is to define the agency's aims and to set priorities for achieving them. This gives external audiences a clear view of what the agency will seek to accomplish and plays a vital role in making the agency accountable for its policy choices. The leader's statement of ends and means also guides the agency's staff in allocating resources and developing projects. Appointees who lack broad knowledge of the economy and the commercial forces that shape competition are in a weak position to carry out this task effectively.[11]

Communicating Agency Themes. As the main face of the agency to external and external constituencies, the leader must master the vital role of communications. Working with a foundation of well-defined goals and priorities, the leader must appear frequently before external and internal audiences to explain the institution's program, respond to queries, and discuss specific initiatives to execute the agency's substantive plans. Every appearance within and outside the agency is an opportunity to frame the agency's program and build a positive brand. There is no such thing as a routine speech or internal workshop that can be mailed in.

Audiences inside and outside the agency form deep impressions about the institution's quality based on their perception of the thoughtfulness and knowledge of the leader. The leader should be mindful that each presentation or public appearance may be the only occasion that some members of the audience have to observe the speaker. Not only do external audiences measure the agency leader in each public engagement, so too do the agency's staff. It is inspiring for agency personnel to see their leader excel at a public platform. It is disheartening to see a leader sleepwalk through a speech or stumble about for want of good preparation or understanding of the agency's mission.

10 A recurring source of unhappiness for agency leaders is the tendency of their friends to send messages that vividly discuss the inadequacies of the leader's colleagues or important public officials whom the leader deals with regularly. These messages generally are fair game for disclosure.

11 As part of the pre-appointment self-assessment described above, appointees should ask themselves why they want to take the job. Good answers to this question spell out the substantive ends to which the leader intends to apply the agency's authority and identify possibilities for institutional adjustments that will improve the functioning of the agency itself. Bad answers focus on enjoyment of the glamour of high public office and the possibilities for professional advancement once the tenure in office ends.

Respecting and Learning from Past Agency Accomplishments. There is an unfortunate tendency in many areas of life for the heads of organizations to demonstrate their genius by belittling the earlier work of their institutions and those who led them. Too many agency leaders have concluded that the best way to magnify their own achievements is to show how badly previous agency heads performed their duties. An inclination to vilify the past is accentuated by partisanship that is an inevitable residue of a regime change.[12]

The technique of mocking the past to burnish an incumbent leader's image imposes real costs upon the agency and, often enough, the new appointee. The disparaging behavior undermines the morale and trust of professional staff who must execute the new leader's program. Even when an agency has encountered hard times (owing, for example, to the improvident selection or execution of projects), it is rarely appropriate the leader to denounce the agency or its staff. Few agencies are utterly bereft of positive accomplishments. A leader inclined to denigrate the past may well overlook policy initiatives or techniques that deserve emulation. It is not only dishonest to disregard earlier achievements, but also foolish in that it impairs the implementation of the new leader's program. Leadership predecessors may have devised programs and operational techniques that can serve to accomplish the new appointee's objectives. A leader who ridicules the institution's past management and programs degrades the agency's reputation in the eyes of the larger public and key decision makers who can determine the success or failure of an agency's programs. Among other effects, such behavior can reduce the respect that is necessary for an agency to gain deference from courts.

Good leadership embraces past accomplishments and respects those whose efforts yielded policy successes. Honoring past work (and learning from it) does not preclude new leaders from adding their own initiatives to the policy mix. An impressive example of good practice comes from the establishment of the United Kingdom's Competition and Markets Authority in 2013-2014. The CMA was formed by combining two existing institutions, the Competition Commission and the Office of Fair Trading. Lord David Currie, the chair of the new agency, and Alex Chisholm, the CMA's Executive Director, took care to praise the work of the predecessor agencies; they defined the mission of the newly created institution to do "even better." This approach did not

12 William E. Kovacic, Politics and Partisanship in U.S. Federal Antitrust Enforcement, 79 Antitrust Law Journal 687 (2014).

diminish the stature of the two new leaders inside or outside the CMA. Their behavior increased confidence in their leadership and got the CMA off to a good start.

No Sycophants. As suggested above, new leadership appointees should discourage sycophancy that treats all of the leader's ideas as invariably wise. To build a culture of constructive, critical inquiry. a leader must welcome candor in principle and in practice. Senior officials who urge subordinates to tell them what they need to know sometimes respond badly to advice that collides with the leader's preferences. The agency leader has no obligation to follow the advice of everyone who offers an opinion. After all, the agency leader has the mandate to take decisions. The leader's obligation resides in listening carefully to opposing views before acting.

Accessibility to the Agency's Staff. Agency leaders should make a habit of engaging personally with the staff. Agency personnel usually welcome contact with the chief official. Accessibility comes in a number of forms. One occasion for contact is meetings on cases or other projects. When the leader receives briefings, the leader should invite junior case workers in addition to heads of unit. Another method to demonstrate accessibility is to spend a set amount of time every day reaching out to agency personnel – for example, by taking meals with staff in the agency's canteen or walking the hallways to stop in the offices of agency personnel. There is a lot to be learned from leaving the bridge of the ship and visiting the lower decks. For example, in the engine room where case handlers toil, the leader may gather important information that senior leaders filter out when they brief their superiors.

In reaching out to the agency's staff, it is important not to overlook those who do the unglamorous, bind-the-scenes administrative work that supports the agency's programs. This is especially true for back-office support functions (e.g., budgeting, facilities maintenance, human resources) that form the agency's essential administrative infrastructure. The people who perform these functions deserve recognition; taking them for granted is a serious mistake. Gulliver woke up one day to discover that he could not move because the little people he had underestimated had tied him in knots.

Praising Good Work. One important way that a leader can connect with the agency's staff is to applaud good performance by professionals and the administrative staff. This can take the form of an email, a phone call, a personal visit, a video call, or, even better, a written note. The leader can reach out to staff whom the leader has observed in action or ask senior managers to point out good work done within their units. Even relatively simple gestures of gratitude by the agency leader can generate good will that inspires better agency performance.[13] Never underestimate the value, in any language, of saying "Thank you."

Accepting Responsibility for Failure and Distributing Credit for Success. It is worth repeating the observation presented in the list of leadership desiderata above. When things go badly, effective leaders step forward to take responsibility. They do not blame subordinates. When things go well, effective leaders assign praise to the agency team that did the work. The effective leader takes satisfaction for creating an environment in which the staff can thrive and carry out projects successfully. Leaders should praise publicly and criticize privately. If the staff sees that the leader defines success in terms of team achievement rather than individual glory, they are more likely to embrace a norm that encourages selfless collaboration.

Engaging with the Political Process. A large literature about competition agencies emphasizes the importance of maintaining autonomy from the political process. This advice is sound to the extent that it suggests that agencies must take decisions to prosecute conduct or to take decisions on liability and remedy without political intervention. If courts perceive that political leaders have determined the choice of prosecution targets or the resolution of disputes, they are likely to ignore agency pleas for deference to their technical expertise.

Autonomy in the use of prosecutorial and adjudication authority does not dictate complete isolation from the political process. Regular engagements with heads of state and legislators are necessary in order for agencies to be accountable for their policy choices and to obtain necessary funding, to obtain upgrades to existing powers, and to perform advocacy functions. The agency leader is an indispensable participant in the engagement with political leadership.

Take Time to Renew Intellectual Capital. Leading an agency can feel like being dropped into the center of a cyclone. The urgency to address the myriad matters, planned and unanticipated, that arise each day can deny leaders the

13 In my time as the FTC's General Counsel, the Commission's Chair (Timothy Muris) regularly sent short written notes of thanks to agency staff. I recall how often the recipients framed the Chair's notes and hung them on their office walls.

time needed to learn by reading and by attending events that expose them to new ideas. A number of the agency heads interviewed for this project noted that they take time each day to read as a way of gaining a better perspective.

Preserving Physical Health. Coping with the responsibilities of a leadership position is physically and emotionally draining. It is easy to abandon good habits – a sensible diet, adequate sleep, and regular exercise – that are necessary to sustain strength and generate the energy needed to endure a demanding routine. Attention to good health ensures that the job does not wear the leader down.

Adhering to the Ethical Rules. Most jurisdictions have established an extensive array of ethical rules governing the behavior of public employees and agency leadership. Among other focal points, the ethical codes deal with conflicts of interest, the preservation of confidential information, the use of government property (e.g., computers and mobile phones), acceptance of gratuities from external organizations, and reimbursement for expenses incurred in the course of official business. Scrupulous adherence to these restrictions is essential. The ubiquitous observation from outside and inside the agency also means that violations will be detected, reported, and punished. It is never sensible to proceed on the assumption that nobody will ever know about a transgression, even a minor infringement.

Failure to abide by ethical commands can result in the leader's dismissal or, in extreme circumstances, criminal prosecution. The experience of leading an agency resembles mountain climbing. The views from the leadership summit can be wonderful, but a moment's inattention to the requirements of good climbing practice can be fatal. One misstep, and it is a long way down. Falls do not merely endanger the inattentive climber. Beyond the consequences to the infringer, ethical lapses tend to be widely publicized and damage the agency's reputation.

Learning from the Experience of Other Competition Agencies. The experiences of the world's 140 competition law systems have generated a large body of knowhow about policy implementation beyond the walls of any individual competition agency. Although conditions in individual jurisdictions vary, there is a remarkable commonality in the types of implementation issues – for example, concerning agency organization, governance, priority setting, and project selection – faced by competition agencies. Agencies can proceed down the learning curve of experience more quickly if agencies can consolidate their learning.

Agency leaders can share experience with their counterparts in a variety of settings. Among other fora, these include bilateral consultations, regional cooperation and governance bodies, and larger multinational networks. Discussions about highly sensitive topics (e.g., coping with pressure from political officials) are best conducted in smaller groups where agency leaders are more likely to discuss their experiences candidly. Academic hubs and international organizations perform a useful service by convening workshops and similar mechanisms for conducting smaller group discussions on management for agency leaders.[14]

The leader's engagement with other authorities is generally beneficial, but one caution is appropriate. Leaders must keep in mind that performance of their own competition systems is their principal responsibility. Participation in international gatherings can become a strong attraction for the learning they facilitate and the encouragement and support that international gatherings provide to individual agency leaders. An agency leader must be selective in balancing participation in international engagements with the need to attend to the core mandate – the competition agency's domestic agenda.

Conclusion

Many factors cause competition agencies to rise or fall. The quality of agency leadership is paramount. Great leaders make the most of existing authority and resources and pursue institutional upgrades that improve performance over time. Great leaders can guide thinly funded, underpowered agencies to achieve surprising levels of policy success. Mediocre leaders can bring well-equipped agencies to a standstill or drive them into a wall.

The role of agency leadership is extremely difficult. Theoretical discussions of competition policy often lack realism because they overlook practical implementation challenges. From 1979 to 1983, I worked at the U.S. Federal Trade Commission, first as a junior attorney with the Planning Office of the Bureau of Competition and later as an attorney advisor to a member of the Commission. I then spent three years with a law firm and fifteen years on law school faculties. As an academic, I generously dispensed advice about what competition agencies should do, much like a journalist who reports on sporting events and critiques the players and the teams, Upon returning to the FTC in 2001 as General Counsel,

14 From time to time, the competition law program of Fordham Law School's Corporate Law Institute has conducted excellent workshops on selected management issues for competition agency heads.

I realized how much I had forgotten from my first years at the agency. I had lost touch with how much harder it was to implement policy – or to lead a major operating unit – than to write about it. In other words, there was a world of difference between watching the sport and playing in sport. On the playing field the game is fast, bewildering, and rough.

This volume seeks to enable agency leaders to excel as policymakers. The interviews with enforcers suggest that good leadership has two major ingredients. The first is the appointment of individuals whose knowledge, professional experience, and personal traits have prepared them to lead a competition agency. The interviews reveal characteristics that put an appointee in a better position to surmount the formidable challenges associated with defining goals, selecting a strategy, managing a significant organization, communicating the agency's program to external and internal constitutions, and inspiring agency staff to implement the chosen strategy. An appointments process that consistently gives primacy to these characteristics in selecting candidates greatly increases the competition system's prospects for success.

The second major ingredient of leadership success is the application of practical knowhow derived from the experience of those of who have led competition authorities. Successful competition agencies and other organizations progress by learning from earlier success and failure. Agency leaders can benefit substantially from studying the experience of their predecessors and from the heads of agencies in other jurisdictions. The interviews in this volume capture valuable information, hard won through actual experience, about how leaders can best carry out the daunting, myriad responsibilities that come with the job.

Skaidrīte Ābrama*

Competition Council Of Latvia, Chair (2012-2020)

You have been the Chairperson of the Competition Council of Latvia, initially appointed to that position in 2012, reappointed in 2017, and has been one of the most formidable leaders of competition agencies, especially among the cohort of the many new agencies – nearly one hundred – created since the late 1980s. I would like to begin by asking what path you took professionally to the Chairperson position of the Competition Council; what is the path that brought you there?

My path has been very diverse. Until 2004, I never thought to work for a government agency, or for a competition authority, and to do something with competition policy at all. I was prepared to work for business. Latvia gained independence in the early 1990s, and, thanks to a Swiss foundation established by the government, 10 people from Latvia, 10 from Lithuania, and 10 from Estonia received a very good postgraduate education in business and economics. It lasted one year, and we studied subjects we didn't even understand how it works in practice. We were prepared to be business advisors in the new market economy in our countries.

Where did you study?

Studies were organized in Riga, Vilnius, and Tallinn. The lecturing professors were Swiss, excellent professionals, and they came to the Baltic countries. I started to work for business after finishing this education. My three previous jobs led me step by step to this side of the table. My first job was business editor at a newspaper. The newspaper went bankrupt. Then, I was marketing director at one of the most popular commercial radio stations in Latvia,

---

* Interview conducted on 25 July 2019.

established by a large German broadcasting and advertising company RMS. My third job was establishing a Latvian subsidiary on behalf of a German organization, International Bund, which had 12,000 employees at approximately 300 branches in different countries. I got superb international training and work experience. This was the time when a market economy was developing in Latvia.

What was common among such very diverse jobs? Business development. I was always responsible for business development, business strategies, relations with clients and with competitors, financial management, and personnel management. Above all, there were competition issues. In all such positions, I had to think about competition: how to be better than the competitors, and how to succeed in business. I got more of an academic interest in competition strategies, but not from the point of view of competition law and regulation only.

I studied again at the Latvian university in a Master of Business Administration program. I wanted to go deeper into competition strategies. So, I learned about the competition regulations and the Latvian Competition Council. It was early 2000. Before that, I knew very little about the Competition Council. So, I thought, "Oh, there is law, regulation, but a lot of business people at that time did not even know what the Council was doing, what is permitted, what is prohibited by law". That was me in 2000. I wrote my Master's thesis about competition strategies. I looked on the web page of the Competition Council, and then I saw the decisions. And I thought, yes, I have to say something.

When I saw a vacancy on the board of the Competition Council, I applied immediately, despite having a stable, well-paid job, much better paid than a board member. In 2004, I was appointed. I came with my theoretical knowledge of competition strategies and my practical experience in business management. Sure, my diversity of jobs helped me to work at the Authority, also to bring into it some kind of new business culture, and business thinking. Such as to be faster, more efficient, to not have fear of communicating with different audiences.

I was not reappointed for a second term. It was very 'interesting' why not. The Competition Council is supervised by the Ministry of Economics. The Minister at that time wanted to have on the Board his party member who had lost his job in the Ministry. Afterward, I worked for two years as a competition chief economist. It was a very interesting time. I worked together with case handlers on economic cases, which I liked, as proving abuse of dominance or reviewing mergers. When the previous head of the Authority resigned, I applied, encouraged by colleagues. Since 2012, I have been here.

This is an impressive background because part of what we're interested in is what kinds of background and preparation make for a good leader. But your background has a number of fascinating features. You were experienced in media organizations, so you knew something about the role of dealing with media organizations; you were a senior manager, so you were accustomed to the things that come with being a manager; you were trained in the academic discipline in some important ways; and you had been at the agency before. In some ways, it seems to me you were at just the right moment and you were just the right person when the call came in 2012.

Yes, it was not a straight-going career path, always with some diversions. In some positions, I had to start from scratch. I could use the knowledge gained before, however, there was always something new to learn. I always have had an inner driving force that makes me go forward. Not to stop at what I have achieved but learn again and again. And I like lifelong learning. Looking back, I think it's the best combination – my diverse jobs all had something in common. And then, I ended up being on this side, as a competition law enforcer.

But with a broad background in business, too.

Yes, here it's important to understand the way of thinking of the businesspeople.

And the knowledge about the economy that you accumulated from all these positions as a businessperson, too.

It just helped me a lot, not only in decision-making but also in managing the Authority. As I said, when working for a business, I have always been responsible for achieving strategic and financial goals, for efficient spending of money, for staff, and on how to attract, motivate, and retain good people.

When you came to the Office to be Chair – you'd been on the Board; you'd studied the agency – what was new and different about now being the head of the agency? What challenges were different for you? What was new in having to be the person who is the face of the agency?

The first thing I thought about when I took office was – I need to maintain inner peace and self-control in any situation, no matter what may come, from outside or inside. To withstand not only heavy workload but also stress. If the authority does what the government or politicians do not like, they usually criticize its head, and this can end up even in his dismissal. In my case, I have been close to it several times, especially when we started taking action against public administrative bodies that violated the principle of competitive neutrality. Speaking about managing Authority, from the first day, I was trying to promote initiative in people. I want to let them feel more involved and united. Civil servants are rather not very active in coming up with proposals for improvement, and changes. They usually wait for what the head would say and then they would do it. People with good knowledge and experience, however, most of them are quite passive. From the very beginning, I told my staff that I would appreciate their initiative.

How did you communicate that to your larger team, that you want them to be more responsible for developing matters, for giving you ideas? Did you do that mainly by working with those who were there and bringing them to a different attitude? Did it involve bringing in new people from the outside, maybe more with your background? How did you encourage a staff whose culture was more passive – "I'm going to wait for the boss to give me instructions" – how did you change that attitude?

If you start working as a head, you need a key team around you who understands you, who supports your ideas, who has the same values. You are not a fighter alone. When I presented my priorities to the staff for the first time, I made it clear that we have not only to focus on strong enforcement, but we also need to do more communication, to promote a competition culture in the society. We have to go out and present what we are doing, to educate and inform market players, and public administrative bodies. Many of the old staff argued, "No, we are only enforcers. We need only to do cases and not give such public speeches or presentations." However, there were people who said, "Yes, we will change the culture of our authority."

I had a very good key team that supported me and the culture of the authority changed. We managed to recruit young people full of energy and zeal. We reassessed both the duties and responsibilities of employees. We started to organize training courses – communication, public speech, and presentation techniques. Every year we prepared a very detailed work plan that included an extensive communication and personnel development part. We started to evaluate on a regular basis each individual performance, conduct regular interviews with them. Initiative, innovative solutions, and work ethic were especially assessed.

People were informed what the managing staff expected from them. Also, the bosses received feedback from employees about what they were expecting from them. All in the office know that they can come to me anytime when my door is open, and we can discuss different issues – professional, and personal. Or criticize me if they think I did wrong. I am not afraid of criticism, it helps me improve myself.

And the people changed their attitude. They started to come up with proposals. Some of them were quite innovative at that time. Such as resolving less severe infringements by warning or mediation, or – claiming for recovery of the fine against the company that has taken over assets and liabilities of cartelised business. Huge attention was paid to personnel matters, which was not done before. So, we introduced the tradition of an annual celebration of the Authority's birthday, November 12, with an award ceremony in 4 categories.

Like the Oscars, but more important.

4 Oscars, yes! One is for the most complicated case of the year, another for the most significant market inquiry. The third goes to the team with the best performance, and the fourth award to the most active, creative employee. It's a very good tradition. The institutions need to have such traditions. That helps motivate people, they know that their initiative and good performance will always be praised. So the people get common values. They have information on what is going on in other departments, what are the successes, and also the difficulties of their colleagues.

Do you do other things to acknowledge good work? You have a group of 50, and with 50, I'm sure you know all of their names.

I believe it's very motivating to give people the opportunity to represent the Authority, present their personal achievements, both locally and internationally. Such as accomplished complex case investigations or market studies. Or an innovative approach adopted in assessing price excessivity by the court. Of course, I know all the staff not only by their names but also by how many of them are doing in their personal life. Hobbies, interests, what their children do.

You know them on a more personal level than if you had maybe 800 or 1000.

Clear, it would not be possible with a staff of 1000.

Do you do other things? If you see something that you like, will you walk by an office and say, "Good job?" Will you go to someone who helped organize a conference and say, "Our event really went well; thank you?" Do you do these sorts of things, too?

I try not to forget this. I have learned that it's very important to say thank you, otherwise, people react very sensitively, they feel insulted, and underestimated. To understand the work environment and atmosphere in the Authority, we introduced an annual staff satisfaction survey.

Every year internally?

Yes, every autumn, and anonymously. The very first survey, a few months after I took office, gave me quite a lot of unpleasant information on mistakes made in personnel management in the past. And what kind of improvements people are now expecting.

Can you give me some examples? What did you learn?

People indicated that they lack information about how the promotions or salaries have been reviewed. Or quite a negative assessment of the work of some senior executives. Employees also answered a question about what motivates them at work, and values such as usefulness of work, professional development, however, prevailed over pay.

And, again, people said they need to hear "thank you" more. I thought "Oh, how is this?" I usually say thank you at the board meetings, when the case or market inquiry is accomplished and a decision is made, and that's not enough. Then I understood that people need more, so thanks also for smaller things. They need regular feedback from their heads, also informal communication.

We regularly discuss the progress of case investigation or market inquiry at board meetings. With case handlers, legal advisers, and economists. And I see, it's a very hard, very demanding job they do, with all those dawn rides, court proceedings, etc. They are the ones who actually conduct the investigation. Acknowledgment helps raise individual responsibility. Also in the sense that people from the executive body should have responsibility for the decisions the board will take. And not just say, like "It's your decision. The board decides if there has been an infringement or not." We all need to work together as a team.

One thing you've mentioned is the importance of having a culture in which people are praised for good work but encouraged to improve where they could do better, the role of constructive criticism. You mentioned that you encourage people to talk to you. How do you do that in practice? How important is your own inner team as a sounding board for you in deciding what to do?

It's important that a head talks directly to the employee. Especially if there are unpleasant things to talk about, then I never do it by email or written orders. Just meeting face to face. It's not an easy task. Constructive criticism in my view also means talking to the person in a motivating way. I always keep in mind that professional things must be separated from personal ones. It requires being well prepared in order not to provoke emotions, offend a person's self-confidence, or destroy their willingness to work. Instead, we try together to look for reasons that hinder to do the job properly.

Once again, the main thing is that you as a head have to talk to the people and invite people to talk to you. Nevertheless, when working with people, I need to hear other opinions, advises. My team which I listen to is, basically, the personnel manager and chief executive. We are quite different, but as a team, we complement each other perfectly and it helps find constructive solutions. Such as do not rush to fire an expert with lower results, but offer to change a specialization or department.

I remember, earlier I thought: we all need to do our tasks fast, efficient. I understood over the years that people are very different. Not all experts have the same speed, analytical skills, but they may be able to do other things better. In my Authority, if we see that the person isn't in the right place we usually give a chance to prove their abilities in other matters. There have also been cases when after the second chance I told a person, even to a high-ranking official – you have to look for another job. Of course, it's not easy to say, "It has not happened, so maybe it's not the best place for you." It's important not to kill with too much criticism.

Over time, I have also realized that it is important for a head not to impose, push own ideas on the staff, especially if serious changes should be implemented. Just to give a hint as to where to change something. And the person has to take it on and say, "Yes, I have decided to do it and not you."

The importance of the skill in management comes through so strongly in your observations. That is, sometimes again when we think about competition law we think about having deep expertise in the substantive subject matter, but you're pointing out to us how important the capacity of management is to being an effective leader, and you've underscored for us – almost as though you were the head of a sports team, you're the head of a football team – you have to have a good idea of which players should play which positions.

In principle, yes. However, as I said, personnel issues are so sensitive that I need my inner team to consult, discuss.

So, it's evaluating your talent and not expecting someone who is maybe not skilled in a certain position to play that position; put them in a position where they succeed, but also encouraging them to think about the best way to do the job and to come back to you with ideas so that they feel at some point that "These are our ideas, too".

Exactly. It's so important. The training process of new case handlers at the Authority is time and resource-intensive to start all over again, recruiting new experts over and over again. However, I am happy to admit that young people who now come to the Authority are very talented and interested. They are not afraid to investigate complicated cases and do it quickly and efficiently. They have no fear of criticizing their bosses or proposing really good ideas. People who have worked for twenty or more years at the authority mostly are not so open-minded.

Do you play a role in recruiting? That is, do you have a hand in bringing these people into the Council?

I usually participate in the recruiting of middle and senior staff. But I am also informed about candidates who apply for case handlers and other experts. That is within the competence of a chief executive. Recently, when attending a course in strategic personnel management, I learned that we need to trust personnel managers because they are well-prepared to assess applicants and recognize talents. I trust our personnel manager and also encourage other heads of the units to trust her when assessing candidates' suitability for the job. Because of our inadequately low salaries, we cannot recruit experienced professionals from law offices, courts, or universities who are able to work with complex economic and legal issues from the first day. Applicants usually come with little work experience, and then we have to train them on the job. We can not know what the result will be. Whether he or she will be suitable for work, and, if so, whether will stay here after two or three years. Staff turnover is a problem.

But it's good that people want to take your people. If no one wanted to recruit your people, that would be a bad sign. So, it's a sign that you're bringing the right people in the door.

That's true, we prepare good professionals for private business and sector regulators. But filling vacancies, training new employees puts extra strain on the work of heads and other colleagues. I can't go and say to the public "We are not able to accomplish this case within the deadline because its investigator has gone to work for a law firm".

You mentioned, of course, that the Competition Council of Latvia is a council. It's a board. You are the Chair. What special ideas go into dealing with your colleagues? What does the chairperson have to keep in mind in working with the board?

It's my responsibility that all decisions are taken legally, independently, and in a timely manner. Our board has 3 members. Each of us needs to have good knowledge of case law and a certain specialization. One board member has good experience in cartel investigation. With the newest member, we agreed that she specializes in vertical agreements. I usually take a deeper look at cases where economic analysis is needed, such as mergers, abuse of dominance. I also like market inquiries, and studies, so I can use my chief economist's and research project manager's experience. Not for all cases three board members are enough. In complicated cases, I often think, we should have more people on the board, to have a greater diversity of opinions. Virtually, in competition authorities the chair should be not only a general manager but also an experienced expert. How else could I know and explain our cases and studies when journalists start asking for countless details of the investigations during an interview?

Everything that's in the house.

Not only. Everything, what is and isn't in the house. To be able to explain different interrelationships and scenarios for possible market developments.

Do you speak with your colleagues frequently?

Of course. If you could see how our office looks... In between is my small room. Board members are at your fingertips. Board meetings we have once or twice a week, but before or after that we all 3 often come together and discuss concepts or possible scenarios, and other issues. Of course, we are also talking about life... We have rather modest conditions, not enough space, and not even the heads of the departments have separate rooms except me and the chief executive. There are no spacious corridors that I should go 20 minutes to my office [...] My office is in the middle. And, my door is almost always half open, not guarded by an angry secretary sitting in front of it. So I can hear what the people are talking about and join them when professional matters such as litigation or upcoming meetings are discussed. Of course, I do not keep my door open just to listen to what people are talking about, but to show that we have to be open.

Did you think of the design of the physical space – I sense you did – as one way in which you help create a culture; that is, the way in which the office itself is laid out is one way that you send a signal about what you're trying to do and the culture you're trying to create?

I actually like such open-space bureaus where all sit together and if necessary can collaborate very quickly. You are right, it is like a signal that the Authority is open and available to anyone who needs advice. No wonder our stakeholders, clients praise us for our openness. For me, it's important that the place where I work does not make the impression of a bureaucratic, dark space. Recently we significantly transformed and modernized common areas in our office. They are cozy, encouraging creativity, informality. Thus, we demonstrate our culture and attitude. Nevertheless, there is still a lot to be done to promote openness in the whole Authority. Each division has separate rooms and some of their people behave quite separated. I would like them to communicate more with each other.

You need a passport to visit them.

We try to establish new traditions and organize joint events for the whole staff. When I just started working for the Authority – it was 2004 – I found it very strange that a staff of only 50 can be so separated. This was very different from what I was used to when working in private companies. The case handlers didn't know what kind of cases were in other departments or what the chair had presented at the conference. Now we change it. On Mondays heads of all units come together to inform what was done last week, and what is going on this week. Once a week we organize internal workshops for interest groups explaining the latest court decisions or presenting specific legal or economic topics. Thus we try to bring openness and communication culture within the office. Actually, I believe that in such a small Authority it is absolutely necessary to communicate on all levels.

I think this is a great advantage that you've highlighted of a smaller rather than a more massive agency. When you have 50, you don't need the same complete collection of formal hierarchies and procedures. You can in a much more direct way build a team spirit and broader awareness. A disadvantage you have when you go above a certain number – and I'll just pick one; I'll say when you go above a hundred, or certainly above 200 – it's harder to see that everyone knows what we're trying to do, our goals, what projects we've selected to try to accomplish them, and what our plans are for the future. A smaller agency has the advantage of being able to build a more cohesive and intimate commitment to accomplishing specific aims.

I completely agree with you. However, I think the way of communicating with staff that I brought from business could work in larger agencies as well. In business, it's impossible to have a bureaucracy which is typical of public institutions, such as the approval of documents with five signatures or communication in writing only… My staff knows that I hate bureaucracy. From the very beginning, I told them, "If you need to discuss anything, don't write me long emails or send piles of papers, just come to me." I think, even in larger agencies with 100 or 200, if a head had previously worked in business, he would know how to change the internal culture to a more constructive, efficient way of communicating with people.

I think this experience from your earlier career provided an extremely valuable way to think about how the organization behaves, to look at different ways to communicate internally and to create a cohesive spirit that doesn't involve filling out forms, making appointments, submitting memos.

Looking back, I now see that we were on the right track. Public administration in Latvia – it's 2019 – is changing, moving from bureaucracy to more openness, open discussions, and dialogues. But at the time I started, it wasn't such a common situation. Young people also bring a new style of collaboration within the Authority, reducing bureaucracy and formal hierarchy. I'm happy that in my previous jobs before joining the Competition Council, I learned business culture – precise organization of work, and an open way of communication inside and outside the office. My foreign heads trusted me, trusted my ideas. They told me, "You here, in Latvia, know better how to do it". It is the same thing I try to implement here.

I have two more questions for you. One involves your role as the public face of the agency. That is, even though you are part of a board of three, you are the chairperson; you are the most visible focal point for outsiders. What does a leader have to keep in mind in playing that role of being onstage all the time for the outside world? What do you have to keep in mind in playing that role, knowing that the spotlight again and again is on you and they watch everything you do?

This is a small stage. There are so many agencies, institutions, and regulators in Latvia. However, as a person who very often speaks with journalists, the first thing I kept in mind is that I should never say, "I cannot comment. No comments." "No comment" is a wrong comment. Either you know and tell something about that or you can promise later to give more information from experts on it. Once again, I want to point out the importance of efficient communication with the outside world. In our Authority we have accumulated a huge amount of information about the markets, including what hinders development of some of them. And, it's our mission to support and promote competitive processes, taking firm positions against administrative or structural barriers to competition, regardless of who created them – legislators, companies, municipalities. And here, the head has to be strong and visible as the public face of the authority. I do it with pleasure, even if I have gained enemies among the government or municipalities. In general, reputation, impartiality, accountability of authority are greatly valued according to the stance, courage of the head to express a strong competent opinion. Thanks to open communication, my authority is very visible here in Latvia.

Let me pose a final question for you. The day will come when your time as Chairperson comes to an end. These are usually not appointments for life. We are coming to the end of the Ābrama Chairperson era and I am your successor. Here's your successor. Give me some advice about what you know now that would be good for me to know on day one.

First of all, I would like to know if you are really a person who is impartial and neutral, not politically influenced. You must not be a person playing on behalf of anyone. That's very important for the Authority. The second point, you must have a good understanding of and a deep interest in competition and competition law. As a head, you won't have much time to learn the basics of competition law, but you have to make decisions from day one. Third, global trends, the digitalisation of the economy, and the complexity of infringements determine that the processes in the Authority need to be constantly reviewed. It means the head must be able to notice it and accordingly make decisions about changes. But in the end, I would suggest to the new head, "Organize your work so that you have more time for your private space, for yourself." If I look back, I think, yes, my family suffered a lot from this workload because of what I did.

Managing such an institution requires a lot of time and strength. Sometimes I think I do not have time enough to think, I'm only producing and producing. On Thursdays, we have a board meeting. Usually, 5, 7, even more progress reports on case investigations, and market inquiries are to be discussed. Then my night before the meeting is reserved for reading and analyzing the reports. Not enough time to think about concepts, to look for similar cases in competition literature. When I was a chief economist or a board member, I had more time for reading competition articles, deepening my expertise, and thinking. Sometimes I miss that.

How did you try to get time for yourself? Maybe close the door, maybe stay at home half a day – different things. How did you keep time for yourself so that you could think about the way ahead and that you could be the larger person who has family, who has friends?

A very clear schedule. On Saturdays, I try to do nothing for the job. I clean houses, do house chores and go shopping. In the afternoon I walk in the forest, at the seaside, listening to audiobooks, so I can do two things at once. We have very good theaters in Riga, often there are great concerts, so I try to attend them. Sunday in the afternoon it starts again, the job. I draft the agenda for the next week, prepare my presentations, write articles, and read reports. So a very clear split of my week. My working day doesn't end at 5:00 p.m. The day is so full of internal and external meetings, and discussions, that I can work with my papers and reports only in the evening. Then it's quiet in the office, although I am not the only one here after work. So, the whole week is very clear. It runs so fast.

It is like being on a treadmill set at the highest speed. To finish, I think your observation is so important, that if you don't have some time in the week that is entirely your own, if the job is 24/7/365, after 365 you will either be burned out or, sadly, you could be dead. So, I think to realize you have to restore yourself and you have to have time – maybe on the Sundays you get ready for the week – to step back and think, What are we trying to do here and how do we do this the best way, and how do I make everything I say reinforce what we're trying to do?

You know the matter. In the end, however, I have to confess. No matter how difficult it may be at times, I am glad that my career has led me to competition law, and to the Competition Council. Also to our wonderful international competition community where I made great new friends. I love this job and can't wish for anything better in my professional life.

Tembinkosi Bonakele*

South African Competition Commission, Head (2013-2022)

You are the head of the Competition Commission of South Africa. You have helped develop what, by any measure, is one of the most effective competition systems among the one hundred created since the late 1980s. If you look at the top list of successful relatively newer institutions, South Africa stands at the top of the ladder, or in anyone's calculation near the very top of the ladder. I would like to begin by asking you to reflect on the experiences you had before you became the head of the Commission, the experiences that provided in some way good preparation for doing that job. If you go back through your life's curriculum, what experiences put you in a good position to do what you're doing now?

I'm a lawyer by training. Before getting into antitrust, I practiced labor law. I was in a labor law firm that was very engaged with issues of social justice. This was South Africa in transition. When I started with the practice, we had a new labor law in place. That's when I honed my skills both as a lawyer and as a litigator. Then, I went to the United States where I was part of a cohort of young African lawyers who were sent to U.S. law firms to learn a new set of skills. We focussed on corporate law. When I arrived in the United States in 2001, there was a recession and there wasn't much M&A going on, business going on, and the only busy area was antitrust. So, I got into an antitrust group at Clifford Chance in New York, and that's how I got introduced to competition law. I then got back to South Africa and got into contact with the agency.

---

* Interview conducted on 4 September 2019.

How did you come to the agency? How did that happen?

I don't know. Those who were involved refused to reveal all. However, I was recruited by an ex-colleague who used to work at the firm and who subsequently went to work for the Competition Commission. When she was at the Commission, she gave me a call. As I had not previously worked with her, it made this a little bit of a mystery. I didn't know how to reveal my work experience or even my capabilities. But, in any event, they tried to recruit me. I was quite reluctant at the time because I was set on what I was doing in practice. But I felt I needed to contribute, in part actually by exposing us to corporate law, to competition law, and sending us to the United States so we could hopefully contribute to building what was then a new country with lots of opportunities.

What was the transition like coming into a public institution? You have been in law firms, you have had the practice in the labor law firm, you have had the practice in Clifford Chance, and now you're in a public institution, and you're the head of the public institution. What was that transition like for you?

The transition worked quite well for me. I managed it quite well. There was a lot of pressure in a public institution, but a different type of pressure – dealing with the government, for example; dealing with all sorts of stakeholders who are interested in what you do – rather than the private practice pressure, which is meeting clients' deadlines and meeting your fee target. I kind of like the latter, the pressure of service and the pressure of managing expectations about yourself. I deal with that better than having to manage clients' interests. I liked the transition, and I think I was pleasantly surprised by how I managed to fit into the public sector, I have enjoyed it over all these years.

I'm gathering that having been a litigator was valuable background for what you're doing now.

Absolutely. I think that the skills of a litigator are always important, even in management, because we make decisions. After we have a full investigation, we have to decide whether we're going to prosecute the case. I think it's good to have the expertise to assess evidence, the expertise to anticipate what the Tribunal and the courts are likely to say. I think it's usually valuable.

It puts you in a good position when case handlers make presentations to ask the hard questions that the parties are going to pose before the Tribunal.

There are no shortcuts in driving cases, it is a function of detail. It's also a function of techniques. There is a lot of technical expertise involved. Managing an agency, in a sense, is a high-level job, but you still need to engage with the details, and I found that my background in private practice has helped a great deal.

What were some of the transferrable management-related experiences and skills? I assume that when we consider being the head of an agency, sometimes we think just about the technical concepts – what's an abuse of dominance; what's a substantial lessening of competition – but we forget that the head of the agency is responsible overall for personnel, for the budget, for any number of administrative features – carried out by others, but you're responsible for a variety of administrative tasks related to the functioning of the agency. What's different about doing that in the private sector? What about the management experience in the private sector informed doing those jobs in the public sector?

I think that private practice is very good at painstakingly training young graduates on the basics of how to write a letter to the other side, and how that gets settled by associates and partners. I found that's probably one of the things that I brought to the teams I was managing at the Commission, the idea that every document you put out matters, it has to be reviewed, the little things like commas and full stops matter for a lot of that, the presentation, but also the substance of the argument. I find that discipline is not always there in government departments, but I think we have been fortunate to have an agency that has that kind of professional impulse.

I think that is attributable to the fact that a lot of the people going to the agency have been in private practice. I also think that having the experience of working with professional teams is quite important because professionals are a different kind of species. Their expectations, their training requirements, and their motivation are different. I think it does need a set of skills. It has to be understood. I think not every manager is going to have that kind of exposure to managing professionals, meeting their expectations, and motivating them. I learned a lot in law firms about how it gets done. They don't always get it right, but at least there is recognition that managing professionals need a particular skill and a particular approach, and that has been useful. I think this is what we try to do. We recognize that we are within government, but we employ people who are fundamentally professionals rather than civil servants.

How do you communicate these expectations to the staff of the Commission, your expectations about the professional ethos, about how to do things, and how to achieve the highest standards of professional skill? How do you communicate that throughout your agency?

It's very important. It starts with the people you get into the agency. You have to be satisfied that your systems give you the right kind of people. In other words, they give you these professionals who have the right attitude, who have the right work ethic. And then you have to make sure that they identify with the public mandate, and I think this is where it's crucial for agency leadership, regardless of the technical skills that people bring, that they also have an affinity to the mandate and are passionate about public service and making a difference. This is something you have to communicate across all levels in the organization. We're fortunate to have an organization where we can call all the staff.

How many people compose the total staff of the Commission?

There is two hundred and fifty people. So, we are still able to call them into a room and talk to them. There is also a time when they are free to engage with the head of the agency and raise how they would like the agency to be managed, and what kind of agency they would like to be associated with. You have to use all of these platforms to communicate. And, of course, it's important to also make sure that the entire management team really reinforces the messages. The whole issue about culture, although it's set from the top, is that it's very important that everybody feels they have a contribution and believe it.

How often do you meet with your managers? What is your routine? Is this a weekly meeting with the heads of units? Can you tell me how you manage your week with your top managers?

I start with just a meeting in my office on Monday, which is usually a short meeting about how the week looks. That includes my personal assistant who manages all of this area. I find that it's a very important meeting for me because it reminds me what's in the pipeline for that week. We meet every Tuesday morning at 9:00 with top management. It's a meeting where we decide cases. We get the file on Friday. Then, we have the whole weekend to go through it, and on Tuesday we make decisions. This is where we can call the teams to come and present the investigations they're doing, once they have reached the point where a decision must be taken on whether to prosecute or not; whether to refer a matter with conditions, whether to refer that it be blocked; or whether to recommend that it be upheld by the Tribunal. So, all of those decisions take place on cases on Tuesdays. Then we have a monthly meeting where we deal with all the organizational management or administrative issues.

These are all occasions for you to reinforce your expectations, and your goals for your entire institution.

That's right. And we have middle management meetings as well. Middle management meets every quarter. We have an all-management meeting where top officials and mid-level officials meet, and we talk about the actual investigations, on how to allocate resources and how we prioritize and change course where it's necessary.

How do you engage with junior people? How do you engage with people in case-handling positions? Do you keep your door open? Do you walk through the building and say "hello"? Do you invite them to meetings? How does the junior case handler get to know the Chair?

That is the greatest challenge at this time. I have quite an open-door policy. I like talking to people. I like walking through the organization, meeting different teams, feeling the environment, talking to people who are in different areas of our work – IT people, people who are working at our registry, who receive our documents, who interact with people who come and file things at the Commission. I'm fortunate enough that I think it comes naturally to me to talk to people.

When you came to the agency, what would you say were your ambitions for the agency? What did you want to do in this extraordinary position in South Africa?

I thought the agency could make a difference in the South African economy in very specific areas: the issue around inclusivity of the South African economy; inequality always looms large. I think this is one area that I felt we could bring a much sharper focus on. Competition law, being quite a fairly old and traditional field, perhaps is not regarded as an area that would intervene in the economy with the aim of meeting these social objectives, but I always felt that there were particular angles where we could fit the Competition Authority into this challenge. In my opinion, the Authority needed to remain relevant in our context. South Africa was in transition – still is – and the issue of opening up the economy is still very important. I think it would be very difficult to justify the existence of the agency if it was not responsive to the very important contemporary issues in the South African economic evolution. That was the ambition I had, that we would be seen as part of an instrument that could transform the South African economy into higher growth levels but also more inclusivity.

Have you been pleased – maybe not completely satisfied – with the steps that have been taken to realize that vision, to link the work of the Commission directly with the attainment of these important social objectives? Are you happy? Do you see progress?

I'm happy with the progress we're making. I think it's going to be an ongoing challenge because it's not always easy to see the link, the cause and effect between economic policy, and economic growth, and we should let alone inclusivity. I think the challenge is there. But I'm very happy with the progress we have made. I think we have tackled cases in pursuit of that. I think the rest of society recognizes this as a contribution.

Can you mention one case for which you say, "That's the kind of case that's consistent with this aim and I'm glad we're doing this."?

We've done cases, for example, that seek to open up entry into the South African downstream manufacturing, which is quite important for jobs. We've tackled exclusion against a petrochemicals monopoly that supplies key input into manufacturing. We have been successful in opening up downstream investments for things like fertilizer, for example. We have been able to take our cases and win them before the Tribunal and courts, but most importantly to explain them. It's very important for us that after we do a case on fertilizer, we can explain why fertilizer is so important for farmers, including emerging farmers, what is the effect in the long run on the competitiveness of South African agriculture, and what this means for employment. So, you are dealing with an upstream monopoly, but you have to explain why it matters for everybody. I think we've done that fairly well.

Is this an element of building a case that you encourage case handlers or managers to think about, like "Here's our larger goal; one of our most important goals is to connect what we do to the achievement of these important social objectives, and I want you to think when we develop a case where we can do it, what's the connection"? Do you encourage them to do that?

Absolutely. Everyone has to justify why the case matters. There are instances where it could just matter for precedent. That's also fine. But, by and large, tell us why this case is important. This was a very important discussion within the Commission when we started developing a strategy and prioritization because there was a view that we didn't have the discretion to choose what we pursue, everything that comes through the door – pigeon racing, for example, we had a complaint about this.

But I think we ultimately managed to persuade each other and reach consensus that if we are to be effective, we have to do fewer things that we can hopefully do well but, most importantly, that make a difference. This has become a mantra for cases that case handlers make. In that quarterly meeting where people come and discuss their cases, an important element is why this case is important.

I think it's so important for leadership to reflect on how you define your objective, identify the types of priorities that you want to pursue to achieve the objective, and examine project by project how this project is going to fulfill these priorities and goals, and you reinforce that regularly so that the most junior person in your building knows what they're trying to do.

Absolutely. You have to reinforce that all the time because it's easy to slip or forget. All the cases are exciting, even pigeon racing is very exciting. It is very important to reinforce this message all the time before people get caught up in the excitement of pursuing that.

One of the most important things you do in this respect is being the public face of the institution. You're speaking to your team, to build cases that you want, but you uniquely are on stage. The spotlight is on you. Everyone follows what you say. What steps do you take to reinforce this message on the outside so that the larger public, the proverbial "person on the street," understands what you want to do? How do you accomplish that?

I first try and map the relevance, identify the relevance for whatever we are doing, to what the person in the street can identify with. They must see what we are trying to resolve rather than seeing this as just a kind of exercise. That includes taking things that matter to them. We have recently tackled an issue of school uniforms where schools entered into exclusive supply agreements with school uniform suppliers. Those are things that people can identify with, so that when you move into more complex issues, at least you have a lot of people on your side, a lot of people who understand that you're pursuing things that matter to them. I think it's very important that we start on the basis that there is a problem, and this problem affects a section of the population in the society; and, if you explain well your interventions, that section of the population, at least, will understand what you are doing.

What was the role of being the spokesperson for the agency to the media? Was that a major transition for you, or was it something that you enjoyed once you started doing it?

It was challenging because I didn't come from any sort of public relations background. There were lessons to learn. I had to do media training. It's the kind of training that gets scheduled in your diary, but you don't think it's particularly important until the day you have to give a TV interview, and those tips that you get come in handy. It's one of the areas where I had to recognize that it was new, and I needed to learn. It helps a great deal, of course, that you understand the cases because you have to understand what you're talking about. I don't think you can just learn public relations and think that you can get away without it. You have to give them content, and it is actually what gives you confidence as well. I would think that this is probably the biggest thing one needs to take into account.

When approaching these encounters, you have spent lots of time thinking about what the theme is, and what point you want them to take away from this. Instead of giving them a mass of technical details about some intermediate industrial input, you have a clear idea of what you want the headline to be.

That is right. One of the tips I got was: you have to repeat the message you want to get out, and sometimes it doesn't matter what the question is; you just repeat what you think must get out.

You can't do this well unless you've decided in the first place what your agency is all about and to have that set in your mind as you go ahead. Beyond the general media, there are elected officials and appointees who are very interested in what you are doing. They give you a budget; they can change your law. There is an organized bar. There are academics. Here again, they look to the Commissioner. What is it like being the person who deals with all of these constituencies as well? What is your relationship to elected officials for example?

This is one of the most difficult jobs of being an agency head, because not everybody is going to necessarily be happy with you, not all the time, so you have to decide what level of discomfort you can live with. But it is important to take people through what you are doing. If you go to members of Parliament, they always want to see more; they want to see more litigations, more cases. It's important to communicate the message that what you are doing makes a difference and explain what that difference is and what you cannot do. Sometimes we fall into this trap of thinking that we can solve all the world's problems. Often you encounter this with lawmakers, and they'll tell you, "Well, if you have a problem with the law, you must tell us so that we can change it." But you know that even in the law itself there are limits on what you can use an antitrust statute for. I think it's very important that you don't communicate "doom and gloom" because that's going to lead people to want to make changes all the time that might not always be helpful. But at the same time, you have to explain the challenges. All of these constituencies – the lawyers are very important because they have to make the system work and they are your point of contact with their clients. This is one of the areas where I wish I could have spent more time with the legal profession in our country because I think a lot of the issues in the system – whether it is the delay in pursuit of cases or technical challenges – a lot of these characteristics relate to on how the lawyers perceive the agency, how it conducts its processes, investigations, and things like that.

Then, there are also consumers and the rest of civil society, which I think are also quite important for galvanizing support for the mandate of the agency. I think sometimes this is the constituency on which everybody sort of turns their back in the agency, of whom this is the constituency that will be important for you. It's important that they understand what you do, they're kept abreast, they're interested, and you show there is something in it for them. It's not easy because you might as well say where you have prosecuted a cartel the prices go up. So it's not always easy to explain issues. But you can't leave them behind because these are the people that you will need for the long voyage.

Doing all these things, of course, places tremendous demands on you. You are on the job all the time. You are doing work at night. As you just said, the files come in on Friday, and it's through the weekend that you get ready for the meetings that take place in the coming week that you have regularly, the case meetings. How do you create time for yourself? How do you create time to refresh your soul, to read, to think, to keep your eye on the horizon as well as on the matter that's right in front of you, and avoid just getting run into the ground by the routine that can be brutally difficult?

What I try to do, with mixed success, is to engage with academic institutions. I have studied quite extensively, and I find that's a necessary process of refreshing myself, because you are in this job for all the time, and it is natural to be tired, despondent. Sometimes you go through phases. And if I need a break I think engaging with academia, and talking to students, is quite refreshing. And talking to my counterparts all over the world has also been a big source of relief for me. It's useful to know that you are not the only one going through some of the challenges that you do, so attending international conferences and engaging with counterparts has also been a form of a break. I find actually that when I travel that's when I'm most efficient with my reading. So, I think it's useful that I don't stay in the office all the time. That doesn't work for me.

You are the Commissioner. You're not part of a board. What steps do you take inside, consultation with colleagues, to share some of the burden of having to decide, to have a discussion that gives you confidence that you're in the right place?

The one thing that I inherited is this collective decision-making process. Even though the decision is mine, that meeting every week on Tuesday involves all the heads of the divisions within the Commission. They participate as they are going to make the decisions. They criticize it; they can engage with the teams; so, there is a nice and robust checks-and-balances thing that takes place there. I encourage that because it's in my interest that we exhaust the discussion, and everybody gives their input. So, I have the head of legal services and the chief economist amongst this team, and I think this is what helps the quality of decisions.

Most of what we have been talking about involves your job in the agency at home. You also have a significant role across the border with regional agencies across Africa; on the global scale with the Organisation for Economic Cooperation and Development (OECD) meetings, the United Nations Conference on Trade and Development (UNCTAD), and the International Competition Network (ICN). The success of South Africa in building an effective system has made you and your colleagues frequently invited speakers in the larger system to events around the world because people are hungry to learn. Individual countries seek you out, especially those in neighboring areas, to ask, "How did you do this?" […] this gives you exposure to broad experience at the regional and international level – and you learn from that – but it also tugs at you when you have to try to do your job at home. How do you reconcile these roles, the one of the Authority but also as an internationally recognized figure whose advice is keenly sought by any number of observers around the world?

I make sure that I have a laid-back, functional office. I have a head of international affairs who sits not far away from my office; I have somebody who looks after the media who also sits not very far from my office; and I have a sort of chief of staff who heads all of these units daily. I mention this because it's not the capacity that I found there, but it's the capacity that I felt was necessary, that I built up. I have to be very careful in balancing the resource requirements that will make my office effective vis-à-vis the resources that go into what I call the "core business" of the organization. I think that I have a fairly effective backup team. I could do with more resources on that, but I think that's helpful, even if you have one person who does international relations if you're going to do this and do it in a way that doesn't break you. I also am fortunate to have colleagues I have confidence in, so when I'm away I don't have sleepless nights. I know that I have left a capable team and things will happen. There is technology; if they need to consult, they will consult. But I enjoy the fact that I can trust that even if I'm not there, the decisions that are made are decisions that I would have made. I try to share the responsibility with my colleagues as much as I can even on an international level. For an OECD meeting, I appointed one of the managers and said, "You are our point person at the OECD for this meeting, to coordinate all the submissions. Regardless of whether I'm attending or not, you are the person responsible for this coming round of roundtable discussions at OECD." It empowers everybody. Everybody enjoys this sharing of wealth and exposure.

A time comes when your mandate ends, and you move on to your next career. But, before, the person who has been designated to succeed you, says, "What advice would you give me about coming into the agency, about how to behave, about what to do, about how to get off to a good start? What would you tell me?"

It's like a cliché, but people do matter. This is all about people. People inside the agency and people around you will determine the success or failure of the institution even long after you have left. It's about engaging people outside. The government is people. You are coming in with all the technical know-how for this job, but what you're going to need the most is to spend time understanding people, engaging people, and outlining a vision that can be bought by people.

Terry Calvani*

Federal Trade Commission, Commissioner (1983-1990) & Acting Chairman (1985-1986)
Irish Competition Authority, Commissioner (2002-2005)

You have served on the Board as Commissioner and Acting Chair with not only the Federal Trade Commission but you have been a Commissioner with the Irish Competition Authority as well. So in two fascinating capacities you have had the experience of serving on the governing body of not just one but two national competition authorities and derived from that, I think, some wonderful lessons about how to lead. I would like you to reflect for a minute on how it was you came to the Federal Trade Commission and then how you came to the Irish Authority?

I used to tell my students that hard work and perseverance would go a long way to making a successful career, but Lady Luck can also play a role. How did I get to the Federal Trade Commission? I had been active in the American Bar Association Section of Antitrust Law, and in the course of that I had worked with Jim Rill on various ABA projects. One day I received a telephone call from Jim during which he asked, "Terry, are you a Democrat or a Republican?" Before responding, I tried to remember his party affiliation so I could be the opposite. If we were of the same party, I feared that he was going to solicit a $5000 contribution to attend a political fundraising lunch. I couldn't figure it out quickly, and answered honestly: "I'm a Republican." He responded, "Oh, that's great. I'm putting together a list of some names to submit to the White House as possible candidates for an open position on the FTC, and I want to include you". I thought to myself: "Okay, Jim's got 25 people on his list, there are another 25 people with 25 people on their lists." I didn't think

* Interview conducted on 21 March 2019.

much about it. The next week, the White House called and asked me whether I would come for an interview, and the rest is history. The President nominated me, the Senate confirmed me and Chief Justice Rehnquist administered the oath of office.

And then to Ireland.

Lady Luck again. I received a call from Pricewaterhouse, which had been retained by the Irish Government to identify candidates for an open position on the Irish commission. They invited my wife Sarah and me to come to Dublin for an interview before a committee that would advise the Deputy Prime Minister, who would make the appointment. I was offered the appointment on my return to the States. We were soon in Ireland.

A total of 7 years at the FTC, including 8 months as Acting Chairman?

I think something like that, yes.

And then in Ireland the total time you served as Commissioner?

3 years.

A decade of service on multi-member commission, competition, consumer, regulatory authorities? I don't think there is another person on the planet who has that in their portfolio. If you could reflect a bit on lessons, concepts of leadership that were important to you, what made for good leadership in your own experience? What sorts of things should a good leader avoid? What should you do; what should you not do?

That's a big question. One of the requirements is to surround yourself with very good people – individuals who are much brighter than you.

I always sought to raise the average IQ. If I was the baseline, I succeeded.

For me it was very easy to find people who were brighter. For you, I'm sure it was more difficult.

Did you almost deliberately look for people who would not naturally perhaps be disposed to agree with you?

I purposely looked for people who would take different views. In fact, I remember interviewing Jonathan Baker when Jon said very candidly, "Terry, I disagree with some of your views of antitrust." I responded, "Great, I want people like you aboard. You tell me your candid views about the matters before us and I promise to listen carefully."

Jon Baker later becomes the head of the Bureau of Economics and he becomes the Chief Economist at the Federal Communications Commission. Jon ascends to positions of considerable prominence in academia and in government service, but his real start in government service was with you.

We didn't always agree – in fact, we probably disagreed a good bit. But the presence of people with different views made for stronger decision making. If you can't take criticism from your staff, you need to think about doing something different. You don't want your office to have a "Yes, Minister," mentality. You need tough criticism within your office.

That requires your willingness over time to listen carefully even if you're hearing things that you don't like.

It makes for a better product. I would add that working hard yourself is important; it sets the tone. If you work hard, you'll find your staff are happy to work long hours if they see you toiling away with them. Humility is another ingredient, and it isn't a bad virtue for public officials. All of us make mistakes. I know I made mistakes at the Federal Trade Commission and a good number at the Irish Competition Authority. You need to own your mistakes. You need to be candid about what it is that's worked and what it is that hasn't worked.

I assume that is good both for the internal audience you work with, to have your staff and managers see that you will stand up and take responsibility, but also for the outside world too.

Right, that's exactly right.

Nobody expects perfection but they do expect responsibility. That creates a culture that is healthy for the institution.

Healthy for the institution and sets a good role model for the people who work with you.

And I would add on the people who worked with you: it's extraordinary to me to watch the Calvani alumni from the Federal Trade Commission. It is a distinguished group.

Yes, it is.

I think it's no accident that the Jonathan Bakers, the Randy Tritells, the enormously successful head of the Office of International Affairs at the FTC, in many ways cut their teeth in your office.

Yes, and Jeff Schmidt, who went on to be a partner of a major magic circle firm in London.

Yes, and also head of the Bureau of Competition at the FTC.

You know, we all still get together. In fact, this evening is our thirty-fifth reunion. The whole group will have dinner tonight. We do that every year.

If we're thinking of one thing that leaders can do, it's preparing the path for the next generation of leadership and showing people by example.

Yes. But it's the next generation of leaders that also makes you a better leader. Learning goes in both directions. While I like to think that my staff learned some things from me, I can assure you I learned a lot from them.

Other things to do to motivate career professional senior managers inside the agency. What do you have to do to motivate them to pursue a program and invest the effort that makes it successful? Thinking about your time in the United States and in Ireland, how do you catalyze?

Bringing good people from the outside, or even keeping good people on the inside, can be difficult. The public service doesn't pay what you can make in the private sector. However, good people respond to excitement and challenge. Having an exciting agenda is an attractive lure for talent.

When you came to both institutions and as you ascended to the position of Acting Chair of the FTC, my guess is you didn't go to these agencies just for the glory of being called "Commissioner," that you had something you wanted to do.

Yes. This brings me back to the point of an exciting agenda. Unfortunately the agenda of many competition enforcement agencies is set by their inbox: what's come under the transom today, what's been filed. To be sure, you do have an inbox. Most agencies have things that they're statutorily required to do, and you have to do them. But the fact that you have an inbox doesn't mean that you can't have an affirmative agenda. So, to answer your question, if I had to pick a single thing, I would say having an exciting agenda – one that benefits the public – will draw good people. They want to be part of that. It goes a long way to drawing good people, retaining good people, keeping morale up, as opposed to just "Oh, it's another day at the FTC."

You picked out a couple of exciting projects at the FTC. Even though your time as Chair – in some ways, 8 months is like having a cup of coffee – I had the job for a year, and it's enough to say "Hello/goodbye" – but even in the 8 months you had some very specific, noteworthy focal points.

We tried to do so, but my appointment was as "Acting Chair." I, or someone else, would fill that position. And, frankly, you don't want to get too far out in front of the parade. The Chair will want to set their own agenda and not be saddled with yours. They will want to fill open senior staff positions. You owe them that. But we tried to focus on a few things. For example, we focused on anticompetitive abuse of government processes to thwart competition.

An important forerunner of a growing concern over time with the use of public instrumentalities for competition, a global norm.

Exactly. There is no better impediment to competition than the police. Getting in trouble for competing is a good way of dampening competitive ardor. We also sought to try to increase the agency's efforts before other government entities – sometimes welcomed; sometimes not, where we would point out when a proposed regulation or outcome was anticompetitive.

You were young when you came to the FTC.

Yes, probably too young. As I look back, I would have liked to have been appointed 20 or 30 years later.

You were in your mid-thirties, weren't you?

Yes, I was. At the time, I probably knew much more antitrust law than I know now.

Because you taught?

Yes. I knew the law, but I think my judgment, political acumen, and administrative skills that go into running a government agency have improved over the years. Some of the things that I championed at various points in my career, I would temper today. When running a government agency, one needs to be careful to appreciate the realities of the political environment in which you exist. To give you an example, from my time in Ireland, I brought a case that I thought was important. There was competitive problem, and I felt at the time needed to be addressed. But that good case almost resulted in a significant curtailment of the agency's statutory powers. I had stepped on a rattle snake. The respondent mustered a bit of a political storm. I just called it wrong. I failed to take a long view of the competitive environment, and I think my action had the potential for hurting the competition law enforcement going forward. Which is only to say that I think we live in a real world and we have to pick our cases wisely.

I think this strikes me as such a key point for our program here, which is the realization that you have to be aware of the larger context in which you are making decisions. And the notion that you can be autonomous in the sense of being isolated and completely apart from the world. No man is an island. If you are completely isolated, you can become blind and you can simply be bypassed.

And you can get overly confident about what it is you think you know and fail to appreciate what you don't know.

Part of the intuition that I suppose leadership has to develop, if not by formal training, is to be a bit of a political scientist as well.

And also to be a good listener. Thinking about my tenure in Ireland. I asked myself: " Were you better the second time around in Ireland than you were the first time around in the US?"

Yes. How about that?

That's an interesting question. Comparison is rendered difficult because the two environments were different. When I went to Ireland, I thought, "Ah, common law country; the competition law very closely resembles that in the US. This is a piece of cake; I've done all of this before." I got there, and before long I figured out that actually it's a different country, and the legal culture is different. Yes it's common law, yes the legal education is pretty similar. There are a lot of similarities; but also a lot of differences – a different culture, different legal procedures. When we do technical assistance projects to aid other countries in their development of sound competition policies, we need to be sensitive to the cultures in which we are working.

In the experiences that you had in both, you referred to the importance of listening. How do you go about listening in a way on the outside to get a sense of how you're doing, to get a sense of whether the choice of program is right, whether your priorities are right? What is the best way to look outward and listen to the larger world to get a measure of how you're doing and what you should be doing?

Talk to the larger world. You can go and spend all your time talking with your fans who think like you. It's great to hear how great you are and what great things you're doing at your agency, but I think you're better off spending some time with people who don't think you're doing quite as good a job and who have a whole host of things that they would like for you to do differently. Give them a fair hearing. You may decide that you are on the right course, but it is important to hear them out. At least you will understand where they're coming from, and they may think more of you for having got a hearing. And you may find you have an ally on some future issue where an alliance may be important and work to both advantages. But resist the temptation to spend too much time with fellow travelers.

I think the theme inside with your own advisors but outside that you're underscoring and that is so important is you've got to be able and willing to test your ideas in a way that elicits a candid view about how well you're performing and what else you can do.

Right. I agree.

I would like to talk about a couple of other leadership points, one that we haven't touched upon but others that you've raised already. In a decision-making body with an adjudication and decision-making feature, when I think of your tenure especially at the FTC, one way that you led was in writing opinions for the Board. Our larger audience is probably familiar with a case called Hospital Corporation of America1, which was a coordinated effects merger decision decided by the FTC. You wrote the opinion for the FTC with a fairly soaring affirmance by Richard Posner and his colleagues on the Seventh Circuit.

Yes, Judge Posner was very generous in his comments.

You used opinion writing in a way that, I think, elevated the statute of the institution and used that as a way, in many ways, to lead in the formulation of ideas. When you came to the FTC, was that something that you said, "As an academic, as a Commissioner, I'm going to make a point of doing that well"?

That was certainly an important point on the agenda because I viewed opinion writing as an exposition of the reasons for the decision at issue, but also, in a way, as "super-articles." As any law professor knows well, many published law review articles are read by the author, the editors, and maybe a few others.

And you can hear them rattling in trash cans.

Gathering dust on university library shelves, whereas opinions actually get read by many more people and can be read years later too. I thought this was a way of putting ideas out in a more effective manner in the development of the law. That doesn't necessarily mean everybody's going to say, "Oh this is fabulous," but it is a way of getting ideas out and generating discussion. You've got their attention. I look back on an opinion that I wrote addressing application of the rule of reason cases that generated a lot of discussion, some positive, some adverse and some in the middle. But It got people thinking.

In re Massachusetts Board of Optometry2.

I can't take credit for the underlying ideas as many contributed to that discussion. The opinion led many to appreciate this more nuanced approach to the rule of reason. And the decision did provide a roadmap, if you will, for the Commission's own handling of such cases.

But it seems to me that, when you're thinking about the composition of a board, where you've got a collective decision-making body and you're going to be issuing decisions, and you think about who you want on that board, it's a very good reason to want an academic, to have one there who's attuned to this.

Yes, I agree.

As someone who continues to write unread articles and other items, I'm struck again and again about how, when you look at the intellectual roots of so many debates that take place today, these are Calvani's opinions from the Federal Trade Commission.

I'm not sure that is accurate, but my mother would have liked to have heard it.

I am sure of this. In thinking about the way that an agency leads, builds its brand, and contributes to the formulation of policy at home and abroad, this is an undervalued, unappreciated way in which that happens. That was part of your tenure.

I think it's an important part. I don't want to step on anyone's toes, but expertise in law and economics are important qualifications when making appointments to positions of leadership of competition authorities. At least some members of the governing board have this background.

You could have some diversification.

Yes, absolutely. Some of the most interesting FTC Commissioners came with absolutely no background in antitrust, and they still made important contributions. But in the main, I think there needs to be a corpus of members who possess expertise in the field. I know that this is an alien tradition in some places. When I first came to the FTC, I found that some competition agencies had a "Whitehall" mentality: "A fine international trade official can be a fine competition official. What is important is someone who is bright, hardworking and understands the workings of government." There is something to that. But I think substantive knowledge about what it is you do is also important. A fine obstetrician likely would not be a good substitute for an eye surgeon. While the whole board doesn't have to be composed of experts in that discipline, it's important.

I think a reason that it is so valuable to do comparative study, but to study specific examples carefully, is that you can see what you get if you have that representation. I think again and again about what an impact on the analysis of coordinated effects in mergers you had by writing your opinions there. Talking about boards, being on a board, you were on two of them, each with their own decision-making roles and responsibilities. I think we could say that governance questions for competition agencies headed by a single executive and those headed by a board, a college are different environments.

Completely different.

You served on two boards. Reflections on which experience you found more satisfying, and why was one perhaps better than the other, or is it just too hard to tell?

I was hoping you would not ask that question because I am not sure of the answer. The two boards on which I served were really quite different. The FTC was an adjudicative body like an appellate court. The body met after reading briefs and hearing oral argument. Someone in the majority took responsibility for drafting the opinion. If not unanimous, you might have concurring and dissenting opinions. In Ireland, it was completely different. I don't recall an instance where there was any dissent from a decision of the Irish Authority. The Authority operated by consensus. Sometimes that was achieved by compromise. But there was the tradition that "We're going to do this by consensus." There are positive aspects of both. Service on the Irish Commission was, frankly, more collegial than the FTC. That was positive. It had a spillover effect on other things that we did besides our decisions in cases. We were more of a team vis-à-vis the Government, vis-à-vis Parliament or vis-à-vis the European Union. There weren't big fissures on the board. By the same token, FTC opinions, fully exposing differences of views, were also very positive. They furthered critical thought to the betterment of the development of the law.

My own impressionistic view is that the quality of discourse in opinion writing rose in the 1980s when you were there.

Yes. I think that may be correct, but how one weighs –

It may be unmeasurable?

Yes. Let's leave it at that. I like that.

On the collegiality point, can you think a bit about what makes for a good colleague on a board, and were there features of the U.S. process that inhibited the kind of interaction that you had on the Irish Board with your colleagues? Or maybe another way to think of it more positively is, what created the collegiality on the Irish Board?

I think it was this consensus; we are all "in it together." Sarah and I would have dinner with individual colleagues on the Irish Board with about the same frequency. That would not have been true during my tenure at the FTC. That said, my term overlapped with Michael Pertchuk's. We didn't have a whole lot in common in terms of our views on antitrust and consumer protection. But I remember with fondness our dinners with Mike and his wife. Michael was a delightful dinner companion and a great person, except when we were at loggerheads at the agency or on the Hill where it could get tense at times. But Michael was a professional and we left our disagreements at the door when we left the office. I don't know what the current environment is like now, but I would encourage current Commissioners to remember that disagreements do not preclude civility. And who knows? You may be able to find areas of consensus. More importantly, there's the institutional interest of the agency in civility among its leadership.

I think that when you look around the world's 130 or so jurisdictions with competition laws, the collegial governance framework in some form is the leading framework chosen. You're pointing to a number of areas in which conscious thought about how to promote effective governance with a board is a distinctively important issue for boards. This personal dimension that you mentioned, too, developing a sense of common understanding, a bit of empathy, even common cause on some issues, is –

Right, and it certainly furthers finding areas where you can find common cause.

Yes. An institution whose leaders overlook that are missing a big chance.

I agree.

I would like to turn for a second to matters international. A question I think one faces – and certainly you saw some of that at the FTC but also with the Irish Authority – is: in one sense your job is at home, for your own citizens, but it's almost a cliché now that, with the growing interdependence across borders, the multiplicity of systems, the effective development of relationships across them, some standardization, some understanding of norms, becomes more and more important to the effective operation of one's own system. Yet, to do that effectively, you have to go to events, you have to meet people and get to know them. How does one reconcile the demands that are imposed in being the Chair of the Federal Trade Commission or a Commissioner for the Irish Authority but also being connected to this larger global environment?

I had the benefit of a year-long tutorial when I went to Ireland – "Modernization" under Regulation 1/2003 was taking shape. This basically integrated competition law enforcement in Europe and established "Rules of the Road" for interaction between and among the Commission and the Member States. While "Modernization" didn't bring about complete harmonization, it certainly moved the Commission and the Member States in that direction. Although my number one job was the enforcement of the competition laws of Ireland, I spent a lot of time on Advisory Committees talking with people from other Member States about "Modernization."

True, this probably was easier than normal discussions between or among national competition agencies because we were all Member States of the European Union. Focusing on the world at large, it's incredibly important for there to be interaction and exchange between competition authorities for lots of reasons. One is that cooperation may be essential to the discharge of your domestic responsibilities. When two authorities are reviewing a merger and take remedies that are not only quite different but inconsistent and contradictory, you have a problem. That's a bad mark on the discharge of your own domestic responsibilities. Doing a good job on your own turf often involves interacting with other competition agencies.

Participation in the work of transnational competition organizations is another important area. The International Competition Network (ICN) is a good example. Right from its beginning, when it focused on merger review processes, it has contributed to a better competition enforcement world. Another positive aspect, not often discussed, involves shared learning. I remember times in Ireland where we would call up someone in another agency and say, "I understand you've just had a merger in the widget market. We've never worked in the widget market before." We found those informal conversations immensely helpful. This was hugely important, particularly for a small agency that didn't have a wealth of experience in many markets.

And in Ireland you had a very modestly sized staff.

Very modestly sized staff. So that was very important to us. I also think that another important aspect of international cooperation – we touched on this a second ago – is formulating best practices. I remember changing Irish policy because of the ICN recommendation, which made us better and more efficient. The ICN has made a lot of progress here.

You underscore what I think is such an important point for our leaders to think about, which is that in this environment, with lots of very bright people in different places trying to solve similar difficult problems, it's crazy not to take advantage of the other experience and to join that up with your own.

Absolutely. Why reinvent the wheel?

That's a square, a triangle – no, round; someone else has shown that is best.

As we enter into a possible new era of antitrust, I hope that we will embolden agencies to think critically about where we've been before, where we are and where we want to go in the future.

A final question for thought. I'm struck by your comments on how it seems so important for a leader to take stock of their personal values and to emphasize certain traits that go beyond whether you know a lot about law, economics, how to define a relevant market or measure market power. You've spoken about humility. You've spoken about openness. You've spoken about the willingness to test ideas and listen carefully. The importance as well of honesty, being honest to yourself and to those you work with, to external audiences. Am I right that in many ways, when thinking of approaching a job of this kind, it's good to look in the mirror and ask, "Do I have these values, and how do I develop them?" because they may be as important as anything else we've talked about.

You're exactly right. And here is the challenge: you can look at yourself in the mirror and say,"Wow, what a leader!" Sometimes it is difficult to look closely enough at yourself. But when you do, think about the values that you seek to address. Rise to the challenge and say, "I'm going to try to externalize these values and, as imperfect as I am, I'm going to foster these values in the administration of this agency with my colleagues at all levels, and endeavor to instill these values in this institution."

And, I think, to think on a regular basis while you have the job, "Am I doing that?" That is, "What did I do this week to drive home to my colleagues and others by my own example, by my words, that these are things that are the values that will make us prosper?"

Right. And it's important all the time. I know you have championed retrospective studies. And not just in mergers, but generally. "How could we do it better?" This is exceedingly important. "Did we deliver on this objective; and, if we didn't, why not; and how can we be better at doing it?"

Andrea Coscelli*

Competition and Markets Authority, CEO (2016-2022)

You are the Chief Executive Officer of the United Kingdom's Competition and Markets Authority. In your capacity at the CMA, you developed a wonderful program. You are a voice that commands respect and attention in the field of competition law and policy. In coming to the CMA, you had had a variety of other experiences as a manager and now as the Chief Executive Officer of the institution. Which of your life's experiences best prepared you for this initiative?

I think quite a few. In many ways, you never plan your career, and things happen, but I spent a lot of time studying the substance. I did my first degree in Italy at Bocconi, which was already very much about economics, competition, industrial organisation, and also quite a lot of law, history, and politics. I really enjoyed this degree. And, then, I had a scholarship to go to Stanford and do a Ph.D. in Economics, which was an intense course in economics. I was already interested in competition regulation, in terms of courses I followed and in terms of my Ph.D. thesis. When I came to London to teach at UCL, I was already very interested in these issues and I realised quickly that, in many ways, there is a bit of a division of labour. It means that if you want to be a top academic, you need to spend a lot of time thinking about methodologies and pushing the boundaries. It was not as interesting to me as potentially applying things in a policy-making role. So, I decided to go into consulting, and I spent many years advising companies, in the UK, Europe but also a bit outside Europe, on antitrust cases, on mergers, or on Articles 101 and 102. That was very useful because I spent a lot of time learning how businesses operate, whether there are extremely well-organized businesses or not, with amazing internal documents and great data or not. When I then ended up on the other side, joining Ofcom,

* Interview conducted on 23 February 2018.

that business experience was very important. When I went to Ofcom, I was really interested in the agency, its problems and policymaking. Telecoms and media are very interesting sectors, so I really enjoyed doing that. I learned from Ed Richards, who was the Chief Executive at the time. He was very impressive in trying to combine intellectual content with implementation, stakeholder engagement, connections, and leadership.

When I then had the opportunity to join the CMA, first as an Executive Director on the Board and then as a CEO, in many ways, it felt to me that a lot of the things I had done made sense and they all contributed to what I was doing. Obviously, there are other things that I am doing more of, such as media or general leadership, where we try to learn by seeing others doing it and talking to people who can help us and give us good ideas. It is never-ending learning, but I am lucky that a lot of what I have done since I was 18 and started university contributes to what I am doing.

Would you say it was an advantage for you to have had this experience as an academic, as a researcher, as a practitioner advising firms, and as a civil servant, before coming to the CMA?

I really think so. It wasn't planned but it worked very well because I think as an academic. I had years to think about the substance of what we do and that's fortunate because now I don't have much time to replenish my intellectual capital and renew things so I need to be very selective. But there was a time I didn't need to, and I was a voracious reader of various things that are still relevant to what I am doing.

I think having been a practitioner is almost essential to do this job because you need judgment. You need instincts about when to enforce and when to push, when not to push, and how to listen. I think being on the other side and seeing genuinely how varied the situation is on the other side helps you a lot. Otherwise, you can become either too paranoid about the way a business behaves and think there is always an ulterior motive, or you can become very naive about the way a business operates. I think being on the other side allows you a better precision at making the judgment and your instincts hopefully are better. Certainly, having a period in highly performing agencies in a senior role, but not in the top role, is also essential before becoming the CEO of an organisation like this one, because I learned from very good people, like Ed Richards or Alex Chisholm. I was in the room when they had to make some difficult decisions and I saw how they operated. I saw how they thought about various issues, and how they tried to acquire the information. So, I learned some of the skills that I am applying, because I am the one who must make those decisions.

Are there some characteristics of leadership that impressed you from these earlier experiences, what you saw in a manager that struck you as being useful, valuable, and worthy of replication in your own work?

Absolutely, all of us think about some people who were in your position, and you try to replicate what you liked. For me, that applies both to senior businesspeople I worked with, senior people in agencies, and senior academics. It's a combination of that kind of interest in the substance and in the content – and intellectual curiosity – which is essential in this role because you need to keep evolving, and you need to feel challenged in the right way. I think you need to have the humility to understand that you are in a context where there are lots of people you can learn from, or you need to learn from. So, you need to be inclusive in your networks and all the angles that can help you.

I think there is also an aspect of respect or culture that exists both at Ofcom and in the CMA. I think in many ways that in the UK it's probably easier than in other countries to run these types of agencies because the culture of the Civil Service and the government is based on transparency, respect, and input from junior staff members. It's not a very hierarchical structure and has a culture of openness to the outside world that, I always felt, was the right one and I feel very comfortable in. In that sense, when I came to the CMA, I didn't feel that I needed to embark on a cultural change program because most of what I found, I liked. So, it's more about evolving at the margins.

Do you find that in your position, there is a particular advantage to have a deep background in industrial organization economics – starting from your time at Stanford where you had a remarkable cohort of peers. In practice, how much does it matter to you to have the deep expertise in this crucial field for the functioning of the CMA?

It gives me a lot of confidence on the substantive discussions. When you get to this level, the problem is that you are working across many matters and thinking about many things at the same time. Having this kind of deep knowledge allows me to play a role in the discussions on things where I don't have the time to look at a particular detail. If I didn't have this knowledge, I would play the role in a slightly different way, which probably would still be fine. Personally, I still like cases, so, occasionally, I still work directly on a case. I think it's important because I learn new things and I learn how things evolve, but also, I can potentially change some of our processes by seeing with individual cases what we are doing right and what potentially could be done in a slightly different way.

Coming to your current position, you had extensive exposure to the most senior management levels in the institution, you watched senior managers in another important public agency, Ofcom. What's difficult or different about taking the next step to being the Chief Executive Officer?

I think there is, to a degree, nowhere to hide. In many ways, the Board is very useful to me and plays an important role. But I need to do quite a lot of filtering and, then, there are some difficult judgments that, ultimately, I must make as the CEO. My personal approach is to try to share some of these problems with the Board or other people I know who can help me. For example, some of the debates are about how to deal with large digital platforms, in general, and with large digital platforms purchasing competitors. We want to be part of the debate and ultimately we have to make a judgment on some of these things.

As the CEO, you need to play a big role, but having a Board or other senior stakeholders who can help you is very important. I feel a degree of pressure on making some calls, because when you are the CEO nothing is risk-free, so not doing things or not launching programs is an active choice. I think that if you are one or two levels down, you can hide a bit more, saying: "Well the Board, or the CEO, decided not to launch this particular program, it wasn't really my active choice". There is an important difference. But if you have a healthy top team around you, if you have a good Board, I think you share quite a lot of this pressure in a very positive way.

I take it that formulating early on a good team of advisors, to surround yourself with people who will be candid, thoughtful, and effective in bringing issues to your attention, is very important to your success.

It's essential because in many ways you have a sequence of knotty issues coming and you need to be able to share the load with your senior team. I believe in a mix of being across everything and then doing some deep dives in only a few matters. Otherwise, you are not adding value. I think it is important to have a degree of knowledge about everything. But then on important matters, I will be the lead on some, and for others, it will be my key deputies, and I want to be in a place where I trust them. I know they are going to do a good job and I am not going to second guess because a lot of what we do is evidence-based, it's case-specific, and there is a lot of knowledge linked to it.

Is it important for the leader to do the occasional deep dives, not simply because of personal interest or intellectual curiosity, but to get an idea of what's really going on in the heart of the institution?

Absolutely. Sometimes, the organisation can find it unsettling to have the CEO be the key part of a big decision on a specific case, but I think it is important to keep yourself close to what is happening and be able to make the right decision if you need to make some changes to process. For instance, I am doing one of these case decision groups in one of our pharma cases – which is an important case – but also I am seeing a number of things about the process. Then, when I decide with others about whether we want to flex certain things, this puts me in a much better position to judge the type of changes we want to make.

Is there any rethinking you have to do about your role or a broader appreciation of it that comes from being on stage all the time internally, everyone pays attention to the CEO? They notice whether you wear the same tie 3 days a week, they follow where you go, they notice if you go into this coffee shop all the time. Externally, you are in a crucial way the face of the agency, reporters ask you questions, not always the ones that you want to be asked, but you have to be basically ready to go all the time with this sort of ubiquitous observation. Was that something that you had to adjust to?

Yes, it's something and in a sense, I am still adjusting to that. I think it's one of the big changes from the previous roles. What I am trying to do is – and even if I look at the last 2 months compared to where I was in the summer – to be more selective with what I do. I try to spend a day, or a day-and-a-half a week if I manage, at home actually reading for various things I need to read, but also thinking a bit proactively; because there was a time when I felt I was constantly in this kind of cycle from a meeting to another meeting, from a decision to another decision and I felt my ability to actually influence was suffering because I didn't have enough time to properly think about things.

Also, I am thinking a bit about personal resilience. If I have a long day, if I can get home and go for a run it's the type of thing that I think really helps, because it is draining and it is quite exhausting to be constantly on stage, constantly chairing and deciding. So, I think you get into a world where I would say it's quality rather than quantity. You need to think about what you really need to do, how to do it well and then build some space around it, where maybe you work from home or go for a run rather than just being on all the time, because it's just not possible otherwise.

I think people tend to forget or don't realize what a fast treadmill this experience is, and they forget in a basic way to take care of themselves. And I sense from what you are saying that a conscious choice that you make is, "I have to be able to continue to maintain my health, my fitness, my energy" and that's a deliberate part of your schedule.

Yes, absolutely! And it's difficult – when you read about CEOs in much bigger organisations, they would say the same. It's always a challenge, but I think it is very important to try to do that. So, I am spending quite a lot on thinking about and trying to do it.

And to protect a space in which you can read and think.

Yes, exactly – I think that is very important. I mean obviously, you evolve into a world where you become extremely selective about what you read, and about the length of what you read. It is one of those things where you realize with age that writing a short article to the point is much more likely to have an impact with senior decision makers, and obviously in a sense if you read about prime ministers and very senior politicians that is an extreme version of it. So, I try to curate what I read, I try to become very selective, but I need time, when I am at home, not looking at the iPad, not looking at the computer, not being on the phone and actually reading from the beginning to the end a particular piece. This doesn't happen very often, but it is quite important and similarly, in terms of Boards and Executive Committees and the sort of committees I chair, you need the time to read the papers and properly think about them because that is really where you add value at the end of the day. You need to take decisions, but the decisions need to be informed and based on having been thinking about things. I think otherwise, there is a real risk if you just start doing it in a very superficial way, because you are just too stretched.

Do you keep time for yourself to read outside the area of competition law and policy?

I do a bit. I like to read fiction and I find at the end of long days, to have an hour to read a good book which is not about politics or competition law; I think it's actually very good. I am finishing Eugenides' *Fresh Complaint,* which is a collection of short stories.

So, to refresh the palate to...

Yes, to think on something which is good, which I enjoy doing, which is different from what I do in my day job – because I have always been very interested in politics, policy, history, newspapers and what we do. So, in many ways I could continue to do that, but I think it's quite healthy to mentally – occasionally – have a break and be in a different space or do something different. And I love going to the cinema, I love football, so I do several other things in London, which have nothing to do with my job, and which are an important part of replenishing my energy levels.

What's the hardest thing about the job for you, the most difficult?

I think it is this nagging sense that you are constantly making decisions even when you are not making them and that things take a long time in our world. In many ways, if I think about my tenure, probably I am taking right now some of the key decisions that will affect my overall tenure. So, it's this sense that you think you would always like to acquire more information, to talk to more people to have more views, so that you can make the best possible choice, which obviously you can't. So, you must be selective, you have to think about who you talk to or what you read, what kind of input you seek.

As an academic, there would be a tendency to want to study more, but you can't do that unless you want to decide one matter a month.

Exactly, – so there is that balance and luckily part of my brain is academic because this is what I did for part of my life, but the other part of my brain is very much on results, outcomes and in many ways very pragmatic, very incremental. So, I try to combine the two instincts because I think I have a very strong sense that I want to add value and to do something concrete – very much try to show that we have moved particular industries from 'A' to 'B' because of our intervention in a way that we could. I can be somewhere in the country and explain to an average person, who doesn't even know what the CMA is, that we have actually done something useful. So, I try to combine these two things, which in a sense is never perfect but you try your best.

We talked about the hardest thing. What is the best part of the job? What is it that gets you up in the morning with a bounce in your step?

I think in many ways it's almost a flip side of this. It is the fact that you are in a well-functioning, strong organisation in a context that is very supportive of us trying to do the right thing and you do have the power – in a sense it's earned power and it's power shared with others in a very democratic way – but as a CEO you do materially influence what the agency is going to do, this has a real impact on people, and you can actually improve things. That is a fantastic luxury and in many ways; I am very grateful that I am in this place doing it. I think it's a big responsibility but also a great feeling that you can do something useful.

I have two more questions; one deals a bit with preparation. How to do the job? How important is it to be a political scientist, at least an amateur political scientist? The CMA has a significant degree of by custom and by law independence. You take your own decisions, yet you operate in a political environment that has a keen interest in what you do. It's pressing demands on you for what to do, it's part of the larger life's preparation. How important is it to be at least at some level a student of the politics, of the political evolution of the nation?

I might be naïve in a sense – growing up in Italy you think about political science very much in a Machiavellian way, which is very much thinking how I can get a particular angle on things – and the way I am interpreting it here is very different. It's much more being out there, talking to lots of well-meaning MPs from all political parties, to understand what they get from their constituents, what their concerns are, and taking them very seriously. Again, I think the advantage of operating in this country, where democracy is working very well in my view, is you talk to lots of well-meaning, reasonable people challenging you in a constructive, positive way and I think to me it's a main source of inspiration in terms of things we should do, or we should do differently. So I really like to do that. And I think if you do that in good faith, if you are open and try to help people – if they come to you with concerns, you try to explain that either you deal with them or explain why you are not dealing with them – that creates relationships that are very helpful for the organisation as a whole. I think you should do it anyway because it's a very important aspect of what we do, and if you do it in the right way it really helps the organisation. So that is what I am trying to do at the moment and obviously the Chair plays a big role in it, and other Board members, but it's an important part of what a CEO needs to do.

The day comes when you move to another stage in your career, part of the continuing journey that you embarked on long ago and you are talking to your successor, a prospective successor or someone who is thinking about coming to a position of public responsibility in a similar institution in another time. What do you know now that you wish you had known on the first day, that you would want to convey to them?

In a sense, I am still reasonably new in post and still learning. I think that one of the big lessons in my mind, particularly if you come from the private sector, is that at the end of the day these institutions have lots of processes – and there are good reasons for that because you are exposed to many challenges at many levels. I think in my mind, the role of the CEO is to be very focused on decluttering, on trying to break down processes, simplify things, and try to create energy and dynamism in the way things are done. I think if you are in a private sector environment, in a competitive sector, you have to do it because, in a sense, if you are less efficient than your competitors it shows up in the numbers. As a public agency, this might not immediately show up, so I think you need to be the actor who is constantly challenging the institution in a constructive way, understanding the institution well but to simplify, declutter, speed things up, and increase the level of energy and dynamism, because the system as a whole will always put in more challenges to you and slow you down. So, unless you create this force on the other side, there is a real risk, I think, that the agency becomes a bit too slow in dealing with the challenges coming to us.

Carles Esteva Mosso*

European Commission – DG COMP, Deputy Director-General (2014-2021)

You are one of the great enforcers of the past quarter-century-plus. You are now a partner at Latham & Watkins but have served for over 25 years before that with the European Commission in a number of positions that deal with competition law and policy at very senior levels; you have extensive experience in merger control, in State aids, and indeed as a senior adviser to the top leadership of the Commission. As a way to begin, could you take us on an autobiographical journey, telling us a bit about how you came into the field of competition law and policy and covering some of the highlights of your tenure in the European Commission, please?

My career has mostly taken place within the European Commission. It has been the typical insider career. I started as a lawyer just after university, but I joined the Commission very young. At the beginning, I was a case handler in antitrust dealing with financial services. I joined the Merger Task Force after learning all the niceties of Articles 101 and 102. There I dealt with cases across all the spectrum of industries. At the time, merger control was still not structured by sectors, a Task Force was dealing with all cases. I moved because Commissioner Mario Monti asked me to join his cabinet, his private office. I think this was a turning point in my career. I spent 5 very intense years advising him on cartels, on antitrust, on mergers; and this was a period of great change in competition policy. That is when the modernization of antitrust was enacted. That is when we reformed the Merger Regulation.

* Interview conducted on 21 January 2022.

Can you remind us of what year was your first year in the cabinet of the Commissioner?

Commissioner Monti was Competition Commissioner between 1999 and 2004, if I am right, so this was the period that I spent with him.

An incredibly significant period in the development of competition law and policy in Europe and globally.

The modernization had been started by the previous Commissioner, by Commissioner Karel Van Miert, but Mario Monti was the one who concluded the discussions with Member States and started to enforce it. The merger review started at that period, and we concluded it before the end of the mandate. So, as you say, a very important period for the reform of competition policy.

After the time with the Commissioner in his cabinet, what came next for you?

After this I came again to DG COMP where I started to have management positions, first in merger policy; then I enforced for a while the merger instrument as the Head of Unit for the Telecoms and Tech Sector, where I was involved in cases like Google/DoubleClick, Nokia/NAVTEQ, some cutting-edge issues at the time; and then I was appointed Director for Policy, where I was in charge basically of the development of policy in all the areas of DG COMP, coordination of enforcement, and also at that period I was in charge of the relations with national authorities and of the international aspects of competition policy. It was a great period in which I met a lot of people – I think it was at that time when I met you, Bill – and I could develop a real overview of what DG COMP was doing in all areas.

Then, I was appointed Deputy Director-General for Mergers. I stayed there for 5 years. In a certain way I see a continuity in all this career. I spent time with Commissioner Monti helping to reform the Merger Regulation, then time in the policy function dealing with implementation and developing these reforms, – the Guidelines on Horizontal Mergers and Non-Horizontal Mergers, the Guidelines on Remedies – and then I had the opportunity to be in charge of all the enforcement merger capacity of DG COMP. So those were 15 years with some coherence that I enjoyed very, very much.

After this, I still was asked to be in charge of the State Aids Department. I did that for my last 2 years at the Commission. It was a pretty special moment. This coincided mostly with the most acute days of the Covid-19 pandemic, so it was a period where the State Aids world changed substantially. We had to find a way to support the economies of Member States to waive the negative impacts of the pandemic, but at the same time to put in place a common framework in which this support would be granted to maintain a level playing field in Europe. So, it was a period of change, and I would say an interesting management challenge for my last 2 years in the Commission.

Of all of these positions, before looking at some of your broader observations, which was the most challenging?

I would highlight two of these positions. Certainly, the 5 years at the cabinet was a period of change and also a period of difficult challenges. This was when the Court annulled 3 prohibition decisions in a few months' difference, and we had to react to this. One of the great merits of Commissioner Monti was to transform this challenge, this crisis, into an opportunity to really revamp the system of merger control in Europe and make it much more, let's say, resilient to this type of challenges in Court. So, this was a fascinating period to be there. And also, my 5 years at the helm of Merger Control were a highlight of course, a moment to put in practice all that I had learned during the previous years of my career, so I enjoyed this very much.

Looking at this fascinating progression from your time as a junior case handler and looking at the positions that you ultimately ascended to in a senior leadership role, can you say a bit more about how the earlier responsibilities prepared you to be an effective leader when it came to assuming ever-more-demanding senior leadership roles? I guess another way of putting it is: Is the path that you followed a good path for a manager to take in the progression towards greater responsibility?

I'm sure there are many good paths to become a manager in a competition agency. My one was the insider path, and I think it has certain advantages compared to someone who would come from a different position directly to the top. Maybe if you come from the outside, you might have a stronger drive for radical change, but I wonder whether you have the tools to make this change sustainable and long-lasting. When you have grown through the organization, you know the persons, you know the real constraints, and you know what are the levers that you need to use to really ensure that there is real and profound change. And also, you have seen others do it. You have seen others making right decisions but also making mistakes, yourself you have made mistakes, so you can use all this background, all this baggage, to try to do it better at the moment that you have the responsibility to run the network.

Did it help you in your later career to have started as a case handler, to have worked in the engine room, not on the bridge of the ship but in the engine room? Was that useful to you? Did you continue to draw on those experiences as your career went forward?

I think understanding how the cases are run on a day-to-day basis is fundamental because it allows you to have realistic expectations of what people can do, to be demanding as to what you think the teams can deliver without being unrealistic, and also because I think you cannot be a manager in a competition agency without keeping very close contact with the facts and the cases. Obviously, you cannot deal with all of them, but the key ones, the ones where the reputation of the agency will make or break, for these ones you need to be able to get into the facts, get into the details of the cases, and if you have been a case handler before, you know the basics of the task. But I would say that another experience was also very useful, and that is the cabinet experience. I would recommend for those who want to have a similar career in the Commission to try to have an experience in a cabinet, because at the end the decision-maker is the Commissioner. Understanding the constraints, understanding the way a Commissioner operates, is very useful afterwards to provide good advice to the Commissioner as a senior manager in the Commission and to avoid pitfalls that maybe you would not recognize if you had not spent some time helping the political level to make decisions and to run their day-to-day business.

You observed senior leaders who indeed occupied the top spot in the Directorate. You had your own major roles as a manager. Can you give us some general observations about what makes for a good leader in the front office, in the position? Reflect a bit on the role of the Commissioner. What characteristics do you want to see in a person who takes that position? What do you want to see in that person?

First of all, you want to see vision. Maybe vision is too grand an expression. You want to see the clarity of purpose; you want someone at the top who can explain what are the values that matter for him, where he wants to go, where he wants to bring the organization, and that he can convey also what he expects for the people working for him, and that he can convey all this internally, but also externally to a stakeholder. That is the first thing. Second, you need a degree of people skills, to put it in a single expression. You need to be able to build teams, to empower the teams, to guide, to coach them.

In the end, you cannot achieve anything on your own unless you are able to build a strong team around you. And finally, at least in the positions where I was, you need to be also a good adviser. You need to be able to provide relevant advice on different cases and present options and their pros and cons. Competition policy is not a science; there are always alternatives, with their advantages and disadvantages.

I assume it's important to have a Commissioner who will listen to the alternatives too and will encourage advisers and others throughout the institution to say what they think. I mean the Commissioner, as you say, is the appointed official who will have to decide; but I assume it's important for that person to listen even to advice that might not immediately fit the initial preference, but to be a good listener too.

And I think that a key responsibility of the managers is to provide the Commissioner with well-argued options in order for him or her to make the final decision. When I joined DG COMP, this was not at all the case. There would have been long discussions within the administration and then the Commissioner was presented with a single choice, like "this is the right decision." This evolved over time. We introduced the Chief Economist's Team to be able to provide advice also from an economic perspective. There is also a Hearing Officer who provides advice on procedures. The Legal Service provides legal advice to the Commissioner. The DG and all the services around would in every important case provide a panoply of possibilities for the Commissioner, sometimes even too many. But, now to be serious, there is always a choice within reasonable alternatives, and to really reach good decisions it is important that several people present their views on these different choices and the Commissioner then really has a good basis to make a final decision.

I think you've touched on this already, but what brought about that change in decision-making culture, to increase the streams of advice coming to the Commissioner? What brought that about?

Certainly, the merger defeats in 2002, the 3 cases that you mentioned, made us reflect a lot on what type of organization we wanted to have in the future to avoid these types of situations. The introduction of the Chief Economist's Team was one of the ideas. Also, what we call the peer review panels, these panels of "a fresh pair of eyes" officials that would revise the proposal of the team to see whether these proposals hold or not and then present these alternative views to the Commissioner. All these were mechanisms that we introduced at that time in order to ensure that the decision-making would be more diverse, would incorporate more diverse views, and therefore would be more solid. I think when you look at the track record of the Commission in the recent years probably this was a good change to have incorporated.

Quite often in life I think you learn the most about people when times are bad rather than when times are good. When everything is going well, the love just pours from the sky and everybody's happy; but when you face difficulties, crisis, you perhaps see more deeply into the souls of individuals and see what they do. You referred to the reaction of the Commissioner when these 3 defeats came about. Of course, the way they are portrayed externally is that the universe is falling to pieces, that the roof has caved in. Tell me a bit more about how the Commissioner responded to this; that is, as a human being and as a leader, how did he respond to this and bring about the changes that made such a difference?

As you know, Mario Monti was a leader of great integrity, so he took these defeats very seriously. At the same time, he understood that this was an opportunity for change. The merger review had already started. It's not that it was started at that moment – there was already a reflection on how to improve merger control – but that that moment it got a new impetus. There was a mix of proposals that were coming from DG COMP but also proposals that were coming from the Commissioner himself to strengthen the system, so he took a very direct and personal interest in this. Altogether, in a dialogue with DG Competition, the result was the proposal for what would become the Merger Regulation of 2004 plus all the processes that were developed around this and that have continued basically to this day.

And I think, as you mentioned, in the face of difficulty to see it as an opportunity to carry out needed reforms; instead of giving in to a sense of despair, to think about how this is an opportunity to make things better going ahead, and perhaps to put in place changes that might not have been accepted otherwise. I sense he had a strong intuition for this. In building and communicating with the team within the house, what are the best ways that a leader can do that, how to be an effective exponent of your program, how to gain support for it? What do you do to make that happen?

I think in competition agencies, or more generally in enforcement agencies, the teams have a very particular position because you really want them to be applying the law in an impartial and fair way; therefore, you want them to be empowered to do this, to take responsibility on this. You need to find an equilibrium of empowering the teams but at the same time ensuring that these teams would not really become too attracted to one particular outcome. You want them to maintain their impartiality; to maintain the approach that we discussed before, the idea that there is not only one single outcome but there could be several outcomes that would all be reasonable. It's very important to have this communication, I would say, from the beginning, that the team has to do this thorough job, but at the end the decision will not be made by the team. This needs to be understood – if not, this could lead to frustrations – but when this is understood, I think you have an agency that works better because there is a team that is doing the groundwork; but then you have also the possibility to have decisions that ensure a coherent approach around cases and that incorporate a policy thinking in the evolution of cases. You need to achieve this equilibrium, which is not always so obvious.

Do you think it was important to the Commissioner for you to spend lots of time individually with members of the Directorate – that is, to have the proverbial open door or to have a regular process by which you get to know the individuals in the organization better than you did before? Is that one-on-one contact important to build the team and as part of your communication strategy?

No doubt, also for the reasons I've mentioned before. Even as a top manager, you want to be involved in the cases, and the best way to do that is having long discussions with the teams, with team members in some cases, and to be a good listener. I think to be there you need to listen a lot and to ask questions and ensure that people can express their views. Sometimes the shy guy at the table is the one that will have the best insight, so you need to ensure that this person also is empowered and is comfortable to speak. So yes, I think at all levels of management a good attitude to listen to people is fundamental for success.

In carrying out modernization, just to mention one other major transformation that takes place in addition to the significant internal reforms that took place within DG COMP, what was crucial to bringing along the Member States? Many of the Member States have long and proud traditions. I think they like to see themselves as being peers rather than in any subordinate relationship as members of this network. The European Competition Network was a new approach to ensuring that this remarkable delegation of authority would operate effectively. What was important for the Commission and the Commissioner and those of you in senior leadership positions to gain confidence among the Member States that this was going to make things better? How did you make that work?

In the antitrust modernization there was a fundamental tradeoff that was in the interest of everybody. On one side you had the decentralization toward Member States, they could apply Article 101(3), but on the other hand you had a series of measures to ensure coherence of application that would also be part of the package in Regulation 1/2003. At the end of the day everybody had something to gain in this tradeoff, but it's true that to get there, there was lot of dialogue, a lot of discussion multilaterally with all the national competition authorities, but also very often bilaterally to try to address particular concerns of the one or the other. It's in these situations where you see Europe at its best, trying to understand the difficulties that each Member State would have to move forward, to find solutions that would keep the group united and would allow all to move. There are things to improve, things to correct, but overall, I think modernization was a great success and has helped to have a much more, not only coherent, but also widespread enforcement of competition in Europe as a whole.

I think you've touched on it, but I was going to ask: Compared to the initial goals and expectations, what has turned out better than you expected?

You've seen very little conflicts on case allocation. In these almost 20 years you can count the conflicts – well, very few of them – and this I think was one of the big question marks of this package, how this would develop. On this front, much better than expected. On the coherence front also, it has turned out well. Of course, there have been here and there some areas where not all Member States are aligned in their national enforcement, but overall, I think there has been a clear push towards much more coherence in priorities – 20 years ago, cartels were not a priority in many national enforcement plans – and much more coherence in the interpretation of the rules. There are still things to improve, but overall, I think it was better than expected.

Of course, that is taking part in parallel that we assume this conversation is a breathtaking expansion of the membership of the Union. The only people who think that was easy have never been involved in doing that. That was an extraordinary adjustment I'm sure for all the Directorates, but yours as well – that is, to accommodate the admission of many more Member States with varied traditions, varied degrees of administrative capacity. That had to be a difficult management challenge as well.

It is often forgotten that modernization coincided with the enlargement of 10 new Member States at the time, plus others that have joined afterwards. So, it was a Big Bang moment. It was a moment of change on many fronts. In a certain way for many of them – some of them had of course already antitrust enforcement in the past – it was also an opportunity to develop a really modern system of antitrust enforcement. I think again we can see a good integration.

We've talked about the relationship inside the European Commission, among the Member States inside DG COMP. Another dimension is the relationship with external constituencies – with the bar, with the academic community, with business organizations, with other countries and jurisdictions. What attributes make a leader effective in dealing with that environment? You were part of that process. I would hesitate to even guess how many speeches you gave over the course of, say, your last 20 years in leadership positions. You've stood at the podium. What attributes are important in dealing with this external audience that looks at every word you say, has its own high expectations, its criticism – you're never doing a good enough job? What state of mind and ability do you have to have to act in that environment as a representative of your institution?

I think there are two precise interactions in relation to stakeholders – you need to communicate but you also need to listen – and I think the two aspects are very important. In terms of communication, you need to be able to articulate the changes that policy is going through. Sometimes those are easy to present, such as a new legislation or a new guidance; but for some others it's more about explaining what you are trying to do – following certain trends in enforcement, things that may not be so apparent to the public, maybe only to the people who really follow what the administrations are doing. I think part of the job is to divulgate, to give transparency to what you are doing and to what you want to do, to give in part legal certainty, to give in part predictability to the stakeholders that have to interrelate with you. You do not want to surprise people. You want people to understand what you will do when a case arrives on your table. That is an important part of the communication. But it's also about listening, about understanding concerns, and about being open to integrate these concerns when possible.

You've mentioned competition authorities around the world. I think one of the really satisfactory aspects of my years as Policy Director was to be involved in all these discussions. The International Competition Network (ICN) had already been established, but it was a period when the ICN was being developed, so how to develop this ICN without binding tools? Simply by ensuring that everybody around the table agrees on some basic principles. This required quite a lot of dialogue, quite a lot of understanding, and also maybe being able to see what is essential for you and what is maybe accessory and being able to compromise on the accessory aspects in order to agree on the essentials. I think the ICN made quite a lot of progress with these attitudes of many people around the table.

How do you operate in an environment where occasionally your international partners suggest directly or indirectly that you're doing your job badly? Not to pick on any one country, but let's imagine a large country in North America that from time to time says publicly, "You're on the wrong path." How do you respond to that? What does a leader have to do in responding to that kind of criticism, sometimes very pointed? I was never a participant in throwing those rocks myself, but I watched fellow countrymen do it. How is a leader supposed to cope with that?

You're pointing at a period that we all lived very intensively. I think there are two reactions. One is maybe an internal one, really to say to your interlocutors, "Look, we are open to discuss all this, but maybe it's easier to make progress when you discuss these things behind closed doors than when you make your position so clear in public". That is an important reaction to set a good path for future relations. But also, there is a need to react publicly. Very often these statements are based on misunderstandings, are based on simplifications, so it is important to react, to put the record straight, and then privately try to advance without less public noise, which is always possible.

If you had to think of specific steps that authorities could take today to increase that understanding – and I think you have put your finger on such an important condition, which is, to put it bluntly, ignorance – ignorance about process, ignorance about context, ignorance about motivation. How do we overcome that? What kinds of steps can we take to do better than we are doing today to achieve that deeper awareness of why things have happened and what those things are? How do we do that?

First of all, during my period in DG COMP I have to say that the situations that you mentioned have been the exceptions, not the rule. Normally, the cooperation among agencies was functioning reasonably well. There were good discussions and in most of the cases these led to convergent approaches. So, let's not give too much dimension to these conflicts that normally are the minority of the situations.

Now I think dialogue, at all levels of the agencies, is what is needed to understand each other better, to understand each other's processes better. Sometimes we believe that we understand the systems of other countries better than what we do because we try to believe that they have things by default like ours, and this is not always the case; you always discover new things that you were not aware of in other countries' competition systems, so there is a need to improve this knowledge.

There is a need also to have discussions at the top to align goals and objectives. And then, on a case-by-case basis, of course there is a need to have discussion between the teams to try to align, to the extent possible, the approaches. That doesn't mean that in all cases you will always arrive at convergent situations. Sometimes the markets are different, sometimes the concerns are different, but as much as you can it's important that agencies talk to each other and try to give coherent messages to companies and to advisers because that is also part of the job of a competition agency, not to make these deals more difficult than what they are already.

Did you feel a tension in your time at DG COMP between the demands to serve the immediate needs of the community, to work on your work at home, your main job, but at the same time to interact with this larger international world – not simply in the context of the ECN, but in the context where today over 130 institutions around the world, more than that doing competition law – did you find a tension in deciding how much time in senior leadership beyond your position as head of policy, but how does a leader decide how much time, roughly speaking, to work on the main job at home but also the part of the job that involves these external connections? If you want to go to an international meeting, you can go every week. How do you decide which of these two functions to focus on?

When you are in these positions time is always missing, so you really need to make compromises. Obviously, your main responsibility is to ensure that enforcement at home is done properly, but you also have very good teams that can take care of the day-to-day cases and you don't need to be on the cases every day. This gives you some scope to engage with the stakeholders and to engage with international counterparts. But it also depends a bit on the time. There will be moments when you have more to communicate, moments when you have more to explain. Let me simply give an example. I think at the time when we started to focus more on innovation in merger assessment, some of what we were doing was misunderstood, so at that moment there was more of a need to go out and explain what we were doing in Dow/DuPont or in similar cases, to go out and discuss with other authorities how they would approach this type of development, while in other moments maybe there is less necessity to engage and discuss. But this is an important component of any senior management job. It cannot be left aside.

Before going to some closing questions, can I ask: If you look at your time and you look at things that you worked on, what handful of things gives you the greatest sense of accomplishment and pride?

You always tend to think about one case here or there. Certainly, in my period there were major cases – I've mentioned innovation cases; Siemens/Alstom; maybe the recapitalization of airlines when I was in State Aids. At the end of the day, I don't think this is what really gives you satisfaction. To me it is more what I mentioned before; it's the continuity in being first next to the Commissioner when the Merger Regulation was reformed; being able then to implement it, to develop guidelines, and then to apply it. It was this contribution during 15 years of developing a merger control system that works. It's not something that you do on your own, you do it with many people; but having been part of this endeavor for 15 years and seeing that the system works reasonably well is probably one of the major satisfactions that I would get from my time at the administration.

Would you say that it is a good team to have the mix of insiders with this long view of what has taken place and how things have unfolded, with occasional introductions of insights from outsiders who come in – that is, with other ideas, perhaps unconventional ideas? For a competition authority is that a good mix to strive for?

It's always good to have views from outside sometimes to relativize some of the debates that in agencies could go for years, sometimes to bring new perspectives and new ideas – certainly that is useful – but also what the insiders bring is necessary; so, it's a balance between the two views that achieves the best results, no doubt.

Certainly, in our many conversations a theme that has come up is the importance for the institution to have the memory of what it has done, why it has done it, things that have gone well, things that have fallen short but how to improve them, to have that one standing memory; but this injection of new perspectives as well, to bring those together. A final question for you: Imagine the day that you were leaving the office – and I suspect in some ways that was a bittersweet moment, to look at all of your colleagues, even in a pandemic where you don't quite look at them in the same way – and you are having the one-on-one discussion with a successor, senior management. On the question of management and leadership, when you look back at what you have learned, what advice would you pass along to them as they begin their first day? Maybe it's a person who has also been an insider, but they haven't had the job of being the boss. What do you tell them? Something that you learned, things you learned, in the course of a quarter-century that might not be evident to them coming into this new senior role. What is your advice to them?

That is what I would say to anyone who gets to a position of power: Don't stay there simply to manage things. Try to bring change. Try to improve the situation. For this, first, don't think that you have all the time in the world; the time goes quickly, so use it. But also, don't rush; sometimes rushed changes are not sustainable. Second, don't believe that you have it all under control even if you are in charge, because there are many, many uncertainties that could derail even the best-planned change programs. Look at the pandemic. I was 6 months in State Aids and suddenly this arrived, and we had to start from zero. So that would be my message: Use the position to introduce change, do it responsibly, but don't wait too much.

Allan Fels*

Australia Competition and Consumer Commission, Chairman (1989-2003)

You served for many years as the Chair of Australia's Competition and Consumer Commission (ACCC). You have had a broad range of experiences outside of competition law and policy, and it's no accident that you have been sought out again and again by governments to provide advice and guidance on a whole host of crucial public policy challenges. You had a formative role in creating the Australia and New Zealand School of Government, which is a repository of knowledge for civil servants in those two countries. I would like to start taking you through the path that led you to the ACCC and the chairmanship of the agency. Can you tell us a bit about how it was that you came to be the Chair?

I was on a dual track: an academic, including some teaching in competition law; but I also was for many years a regulator, often part-time, for about 20 years before I became Chair, of various Commonwealth government, state government, regulatory things, in telecommunications, aviation, agriculture, sometimes the Price Commissioner, and so on. I found that a tremendously useful and somewhat unique background for my start at the ACCC, which previously had been headed by good people, but their background was entirely corporate law. They were not so used to engaging with the public, the community, the media, and dealing with that, let alone the intricacies and tricks of dealing with the government and the departments and the ministers that sponsor you and the other ones. And also, I had a fair bit of experience in actually running regulatory organizations, so I had some idea of the managerial challenges.

---

* Interview conducted on 28 June 2019.

I want to draw out a couple of points there that strike me as terribly important for thinking about how good leaders develop. I take it that the backgrounds that you referred to, having had extensive experience in public-sector regulatory bodies, was very important for coming to a new public-sector regulatory body. It was a start-up institution, but that background in public-sector regulatory functions and serving as the head of those institutions was a very valuable background for you in coming to the ACCC.

That is right. I kind of had the idea from the start that there are really 3 things you need to look at. One is: what would be of value to the community? What is the real contribution that the agency is making? And then, also, what do you do about the political authorizing environment? It's the source of your legitimacy and authority, and it's something you have to engage with, sometimes cautiously, but you certainly need to understand it. And then the other thing you think about is: What can I do? What is my actual capability of getting the results which I think would be of public value – the resources, the skills, the legal powers – and what role do other people play in helping you achieve your objectives?

Thinking of good traits for a competition agency leader, the broad knowledge of the economy which you acquired in these positions is quite valuable.

Yes. I was the first economist appointed as Chair of the ACCC. I started at the Trade Practices Commission. That meant that I had a somewhat different perspective. First of all, economics, as you know, is a system, it looks at the whole system, so I immediately thought about general priorities. It was really obvious to me that the priority should be the sectors not exposed to international trade; generally competition from abroad took care of them. It was in the non-traded goods and services sector that the priorities clearly existed, so we tended to give much more attention to that. Of course, I also understood the need to get more economic analysis into various issues, and somehow to link that properly with the law. I was aware from the start that economics has its own deficiencies. Just to give you one example, very early on there was a spectacular business crash of a new airline in Australia, a new competitor, and we were asked to report on the immediate causes of it. So we hired an economist who wrote an excellent essay on the need for an open skies policy in world aviation policy. However, this was an excellent essay, but completely irrelevant to what we were asked to report about, the immediate causes of the collapse and so on. So we need economists, but we need them to come up with work that is operationally useful and often in a situation where in the jargon of economics you're looking at third-best policy – you know, there's ideal; then there's near-ideal; and then somewhere down further you have to apply economics in imperfect situations.

I'm guessing that, by the time you came to the ACCC, not only were you professionally trained as an economist and well-practiced in that field, but you had become a political scientist too in a way that, as you were mentioning before, you had a broad understanding of how government works in all levels of the country and how the political context part of what, I think, you've called the "enabling environment" at different times, is a crucial consideration in formulating your own program going ahead.

That is right. From the start, I knew that the ACCC was dealing with huge disputes over really valuable property rights and there is no avoiding the fact that there is conflict and that different sides of the argument will try to influence you in every way, whether through political influence or through the media or other things. Above all, it seemed to me that I should use the media as an instrument to strengthen the power of the Commission in the public mind and politically, that we should be out there explaining to the community, to the media, to everyone, what we were doing, why it was needed, and so on. But, of course, it's not a matter of calling a meeting of the media to discuss those abstract questions. You do your education through cases and the strategic use of them. A case is great for media publicity because it involves conflict and confrontation. The media loves a fight and they will cover it, and most often you will come out the winner in these debates – not always, but it's worth taking the risk. Also, in talking to them you have to try to tell the human story. They're not very interested in whether some particular subsection of the Act has been breached by a particular technical action, so you want to offer the human bit. Early on we had a case where two friends used to play golf every Saturday, and then one of them changed jobs, and suddenly they realized they were competitors, and at the nineteenth hole at this golf club, they started getting a cartel arrangement going. That is a very good way of getting over to the public what is involved in a cartel. Also, we strongly emphasized our consumer protection role.

ACCC has the dual competition and consumer role.

The dual role; that's always very popular. To use the language of long ago, it's "motherhood" – I think it's "parenthood" these days. So these rather easy consumer cases – first of all, they're easy to explain to the public; they get over to the public that you, the regulator, are on the consumer's side. Then, later, when the debate is on about a more complex matter, a merger that you have rejected or something like that, it's difficult for the public to fully grasp the issues but they still think, "Ah, that person, he is on the side of the consumer". I will give him the benefit of the doubt on this one. To get the story over, it's a matter of exploiting the cases. Now, of course, business hates it. As far as business is concerned, there's a case and there's an outcome and once the fine is paid, or whatever, they want to move on. That is just the beginning of it for the regulator; you want the whole public to know it. You want to explain why that case is relevant to everyone in business and why the regulator could come to your sector next, and also getting over to the public, to small business and to farmers what it's all about.

I take it that a conscious element of your approach in the ACCC was for the full range of things that the ACCC did, to always be aware of how you're going to convey the meaning of this to the larger constituencies outside of your institution, including the broader public.

That is right. As soon as we sniffed a case, I was already thinking of the relevant headline. I did have a great education in the United Kingdom. I wrote a whole book about a great UK institution, the National Board for Prices and Incomes, which was headed by a very skillful politician, Aubrey Jones, who was also a journalist. He had a similar thing, that he could immediately see at the beginning of the case how you were going to explain it publicly. So we also made it pretty clear to the staff: do the technical work; win all the technical issues in court, or whatever; but be ready to explain in plain language what's going on and the wider implications. Again, for example, if there was a cartel that you caught, you would find out where they met and then you would take photos of that meeting venue. We had a good cartel in a couple of our well-known hotels, so we sent –

Without naming them, were there well-established hotels that they chose as a matter of course?

They were sort of interesting hotels. They were rather popular – not the top-order ones, not global names that you would think about, but very well-known local drinking institutions. And also in those places it's a little bit harder to hide, so normally they took some precautions not to be seen there, whereas in a big hotel it's very easy.

The great benefit of, in a sense, having done similar things before, being the head of regulatory authorities, being aware of the management side of the job, which might surprise you if you had not run a major institution as well; you're coming to the Commission – you've hinted at some of this – what was your strategy for how to use the authority that you were now coming into?

I've been in a number of institutions and in each one of them, the strategy has to be a bit different. You know, you're path-dependent; you start at a certain point. When I started at the Prices Surveillance Authority 3 years before the Trade Practices Commission – ultimately that was merged into the Trade Practices Commission to form the ACCC – it was clear to me from day one that a complete upheaval, transformation, and process of change had to happen starting at the top levels of staff, and a total change in culture, and a different view of what they were trying to achieve.

At this point, what steps did you take to formulate an understanding of what needed to be done? Do you read in advance, but you go for a while and observe, and then you draw conclusions?

In this case it happened that I had been a part-time Commissioner on this and I sat through the Commission and the previous Chair, who was generally an excellent person, misjudging the environment they were dealing with totally. I did hear from all the interest groups – business, unions, governments, both sides – what they thought about the Commission, and they all thought it was doing the wrong thing. So I learnt a lot from the political environment. At the same time, I was trying to be serious about the economics of it. So, just on that Prices Surveillance Authority, of course I understood, from an economics point of view, that you have to be very careful with price regulation. In fact, the price regulation I inherited was regulation of sectors that didn't need much price regulation, oil, banks and so on – maybe they needed a little bit, but not too much. At the same time, there was pressure from the government, the unions, and so on, for it to do more as a counterpart to a lot of wage restraint that was being asked of the unions. I identified a number of excessive prices that were the result of preexisting anticompetitive restrictions. For example, in Australia the price of books, CDs, and a whole lot of other things, has been much higher than elsewhere because of certain import restrictions. So we made a huge campaign focusing on the higher prices, doing comparisons with overseas and attacking the underlying anticompetitive drivers. Our staff did a good job on economics.

Then also, I lived through the oil crisis of the 1990s during the war, when unfortunately you had to let the prices go up. But I was very careful how I announced price increases. I certainly didn't want to be the public relations arm of the oil industry. I tried to develop a kind of approach to the media where I seemed to be very much on the public side, warning and threatening the oil companies, and expressing concerns. But actually, there was no choice. You had to let quite a few prices go up, but then you made a fuss about how quickly they went up and when they were coming down, make sure it happened quickly, and things like that. That was a different need for that organization. When I worked at the Trade Practices Commission, which was the core part of what is now the ACCC, I felt it was on the right track. The staff were broadly on the right track, they understood what enforcement was about, but it needed to do more and better faster. It wasn't a radical upheaval of strategy; it was just a big expansion. In year one, or the year before, there had just been 5 cases. Within two years we were running 50 cases. We took it straight up. Because the previous commissions had been a bit slack, there was a lot of low-hanging fruit and easy targets, which we exploited to the fullest, and we took the legal and business community a bit by surprise. They caught up later. But we did really step up the activity and, associated with that, a lot of publicity. At the same time, I was also anxious to get the law changed. That came about because – I did know the Act fairly well, but on day one I kind of did an Economics 1.01 look at the Act. It was just obvious to me that the dominance test for mergers was the wrong one; it should be a competition test. It was obvious that the fines were too low; they should be put up and possibly criminalized – that happened later. There was no divestiture part – there still isn't – but there should have been. Some of the wording in the Act was really weird. Abuse of dominance required a "full purpose" test and effect was irrelevant. And there were a number of other quite important statutory changes which I pressed for quite hard from the very beginning. Each one takes about 5 years of campaigning to get each one through, but on the whole they've gone through.

When you arrive you have a view about where the existing institution and the newly established ACCC should go, but you inherit a large staff and, as you were suggesting, a culture, a state or mind that's a bit more passive, not so prone to look for opportunities to seize upon violations and to deal with them. How did you bring your staff along with you? How did you change the culture? How did you bring managers and staff to embrace the new role for the newly reconfigured institution?

It was mainly at the level of conveying to them what the mission was about, demonstrating a bit to it publicly. The fact that you get on the television with their cases hardly ever happened before, and actually they learned quite a lot from just watching you on television explaining what they had done. Suddenly they saw the importance of it, and their families at home might suddenly congratulate them.

The Commission was doing quite a good job but it was a bit slow, so I wanted to speed that up. I had a fellow Commissioner, Allan Asher, who had a similar view. At that point, we actually got right down into the trenches. Generally, my approach is delegation, but early on we intervened in staff writing letters. We made sure that information demands were sped up; much tighter deadlines were imposed. We put much tighter reporting-back requirements on staff. We had to roll up our sleeves and, to an extent, do it ourselves and get letters, change them, make them more demanding, and so on.

Having said that – because that was meant to be an early demonstration of what we were on about – I was mainly interested in getting over the general mission of what we were doing. We were there to uphold the law without fear or favor. That was the key message. Fortunately, we had a good law, and we also had to uphold it intelligently enough; but uphold the law without fear or favor, with integrity, that would bring good results. They responded to that very well.

Did you spend lots of time with staff people across the span of your chairmanship, especially in the beginning, working with groups, one-on-one encounters, so that you had a chance face-to-face to demonstrate what you want?

When I started, we had about 200 people, that was easy. It went up to about 600 by the time I left. The Commission doesn't draw a sharp line between Commissioners and staff, as some organizations do, so the staff would bring in their reports. Actually, if something came up, the Commissioners would be immediately involved in figuring out how to go forward, what issues to investigate, etc.; and as issues arose during the investigation, the Commissioners were quite involved; so they were involved in the operations. Now, it may sound a little bit contradictory, but it's not – I was a strong believer in delegation to staff. One of the reasons why our output was a little bit low when I started was that we had a tradition of usually the Chairs – so usually pretty bright people – doing full quality control. Nothing big happened without every detail being checked by the Chairs.

Now, I much prefer to take the risk. So the staff were given a much bigger delegation. Of course, sometimes that went wrong; but, on the other hand, they got their head, they felt their responsibility, they generally did a great job unimpeded as it were by detailed oversight by me and the other Commissioners; although they did have to report back to us all the time what was happening. Inevitably, delegating a lot can lead to some things going wrong. But what actually happened was that our output surged, and that meant that these mistakes were buried by a lot of successes. Also, even if a case went terribly wrong, you normally had 4 or 5 that you could immediately get on with, and the media and everyone would quickly forget whatever things had gone wrong prior to that.

So, through the whole time, you had a big inventory of matters.

We had a big lot. In other areas of policy, there is a bit of a thing you've got to do, which is to have in your top drawer kind of a set of policies that are all ready to go when the right crisis happens – you know, you want a power, but you can't get it now; but with a crisis you have it ready to go. Now, we weren't quite like that. We just had a flow of cases, but you could speed up one or two if you needed to or slow down where things were looking difficult and so on. In terms of priorities – that's another aspect of it – people talk at these competition meetings about having priorities, and orderly priorities in this sector and that form of behavior. It's much more complicated than that, as you know, because you can't control the cases that come in. There are certain cases that land on your desk in the morning and you think, "This is the last case on Earth I want to do". But it happens to be on your desk; you can't avoid it; you just have to handle it, even though it might be low on your priorities. There might be another sector of the economy where you would love to run a case, but there's nothing there or there's no evidence that would back up your suspicions that would warrant litigation or whatever. So this playing with priorities is something that's subject to real-world problems.

The other thing I would say about priorities is that I'm not very keen on a strict economic approach to priorities, where you decide to take action if it's going to save X dollars for the consumer and that kind of thing. The main reason is that the priorities need to be broader. Firstly, where there is a blatant breach of the law, you've got to take action irrespective of the economics.

That's a direct challenge to your authority. You can't move the fence down there.

Yes. And usually it's a pretty good thing to play publicly and with the government when there's a blatant form of behavior. The second point about strategy is: don't just think of the case in front of you, think of the uses of it more widely across the whole economy. Certain things, you just know that you can have a big impact with them, whether it's a straight case or whether you're trying to get into a new area.

And in giving guidance to your staff, your managers, these are criteria you encourage them to have in mind.

Yes. So we did have priorities and currently the ACCC has its priorities. It is a mistake just to sit back and let cases come in and all of that. You have to have a good sense of priorities, but you also have a good sense of reality in what has to be dealt with.

You governed as part of a board. A number of agencies have a single executive. You were one of five, I gathered, throughout the time. What are some of the special considerations that go into being the Chair of a college, bringing a college around with you and using the experiences that your colleagues bring to the job?

You have to work with them. I certainly always wanted them to feel that the Commission, as a whole, was taking special account of their concerns. If one of them had a special concern, even a hang-up about something, you would seize the moment when you could give a little bit of room to them to have their view of the world implemented. Of course, on a slightly more flippant note, when you get your chance, you talk to the government about who they're going to put on your Commission. That is useful. But also the government needs to listen to you because you need a balanced team – some economists, some lawyers, some other people. We sort of allocated Commissioners to different fields of specialization. We always had a mergers Commissioner, for example, who I worked with really closely. Obviously – the Chair is involved in mergers law – but ultimately merger decisions went from the mergers committee into the full Commission and so on. Likewise, we had an enforcement Commission, and one or two of the lawyer members played a dominant role in that. And we had various other sorts of delegations of roles for Commissioners, and on the whole that worked. Now, in Australia – possibly elsewhere – one of the ways of getting real talent into the show is getting talented Commissioners. You know, often, with the salary levels and other things, that's the only way of getting really top people onto the Commission. So that was another factor in it. We did have some businesspeople. They're quite hard to capture. Way back, 20 years before I was on the ACCC, I was on a body that had mainly businesspeople – it was a price regulation thing – and we had a fair bit of trouble in, first of all, conflicts of interest. At a later time, we had a man who was involved in the computer industry and practically every firm involved he had a conflict of interest. But also, we found the salary attracted low-level businesspeople, the less-smart ones, who kind of tried to give lectures to big business who knew a lot more about business, how to operate it and so on. On the other hand, they did have a commercial feel, a bit of a sense about what was really going on.

I would like to focus on a couple of things to basically wrap up. One is you've had a remarkable career after you left the ACCC. You've had a chance to focus on many different areas of public policy. I wonder if you could think about other thoughts about what makes for an effective regulatory agency and what our governments have to do as a whole if they want to put regulatory agencies in a position to operate effectively.

First of all, they need a commitment. There is almost a moral point to it. If I were asked "What are the most important attributes of a regulator?" there are many: competence, intelligence, and all of that. Then, above all, a commitment to the job and a preparedness to do it no matter the hardships, the criticism, the interest groups, and so on. I rank that as pretty high. And to be ready, of course, for confrontation. Now, as the ACCC expanded, we started to attract a lot of staff from elsewhere in the public sector. They would come over thinking it would be a glamorous job, but they had to learn something: this is not like other areas of government where you would go out and be helpful to people, provide a service; this is an area of government where it's enforcement and it can be pretty ugly, nasty, unpleasant, and you have to be a bit yourself.

Did your work before coming to the ACCC prepared you for that dimension of it? That it is not a sport for the timid, that it becomes very personal; it becomes, in some instances, a bitter contest?

Yes. I had done a fair bit of price regulation before that, and it comes out there very much. I felt much happier with competition because I thought I was doing a good thing. With price regulation, you're never quite sure if you're doing harm or good when you restrain prices.

But if you want to do things that matter in this field, you cannot suffer from pervasive self-doubt and a shyness that makes you withdraw. You will be in a tough arena and you have to be ready to take the blows.

Yes. And your KPI (Key Performance Indicators) is the number of complaints about you. As soon as someone complained about me, I would thank them, I would let the public know, and it would turn the Commission into a public hero, the fact that they were being criticized.

A final question for you. You're talking to your successor, to someone who is ready to come into the role as Chair of the ACCC – or perhaps, given the many other agencies you've spoken with around the world, someone who is about to ascend to the position of leadership. Some parting advice that you give to them?

It would be to stick to the fundamentals. There is a law there. It's basically a good law. Uphold it without fear or favor. That is the key message. But in the area of competition – and even a bit in consumer protection – do so intelligently, not in a way that qualifies your underlying commitment to applying the law, but use the tools of economics – legal analysis, and other things, some understanding of business – use all of them to do the job properly but with integrity and commitment to serving the public.

You've done many things since leaving the agency. When you look at the span of experiences – maybe there isn't a favorite – do you have a favorite? Do you have an experience across the entire range that you look back on and say, "They're good ones; that was especially satisfying?"

At the ACCC, our first really big cartel case still fills me with satisfaction. It was a hard one. We hung in there very tight through a pretty unpleasant time, and then, at a certain point, they cracked, and we also got a spectacular rise in fines as a result of that. Beyond that, I've done a few other things. After I left the ACCC, running a school of government, training people from around the world.

John Fingleton[*]

Ireland Competition Authority, Chair (2000-2005)
UK Office of Fair Trading, Chief Executive (2005-2012)

You headed the Ireland's Competition Authority, and then the Office of Fair Trading (OFT), which is one of the predecessor institutions for the current Competition and Markets Authority (CMA) in the UK. More than anyone else, you have had a breadth of experience in running these institutions, and later ascended to the position of Chair of the Steering Committee of the International Competition Network (ICN). One thing we like to begin with is the path that takes one to a competition agency and the kinds of experiences that put you in a good position to do the job. If you could reflect on the kinds of experiences you had before going to the head of the Authority in Ireland, but also to the CMA, what kinds of background tend to help a person do well in this leadership position in an agency?

I was an academic economist in my mid-thirties when I was appointed to the Irish Competition Authority. Over the previous 10 years I had taught microeconomic and industrial organisation at Trinity College, Dublin. I first got involved in a practical way when I gave expert evidence in the *Masterfoods vs Mars ice cream* exclusivity case. That introduced me to a world of competition law and economics which I had not been aware of. I also advised the telecom regulator in Ireland on how to interpret some of the guidance on significant market power that was coming out of Brussels. But there were probably two really formative events. One was writing a book with Eleanor Fox, Paul Seabright, and Damien Neven on competition policy in the Visegrád countries – Hungary, the Czech Republic, Slovakia, and Poland.

* Interview conducted on 15 July 2019.

It was commissioned by the European Commission in advance of them joining the European Union, to assess how they were doing on competition law in their domestic countries. We took a slightly different tack with that book. Whereas previously we would look just at the substantive law, we actually looked at the staffing in the agencies, what their qualifications were. I don't know if it was the first piece of work on agency effectiveness, but it was certainly an early piece of work looking at what would make these agencies effective. That got me interested in that aspect.

The second thing was that I had always been a bit of a campaigner as an academic. There was a dreadful restriction on the supply of taxis in Dublin, and I had agitated about this for quite a long time. I saw it as a very simple economics problem, but a quite difficult public policy problem, that these taxi drivers had licenses – you call them medallions in New York – that were worth a lot of money and were refusing to allow anybody else in, and they had a huge stranglehold over the politicians. As people from France, Paris, Rome and other countries will know, politicians who upset taxi drivers end up with blocked streets instantaneously. I came up with a proposal, which eventually I published in a book, that the government should give every existing medallion holder a second medallion. In this way, the public would have no sympathy for them because they would have got something valuable given to them; and they wouldn't be able to resist selling them if they couldn't use them themselves, and so it would double the supply. The government followed that recommendation and that led to a court case which liberalized the market.

Through doing that and through a number of other pieces of advocacy, I developed a public profile in Ireland doing what you would call competition advocacy. The Competition Authority wasn't doing it. So, when the job became available –

With media work, too.

With media work. My first press release, I remember, was a 17 page document. I had no idea what a press release looked like. A friend of mine, who was a journalist, took it and converted it into a one-page document. The academic in me was horrified because it was so simplistic. But that was another useful learning. When you're running a competition agency and you have to communicate with the public, one of the things you have to remember is that there are only two or three sound bites people are going to remember from what you say, even though your agency has written a 200-page report. More generally, much leadership is about the ability to simplify the complex.

When I started at the Irish Competition Authority, I had a strong economic grounding, but also, I was really interested in competition advocacy. That was a time when, I think, competition advocacy was still only emerging as a sort of a discipline. Mergers, cartels, and abuse of dominance were the 3 main pillars. During the 2000s, many agencies added competition advocacy as the sort of fourth plank, and Ireland was no exception.

In summary, the combination of having worked with the telecom regulator and having worked on agency effectiveness in EasternEurope gave me some knowledge of the institutional issues and an interest in advocacy, in addition to core competition law background.

I mention that the book that John referred to with his coauthors, Eleanor Fox, Paul Seabright, and Damien Neven on the Visegrád competition authorities is still, for my own judgment, the best detailed case study of a group of agencies. I can see how in that exercise it gives you a very good set of insights into questions to ask about how the agency is performing.

It was funny because one of the things we realized was that, at that time, the agencies were used to absorbing people as unemployment was high. We would ask how many people they had, and they would say, “Well, we have 60 people.” A smaller competition authority in a Member State of the European Union might have 15 or 20 people. Then, when you asked deeper, you discovered quite a few of them were drivers. So, you began to understand very quickly that you shouldn’t just count the number of people in an agency; you have to work out what experience they had and who was doing the relevant competition-related work. Of course, that was at the very start and many of these agencies evolved very quickly.

No question, the pool of overhead people and the people who actually do operations are really important. Certainly, going to the OFT, you’ve had the experience of being the head of an authority, and that had to have been useful in the sense of doing it once again in a different setting.

There were lots of things I did well in Ireland. The Competition Authority was not particularly well-loved by the government when I started, and we put it on a solid footing, we did a lot of competition advocacy. But one of the things that I learned, by error rather than by doing it, was the importance of project management. I didn’t come from a background with disciplined project management techniques. What academic has a Gantt chart that is charting out whether they're going to publish a paper? The process of academic discovery isn't done in that sort of project-based way. When you have committed publicly to completing a study of competition in the legal profession by date X, you must think about how you marshal the resources and management to meet that deadline. The OFT already had good project management discipline, but on a different scale and my experience of sometimes getting that wrong at Irish Competition Authority was useful learning.

Second, I had a good understanding of the politics of competition policy. The Irish deputy prime minister, Mary Harney, appointed me before she had ever met me. The one thing she said to me when we first met was, "Don't turn this into an academic thinktank." After about half an hour talking to me, she thought that was what I was going to do with the agency. That was good advice. Later, she advised me when talking to ministers that I should get them to like me first. If they like the person, they are more likely to like the policy. That was invaluable advice to somebody like me who can be over evangelistic and forget the starting point and broader context that a politician has to address.

How do you do that?

It is about understanding the problems they are trying to address and how greater competition can assist with that, but also what problems greater competition might land on their plate or not address. That might require a different set or sequencing of interventions. But in essence it is about offering solutions rather than proselytizing.

I had some really interesting experiences with that in Ireland. One related to the state-owned monopoly of airports in Ireland. The Minister for Transport called me in for lunch one day, and he was having an awful problem with the company running the airport. He said, "What could we do?" I said, "Well, you could break them up, but they wouldn't like that." I explained how it might be done and what benefits it would bring. And so, he did. When I went to the OFT, I asked why all the airports in London were owned by the same company and that started the process that led to the break-up of UK airports. In the UK, the competition agencies (the OFT and the Competition Commission, now combined to be the CMA) had an instrument to break a monopoly, whereas in Ireland it had to be done by a minister.

The second example was that I was contacted to go on the radio one morning at short notice. The Minister of Transport had announced he was liberalizing the bus market in Dublin; he was going to make 10 percent of the routes available to private competition. I said on radio I thought this was far too modest and that much more of the market should be opened. Immediately after, the Minister's office asked to put though a call. This was not usual, and I was nervous given I had just criticised him on national radio. To my surprise, he expressed gratitude. All other commentators were strongly critical of even this small measure, and he explained that having me on the other side of the argument pushing him to go further was extremely helpful.

Some of it was serendipitous, but it is about trying to get to have good relationships with politicians. So, in Dublin and in London I did a number of things. I met politicians regularly. I tried to get on with them well. If they wanted me to speak at an event or attend something, I would do that. You build a rapport with the politicians because very often you have to have difficult conversations with them. I would also talk to them about what work they thought we should be doing, what they think their constituents and their party were concerned with. Mary Harney, the Irish deputy prime minister, was a master politician, and I learned a lot from her in that job. So, when I came to the UK, that was a very useful lesson. The media in Ireland is very different than in the UK, but I had done a lot of media work in Ireland, and when I went to the UK, I adopted quite a different approach. In Ireland, I had a very high profile; I was a reasonably recognizable figure, I guess, because I was on television a lot. In the UK I decided that wasn't what I wanted to do. The British media can be very vicious. But also, I thought it's a bigger agency, so I adopted a policy, which the CMA still continues, of really putting the staff who had led the work in front to speak about it – not just because I didn't actually want to do it – I couldn't do all of it – but also I didn't like the culture of the one person being responsible for everything. They knew more about it than I did. But also, it was hugely motivational. Sometimes, we were struggling to attract talent. Actually, one way to get really good people in is that their family and friends see them on the news and see what they do, and they feel really good about what they're doing. They already felt good about what they were doing, but it's just that extra recognition. So, things like that I reflected on from Ireland also influenced what I did at the OFT. I think CMA does that, but the other regulatory agencies in the UK have adopted that practice over time.

One thing you've described in a very informative way is your relationship with politicians. As you know, there is a literature on regulatory agencies and competition agencies that speaks again and again about independence and talks about it almost to suggest that the appropriate role of the agency is to be aloof from the political process. I gather that you concluded that it's a terribly incorrect assessment of the relationship between the agency and the political process. Where have we gone wrong in some of these conversations about independence?

I think you can be politically independent and be on very good terms with politicians. You have to make the decisions on the basis of what you think is the right thing, and process helps with that, because there is a documented process. Only once in my time at OFT did a minister try to interfere with any enforcement decision and, the moment I mentioned independence, they backed off apologetically. The OFT did many market studies. These looked at how markets were operating and often resulted in recommendations to the government about legislation. In the process of deciding what areas to study, we would talk to civil servants, consumer, and business groups so as to understand what markets were causing them concerns.

To answer the second part of your question about where we've gone wrong, at the 2013 ICN Conference in Poland I said that I thought that competition policy was spending too much time talking to itself and not enough time talking to the rest of the world. I still think that. We have these incredibly arcane debates, and the United States is probably the guiltiest of this. The legal debates about process inside the competition world in the United States were so arcane that even reasonably specialized people like me could find it very, very difficult to understand, like decisions about Daubert rules, or whatever that process issue happened to be that was very arcane, a matter of law for the outcome. I felt that we had gotten into a rut where the competition world had grown and been a victim of its own success and become sufficiently big that it didn't really need to feed on anything from outside; and consequently, there wasn't the right dialogue with politicians. Today, I still think that dialogue with politicians is challenging for competition authorities. In some cases, it is leading to a reduction in independence. Unless you are very clear about what your mandate is and what your role is – but also push back to politicians what you think you can help them with but where the limits are – if you're not very clear about that – and also with the public because ultimately politicians are influenced by the public, so you need to influence the public directly – I think competition policy has struggled with that, and that is partly being a victim of the success I think in the 2000s.

You point to the larger environment in which the agency operates. What can an agency leader do to remain aware of adjustments and changes in this larger atmosphere that affect the definition of what the job is, to maintain the agency's connection with developments that are important to competition policy but also to its ability to be an effective element of economic policymaking? How do you spend your time to remain aware of what these changes are and adapt?

It is always difficult to spot the differences between something that is part of a normal cycle and something that is a trend in a different direction. So, you can sort of see as new ministers come and go that some are more politically interested, and others are less. But then, sometimes you have a situation where all politicians have become more interventionalist or more interested in intervening in what you do. Distinguishing that can be very difficult, but there are a number of things you can do. First is to keep very close to a wide range of stakeholders, and especially consumer groups, which change over time depending on the level and source of their funding. In the 2000s, the UK government funded an excellent consumer research and advocacy group that was later disbanded. Consumer groups "Which?" in the UK produced a magazine which funded a great deal of consumer research and advocacy. This meant that they had deep expertise sector by sector. The internet has changed that, with a broader and more fragmented system. There are positives and negatives, but it means that competition agencies need to work hard to keep up with consumer insights and understand who best represents their interests.

Second is to understand the politics and pressures on politicians. In the UK, in addition to formal parliamentary committees, we have many "all-party" parliamentary groups on specific issues. It is important not just to engage with chairs of the formal select committees, the parliamentary committees that scrutinize legislation, and give evidence before them, but also to talk to the more informal groups.

Third, it is important to engage with business leaders and their representatives. Usually, they want to talk about process. You have to keep your ear to the ground, and the agency head has to do a lot of that work. These people are often important people. Your team at the agency can do quite a lot of work. And then you do the research. You try to understand what's happening in the world; you try to understand where customers are vulnerable. One of the things, for example, I think the UK still hasn't done well – and I've spoken about this within the regulatory network in the UK – is trying to join up with the people who are vulnerable in finance, in banking and credit, in insurance and energy, and in other areas, are the same people or whether they're different people in each market. If they're the same people in each market, the issue is actually about addressing those people, and that might be much more of an issue for politicians to say actually these people need help and no one regulator can do it. If, on the other hand, you discover that there's a difference and other people are being ripped off in each market, then you think it's probably market-specific interventions. In the UK at the moment, I haven't seen the research that informs that debate.

I've also thought that when competition authorities are suggesting reforms, they might look more carefully at the distributional impacts in two respects. First is prioritisation, which already happens. We brought a case in the UK on unauthorized overdraft charges in banks which predominantly affected poorer people. A clear part of our prioritization criteria, the principles at the OFT at the time, was that if vulnerable and disadvantaged consumers were disproportionately affected by something, we would more likely look at that. Second is impact which I do not think does happen much. Suppose a competition policy intervention significantly increases consumer welfare but leaves some consumers worse off. Should the agency try to calculate that impact and communicate to the government who may be better placed to target redistribution? I do wonder if the fact that agencies do not do this can lead to greater unhelpful political intervention later.

You worked hard to put the OFT in a position to look over the horizon and do the research that would inform judgments about which tools to use, how to go about using your power, a major emphasis on investment in building an understanding of what's taking place. Am I right that that was an important focal point of your work at OFT?

Yes. We did a number of things. One was that we introduced prioritization principles for the first time. We didn't call them "criteria" because we were afraid we would get litigated on them, but we thought it was really important to be clear what we would prioritize and what we would not. Second, we had a very strong program of evaluation where we were trying to learn from what had worked and what had not in the past. We generally contracted the evaluation out to independent experts so the results would be trusted, and that we were not seen as marking our own homework. We tried to learn from that. Third, we developed a horizon-scanning unit that tried to look at future issues. At one stage we attempted a project to try to look at all the sectors of the economy where productivity growth was low and ask questions about whether that was linked to e-competition. We found that a really difficult thing to do at the time, but we were nonetheless trying to do things like that. Not all of them worked. Fourth, we undertook a big project interviewing people in businesses and in law firms about compliance to understand the impact that previous competition policy decisions had on company behaviour. We know that the reason to enforce law is to encourage others; so how many others were we encouraging or deterring? This is a question competition authorities weren't asking. So, you ask the question, and you discover these quite high multiplier effects. But you can go to a more granular level of detail and say, "Well, what is it that's going to drive that? Is it the fines? Is it the potential of imprisonment in the case of hardcore cartels? Is it the directors' qualifications? Is it reputational damage?". Really interesting stuff emerged. First, the deterrence effect was substantial. But there were very different perceptions of what drove that. Lawyers thought the fines drove it, but the companies were more focused on personal criminal sanctions and reputational damage. So, the fines were not that important to the companies. The fines, even in the UK and the European Union, are huge, but they're not often huge relative to the companies' perspective.

The gains, yes.

The reputational damage is often far more significant. So, understanding that and understanding how you play with that to better achieve the outcomes you want – because the outcome is not how many fines you impose; it is how many companies don't engage in anticompetitive behavior.

When you came to OFT, were these ideas about things that you wanted to do – the development of prioritization principles; a better evaluation program; a better way of diagnosing where we can use resources best; compliance – part of a larger strategy you had in mind when you came to the CMA?

A lot of it was there. A lot of it was in my head, and there are two reasons partly why it was in my head. One was that I had not started as an industrial organization economist, but I was more general microeconomic theorist, so I came to look at a lot of these things from a "Have you solved some of these problems?" – not from a pure competition perspective, but from a core microeconomic analysis perspective. You can think about prioritization, about resource allocation; how do you allocate these resources efficiently, and so on. The second thing was that I had spent 5 years at that stage in the Organisation for Economic Cooperation and Development (OECD) Competition Committee, and I spent a lot of time looking at what other competition authorities were doing and comparing them to what we were doing, trying to learn from them. That probably made me think about things like evaluation. Many of these ideas had already been planted in the OFT by my predecessor, John Vickers, and Amelia Fletcher, the Chief economist. So, in some cases, I just continued or boosted initiatives they had started.

Other things like prioritization became immediately clear. The OFT had opened a large number of competition cases but later rulings by the CAT (Competition Appeals Tribunal) had made it more difficult to close cases than to open them. We had over 30 open cases but the capacity to do many fewer. And many of them were not strong cases but the CAT had given complainants very strong rights over any closure decision. This was frustrating as we felt that competition overall could suffer from being distorted in this way. I came up with the idea of closing a large number of them at once on the basis of a single prioritisation decision, rather than on the merits of each individual one. To do that, we needed some principles for prioritising, which ones to continue and which ones to close. It was much more difficult for the Tribunal to review our internal resourcing decisions. Having done that successfully, it was obvious that we should use a similar set of principles to prioritise the opening of cases.

A number of these things involve changing an internal culture, changing attitudes. How did you go about bringing the institution toward thinking about things in this way?

When I was in Ireland, I went in with that project management experience and came out of it understanding the benefit of it. I went into the OFT without really having proper change management experience in a large organization, and the way I changed the culture was by having an enormous change program. That had a huge impact on the organization. I think we had 35 percent staff turnover in the year after the change program. We lost a lot of people as a result of that. In the long run, that was probably quite a good thing. The people who stayed were very resilient and committed. And we got to hire many great new people based on values and culture. Second, we put together great teams. When I arrived there, we had a competition silo, a consumer silo, a market silo, and a legal silo, and they really didn't work well together. We had one team working on customer protection when using credit cards, another team working on consumer credit regulation, and a third one working on interchange fees in the credit card market. They had never talked to each other ever about it, and yet they were all working on Visa, Mastercard, and related matters. What we did was that we basically threw the whole thing up in the air and created a move to sector-based units that did all of the competition, consumer, and markets work. It solved problems, but it created other ones. It created a huge disruption in the organization. Of course, if you could go back and do it again, I think I would have probably gone and spent a bit more time studying change management and thinking about how to do that. Also, I would have probably questioned whether I needed to do all of it to get the results I wanted. I am not sure I always got the balance right between getting people to change and changing the people. In the public sector, it can be difficult to move senior management. Those are really difficult questions, and they're very organization specific. But I learned a lot in a way that was very expensive for the agency. In the end, by the time I finished, we were doing 7 or 8 market studies a year that finished within six to eight months, whereas when I started, we were doing 3 or 4 a year, and we had 40 percent less resources after 7 years and were far more productive. So, it did pay off in terms of productivity within the agency.

I imagine it's very taxing for you, too, as the leader. In a key sense, it's a hard job anyway, but someone coming into the job has to be aware that you will be called upon to make difficult decisions and choices, and you will not be everybody's friend as a result.

I have boundless energy and I can be very forward-looking. Although I can be quite irritated by small things, large setbacks don't upset me as much as small ones. I think I just had the sheer energy to push through all of that and bring people – well, not everybody – but brought a lot of people with me. I think that positive energy takes different forms in different people and is an absolutely central thing if you want to lead an agency. You have to be able to look forward. Of course, you try to learn from what has gone wrong, but you can't let it get to you in a way that doesn't stop you taking risks in the future and be prepared to do that in the future. You have to go in and convince the team that they're going to win, even if you have doubts about that, because they're more likely to. There is that wonderful scene in Henry V by Shakespeare, the "Once more unto the breach, dear friends" speech, where the British troops are wearied and battle-worn and outnumbered four-to-one by the French who are mounted, and he gives this great stirring speech that reaches into their emotions, and they beat the French against all the odds. So, it's understanding how to motivate people at the emotional level as well as the intellectual and rational level, and bring them with you. There are lots of things I didn't have as a leader. I wasn't a great manager. I'm not really good at line-managing people and checking objectives and chasing up whether people have done what they said they would do.

I guess you can surround yourself with people who can do these things subject to your guidance.

Yes. Of course, over time you learn what you're good at. I was probably slow at learning what I was good at, but I was good at visible leadership, being out there motivating people. I was less good at telling them on a detailed basis, "This is what you need to do in the next three weeks." But yes, I had a team around me that did that, and it was very important.

One of the other things I learned over the years was picking people who are very different from yourself and learning how to work with them. Of course, it was a learning experience at the Irish Competition Authority. We did some team building and did this Myers-Briggs personality type, and I discovered that most of the people I had hired were pretty much similar to me. That is a disaster. You really need to hire people who are different.

I changed that at the Irish Competition Authority, and made sure that every interview panel was pretty diverse. By diverse, I mean diverse in terms of different types of people, different ways of thinking. I would make sure there were people on the panel who would bring enormous diversity to that. As a result, I hired in people who initially I found it very difficult to work with at a senior level, but actually were a really, really good counterpoint to what I was good at.

And I gather you became a good listener, with some patience.
The point of having the ensemble is that you do have to overcome perhaps an initial resistance in your mind that is: "This annoys me; it's a point of view I don't like", but the point of having them all there is that you do listen and reflect.

I don't come across immediately as a good listener because my initial reaction to everything is to fight it, which is sort of usually that pugilistic thing. But I think

I'm a reflective listener. When somebody says something, my first reaction is to think "That's wrong", and afterwards I often think, "My goodness, they made a really good point". So very often, people don't experience me as listening, but I listen more than I appear to. But I don't think being a good listener is one of the things that people who know me well would be the first thing they would say about me.

It occurs to me that one thing that a person might consider in coming into this job is the self-assessment: "What am I good at? What do I do well? What are gaps, and how do I fill them with my own work and with others?" A good part of coming into the job is knowing who you are.

One of the things I've done over the years – and I continue to do it now – is coaching and doing team-based coaching, getting somebody who is an expert to come in; and, whether it's Myers-Briggs or another framework, taking you and the team through some sort of not just self but also team awareness exercise: "What you're good at and what you're not good at?". I did a huge amount of that. I did that in Ireland, I did a huge amount of it at the OFT, and I still do it with my team in my current business, really trying to uncover two things: what is your purpose?; and what is your preference? Your purpose is what really motivates you as an individual, and that's important to understand. The second is, what are the things that you are really good at doing and do easily, and what are the things that you're not good at doing and do with more difficulty? That is sort of like whether you write with your right or your left hand. Most of us learn that quite early on. Sometimes you have to try to write with your left hand – you break your wrist, and you have to do something – but, of course, you're going to then rely on other people more in that scenario. So, you have to learn when do you have to do something you don't like doing and when do you just play on your strengths. Having the right team around you is a big part of that, but you have to get them to do that with their teams and cascade that throughout the organization.

You've touched upon so much of this already that you can say "asked and answered" – but you are talking to a successor who's coming into the work, someone who is contemplating coming to the leadership role in the agency. What advice do you give them? Things that you know now that might have been good to know on the first day.

I think self-awareness is a really important one. You have a period when you start running an agency where you get a clean period, a free zone to do what you want: think carefully about how you use that. You have to assess your senior team. You have to build relationships. The people who you might get on best with in the first month may not be the people who are the absolute treasures that you need to rely on. One of the things that I think is really important is to value those people who have been with the agency for 20 or 30 years, because they've seen it all, and know who they are.

One of the things I learned as well was: I know who the smokers are because they're outside the building and they pick up all the gossip of what's going on in the organization. So, always make sure you know the smokers, talk to them and find out what they know.

Do a lot of learning in the first few months and then make the decisions you want. In the first year you should try to have the team you want and do what you can to make sure you have the team you want. A lot of them will probably already be there, but you really want to make changes, and getting that right is probably the most important thing, because ultimately, it's the people who deliver.

Peter Freeman*

UK Competition Commission, Chairman (2005-2011)

UK Competition Appeal Tribunal, Chairman (2011-2021)

You served as the Chair of the Competition Commission in the United Kingdom from 2005-2011. You also currently serve as the Chair of the Competition Appeal Tribunal (CAT) in the United Kingdom, so you have seen the experience of leadership both from the position of one who headed the Agency and now who reviews decisions of agencies that come before through the appellate path up to the CAT. Before going to the Competition Commission, you served for a long period as a partner of the Competition Practice in private practice. Can you take us on the path that led you into competition law and led you to the Commission?

First of all, I must just say that I'm here under total false pretenses because I'm not an enforcer anymore, and I have absolutely no pretensions to greatness, but it's a pleasure to be able to share some experience with you. I think the answer to your question is that 30 years in private practice running a law firm's department, particularly an international one, that included most European countries, was quite an experience, and it's more than adequate preparation for the public sector, where, on the whole, people behave quite well quite a lot of the time. I wish I could say the same for the private sector, where they make a science of behaving quite badly sometimes. That's part of its stock in trade, of course. But toward the end of my time, I was increasingly advising regulators and authorities, and I came to be more sympathetic to their problems, I think. That meant that I was quite attracted by the chance of moving across. When

* Interview conducted on 3 December 2019.

I did it in 2003, that was quite unusual, and there were all kinds of silly headlines in the legal press about "City Lawyer Takes the King's Shilling," and things like that. But that soon passed, and now it's actually quite common, so I would like to think that I, at least, blazed a trail.

It had to have been a great benefit, not simply for the Commission but more generally for competition authorities or regulatory agencies, to have the benefit of that life's experience in counseling people day-in and day-out regarding specific problems in the field but also to become an astute student of the economic system, the interaction between the legal regime, the political environment. Indeed, this is ideal preparation.

Yes. Well, in private practice, you really are just a team worker. You build teams; you run and organize teams. If you try to do it all yourself, you make mistakes extremely quickly, and that certainly was the pattern of work at the Competition Commission, so there was quite an easy transition there. That is getting the best out of people, which is not always done. I was on the other side from Sir Derek Morris in a big SME (small and Medium-sized Enterprises) banking investigation, representing a bank, and we gave him quite a difficult time, I think. He said at the end, "Well, if you really want to help us, come and see it from our side and see if you can do any better." That is really what set it in motion.

When you come into the Commission, what is the most notable adjustment that it involved from you? Lots of excellent preparation; what was new?

I think that the fact that the teams in the Competition Commission were very able. They worked on the whole for rather little money, and they were obviously motivated by something other than the profit motive. It didn't take too long to work out what that was, and it was to try to do a good job impartially. They were genuine public servants. I had a lot of respect for them, right from the start.

On the other side, you tend to think of them as the enemy, but that's false demonization. They were genuinely trying, particularly in the Competition Commission, to get to the truth, and they worked very hard to do that. That was the biggest difference I noted, and it was a great privilege to come and inherit that and preside over it and work with it.

It is a first-rate team, both managers and case handlers. It's case handlers I say, those who do the decision-making work, the researchers. You came to an institution that had an exceptionally strong pedigree.

Yes. It was doing very well, and it had a sort of self-confidence as well, which was helpful. All one had to do was not mess it up.

Did you have some thoughts about adjustments to the way of doing things, some change, maybe at the margins, but some thoughts as an outsider about how something working quite well could be made to work even better?

I started as the Deputy Chairman. For a while, I was the only Deputy Chairman, in 2003, for the first two years. I was trying to get the Competition Commission to think in a European way, because the big challenge at that time, with the EU-style prohibition system just having been introduced, was to knit together the two paths of the UK system, the administrative system, which had a direct line of inheritance from the old monopolies and mergers investigations, which were advisory, with the new European framework, where Regulation 1/2003 had just come in and everyone was talking about how we should all do things in the same way. Fitting the markets investigation regime, which was the sort of jewel in the Competition Commission's crown, into the European system was not straightforward. Some even argued that it was illegal, that we were doing things that were already covered by Article 102, as it became, but were not sanctioned by it. I think we overcame that, and I had to try to contribute to that. That was quite a big change, I think.

Could you say a bit more about how that was fitted into the larger framework, notably the markets regime? How did that come to be seen as simply incompatible for the larger framework?

We had a lot of backing from the government at the time, which saw market investigations as a very powerful intervention, and the system was the brainchild of the Blair/Brown government; they were very keen that it would work. Equally, they were keen that the EU-style prohibition system would work as well. They didn't see anything incompatible between them, but of course the key difference is that a market investigation is looking ex post at conduct, if you like, but it looks forward. It doesn't punish; it doesn't condemn; it does prohibit, but it prohibits with future effect, not for the past. Generally – and this is more and more important nowadays – it doesn't give rise to direct private action liability. It is an investigation. The difference, of course, from EU-type sector inquiries, which were there but were a bit moribund in my view, is that the actual remedies are inherent in the system, so if you find an adverse effect on competition, you can take steps to remedy it; and a lot of attention was given to that.

I may say we also had to defend the system in the United States, where it was thought that it might possibly be a little unfair to take steps against a corporation when it hadn't done anything wrong. This was "no punishment without law", and I think again we took quite a lot of trouble to market the markets regime, and say, "Look, it's not quite what you think it is." Companies may not see it like that, but it is a partnership, trying to find out what to do about a market that is not working well. It has, I think, survived its decade since induction, and I hope that it continues. It was easier with two authorities than with a combined authority because it thrived on having one authority choosing the markets and the second authority investigating.

I share your thought that it has survived the induction quite well. Internationally, one notices an increasing amount of attention given to how the markets regime in the United Kingdom functions. And I think an increasing admiration for the flexibility it provides to solve problems without having to force specific circumstances into a traditional competition law framework, but to do it in a way that is subject to rigorous quality control, demanding standards, and review by the courts. I see more and more countries saying, "I'd like one of those."

That was what we found, the more we talked about it. It got more and more attractive, whereas it started out with people saying, "What is that? That seems very odd. That is not abuse-of-dominant position, so what are you doing?" I don't think that is said anymore. Indeed, I came to a conference in Le Louvre in Paris, around 2007, where the subject was, "Could market investigations work for France?" Of course, I said yes. Actually, I said "*oui*!".

Exactement. I think it's a testament to the hard work and thoughtfulness of the Commission in this formative period that this distinctive device has emerged as such an important focal point for discussion, and I would say that the prospects for further emulation and adoption are quite strong.

But it was essential and remains essential that the principles of competition analysis that were applied in those investigations were the same as are applied in monopolization and abuse-of-dominance cases. That was where we were very keen to be allied to the Organisation for Economic Cooperation and Development (OECD), the International Competition Network, and the European Competition Network (ECN), although the Competition Commission, because it was not a designated Authority, was not technically a member of the ECN. So we attended by invitation, along with the delegates from Norway, as I recall. A slightly awkward status, but I think we made a success of it. And that was the purpose of it, so that we would be contributing and drawing on doctrine.

Because I think this is an area where we're going to see growing international emulation, I would like to ask, how did you go about deciding what the analytical framework would be? In the 2000s, when this was being developed – of course there is a long history in the Commission of doing excellent market analysis, studies – but how did you decide how this instrument would be applied?

The difference from the old monopoly inquiries was that there was much more procedural correctness and transparency, so the debate was conducted with the parties in an open way. The old Monopolies and Mergers Commission (MMC) was excellent in many ways, I am sure and could analyze to a very high standard, but on the whole, it did not share the analysis with the parties. It gathered information and comments; they disappeared into a sort of opaque crystal box, and then out came the answer. As a recipient of that, I found it very frustrating. I think Sir Derek also had experiences like that, and he really brought in the new procedures, which meant that every bit of information was collated, summarized, and put back to the parties from which it was taken. Each stage was documented – provisional findings, proposed remedies, comments received, that sort of thing, and then, at the end, we took a decision. They wanted to comment on that too, but I remember giving a talk called, "The Line Must Be Drawn Somewhere."

That is where the markets regime came up against a difficulty, which is that it's very time consuming, and the increasing pressure in the first decade of the 2000s was for shorter investigations, so we must have answers quickly. Indeed, that still remains an issue because the people who refer the markets for investigation do not want the issue to be in limbo, as they see it, for two years, two-and-a-half years. That's a long time. So, if we can reduce it to 18 months or one year, that is much better. But of course, that makes conducting the investigation very much harder, and the Commission did lots of things to try to truncate the processes – or to run them in parallel, but there is a limit, and I think somebody at some stage is going to have to make a choice: you either want this regime or you don't. If you want it, you've got to give it time to actually work; if you don't do that, you're going to risk being accused of just taking arbitrary decisions on inadequate information without a proper analytical framework. You can see that beginning to emerge at the moment, where, as I'm sure you know, we're going through a slightly populist phase where people want instant answers very quickly, and the market regime will struggle to produce that, I think.

It seems to me that it's so important to draw attention to the wonderful examples of how it has worked, worked well because of its careful, deliberative process – the first-class research, rigorous testing of evidence, and testing of theory – to make superior policy outcomes take place. You can't do it in a rush. Indeed, you do have to make a decision about what it is you want to do.

That is for the policymakers to do. I know that is an issue at the moment, and I would encourage them to not duck it and not fudge it. I should mention, of course, the other strength of the regime is an inherited aspect, which is the panel system. I'm not sure anybody in 2002 would have sat down and invented the panel system, but of course it came from the old MMC. Actually, if it is properly deployed, it's very powerful, because you had part-time people who worked for very little money who would be engaged as a panel of members under a full-time chair for each investigation, and their role would be to take responsibility for the investigation, but also to challenge the analysis and the evidence as it came in. It was a quite healthy debate. It wasn't just the Commissioners deciding at the end of the day; they had their sleeves rolled up, and they were in there. The hearings were in a panel format with questions from everybody, trying to get a representation of different disciplines on the panel. One job of the chairman was to make sure the panels were properly representative. If it worked well (although it could sometimes work badly), it gave the Commission just that extra bit of independence and strength. It meant that whatever the companies thought about what we did, they couldn't complain that it wasn't objective and that it wasn't fully open. They could see what was going on. They might not like it, but they could put their point of view.

They would have to respect the process and the intention and the quality of the work done, even if the outcome didn't please them.

Yes. We were immune from the fashionable criticism of being "faceless bureaucrats." We were bureaucrats with faces. So that is the markets regime. Of course, the mergers work was of a similar high standard. Again, there needs to be enough time to do a phase II merger investigation.

If I can point to an extraordinary accomplishment, by no means the sum of what the Commission did during your time there, which is airports;

a globally recognized example of how this mechanism can deliver remarkably effective results because of its special structure. It is taught around the world now as an example of a policymaking innovation that works well.

Of course, the Commission had a regular regulatory role for airport pricing, which unlike some was not voluntary. Therefore, there was a regular diet of airport cases. But this was about ownership. This was a different issue.

I didn't personally do that investigation. I put somebody else in charge of it. I think I was doing Groceries at the time. It went through the various issues. It found things wrong with the then-common ownership by Ferrovial and British Airports Authority (BAA) of Heathrow and 6 other airports, and it ordered divestiture. Divestiture was very rare and very controversial, I think, as the remedies always had to be appropriate for the mischief that had been found. It was not a sort of standard shot in the locker, but it was thought to be appropriate here; if the issue was that the airports were not able to develop independently, common ownership was clearly the problem. During the inquiry, the BAA cooperated fully. They were not unduly hostile or anything like that. They actually put Gatwick Airport up for sale during the inquiry as a sort of offering, but I'm afraid that wasn't enough, and the Commission decided that one of the Scottish airports, and Gatwick and Stansted, should all be divested. That was the remedy.

Airports, of course, is to some extent an awkward case because there was an issue over the complaint by BAA that one of the members – who actually was a finance specialist who had experience of airports regulation, which is why he was on the panel – had an apparent conflict of interest because he was strategic advisor to Manchester Airports Group, which became, towards the end, interested in purchasing one of the airports. That was an issue which, in my view, could have been resolved during the inquiry. It wasn't. BAA appealed to the Tribunal on the one ground that the disposal was unfair and disproportionate. The other ground was that the Commission was biased. They lost on the first and won on the second. That was a bad moment for the Commission. I personally felt that reflected on the whole institution. I had The Daily Mail on the phone saying, "Are you going to resign?" – I think everybody has to have a moment like that. I told them no, but it was then a case of rallying the organization, because they were very set back by that.

Could you say a bit about how you do that? That is, here is the disappointment, there is not an agency on the planet that will not have or has not had such a moment. How do you rally the team?

It's a very relevant topic at the moment, because the idea seems to have come about in the United Kingdom that the Competition Authority should not lose in the Tribunal. It's apparently a sign that things have failed. I have a slightly more nuanced view, which is that you should expect to lose from time to time. The Competition Commission didn't always prevail in the Competition Tribunal. I always tried to learn from the judgments and do the case again because we always could work it through again and get it right. To me, that seemed to work very well, and that is what we did in the Airports case. I actually did not believe that there was an apparent conflict of interest. I thought it had been presented in a way that made it look at its worst, so we appealed to the Court of Appeal, and we got the decision reversed.

At that point, we had a choice: we could have just repeated the ruling, but we thought again (this is a deliberative process), we discussed it and we thought: actually, it's a year old. There has been a change of government. The Airport's policy has changed. We ought to do a change-of-circumstance analysis. So, we reopened the investigation and started again. I chaired it this time, but we came to the same conclusion. That was appealed again, but the decision stuck, that time. It was after I had left the Commission. It was a very strong judgment from the CAT that basically held that the Commission was an expert body; you didn't pick holes in its reasoning. If it makes sense, is coherent, is fair and proportionate, that is the end of it. The outcome of that was a great success, but it didn't look like that at one stage. It looked pretty chaotic. Organizations don't like being in the process of messing things up. So, you are duty-bound either to resign and go, which is an option, but then that leaves others to sort it out, or to stay and sort it out. If we hadn't sorted it out the second time, I would have taken responsibility and gone.

But internally there was an awareness based on the commitment from senior leadership that, "We're going to see this through."

Internally, yes. I think that was the job of the leaders. We spent a lot of time discussing leadership. In my view, leadership takes place from the front and not from the back office. You have to be there; you take it on the chin; you talk to the press. I did that a lot. You explain what you've done in simple terms, and quite often you can deal with a lot of the issues. The staff, who do the analysis and who feel that they need somebody to shout for them, appreciate that greatly in my experience. If you don't do it, they feel very let down.

I think that is such a valuable lesson. You do not lead from the rear; you do lead from the front, and when they see you in that position of leadership, they so often measure you not on the best day of the agency but the worst day, when things are not going well.

There is this difficult issue of sort of projecting your personality onto the institution but being very aware that actually it's the institution that is powerful and not you; so, you should not fall into the trap of thinking that you have suddenly acquired extra life and immortality. You are only as big as the office. It's the office and the institution which carry you through.

And to keep that at the front of your memory every day you walk in the door.

Yes. But the thing about the Competition Commission was that it was very easy. It was a non-hierarchical organization, and that was inherited from the old days. Once we got rid of the feudal idea that the members were in some way superior to the staff and we had put them all on equal footing, there really wasn't any issue about, "You're senior to me, and you've been ordering me around." Everybody's voice counted, but senior people made a point of going around and making sure that even the most junior people, the people who did the paperwork, and so on, were fully integrated into the team. That is because we had a single format for investigations and a prescribed way of working. In an organization which has to do other things – decide what to do; prioritize – I can see it's much more difficult. But we had a very privileged setup.

I would guess that, from your time in private practice, you probably saw time and time again that to build an effective team requires consultation with the whole team, their involvement, junior people, senior people.

Absolutely. And there is good in everybody. There were some awkward characters in the Commission, make no mistake about it. Somehow or other, they had to be integrated into the whole arrangement, what they could contribute had to be extracted from them, and they had to see that they could actually put something back as well.

If I could go back to a point you mentioned before, which I think is significant for decision makers and agencies, is the question of how often are you expected to prevail. The notion, as you mentioned, that you would always be successful, that your success rate would be 100 percent, is astonishing. If it were sport, I suppose you could do that if you were a football team and you have scheduled nothing but nursing homes, but then someone might raise questions about your strength of schedule. There would be no glory in having an undefeated record if you're thrashing middle schools or other lesser opponents. Do you have any advice you would give to the leader of an agency about what is the right way to look at success, litigation failure? How to think about this, and what level of success you should achieve?

I think, starting at the far end, you shouldn't put litigation success into the balance at all, because if you do your work well and soundly, the litigation, if it comes, will run its course. There are strong incentives on companies to resort to litigation. The system is, in a sense, designed to give them that right, because the Authority has such extensive powers which severely interfere with corporate life, that you can't have a system like that in a democracy without some form of redress. So, the redress has to be there. If you spend the whole time thinking, "Gosh, I might lose this case, I'm not sure I want to do it. I don't want to be seen to have lost against this company", I don't really see how you can do the job. I say that with some hesitation because I remember being myself in that position and taking those decisions with that feeling. All the cases we had to do were given to us, and we had to do them. Is the litigation risk disproportionate at the moment? Looked at objectively, I know it is being said that it is, but I don't see that. I remain of the view that competition cases are very hard and challenging to mount. The law and the economics analysis has become very complicated. Companies who are attacked, particularly if you're dealing with abuse-of-dominance cases where there is a lot of judgment involved and when it's not just a question of "You were caught red-handed; let's hear your confession", there's going to be a fight, and then it is down to the Authority to fight as best it can. That is the system. You don't have to have a prohibition system like that with penalties, fines, and terrible consequences. We have chosen to have it. For a while, I think we quite gloried in it and thought it was great. Some of the difficulties that have come to light in recent years are because, on issues like excessive pricing, predatory pricing, exclusionary conduct, and all those favorite topics, opinions can differ. It is the strength of the analysis that prevails. So, it is inevitable that an authority will not win every case. On the other hand, if it is seen to be doing its analysis in a sound way, gathering evidence in a fair way, and assessing it properly and openly, whether it wins or loses on appeal is an irrelevance. In my view, the better argument in the end will prevail.

As you were saying before, it is so difficult in the modern world to keep one's eyes focused or keep the policymaking overseers focused on this longer term.

I've got some sympathy with them on that because the politics have changed. Again, I was lucky to be in an institution when – I wouldn't say it was a honeymoon period – but there was broad consensus that this competition regime, arm's-length authorities, government staying out if it, ministers saying, "No, you do that; we will cover your back". That was okay for about 10 years in fact, and that is quite a long time, but there are signs of a reaction now. There is more short-termism. Ministers don't like to be told that they have lost the power to take decisions or control them or influence them, as I think they are very firmly told by their civil servants. Instead, they want results, and they want them quickly.

The glaring example of that is in the energy markets investigation done by my successor, Roger Witcomb, who was placed in a very difficult position. He oversaw a very carefully analyzed, evidence-based inquiry and came to the view that capping energy prices was inadvisable except in a few cases. There was a minority report by Martin Cave, who is certainly not to be discounted in any way whatsoever, but that was the majority view. And then the politicians intervened. First of all, the opposition said that wasn't good enough. Then, the government legislated, and the Office of Gas and Electricity Markets is now trying to make sense of the price cap that it has had to introduce. That is not government letting competition authorities do competition. It is intervening, saying, "Sorry, there is a political overriding demand, and we must see to it." There you are. I'm not quite sure where that leaves the system. People have gone very quiet about it, but it is there on the record, and it's something that we all ought to be quite concerned about, in my opinion.

I think you have put your finger on a very serious difficulty. It's not clear where this is going, but it's distinctly uncomfortable because you have the institution doing a careful technical analysis – it's not being heartless, but it's doing good technical work – and then it's told, "That's the wrong answer, and I'm going to superimpose another one." What do you do next time?

To which the response might be, "Well, why did you bother with the investigation in the first place, if you know the answer?". It has raised a question mark over the evidence-based, economics-based competition analysis which is at the heart of things. That may be because that has become an extreme form of science, which is not readily comprehensible to the average citizen. That is the big challenge for antitrust with a small "a." Maybe we have been over-sophisticated in our solutions. They are justifiable and evidence-based within the confines of the analysis we have chosen for them, but they may not resonate, and I think it's the risk that competition and antitrust do not resonate with – certainly not with the business community – but with consumers. The population at large simply doesn't understand what is being done, and this is ironic because we are operating in the interest of consumers.

On their behalf, yes. In a way, I think the entire system is on the back foot on this issue because so many agencies are wrestling with great unease and thinking about how to respond to this fact, this adjustment. What is your appropriate relationship with the larger political process? Are you responsive to basic changes in public moods? How do you adapt your methodology to be more responsive, where you're aware of the professional dangers of being too responsive? I sense that this is an area where we really haven't found a way ahead. It is reflected in the agenda of the OECD. There are a couple of panels that deal with the question, "Is competition good for you?"

"Is competition good for you? Is competition the answer for everything? And can you explain your competition solution in everyday language?" Because if you can, then you can discuss it along with other policy options in an everyday way. After the Groceries inquiry, which was a competition one, I remember being on, I think, Channel 4 News, and I was asked: "Well, why haven't you dealt with health? Why haven't you dealt with the environment? Why haven't you dealt with all those trucks carrying goods all around the country, shipping merchandise from warehouse to warehouse? Why didn't you deal with that? You had all the information. You had the people in front of you." And telling them "I'm terribly sorry, but we're a competition authority, and we decided the market was competitive," was so obviously unattractive that you hardly dared say it, but said it had to be. That is leading the impetus for a return to a public interest test. Okay, we've got these authorities. They're very powerful; they've got all kinds of instruments. But why does this have to be competition all the time because there are other glaring issues that they are in a position to address, all for consumer protection. That's the way in. But then, it's not that difficult to add some more, and I can see pressure for that too.

Is that – perhaps not a vulnerability – but an issue that can arise with the market's regime when an outsider, a Member of Parliament, a Minister, looks at this framework and says: "My goodness. This is a magnificently flexible device that's concerned with problem solving. Go fix the problem, and don't tell me about your concerns about certain technical niceties that might arise in your field of interest. We have given you a broad mandate with inherent scalability and flexibility. Fix the problem."

Then the question arises, "How am I going to be held to account, and by reference to what standard?" You may get it right half the time, but you may get it wrong the other half, and those people, their interests will not be assisted by your methods, and that will, in the end, bring the system down also. Just being more flexible is not the answer, I'm afraid. You've got to have some reason for doing things which makes sense according to some coherent intellectual framework. What I was saying earlier was not that the competition framework is not coherent. It's just that it has become very sophisticated. Can it be simplified in some way? That is difficult because it is data driven. Data is complex; data is enormously voluminous. Can you find a way through that? We all yearn for cases where the answer is very plain, where it depends on a few salient facts and you can decide it on that basis; but that is, I fear, not the norm.

Are there highly effective treatments that would not be so laborious and expensive to carry out, and time consuming as well? I would just say that one other thing that struck me with the market's regime is dealing with expectations once you announce you're going to undertake a study, an inquiry. There seem to be almost immediate beliefs that you're going to fix it. You'll make it right in some sense. How you shape those views to have an acceptable balance between ambition and realism is a great challenge for the Competition and Markets Authority (CMA) today.

Well, the CMA has internalized all that as the solution to the rather uncomfortable equilibrium that was existing before. The decisions on references were, on the whole, made by the Office of Fair Trading (OFT), and the decisions on matters referred to it were made by the Competition Commission. They weren't always what the OFT expected, wanted or had asked for. Those caused issues. But I don't think bringing the two aspects of either mergers or markets into a single authority necessarily fixes that. It ought to make no difference to it at all. I think it's a little early to judge whether it is making a difference.

A couple of additional questions. One to look in the larger international framework, where certainly being an observer or participant in the gatherings of the European Competition Network, being a participant in a variety of different international events, including OECD meetings, you spend not every day of the week, but a notable amount of your time engaged in examination of the larger environment in Europe and around the world. Can you talk a bit about the value you saw in that kind of comparative study?

It became more mature. But I think it took a big knock with the financial crisis. I remember meetings with people looking aghast at each other and saying, "What did we get wrong? What did we do? Where were we? Why weren't we watching?" And that is still working through, I think. As I said, I referred to a "honeymoon" period. I think there was an international honeymoon as well. On the whole, everybody was singing from the same sheet, saying the same things, getting very good in some cases and very interested in sharing best practices. There is more of a strain now. There are too many divergent tensions to make it altogether easy. On the other hand, it is still extremely valuable. There is nothing particular to one country or one group that makes them better at doing something than their neighbors. There is always something you can learn.

There are a lot of bright people trying to solve these problems.

Absolutely. There is a great spirit of common endeavor. That is why I was very concerned to keep the Competition Commission in that circle and not to be British isolationist and say: "No, we do it like this. We do understand what we do, and you'll want to do it like us." That was not my approach, and I don't think that has been the approach of the CMA either. It's obviously going to be under pressure with Brexit as to how we remain aligned while being told that we shouldn't be, but I think the willingness and the spirit are there.

I believe so. I think the important point you mentioned earlier about how the familiarity and understanding that comes from the repeated engagement gives other jurisdictions an opportunity to see options that have not been visible to them. One of those is the markets regime in the United Kingdom, which offers another approach. In talking about things digital, there is a great conversation: Do we need a new institution? Should we create a new regulator? What might we do? A solution that I think a number of countries might consider is that this is a way of trying to solve problems in a rigorous manner, but in a way, that is not again cabined by existing doctrinal approaches to dealing with Article 102 or its variants. That process of adoption, awareness, learning, and emulation couldn't have taken place without the UK's expansive engagement internationally.

Having now done Article 102 cases at the Tribunal, one is conscious of how very precise the structure of Article 102 is. It's a linear process; you have to go through the steps, and each step leads to the next. The markets regime is inherently more flexible. You look at the situation in the round and come to the final analysis where you bring everything together right at the end of the process. You obviously go through procedural steps in a linear fashion in order to be fair, but you are very careful not to make up your mind until the end. I think that this is a strong argument; but of course, it's not either/or. We need to do things like making sure merger control is sufficiently smart, that it doesn't let through things which are later going to come back to haunt us, but at the same time not simply banning all mergers that could be argued to be anti-competitive. But the markets investigation regime seems to me to be the obvious way to deal with the Google, Amazon, Facebook, and Apple (GAFA) issue. Of course, the argument against it is: "Well, it'll take a long time," but the more you delay, the longer into the future the solution comes. I have to say, that is just a re-run of the banking and energy markets investigation cases, which were overdue in my view when they occurred, and suffered from being overdue. The argument that you couldn't wait for the answer was just false, I thought, particularly unconvincing, and the same is true with the digital issue. Of course, things will change during one-and-a-half years, two years, but it will come around very quickly, and we might all benefit from a bit of sober analysis.

Let's have some hope that can count.

That is not to cast any disrespect on the various expert reports that have been put out. These are all very interesting, and I have read them very carefully, but of necessity they are not legally structured. They don't take evidence in a formal way. It's not always clear what evidence weighed or didn't, and they come to a decision which is not binding. It's just a report. They are part of the process, but they're not, in my view, a substitute for a properly structured market investigation. A sector inquiry in Europe would be equally interesting, but I would also recommend the market investigation route. It does work.

If I could ask a closing question to you: in so many ways, you've touched upon this, but imagine that the new head of an institution is seeking your advice.

There is no exact ancestor of the Competition Commission. The functions have merged into another institution, and it's a different framework, but thinking generally of someone coming to this leadership role, what thoughts do you give them about how to look at the job and how to approach it in a way to do it as well as they possibly could?

All the management and leadership behaviors that we talked about earlier, which I think are necessary qualifications for the job. I would have hoped not to have to spend time telling the new incumbent that they are important. I would hope that that had been dealt with in the appointment process. I think I would say this: there is a great tendency nowadays to regard the headship of these institutions as something that can be done by a generalist, an academic or maybe a politician, somebody who can represent the authority in the political world. That is certainly a very important function, but it is equally important that the individual is also respectful of and willing to engage with what competition law actually is and does, because if they're not sympathetic to it, they will not, in the end, command the respect of their organization, and the organization – rather like an orchestra that doesn't like the conductor – will find its own way of working some form of revenge. The best authorities are ones where there is common purpose, unity of aim, and mutual respect. That is the job of the leader, to encourage and nurture that mutual perspective. That is what I would say. It sounds awfully pompous and high-minded, but there are leaders in there doing it. It's pretty vital.

Douglas Ginsburg[*]

US Court of Appeals for the District of Columbia Circuit, Judge (1986-2001) & Chief Judge (2001-2008)

You are the former Assistant Attorney General for Antitrust at the Department of Justice. Before that, you had a distinguished career as an academic. You have continued to write and are still teaching students, and indeed judges and enforcement officials around the world from your position with the George Mason University School of Law. You also have vast experience watching how agencies develop in a variety of different ways. As a starting point, can you describe a bit about what your path into antitrust law and to the Department of Justice Antitrust Division was?

I really didn't know anything about antitrust when I entered law school. I had some economics courses, but I was at the University of Chicago from 1970-1973, which was a period of enormous debate, development, and ultimately influence, with respect to the economic analysis of law generally and even more particularly with respect to antitrust. My professor, Phil Neal, did not purport to have any economic understanding – although I later concluded that may have been a pose – but my classmates were people like Frank Easterbrook; George Priest at Yale; Burt Foer, who went on to find the American Antitrust Institute; and half a dozen other names that you would recognize if only I could recall them as quickly. So, it was an extremely exciting time and an exciting course. A few years later, 2 years out of law school, I got an assistant professorship at Harvard Law School and got in line to teach antitrust. Philip Areeda was teaching it, and a vacancy opened up when somebody – I think it was Steve Breyer – went on the Court, so I started teaching antitrust at Harvard in the late 1970s.

* Interview conducted on 10 April 2019.

You were also teaching courses in economic regulation. Were financial services one of your courses?

I did Economic Regulation of Business, which was the successor to Public Utility Regulation, Regulation of Financial Institutions, and Labor Law, so it was a coherent bundle there that made a lot of sense. Phil Areeda was very gracious in welcoming me to the fold and giving me a few tips. A few years later, in 1983, I was at a classmate's wedding, and I ran into yet another distinguished antitrust classmate, Ron Carr, who was Deputy to Bill Baxter in the Antitrust Division. I told him I was looking to spend a year or two away from Harvard. I had gotten tenure. He said, "Would you take my job?" I said, "In a trice.". Two weeks later or so, Bill Baxter called and offered me the position as his Deputy for Regulation and Economics.

Can you say a bit about what you learned from Bill Baxter, watching Bill's tenure as the head of the Antitrust Division and his enormously influential time in the Department?

Well, anyone who knows Bill, without being in that position, could learn, first of all, to waste no words; second, to think before you speak, for which he was famous; and third, if you could be as honest as he, you do so at your peril. He had no social graces. He was totally honest. In terms of antitrust he was quite rigorous in his thinking, very well organized, and he was really sort of a model of clear analysis.

I was running the AT&T case then. We were looking at the divestiture on January 1, 1984. Bill left the Division – I had come in on September 1st and he left in December or thereabouts, maybe late November – and left me with the divestiture to manage, as it turned out to be rather easy. But it was a sort of lesson in having confidence in your immediate subordinates and giving them enough rope to hang themselves. He had eliminated a great number of people. He took the Division down from about 800, maybe 750, to 550. That was another lesson in itself, not to allow an agency to get bloated and overstaffed. So, when he left, we were lean, and we stayed that way for quite a while, long after I left.

Now, one of the downsides of that was that the people leaving were not distributed in an organized fashion, so we had a large number of sections that were hollowed out. Where there should have been 20 lawyers, there were 12, and that was not uncommon. After a year as his Deputy, I left for a year to run the Regulatory

Review Program at the White House, then came back when Ed Meese became Attorney General and was his Assistant Attorney General for Antitrust. So, I was in the uniquely favorable position of knowing the people, many of them, and knowing some of the problems, and having a trusted ally who was holding over from Bill Baxter's time, Rick Rule. Rick was Bill's Special Assistant and I made him my Deputy.

Before I came on, September 1, 1985, for my second tour of duty, I spent a month with my family on a vacation, which was devoted to 2 enormous briefing books, one the AT&T case because I had been away for a year, and one on what I asked for, which was a complete reorganization of the Division. Because Rick was on the spot and knew the people – he worked with the executive officer, who was the chief administrative person – and put together a plan so that – I came back on Tuesday after Labor Day – on Friday we abolished all sections, all section chief and assistant chief positions were unfilled, and Monday we had new sections with new chiefs and assistant chiefs. No one was fired, but those who had lost their positions as chiefs and assistant chiefs almost uniformly went out into the private sector or found another government job. Some stayed on. Especially some of the assistant chiefs were fine with that. That really enabled us to shrink the number of sections, fill them up to full staff, reorganize them in terms of subject matter to reflect contemporary current problems or clusters of issues instead of working with allocations of responsibility that were 15 years old and really didn't make any sense anymore.

I suspect it's something that a number of institutions find hard to do. They become path-dependent, and they don't revisit the assumptions that lie behind the organization, and they get stale.

Somebody comes in as the new head of the agency and needs at least a year to learn the territory, who the people are, which ones are doing a good job, who are not. At that point they may be – in our government 2 years is the average time for a political appointee, so the payoff from doing the reorganization and taking all of the heat and resentment that goes with it is very low compared to if they're going to be leaving in a year. So, it's not something that they would ordinarily be inclined to even look into doing. I was just uniquely fortunate. Now, it can still be done, and others have done it, even after they've been there a year or even longer, in other agencies and around the world. It's never too late to do it, it's just harder. Path-dependence, as you said, is very easy to live with.

You say, "How much time do I have?" I guess, to quote Don Draper from Mad Men, "Is this the hill you want to die on?"

Right. But, if you are somebody who is going to be continuing in public service – say, like Bruno Lasserre – there is no downside then. You've done a good thing, and you move on and do another good thing. When I was finished with the reorganization, I had 6 Senior Executive Service (SES) positions, super-pay grades, that I was able to turn back to the Attorney General to use elsewhere. That is how much more efficient we were.

That is a striking change. Other aims that you had coming into the Division – the restructuring, the realignment – that you wanted to do clearly in your mind when you came back?

One thing I did – and I would have done even if I had not had the years' experience – was to elevate the position of the Chief Economist to Deputy Assistant Attorney General, my Deputy. I had 4 deputies. There had been 3 when I came in. I made Rick Rule into one of them, who succeeded me as well. I was interested in doing a lot of non-day-to-day things – drafting legislation, working it through the administration process to get it approved, working on some interagency projects – and so I was very happy to let Rick, who knew the operation, run the day-to-day. He was the chief operating officer, and he was very well-prepared therefore to become Assistant Attorney General. That freed me up to do a few other things. But one of the key ones was to elevate the Chief Economist to the level of a Deputy so that, as Assistant Attorney General and the final decision maker, I was receiving input both from the economists and from the lawyers on an equal plane. The long history of economists and agencies is that they are long viewed as "case killers" because the lawyers say, "This is a case we could win," and the economists say, "But it would be wrong." So, if the lawyers have the last say in reporting to the final decision maker, the economics recommendation gets subordinated. So, I wanted to put a stop to that.

Just mention, if you might, who your economist was. Who was the first?

It was Rick Warren-Boulton. I will talk a little bit more about economists generally, but I will say I was just thinking to myself why didn't Bill Baxter do that, because he was a great believer in the role of economics in antitrust analysis. I think I have the answer. I called him one day. He was back at Stanford, teaching, and I was about to dismiss a power wheeling case where a utility had refused to accept power from an adjacent system on one side and wheel it through to another system on the other side. Just as I was about to sign the papers, it occurred to me to ask: "Well, why didn't Bill dismiss this? Maybe I'm missing something.". So, I called him at Stanford, and I asked him the question. There was a characteristically long pause, and then he said, "One can do only so much." I signed the papers before we hung up with some pleasantries. So why didn't Bill make him a Deputy? It was surely because one can do only so much.

Now, on the economics front, running that group – we had almost 60 PhD economists – this is very important as to how you think about them. The tradition here at the Justice Department and at the Federal Trade Commission and at many places around the world, including the European Commission, is to bring in a topnotch academic industrial organization economist, take leave from his or her university, and come for usually 2 years. These are the top people in the profession. That is an extremely important approach because it's a 2-year seminar for all of the other economists to work with somebody like that. The outside experts with whom one deals in cases respect this person very highly and I wouldn't say necessarily look up to him but always regard him as at least a peer, never look down. That is important. It elevates the quality of the whole operation. Plus, they can hire first-rate people, and first-rate people will come because even when this man leaves, there will be another one who will be another world-class leader, an economist.

The care and nurture of a group of 55 or 60 PhD economists, or in a smaller agency 5 or 10, requires some attention because you're competing with university positions, where somebody who's got a PhD – they're at one university, they might move to another – they're not going to give up academic life suddenly, but you want them to come in and stay for a while – not the leader, but the staff – so you create a semi-academic environment. They have to work on cases, they have to get the work done, but you also give them time for writing. That is essential. And you have guest speakers come in – your Chief Economist takes care of this; you just make sure he's knows it's what you want – so that they remain current on the literature, part of the academic community, and mobile, so they feel they can leave to a good position if they want to, and staying on for 3, 4 or 10 years is not going to prejudice them.

You mentioned one way in which you make sure that their ideas are incorporated into the decision about how to act is to put the Chief Economist on the same plane as the other deputies. Other steps you found useful in seeing that the perspective was integrated into the investigation process and the formulation of recommendations?

That was the last step in the process, that report. The first step is a requirement which I imposed, that every time a file is opened an economist be assigned to that matter. As soon as one decides to have an investigation, then an economist is assigned to the matter. There will be a team of layers, but usually one economist, and that economist, of course, may go back and consult within the economic analysis group to get input from others and has a supervisor who is going to look at the work and so on.

Did your interest in these matters of organization come as a consequence of being a scholar and teacher? Where did your interest in this dimension of policymaking come from, the way in which structure and organization can shape substance?

Well, I'll back up a bit and just say when Bill Baxter was at his confirmation hearing in the Senate, having been nominated for Assistant Attorney General, he was asked by one of the senators about his experience running an organization, and he said, "I've never run an organization larger than my secretary." And he wasn't really interested in doing that, so that is part of the reason there was no reorganization during his time. But I had had a year of observing this. It didn't come from any academic contemplation. I had a year observing the Department and seeing that it needed some attention, I had the benefit of Rick's good advice, and then I had the benefit of a year at the White House, where my particular position gave me – it was sort of like Bentham's synopticon: the center of our government is a complex of the White House, the Office of Management and Budget (OMB), which is part of the Executive Office of the President, and the Treasury, and from there you look out at all the spokes, and the spokes are the agencies. I dealt with agency heads from all around, and I picked up some sense then of some of the pathologies they were telling me about in their offices.

In the White House you had quite a panorama over the regulatory state.

Yes, exactly. I think that helped a good deal.

Other priorities that you had for yourself in the position? Things that come to mind for me are the extent to which this is a critical period in the rollout and enhancement of the criminal enforcement mission of the Department of Justice Antitrust Division.

It was flowering when I got there. At some point, either when I got there or before I left, we were working 130 grand juries simultaneously. These were open investigations. That is a lot for a staff to run. So, that was a very vibrant program, and it had been for not just Baxter's time but even before him.

The difference between then and now is that we were discovering a lot of relatively small local market price-fixing conspiracies – asphalt paving of roads is a market that is geographically limited because you're delivering hot asphalt; you're moving heavy equipment, so maybe it's a seventy-mile radius or something around a town, and there are not going to be more than 3 or 4 vendors except in a big city. Those were just rife with price-fixing conspiracies, some of which went back two generations. Procurement around military bases, providing milk and other things to a military base, collusive tendering was rife. But these were in dollar amounts small matters. Although they were all worth doing, we were sometimes criticized for focusing on small matters. Well, of course, if there was a bigger one, we followed it up. But that all changed after I left, in 1993, when the leniency program brought in and revealed large international cartels in huge-volume substances like vitamins and so on. We just didn't have the technology, the leniency program, with which to do that. It made a huge difference.

And quite an innovation in enforcement.

Yes, and well imitated around the world now. Although that imitation is uncoordinated, people are stuck trying to manage their exposure, getting markers in different countries for the beginning of their leniency application.

As you stepped out, was there unfinished business that you wished you had more time to work on or to pursue further?

I will say one thing I intended to do when I came in but found impossible was simply to keep up with the literature myself. When you go into a government position like this, you're there because you've built up human capital, and you're not building it up, or even replenishing it, while you're there; you are amortizing it, depreciating it, and then it comes the time to leave.

Were there any things you could do to regenerate that a bit? That is, I think, a question that a number of officials face is, "I feel like I'm on a treadmill running for my life all the time." Any techniques you could use or suggest giving yourself a bit of space to restore the capital?

Well, not enough, I'm afraid, not to sit down and be able to read journals every evening or something like that. Because I was able to delegate so much to Rick, I did have time for interagency projects, including fending off some bad initiatives from other agencies, because I thought those were very important things to do, and, having been at the White House, I could see how the apparatus worked, and I wanted to do that. Other than that, I wouldn't say there was any particular project that I had in mind and then wasn't able to stay to do it.

If we sum up some of the observations by assuming that you're talking with someone who's newly nominated, is in the queue to be nominated, or is making their way through the Senate confirmation process – or in another country they're on the glide path, if there is a glide path, – into agencies as opposed to being shot at all the time, thoughts you give them about what to expect, what to think about, things you know now that they ought to know on day one?

First, talk to your predecessors; they know a lot. Their information isn't necessarily going to be stale if it's structural. It can be very helpful. Second, talk to peers in other jurisdictions; I learned a fair amount. When I was the Deputy, I was involved in overseeing the Foreign Commerce Section. I was at the Organization for Economic Cooperation and Development (OECD). I didn't know anything about OECD. I'm not sure I knew what it stood for – I think I did – when I came in in 1983. All of a sudden, I'm the Chairman of the Committee of Experts on Restrictive Practices. I asked one of the OECD staff why it was called that – or maybe it was the head of the Section, Chuck Stark, at the Division. Anyway, the answer I got was, "It's just as well nobody knows what we're up to, what we were doing." I think we were 18 countries then, and it's now 35. It's doubled. That was an eye-opener because it was an opportunity to share and learn experiences from people in other countries, some of whom had a lot of experience – like the Bundeskartellamt had a very active enforcement program for 30 years at that point; the OECD staff themselves; Canada had an active program. So, it was very informative for me.

At the time, what dimension the world outside the United States played in the program of the Department, the international ingredient?

We had a couple of bilateral agreements already at that point for cooperation. We actually had a couple of treaties, too – or mutual legal assistance treaties (MLATs), I guess they were. We had good relations with a number of agencies around the world – Canada, Australia – not with the United Kingdom because we were in great tension over the effects doctrine, which they had not adopted at that point.

I had the experience of negotiating with my counterpart at the Department of Trade and Industry (DTI), who later went on to be the president of British Airways, a very able man. I'm afraid I was not entirely diplomatic because I said: "Well, suppose that there is a conspiracy formed in Switzerland to fix prices in the United States, but all the documents are being kept in the United Kingdom. Would it be possible for us to get access to those?" I was told that would be utterly unacceptable. Then I said: "Well, tell me this. Exactly what is it that differentiates the United Kingdom from a banana republic?". Then the meeting broke up. Then, as we were leaving, a senior fellow said, "Meet me at my club in an hour for a drink," and we put things a little bit back on track. [Laughter] We did not reach an agreement. That took some later time.

Looking at the experiences of peer organizations at the time, the time you left the Antitrust Division, what did you see to be the key issues for the Department to improve going ahead?

One was unique to us. Under the AT&T decree we had been cast into a regulatory role. I had a staff of around 6 lawyers who did nothing but work on the administration of the decree because every time a telephone company sought permission to go into a competitive business, a non-tariffed business, the judge would then automatically refer that to the Department for our position on it. I was determined to get rid of this totally inappropriate responsibility that had been thrust on us by the Court. And, indeed, I drafted legislation with someone from the Office of Legal Counsel to pick up the decree and move it whole, by law, and make it a regulation of the Federal Communications Commission (FCC). There was a constitutional problem about interfering with a Court judgment. There were political obstacles. We didn't get it done. I spent some time on it, we didn't get it done, but not too many years later the Congress did effectively something like that.

Are there reflections that you derived from your time as a judge, Chief Judge of the D.C. Circuit for a long period of time, but a long period of observation where your court has a remarkable perspective on regulation, the regulatory state? Other thoughts about what distinguishes a well-run agency from one that is deficient, practices and techniques that increase confidence in what they're doing?

There are still some agencies – I'm not sure if there are today, but there had been in my time as a judge – that were totally lawyer-driven and missing an opportunity, or even an obligation, to subject what they're doing to some economic scrutiny, and the leading offender was the Securities and Exchange Commission (SEC). I wrote an opinion – well, I should say in 1996 the Congress passed a statute requiring the Commission before it issued a regulation to consider 4 matters, including the effect of the regulation on capital markets, on competition, and on two other things. They had never implemented the statute; they essentially forgot about it.

In a case brought on behalf of an industry association protesting a rule, that was pointed out and we sent the matter back to the Commission to deal with this, to do the right thing. They did a sloppy job in 2 weeks, in a rush, because I think the Chairman was leaving and wanted to get this done before he left. We reversed it again. There were ultimately three of these cases, maybe four, and after the third or fourth one, whatever it was, came out in August of 2011, there was a scheduled hearing in April of 2012 in the House to ask the SEC what they had done in order to comply with these directions. The answer was a press release issued on the day before the hearing saying they were building up their PhD economics staff, reorganizing to some extent. There was a long-single-spaced memorandum to the Enforcement Division and the economics group on how they were going to proceed henceforth – and they did; they pulled up their socks.

Now, I had every confidence that they would do this because I had seen in my position at OMB running the Regulatory Review Program the Environmental Protection Agency (EPA) had done it, the Federal Energy Regulatory Commission had done it, the FCC had done it. Surely the Securities and Commission Exchange could do it. That was my legacy for them as a judge. But we get more competition cases in the D.C. Circuit Federal Court of Appeals from agencies than we do from Antitrust because a lot of the statutes require attention to competition. The Federal Energy Regulatory Commission, the Federal Communications

Commission, and now the SEC, are all 3 required to do some economic analysis of competition issues. They may not be as deeply expert as the FTC and the Antitrust Division, but they generate issues, and we review those.

They have some good analysts who do this kind of work as well. I would like to ask an international question and then maybe another. On the international stage, where it has become an expanded part of what you've done – I mean the exceptionally successful program at George Mason, the education program, the teaching program – do you see observable progress on the part of agencies to adopt more effective decision-making processes, leadership? Do you see things that hearten you about the direction in the field globally?

I've seen some of that in specific agencies, not enough to know whether that is a worldwide phenomenon. I was at a program at the National University of Singapore in around 2013 for 8 youthful agencies in Asia. They were keen to learn from each other and from those of us who were visiting. I was very impressed even then with Singapore. They were already doing an excellent job. Of course, in 2013 China was only 5 years into it. I went there in August of 2008. The statute was a year old – maybe it was 2009 then – and I guess the private action provision had just come into effect that month and the first cases were filed. How does an agency deal with this? They've never had a private action before. I was approached during a visit in Beijing at the conference by a young woman who was an assistant to one of the judges and said: "We have this case. It's clearly not a meritorious case, but the statute, the AML, the Anti-Monopoly Law, requires us first to define the relevant market, which is going to be very difficult." I alerted her to an article by Judge William Schwarzer that had been published probably in the 1970s, maybe even late 1960s, on the management of a big antitrust case. He had a lot of wisdom in there, such as "before you start down this road, make sure there is a feasible remedy," things like that. So, it was very easy to say: "Well, look, you must have the administrative flexibility under the law to avoid defining the market in a circumstance where the case is clearly without merit," and I showed her how we would put that and do it. That would never happen now. I mean, even 2 years after that it would never happen again. They became much more sophisticated. Look at their merger decisions. The early merger decisions, the Coca-Cola orange juice case, was completely unpersuasive. Five years later you didn't see that kind of thing. Again, they became much more sophisticated. Even private litigation – look at Johnson & Johnson; look at Tencent. Those are cases that could have been written in my court.

I'm struck as you are at the sophistication of the work. But I also am struck at how – and maybe it's your impression from your role as a teacher overseas, too – there is a huge value in having experienced jurists from the United States, and in your case an experienced head of a major law enforcement institution, doing the teaching at the podium, conveying knowhow in a way that has immediate credibility and impact on the audience.

Since 2014, when I established the Global Antitrust Institute for the purpose of teaching judges and regulators at George Mason – to establish that I went to the dean and I said, "Look, I don't know if there is any demand for this, but I know there is a great need." Well, it turned out there was also substantial demand.

A few years ago, we were in Shanghai, and for a few days we had 200 judges and for the whole week we had 60 judges. They were terrific, by the way. About a third of them didn't even use the translation. But we weren't teaching them the law – they're judges, and they have their own law – we were teaching economics and how it fits into an anti-monopoly law. Of course, being there and being with judges, it gives them an opportunity also when we break out of the formal sessions to talk about things like how one as a judge can proceed; or, if it's agency officials, even more so. So, there is that. I'm trying to think of other agencies where I've seen that kind of evolution. Theirs is the most impressive because it's recent, it starts from zero, and it becomes quite good. That is probably the best example I could come up with.

I just did a program a year ago in Mexico, which was a review of progress in the development of Mexico's system. Two senior officials of the Mexican agency, one past and one current, said: "We'll tell you what helped change the relationship of our agencies to the judiciary. It was the effort of the United States to send its judges," and the two they mentioned in particular were Douglas Ginsburg and Diane Wood. "Two people have been here teaching," and they said, "If you had to point to one thing that changed the quality and tenor of that conversation over time, it was those two people."

Well, thank you for relaying that. It was Eduardo Pérez Motta, who was for, I think, ten years head of the Comisión Federal de Competencia Económica (COFECE), who got this idea. The problem he was facing was this: the judges were unfamiliar with this; it was a new law; they were unfamiliar not only with the law but, more importantly, with the economic concepts behind it. A company that was being investigated would run to a court and seek a writ of amparo, which for us is like a writ of prohibition, to stop the investigation. It's essentially a procedural way for the judge to get rid of this and not have to deal with the substance, so it was very tempting and very frustrating for the agency. So, yes, Eduardo brought Diane and me down. I was down there three times doing seminars for judges, and he said, "Maybe it's just coincidental, but the problem went away."

When I think of the conveyance of knowhow, it is drawing upon this experienced group of jurists – and in your case scholar, jurist, former official in a law enforcement capacity – that has had a remarkable impact. If we were thinking about ways that we could maximize the effect of, let's say, the U.S. perspective or the knowledge we've accumulated, I'm convinced, based on your experience – others, but your experience in particular – that that moves the needle.

Your mention of the experience in Mexico reminds me I should have mentioned Mexico in talking about how seeing an agency come along. When Eduardo became President of the Agency – he's a PhD economist from UCLA, and he had a terrific Deputy, Ali Haddou-Ruiz, who is actually from Brooklyn, and they really shaped that agency and shaped it up. Then, Alejandra Palacios comes in, and I believe in her time 6 of the 7 Commissioners are economists. So, this is a really remarkable flowering of the agency as a result.

Eduardo was very astute. He pointed out, "Competition is not an everyday thing for people in this country, for the ordinary person, they're not familiar with this.". He had a national competition day. One time I went down for that, and we did videotapes and so on, and it was on television, to alert the public, to educate the public about this and to build public support. He needed legislation, and he got it twice. So I think the public support mattered.

We've talked about law enforcement and related things, but, just as a footnote, competition advocacy has a very important function. When I was there, there was a sort of informal division of labor, I would say, in which the FTC did this in state legislatures and we did it with other federal agencies. We would file comments, just like a member of the public could before the Department of Transportation. Now, they didn't listen to us, and they allowed airline mergers that they shouldn't have allowed, but we did get our word in there. We did that at a lot of agencies, more successfully with some of the others. The very first matter I worked on when I arrived as a Deputy was the Department of Transportation's proposed regulation of airline reservation systems. The concepts are still with us, the same problems are still with us, when we look at some of the digital problems today.

They wanted to be the reservation system platform regulator.

I'll tell you something. The papers were due at 10:00 Friday morning on my first Friday. I was handed a 104-or-so-page document at 4:00 on Thursday. I kept the staff through the night, and we filed my document in the morning, and that never happened again. That is a lesson, too.

Antonio Gomes*

Portuguese Competition Authority, President (2013-2016)
OECD, Deputy Director (2020-Present)

You were the President of the Portuguese Competition Authority from 2013 to 2016, so you have had the experience of being in the key leadership role of a national competition authority. Most recently, you are the Acting Deputy Director for the Directorate of Financial & Enterprise Affairs of the OECD, and in that capacity you have had a wonderful opportunity and perspective to look at the activities of a wide range of regulators, continuing your experience in looking at competition authorities. To this I add that you have provided advice on a number of occasions to individual authorities. You have had a key role in the OECD's outreach program. You have been responsible for participating in a host of different projects that OECD carries out around the world to provide guidance to individual agencies, not simply about what to do, but most importantly how to do it well. Let me begin by asking what your path into competition law was and what series of professional experiences brought you to the Portuguese Authority?

I started as an academic. I did my studies in economics, became a lecturer at the Universidade de Aveiro and then was an assistant professor at the same university. At some point, I really felt like doing something different beyond just teaching and researching. I saw an ad for the position of case handler in the Competition Authority in Portugal. That was in 2005. I said, "Why not? It's a recent authority. Why not try to actually contribute to changing the world in a way?". I started as a case handler in the Merger Department of the Portuguese Competition Authority. I was handling quite a lot of complex mergers. I was given the opportunity to lead one of the biggest

* Interview conducted on 3 December 2019.

mergers in Portugal in the telecom sector, where a maverick was acquiring the incumbent in Portugal. I think that gave me the experience, but also the visibility to then be invited to the position of Director of the Merger Department. I was Director of the Merger Department for several years. I had an excellent experience there. Actually, I used to say that merger control was the best thing that a competition authority could do because it was really where you could have the interlink between the economics and the law. It was very much an economic reasoning subject. So, I had that experience for a long time. Then, at some point, I thought, with all the international experience that I have had, why not contribute to the international world? And I have the experience as a senior competition expert at the OECD. That is when I was surprised with the invitation to go back to the Portuguese Competition Authority, now as the President, and I was there for 3 years. I then came back to the OECD as head of the Competition Division. I am currently the Deputy Director of the Financial & Enterprise Affairs Directorate at the OECD, where I continue to oversee the work of the Competition Division, which is supporting the work of the Competition Committee here at the OECD, but I am also overseeing the work of a much larger portfolio, so looking at financial markets, at investment, at corporate governance, responsible business conduct, and anticorruption.

So, when you become the head of the Authority you are no stranger to the agency. Was it an advantage for you in coming in to be the President to have this considerable hands-on experience and familiarity with the institution? Is that a big plus for you?

It was an advantage and it actually cut some corners. I think that I managed to introduce some management changes in the Authority because I knew it well, it allowed me to save some time. But at the same time, it's always difficult when you are, in a way, promoted within the same organization because most of the people whom you are working with were your former colleagues. They are my peers. In that sense, it means that they know you well, there is a lot of familiarity, and sometimes you have to balance familiarity with also some management distance because the decisions you have to take are not compatible with the relationship of friendship that you have with the people around you.

You're no longer just the friend; you're the boss now. And those are different roles.

Yes, the boss now. So, advantages and disadvantages. Actually, I think I was lucky. Things worked out quite well. I managed to create a very good management team to introduce changes to the organization of the Competition Authority.

I was also very lucky to have a group of staff who was very, very committed, and the fact that they knew me also made it easier for them to trust me and for me to trust them in their work.

They must have had a sense that you had shared interests, a common cause for the institution.

It is very important to have that, to have common objectives, a vision, and above all to understand why we are doing what we are doing. I think that you are successful if you really understand. You were talking about the "how" to do it, but I think that, first of all, we need to understand why we are doing what we are doing and then go through the "what is it that we can do and how can we do it?" At the Competition Authority, I think that we had – and that was from a very early stage; it was not just in my period – a clear notion of the "why" we were doing this, that this was good for the country. We were in a mission of public interest, and everyone in the organization shared that view and had this common goal of improving the well-being of people, improving the efficiency of the economy, allowing the economy to be more productive, more dynamic, to promote growth and so on.

When you returned to the agency after your time at the OECD the first time, now coming back as President, did you have specific things in mind that you wanted to do when you approached the job – projects, approaches, a strategy for how you wanted to use your time as chair? Did that inform your judgment from day one?

Anyone who is invited to take such a responsibility needs to have a plan, and I think that the first thing you do – even before actually, because I was leading a board of people, so I wasn't going to be the only decision-maker – but even before talking with the others with whom you are sharing that responsibility, you have to have some sort of a plan of what you want to do. One of the things I've always believed in is openness and transparency. I have always believed that an authority can only gain by being open to society, by being transparent and accountable. One of the objectives was how to reach out, how to not have a competition authority that is closed within itself, even if it is very competent, but that is actually open to society? I wanted to reach out to the environment around me, around the Competition Authority.

How did you do that?

One example is companies, firms themselves. I thought we need to be closer to firms because they need to understand why we are doing what we are doing and why we have a competition law. I realized that, apart from the big companies, all the other companies, especially SMEs, weren't so aware of competition law or of the benefits of competition law and we had to reach out to the business community. For example, one of the things that we developed as a team – and of course it was not just my plan or my execution – was a roadshow across the country called "Fair Play – With competition everybody wins," where we partnered with several business associations across the country, and where we made an effort ourselves to turn a sometimes difficult and complex field that is competition economics and law, and bring it into a more common-language way of communication with the business sector. I think that was particularly successful. Also working with other regulators, legislators, the government, and making them understand exactly why we are doing what we are doing. Of course, I think that any manager of a competition authority wants two things: to increase and improve enforcement and to have better advocacy, especially to foster a culture of competition in the country.

Looking at those things, I thought on the enforcement side that we needed to reinforce, especially against cartels. We created an anti-cartel unit which would be a team that would gain experience in dealing with leniency applications and in dealing with inspections, dawn raids, so that we build up knowledge in order to be more effective in the future. We also trained people to use forensic IT to do searches with electronic means because nowadays if you don't have those capabilities, there is not much you can do.

When I arrived, we had just had a very big dawn raid in the banking sector. The Competition Authority had dawn raided 15 banks in the economy, and it was amazing the amount of evidence that was gathered then. In the first bunch of documents, we had more than 5 million files. Just thinking of how many years it would take to handle that, you need to have the right software to go through the evidence and you need to have people who are prepared to look at that electronic evidence so that you can actually make sense of what you have. Having an anti-cartel unit was a very important element of the strategy.

And of course, on enforcement it was also very important to make sure that we have quality decisions. That meant to have appropriate checks and balances within the Authority, so we needed to have the Legal Department fully involved with investigations, but also to have the economics side – of course not so much on cartels, more on abuse of dominance, vertical restrictions or even merger cases – and it was very important to have a strong Chief economist's team that would be helping to build the cases and also to be a devil's advocate when looking at those cases. So, checks and balances.

And finally, that rights of defense were being respected was another area that we focused a lot on, to make sure that we would not lose a case because of a procedural issue, because we did not allow companies to have a fair procedure.

How did you roll these changes out inside? Some of these involved creating a different organizational structure, maybe a different emphasis. How did you bring your internal team along with you in laying the groundwork for the changes and gaining acceptance for them inside the house?

Of course, you have to rely on the people. At the end, it's the staff that you have that will take the Authority forward or take you as a leader forward as well, and it's very important that you have a good team of managers around you. I focused on both. I focused on having a good team of managers, people that have experience. Most people had experience in the Competition Authority, even as case handlers or former directors. They had experience also in the private sector – our General Director for Investigations, for example, had both kinds of experience; he had been in the private sector, and he had been in the Competition Authority – to make sure that you have a good team of managers that understands your vision and where you want to bring the Authority.

Did you have some freedom inside to decide who these people would be? Did you largely inherit a management group, or did you have some freedom to say "I want to build my team to work with me?"

The Competition Authority in Portugal has quite a lot of freedom to establish its own internal organization, but it's not an individual decision, it is a decision by the board. The board is composed of 3 members, the President and two other members of the board, so of course it's not my decision. You do have to convince others and you do have to take the suggestions of others. We managed to build a team of managers reaching a consensus on what kind of profile we should have, what kind of skills and what kind of competences we should have in the management team, and of course we also sent invitations to people who did not accept the invitation. You have to have not just the first choice, but you need to have other choices – I wouldn't say second or third choices – I would say alternatives. I would say that all the potential options were quite good options.

A good thing about the experience in Portugal is that I realized that there are very good and well-prepared people, to take on those kinds of responsibilities. I also worked with the team, and that requires thinking that, when you have a group of staff, you shouldn't look at the staff in a static perspective but in a dynamic perspective. You need to understand what kind of skills they have currently and what kind of skills they can have in the future, what are their capabilities, and also what are their limitations, and you need to work on those, by bringing them in, making them understand why you are doing what you're doing, making them see what the path might be, being quite clear and communicating about that path. Again, as you said, there was a lot of shared common values and shared common vision, which helped, but you still need to team build around this vision; and also train the people, discuss with the people, involve the people as much as you can; and finally, empower the people. You are not going to do it by yourself. You always need to empower the people to be able to do the work and to be creative, not just to follow orders, because at the end you are only going to potentiate the capacity of the agency if you give them the power to also generate new ideas, to find new ways of doing things, to create new processes, to improve, to be more efficient, to be more effective, and so on.

Several things you've mentioned strike me as so important – to explain to your team why we're doing this, where we think we're going, how they fit in, how they can contribute, how they can grow – so that everybody understands what the agency is trying to accomplish. I take it you spent lots of time, or some amount of time, every week with your staff, that they got to see you. Recalling my own experience as a junior lawyer, but maybe thinking about your own as a case handler, I take it that has a positive impact on the staff to have some time to discuss with the agency leader what they're doing, just get to know you a bit, but also to see your visible presence.

It's very important that a management board or a president or a member of the board is not closed in its ivory tower distant from everyone. Of course, this depends a lot on the size of the institution.

Just for context, you had a total of about how many employees?

90. I think that with 90 employees it's still feasible that you are actually close to your staff, that you discuss with them.

You know all their names.

Exactly. If you have a bigger institution, I think it can make it harder, but still, you need to create the conditions to meet your staff, even if you do it sometimes indirectly. You need to make sure that you are meeting with groups of people – sometimes you are meeting with task forces; sometimes you are meeting with the teams that are bringing a very important case – so that you actually discuss with them directly. It is also very important for them to understand how you make your decisions, why you make your decisions that way, and what are the considerations that you take into account. That also helps them to know in future cases how to actually handle a case, to make sure that the board understands the case well, that it has the right evidence that the board requires for decision-making, and so on.

You've mentioned the fact that the governance structure for the Authority was a college of 3. It's different being the head of a unitary executive body where you alone are the President, the Chair, from being the Chair of a board where you do share responsibility with colleagues. What thoughts can you offer to us about what a chair must keep in mind to remember "I am part of a college" and how you deal with your colleagues who are your partners in this process?

I think the most important thing when you are in a board is that you have to start by understanding the other people who are on the board. You need to understand them. You need to spend quite a lot of time talking with them, understand their views, their approaches, so that you can then better see why they tend to have this kind of approach or this kind of decision. Then there is a lot of work in building consensus. I think that when you have a board, the first thing you want is that everyone agrees on something. Of course, we had majority voting in the board, which meant that there could be dissent, and dissent can be positive as well.

It can be constructive, so you shouldn't also prevent that from happening. I think that, in the first place, you try to make sure that you reach a decision that is consensual across the whole board. But then it's true that sometimes there is dissent. It's important that whoever is dissenting from a majority decision – and it can be the President – that it is very clear, and also that the people who are around the decision do understand why there was a dissent. And also, that you do it in a way that you don't weaken the Authority because there are, as I know from my experiences across the world, sometimes frequent dissents without good robust reasoning can actually undermine the work of the Authority and even its credibility. It is very important that a lot of these things are treated and discussed within the board before it actually comes to the outside world. Again, working with a board is a challenge. I would say it is easier when you are the only one making a decision. But then you don't have the same diversity of views as well, and, by having someone to discuss with, you often end up reaching a better decision.

You create an atmosphere in which the discussion, and even the occasional dissent, is likely to be positive, constructive, through your engagement with your colleagues on a regular basis, remembering that they are part of the governing structure. You have but one of three votes, you do want to solicit their views, you do see value in having a collaborative process and not simply a single person thinking to themselves. The president helps create a set of understandings that will promote a constructive decision-making process, a healthy one, because everyone believes they are being heard, their views are being taken seriously, and that you, in particular, the head of the agency, view this as a true collaboration, not as an individual sport.

Exactly. There is value in actually having a board to work with.

Just a practical thought about how you spent your time every day. Was there a time of day when you would say, "If you want to schedule a time to come see me, my door is open, stop by and talk?" Did you have an invitation to staff and other managers so that if they wanted to come and see you, they could do it, they could schedule, and that you would be available? How did you schedule your day? How did you use your time that way?

I've always had an open-door policy – I think it's quite important – but also, it's very important that you acknowledge that being the President of an institution means that you are quite busy with a lot of responsibilities, so you are not necessarily always available. An open-door policy is a good thing, in the sense that people can go and check if you are available, but it is also very important that you do create opportunities for people to meet with you.

With the managers we used to have regular meetings. There was a weekly meeting with all the managers that were dealing with all the cases in enforcement. Actually, we mixed those responsible for mergers with those responsible for antitrust enforcement. We brought in the Director of the Legal Department and the Chief Economist where we had regular weekly discussions. We also used to have another meeting with the entire management team at least once a month. You have to create these opportunities, as I was saying before, even for people who bring the cases to explain their cases and so on.

Also, it's not all about work. Sometimes it's about how people are feeling in their working environment, so you also need to allow them to set up a meeting with you to discuss how it is going. Sometimes things are not going well with a manager or with colleagues. You need to be approachable, to be able to listen to people, and then of course also act on whatever they are bringing up.

I take it that your approach with your managers in the spirit of achieving better results was to encourage people to tell you what you needed to know and not just to tell you what you might want to hear, that you invited debate, discussion, challenge.

I think that is the only way. Again, I was mentioning just a while ago the importance of having different views to get to a better decision, and I think that you do need to create a culture or an environment where people can freely speak their minds. That is at all levels, even when you are building a case. When I was the head of the Merger Department, for example, I remember quite clearly saying: "There are no stupid comments. There are no stupid ideas. If we are discussing what can be the potential theory of harm in this case, if we are in a brainstorming phase, we should be able to put everything on the table, even if it may seem unreasonable, and let's discuss it. Don't feel shy to bring an idea to the table, whatever it is, let's discuss it, and then let's bring the evidence, the facts and the elements that can eventually say that's actually rubbish. But being rubbish is not a problem. It allows you to improve your analysis and to actually get to a better result."

Is it a big change once you enter the office to be the focal point for the agency, the main spokesperson, the president walking through the aisles and corridors of the office? You are now in one sense onstage all the time, routinely observed by the people inside – it's the President after all, the Chair of the agency. Outside, you are the main public face of the agency. Colleagues and heads of units may appear and give speeches, but you are the principal embodiment of the institution. Was that much of a change for you to be the one who's now the focal point inside and outside?

It was definitely a big change and a change that I had to adapt to. Having that responsibility within the institution was relatively easy because I knew everyone by name, so that wasn't really an issue. When you think about the outside world and when you have to go and talk with the Parliament, when you have to meet the government or when you have to speak with the media, you do have quite a lot of weight on your shoulders. I had a media adviser, and of course in the first week she wanted to know my strategy, my priorities, and so on. I said, "I'm a bevel, a mirror of this institution, so I am not going to set the priorities and the strategy by myself, and I also need to be very aware of what the institution is that I head." I always felt like even throughout my mandate, my term, I really was a reflection of the institution. Of course, I was trying not to portray the institution worse than it was, but in a way guaranteeing or making sure that the institution was operating well also gave me the strength to portray it in a good way, to reflect it well. The more confident you are regarding your institution and the way it is operating, the more confident you will be in communicating, in representing the institution, because you know you are not alone, you know you have 90 people behind you. Again, you are representing the 90 people, but you are actually representing an idea or an objective, a mission, a vision, which goes even beyond those 90 people.

A couple more questions on this wonderful tour through your own experience. Now, you have had a remarkable opportunity to look at a lot of agencies in different contexts – closer to hand visiting them, watching their discussions at OECD fora of different types, including the regular meetings. When you look at this larger experience, what characteristics tend to identify or predict success for agency leadership? Aside from your own experiences that you have reflected on, do you have some additional thoughts on what tends to predict success for an agency leader?

There are many characteristics that a leader needs to have to be successful. We talked about a few of them. I think having a vision is quite an important element and being able to share that vision with the staff because, at the end, there is no leader without a team. Again, I think it is important to inspire people and to actually bring them into what is, at the end, an adventure.

As a leader, you have to be very aware of the potential but also the limitations of the agency, the authority, or the organization that you have at hand. You have to be conscious that you can change them both or you can help change them both. You can expand the frontiers, you can reduce the limitations, you can increase the potential. That requires working with the staff, developing the staff, training the staff, etc. You need to communicate well or at least have a clear message of where you want to go and what you are doing.

You need to be trustworthy. People need to trust that you are doing the job because you actually believe in the job you are doing and that you don't have any other interest beyond the public interest of the mission that you are trying to accomplish.

You spent a good part of your career working not simply in Portugal but in an international environment that is your professional home now – cooperation, comparative work, collective assessment of experience, the pursuit of better practices and techniques. If you are the head of the national agency, you have a number of built-in responsibilities, especially as the head of a national competition authority in the European context, there are necessary elements of cooperation. At the same time, your principal job is in Lisbon, larger Portugal as well – so many demands on your time to do things at home, participate in things abroad. How does the agency head strike the balance between doing your job at home but participating in this larger framework where you can learn things that are good for your job? How do you balance those different responsibilities?

I think, at the end, it has to do precisely with what I said, that a competition authority has potential, and it has limitations and what you are trying to do is to increase the potential of the authority and reduce its limitations. International cooperation and having an international exposure contributes to both, so you have to keep that in mind, but at the same time you need to know that you have a job to do. You have to, on one hand, know that you have to enforce the law, that's your role; you know that you have to advocate in your own country to create a culture of competition; but at the same time, you know that you also have to invest in the future, so you have to keep the present and the future in view.

Being in the international world is often where you can learn new ideas, you can see what others are doing, and you can benchmark your activity against the activity of others. You can get an understanding of what you are doing. Sometimes it is very difficult to get understanding in your own country because not everyone understands why a competition authority is doing what it is doing. So, in a sense, it's good to also have support from your peers in other countries that will make you stronger to go forward. We have learned so many things at the competition authorities from being part of the international family, even on enforcement. For example, I was mentioning a while ago on enforcement of cartels using IT forensics. We don't necessarily need to move out of the country to learn from that; you can also bring the expertise in. For instance, we had a lot of seminars with the French Competition Authority, the Brazilian Competition Authority, the Spanish Competition Authority, and so on to discuss how to use these kinds of tools. Again, it's balancing priorities, and responsibilities. It's not always easy, but you have to do it in a way that you still focus on what your core responsibility is, that you need to enforce the law and enforce it in a robust manner and with good quality. You also need to bring in new ideas, bring in new ways of doing things, learn from others' experience, and benchmark as well.

As you've mentioned on several occasions, having a plan for how this international collaboration can make you better, it can reinforce areas in which you are already doing a good job, it can assist in building strength where, perhaps, you don't have the strength that you want so far. Let me give you a closing question to finish with. You are talking to your successor who is coming in to begin the experience that you've had. What have you learned that you would now pass along to them, that they ought to keep in mind on day one?

First of all, I would tell my successor, whom I've actually gotten to meet, know and have an excellent relationship with, to build on the past, learn from the past, but also always have a look into the future and see what else you can do to improve. I would probably tell her that what I have done at the Competition Authority – or my legacy, what I wanted my legacy to be – would be to hand over an Authority that was in a better shape than the Authority that I received and hoping that she will take the Authority to an even higher next level, which honestly, I think she did. I'm very pleased with that, and I think maybe she took into account some of the advice that I gave her then. I would tell her to enforce vigorously. It's very important that you do it, but in the right way, so that you do keep the right checks and balances; that you do guarantee the rights of defense. Don't rely solely on complaints. Don't rely solely on leniency. Go into the future. Use screening methods, look at procurement databases, and so on. Work with others, don't work alone. Potentiate your abilities by working with other regulators, by working with other institutions. Have good managers around you. It is very important that you have managers with experience, but also managers that you can trust. Don't forget that you have a board and that you need to create consensus and understanding. Don't underestimate the political context. That doesn't mean that you should bend to it, but it means that you need to understand it, you need to comprehend it. Be open to society, be transparent, and be accountable. It is very important that you are open, that you are not closed in your own world. Communicate because you need to gain the society's support. Keep investing in new capabilities, new ways of doing things. And don't forget that your success depends on your staff, so you need to keep working with them, developing them and bringing the Authority to the next level with them.

Michal Halperin*

Israel Competition Authority, General Director (2016-2021)

You are the head of the Israel Antitrust Authority. You have served in a number of capacities in the private and public sectors. You are the head of a very effective and significant institution. I would like to start by asking you to reflect about the path that led you to where you are now in the Israel Competition Authority (ICA). What were the experiences in particular that best prepared you for what you're doing now?

I started my career in the private sector and I worked as an attorney for many years until I was nominated in 2002 as the Chief Legal Counsel of the IAA – then the Antitrust Authority; today it's called the Competition Authority. I was Chief Legal Counsel in the Antitrust Authority for 4 and a half years. Then, I switched back to the private sector for 10 more years, until I was nominated as the head of the Competition Authority. Now, I really believe that the experience of both the private and the public sector was significant in preparing me for the job of General Director of the Competition Authority. As you know, when you come out from the Authority and you try to practice competition law vis-à-vis the Competition Authority, you understand very well what concerns them, how they understand the reality, and you try to make the dialogue work with them through your experience of how they think of things. So this is a huge advantage. And the same goes for the experience in the private sector. So, when you come into the Competition Authority and you have experience with the business community, everything goes into the right proportion. You understand how business works and you understand that the competition law and the competition regulation, important as it is, is only part of what concerns businesses. They have many other challenges – business challenges; other regulatory challenges; they have

* Interview conducted on 23 July 2019.

tax law; they have securities law; they have employment law – and you are only part of the very big picture. This proportion on where you stand in the whole picture of the businesspeople is very good in order to be able to run the show in an effective way. I think that is the most essential thing that it taught me and brought me the right experience to this stage and this work.

When you think about your experience in a law firm, advising clients dealing with this whole constellation of legal demands that you've just referred to, what stands out in your mind about their expectations about what makes for a good agency? I am sure they don't expect the agency to agree with them all the time or to invariably accept their arguments, but what do they see as being good characteristics of the agency and the people who lead the agency?

It is important what the business community expects and it is what we expect of ourselves, or at least what I expect from a good agency, is to be a smart regulator and to do the regulation in a smart way. I think we should interfere as minimum as possible, only in the cases where it's necessary to interfere. But once we interfere, we should do it effectively, and that is, in my opinion, the essence of good regulation. You need to interfere at the minimum; but once you do it, it has to be effective and smart.

I'll give you a short example. When I was Chief Legal Counsel, in the years after, the Antitrust Authority tried many times to impose divestiture remedies in mergers. Each time it failed. Each time the parties asked for an extension, they would come in and explain that they couldn't find a buyer for their business, that there are difficult market conditions, and what do you have? There were all kinds of stories, and the divestiture never worked. When I came into the Competition Authority, when I imposed a divestiture, what I insisted was that it will be fix-it-first. The first time – it doesn't happen so frequently – I was confronted with a case where we thought divestiture was needed. There was a huge argument with the business community opposing us and the business parties on this fix-it-first. It looked horrible to them: it would delay the merger; it would take a lot of time. But you know what? It worked very well. The second time I insisted, there was much less objection. The third time this was the rule. They knew that this was what I would ask for and they didn't even argue about it. It was how we work. I'm very much into putting as little divestiture as possible. It's not always successful. But once you have it, you should insist that it will be fix-it-first. This is one example of how to build a good regulation.

Did the experience give you a better intuition about what a good argument from the affected firms is? Did it sharpen your ability to say, "Here are four arguments. Two of those they had to make them, but those aren't strong arguments. Here are the two we're thinking about"? Does it give you a greater ability to get to the real heart of the matter and understand what is worth discussing?

I believe it does. We are much more open to arguments like efficiency and we will give a lot of space. I'm not sure if this was the case beforehand. We are a little more suspicious about arguments on the due process because we usually pretty much trust our due process – we could be wrong; and, if we are, then we should take it into account – but usually, in every case, we get arguments on due process, and in most cases we don't give them a lot of weight. But there are other economic and legal arguments that have a lot of weight.

I assume it is possible for you to look at them as they're making arguments and say, "Oh come on, it's Michal. I've done this before. I know what you're going through, I understand that, but really, I also understand the kinds of arguments that have real merit to them, and I know that when you're complaining that maybe is professionally your destiny but it doesn't really reflect reality" – do you get some credibility from them because you were in their shoes at one time?

Well, I'm not sure, but I can tell you that my personal style is to be very blunt. When I come into a hearing, it's usually not like I'm sitting there like a judge, listening to what they say, writing down their remarks, and letting them go and saying, "I'll think about it. Thank you." It takes only several minutes to become a dialogue. When it becomes a dialogue, then you achieve much more from the hearing. You can define very quickly what is the real argument and what is really nothing. I'm getting engaged in the discussion and they get engaged in the discussion too. This dialogue brings you right into the heart of what is real and what is not.

It would be a different conversation if you had not had this experience.

I'm not sure whether it's experience or a matter of style. I know that other general directors usually sat very silently in hearings. But it's a matter of personal style sometimes.

Did it help you that you had been there before, at the predecessor institution, as the General Counsel and as the head of Legal Services; that you had had a significant senior leadership position before? Did it help you in acting as the head of the agency?

I believe it did. I was prepared to start running from day one. Even the teams within the Competition Authority were slightly surprised by the speed that I started to decide things and to change things. I came into the Competition Authority after more than half a year that the Competition Authority did not have a General Director. It had an Acting General Director. So I didn't have time with the previous General Director to hear his thoughts on different cases and how he thought things should go on from here. This was a disadvantage. My familiarity with the Antitrust Authority made me able to overcome this.

And it gives you insight into the culture of public administration and public service.

Yes, that is true. Although the Competition Authority is very unique in our public administration. It works like sort of a hybrid between the business sector and the public sector. People are very business-oriented in their way of thinking – they are quick; they are industrious; they understand the need to reach an immediate and a quick resolution – so they are not the typical public servants that you would find in other sectors of the government.

In the experience you had as a private counselor and as a government official, does this give you an appreciation and understanding about the political science of the country, the environment in which the agency is situated, its relationship to the political process, a deeper understanding of the economic conditions that the agency confronts? Did these other experiences, public and private, put you in a good position to be aware of what some call the "enabling environment" that surrounds an agency?

I learned quite a lot about the general atmosphere of the business community. They're not all the same. There are some companies that try very hard to comply, that will be willing to pay a high price not to get involved in any regulatory violation, and that's a top priority within them. They still sometimes find themselves confronting the Competition Authority. With this kind of company, you need to be patient with them because, as we all know, competition analysis is not an exact science, that you always know what the right answer is. They may look at the situation very differently than how the Competition Authority will analyze it, and suddenly they find themselves in a confrontation with the Competition Authority which they didn't want and they didn't expect.

On the other hand, you will find other companies that only look for the way to pass in between and do what they want notwithstanding what the law says. So you have all kinds of companies. Part of the game is to understand what kind of person you are confronting when you are dealing with them. That is not always easy to make, but you need to understand that there are many types of businesspeople.

In some competition systems, certainly the ones I'm most familiar with in the United States and in the United Kingdom, it's not unusual to have people coming from the private sector into a senior leadership position like head of the institution. I would say that those are somewhat unusual compared to the typical path. If I had to make a broad generalization about the full body of regulatory agencies, the competition agencies around the world, the more typical path is that the appointee comes from public service, and with some experience in a public agency. I am accustomed to liking and preferring the openness of the system to contributions from different areas, but I know in some instances, this can be met with resistance. How well did everybody welcome the idea that, even though she is in a sense one of us, she's been here before, she's coming from the private sector? Was there resistance to that?

I didn't perceive much resistance from within the Competition Authority. Even when I practiced law in the private sector and I had a lot of conflict with the Competition Authority and had quite a lot of arguments, they all always felt that there was a lot of respect for the Competition Authority. They knew that I respected them and that I know that they are professionals, and they want good. So I didn't feel any resentment from the team or from the business community. I did get a lot of objections from the press and the public opinion. It even, I can say, surprised me how much objection was brought up to my nomination coming from the private sector. A lot of media were writing about it. A lot of resentment towards the nomination. It was a rough beginning.

I guess one lesson for everyone is that to some extent these are not jobs for the timid.

Yes. I learned that in the first half-year when I was in the position. It was opening the newspaper every morning and reading articles on the different issues where

I tried to change things, and where I had some personal articles on me and everything. But it's also a very good experience. You learn how to deal with the media. You learn how to put what they have to say in the right proportion. You need to listen to them. They have their opinion and it must be taken into account, but it also needs to be put in proportion. If you believe in what you do, then the media can say whatever they want, you need to go forward.

At some point you have to do your job. The best way to establish the content, substance, and validity of your purpose is to do the job, and to do it well. I think in a number of instances, for different reasons, people do face criticism. To have a job with real significance, real power, public resources, you are going to be in the center of attention, and sometimes that center of attention is not going to be favorable. Do you have thoughts for someone who's coming to the job about how to respond to the scrutiny, the media criticism? Is there an approach that you adopted for yourself to say, "This is hostile commentary, but I do want to do this job; I have useful things to contribute"?

First of all, one of the most important lessons for me, and I think for future general directors in the Competition Authority, is that you should not be pressured. You should not be pressured by the media. You should not be pressured by the politicians. You should not be pressured by the business community; they also have their ideas. And you should not be pressured by your own team; they also have their own opinions and they want to press you to a specific decision. One has to be able to take the time and make their own decision. Most of the decisions are pretty easy to make, but from time to time, there is a very difficult decision to make: there is a merger that is touch-and-go; there can be an enforcement case where you are really debating whether it's worth coming into court or not. There are quite a lot of difficult decisions. You need to take the time and make them in your own time after you digest them. There is a lot of pressure on you to make the decision quickly. One of the things I learned is that nothing happens if you take a little more time to think it over.

To get it right and be confident about the path you're taking.

Yes. It doesn't happen too often, but once you have such a case it's important that you will be sure about what you are doing; and, even if you know that it's a close call and there are faults to your case, you are going ahead knowing the faults. That is also very important.

I'm inferring from what you're saying that part of the process of preparation to do this is: to examine yourself and to take stock of who you are, to assess whether you are well-suited to the sometimes rough give-and-take of this process, to ask yourself very clearly: Why am I doing this? If I'm doing this for important, good reasons, that gives me strength to pursue the aims that have motivated me – the dimension of individual personality is important here, and a person might do well to reflect on "Who am I, what am I good at, and why am I really doing this"?

You need to have self-confidence in what you're aiming at. When I came into the Competition Authority, I had a few things that I wanted to achieve and they were important for me. I started doing them one by one. As long as I was confident that that is the true direction, then I went forward. Sometimes I got objections from within the Competition Authority. Sometimes I got a lot of support within the Competition Authority, but then I got criticism from the outside. But as long as you know what you're doing, you go forward with it.

This is a very important trait of good leadership that you're underscoring for us. The importance of coming into the job with a clear idea of what you want to accomplish. Maybe your list will change, but you came in with a careful assessment of what it is you wanted to accomplish. Would you say it is very important to have an idea of what it is you want to do here so that you can hit the ground running?

Yes. But it's not only that. The daily routine of the Competition Authority is very intensive. You deal with dozens of mergers and with a lot of decisions that you need to make. There are enforcement proceedings, taking part in all kinds of steps through the way. You have Parliament that you need to come to. You have a government that you need to explain yourself to. There are a lot of frontiers and there is a lot going on every day.

One of the important things that the head of an authority should do is rise above this routine and think of the farther objectives of the Competition Authority. It's very, very easy to drown in the day-to-day and to work very hard on it, very intensively and not reach the bigger goals that you put for yourself. So part of the job is to put all of this aside and think on a higher level, look at things from above, and try to promote the more far-reaching purposes that you want to achieve.

As you described it, this can be a frightfully demanding job. It's being on a treadmill that is set at the highest level. It starts early in the morning, it doesn't end until you go home, and there is a good chance that you're taking things home with you to read. It spills over into your weekend. It can be so consuming handling the next matter that's coming at you that you barely have time to think and reflect except upon doing the next one and the next one. How did you secure time for yourself during your week, to step back and think, "What are these broad objectives that I've set out?" as you've described them – to restore your emotional and spiritual capital but also your intellectual capital? How did you get time for yourself to renew your sense of purpose and to focus on these larger issues?

In fact, I found this easier than I thought it would be. I think the reason for this is that I am the head of the organization, so I can manage my time. This is 90 percent of the story. If you are able to manage your time, then this is the most crucial part of it. If you need an afternoon with your kids, you just tell your assistant not to schedule any meetings this afternoon. You have some control of your time. That is what I keep telling young practitioners, young attorneys, especially young women when they're starting their career, that the worst part is being young, when you don't have control over your time, and when your boss tells you that he's scheduled a meeting for 6:00 p.m. in the evening, so you need to stay. Once you become the head of the organization, things become much easier.

You have a bit more control over setting that, indeed. Tell me a bit about your management style in the agency. How do you interact with your staff? How often is your door open? How do you communicate with the team inside the Competition Authority?

I would assume that this would be better to ask my team how they see my management style. I believe that my door is always open and everyone can come in at any time and ask any question. In fact, I almost do not work at work; I always talk with people and answer questions. Rarely does it happen that I have a quiet hour to read the paper when I'm in the office. So it's ongoing all the time. The dialogue is continuing. The other end is that I am blunt, I'm not polite, I'm very direct. If I have criticism, I tell it immediately and in the face of the people that I criticize. I don't keep it in my stomach for long. I think people know very well what I think of them. By the same token, I tell them my thoughts and my considerations. When I decide about something, I will usually explain to them what my considerations were coming into this decision, and share my thoughts.

When you are demanding, I take it you explain why; that is, you don't criticize just for the sake of letting them have it; you explain why it's important that things be done a certain way.

Yes. I do try to explain. Now that I am part of the organization and people have a lot of experience with me, they know what I am sensitive to. When I came into the Competition Authority, there were no schedules for any assignments. The assignments were put on the teams and they had no schedule, no deadline. I started putting deadlines into assignments and I would insist that they would comply with the deadline. This brought a lot of tension into the system.

Did people push back?

Many times, yes. This brought a lot of tension into the system. But, after a year, people started understanding how it worked and they started putting the right deadlines. When they said, "I need 3 months," it was because they really needed 3 months. I never argue about that. I just want them to comply with the deadlines they put to themselves. They learned how to do that and they learned to comply with it. It improved a lot.

More generally, many subordinates, employees, will accept the criticism in the way that an athlete will accept criticism from a coach. If you create the sense that: "This is to make us better and we must get better if we are to do our job well. That's the purpose of it. I don't enjoy criticism for its own sake. It is for the purpose of making us a better institution." I take it that's a point you seek to reinforce with your team all the time.

Well, criticism should not be insulting; it should be brought in a respectful way. That's the first rule. Even if you have criticism, there is a respectful way to bring it in. Not all employees get it the same way. I expect everyone to understand that this is part of the work and go on. But I learned from my years in managing this organization that some people get insulted, even if I don't want to insult them, and it's difficult for them to digest criticism. Every employee is different.

Do you change your approach a bit depending on whom you're working with?

If I'm aware of an especially sensitive person, I will try to be more sensitive when criticizing.

I take it that when things go well you praise them too.

Yes. First of all, I have to say the Competition Authority is absolutely excellent. I know that you are somewhat familiar with this organization. They are absolutely excellent. Most of the time they do deserve a lot of praise. They work hard. They're dedicated. They believe in what they're doing. It's really a great honor to be their leader for a few years. I come into the office in the morning with a smile. It's a great pleasure to talk to them. It's a great pleasure to be inspired by them. It's a great pleasure to have an argument with them – and believe me, we have a lot of arguments. It's really inspiring. I think they all know it; and, even if they don't, I keep telling them that. I tell them that much more often than I criticize them. They're really excellent.

How large is your total staff now?

We're about 120. We have about 30 people in our investigation department, which is responsible for the criminal investigations we conduct. The rest are sitting in the main office in Jerusalem, and they are now divided into 3 professional departments: the legal department, the economics department, and the markets department.

How do you keep everyone informed about what you want to do? That is, you have two audiences – inside the Authority and the external audience – but to motivate your team and to move the 120 in the direction you want, how do you go about spelling out to them what your objectives are, what your expectations are, and how you see each one of them fitting into the process?

I have to tell you I didn't know how to do it from the start. I made quite a lot of mistakes in this regard not informing my staff what's going on frequently enough, and I got a lot of rejections on that coming from the employees, that they were not knowledgeable enough about what's going on and what the general purpose is. We made a lot of efforts to improve this. We arrange for periodical meetings of everyone where we try to talk about different cases, a variety of cases, and where I usually talk about the general purposes, what I see for the near future, what I see for the longer future. We dedicate quite a lot of time now to this specific purpose, of making everyone knowledgeable about what's going on in the different circles where they are not present.

You've pointed to a very important consideration for someone who's coming into a leadership position – or maybe someone who has been there for a while – how important it is to repeatedly seek to drive home to your staff "Why we're doing things, what it is we're doing; that this is why we're pursuing this path; this is why we're trying to work so hard; this is the point of it."

There is no waste of energy being dedicated to this mission. I am putting more and more time into it. When I started, I didn't put enough energy on this issue, and today I understand that it is very, very important.

Do you walk around the building just to drop in on people? Do you go to the lunchroom? Or is your door open: you're in your office, you talk a lot to people, they come to see you from inside?

Now and then I do, but not frequently enough. That's one of the things that I should make more time for, dropping into offices of people to hear what's going on.

I suppose that one change that does come about that you've hinted at when you came to be the Director General is you're in charge now; it's not someone else; you're deciding. How do you adjust to that, being on the center of the stage, the spotlight is on you – it's on you inside the building, inside the Authority; and outside? What's it like to suddenly be the focus of attention in this way?

You don't really get adjusted to this until you make your first mistake. When I was nominated for 6 years – I said it when I came in – there must be some decisions that will not go right. You can't always be right in your decisions. So you grasp the responsibility and the fact that you are the deciding person and that you are fully responsible for everything that is going on. Once you make your first mistake and you understand that you made the mistake, that's the minute when you suddenly understand the weight of the position.

How do you deal with media organizations, for example? They gave you a hard time at the beginning. But now that you have a track record, you have a program, how has your relationship with them changed over time and your own understanding of how to deal with the outside world in this respect as the face of the agency?

Things really improved after a few months because I started working. Once you start working and start making decisions, suddenly people become less suspicious of you, of what your purposes are and what your aims are. The media grew to know me, and I think now I am having a much better time with them. But it's not only that. I learned that I need to invest a lot of time talking to the media.

It's almost an everyday job to answer journalists' different questions that they have on different issues. You need patience to talk to them. You need to explain yourself. You need to meet with them from time to time to talk about your vision and what your aims are because, just like employees, when they understand what your vision is and what you're aiming at, they are more supportive. I learned to invest quite a lot of time in talking to them on a daily basis, and I am meeting with them, explaining to them, introducing them to the Competition Authority, letting them speak with the staff. I think today they are much more supportive.

Do you think as you are pursuing individual matters, as you start doing things, the conversation will probably turn more to your cases – not just to you, but to your cases? Do you think, as you're pursuing cases, about how we explain this to the average human being in our country who's going to be affected by what we do? A common critique of competition law has been this process of dealing with the larger audience outside our own walls where people aren't necessarily interested in complex mergers involving producers of intermediate industrial products. They're not concerned that much about two-sided markets, three-sided markets. That is not what they lose sleep over, but they are interested in very basic matters of their daily economic life. How do you communicate to that audience what you are doing? That it is not an abstract technocracy set apart, but a vital and important part of their own existence?

First of all, you need to get free from the obsession of lawyers to be precise on everyday things. The people who are reading and hearing the media or reading the papers are not that interested in all the tiny details that for you is the whole world. You need to simplify the cases that you have very much. You need to find what are the big relevant facts and simplify what you are doing [...] My legal team would certainly object. A general argument that I have with my legal team is on press releases, how it should be presented, because for the legal team it's extremely important that it will be completely precise. But for the audience that doesn't make any difference. So this is a tension within us. We really need to make the message simple and clear [...] We need to adjust to that if we want the message to get through. I really believe that part of our job is to put the message through.

I imagine that you become better and better over time in thinking about how to communicate that when you're talking to these audiences.

I brought a new head of communication into the Competition Authority. When she came in, she was horrified by the way we write our press releases. But now, two years later, I believe we educated her more than she educated us. Sometimes, I look at her press releases and tell her, "What are you doing? You got all spoiled by us. You need to simplify it much more." I am getting better as time goes by.

What is the nature of your engagement with the political landscape of the country, the elected officials, appointees to senior ministerial positions? You operate, of course, not in isolation; you operate in an environment in which the political science of the country is important. How do you engage with those external groups?

This is a complex question. The Competition Authority is very, very independent. We are very little influenced by the political arena. We have now elections in Israel. The Competition Authority will probably not be influenced by these elections. We do have a minister who is responsible for the Competition Authority, but we, as an enforcement agency, and as a merger review agency, enjoy a lot of independence. So there is very little touch between us and the political arena. We do need their support if we want to legislate. If we want to come and to convince Parliament, we do need our political minister.

And you have gotten upgrades legislatively throughout the history of the institution.

On the last day of Parliament, just before it was resolved on January 1st, we were able to complete the latest reform that we needed in the antitrust law, which made it the competition law, and since then we are named the Competition Authority. We were very pleased with this reform going through and that we were able to complete it in time. So we did get support. We are really enjoying a great independence. When it comes to advocacy, the picture becomes more complex. When you work on advocacy, work vis-à-vis the government, you need to be open to them and to be part of the governmental activity. Since we are advocating not through our formal authority but through our professional reputation, we need to adjust ourselves. We work very differently with the political arena when we are advocating and not when we are imposing enforcement measures.

Let me turn to a couple of closing questions. What is the hardest part of the job that an appointee ought to think about when coming in?

What I found hardest was the deregulation processes. I came in with a lot of thoughts on how we should deregulate a lot of procedures in the Competition

Authority, and I was absolutely sure that I am a genius and that everyone will engage in my thoughts and compliment me on my great ideas and will embrace them immediately. It turned out that it got a lot of rejection. It took me a while to understand what was going on because the ideas were really wonderful, of course [...] Part of what was going on is that when you come to public servants who are working with a lot of dedication and you try to –

They're not doing it for the money.

Not at all. They are very industrious and really dedicated, and when you explain to them that they should start tomorrow thinking completely differently, it reflects on how they feel about what they did until today. The feeling that they might not have done the best practices until now gets a lot of rejection. So I got a lot of opposition. I had to work a lot on convincing people to get engaged in the initiatives. Sometimes, I just imposed the changes notwithstanding the criticism that I received. But this was much more difficult than what I had anticipated.

One thing that we've seen from some of our interviews, and it's a theme that appears in some of the literature about public administration, is that there is an art to what is called "change management," especially when you are trying to do something significantly different, when you're trying to carry out a basic change in culture, process, substantive orientation – that can be a wrenching experience. In a number of interviews, our subjects have underscored the same theme, that is, "I had things I wanted to change, some of them more significant, but I didn't have a full appreciation of how best to go about it and how to carry that out." What would you have done differently if you were starting over on that aspect of your job? Would you have spent more time initially listening to people about why they do things the way they do them? Would you have spent more time explaining what you were trying to do? Or was the only realistic way perhaps to say, "We've got to make this change if we're really going to be an effective agency, and let's get on with it?"

I think you need to give the changes time. I think that would be the way forward. You need to allow really an open hearing – not a formal hearing, but a real hearing – of people who are opposed to your suggestion. They need to understand that they are being heard, and you need to be open to change your initial plan accordingly, because sometimes they have good suggestions on how to improve things. It's not like I came in with all the wisdom in the world. So you need the time to conduct a dialogue and to conduct a real hearing on what you want to do. You need to be open to changes. But after this time has passed, you need to decide, and once you have decided on the change, you need to be persistent in it, and you should explain why you are doing it over and over and over again, as much as needed. But you need to be persistent in what you are doing.

As the person who does decide, you have your own thoughts, you do your own work, you do your own study, you read, you think, you reflect. How do you go about developing a sounding board, individuals or a group, inside the authority to give you feedback – and, indeed, in some instances, to say, "Close the door; we don't think this will work; this is why". How do you test your own ideas inside before you roll them out?

I never, never decide by myself. Even when I digest and come up with a thought, I will always speak them loudly to my team, to the management of the Competition Authority. And of course there are people who can be partners in such a dialogue more than others. It's a matter of style of people. But what I learned is that if there's a consensus within the management, what I would try to do is find the person who is not agreeing with me and bring him into the discussion. Once everyone agrees with me that this is the right way to go, that is when I search for a person who thinks a little differently and bring him into the discussion to hear what he has to say.

How do you create an environment in which people are going to be willing to do that? In some organizations, there is a sense that we'll give a boss good news, we withhold criticism or we turn down the volume to a point where it almost doesn't sound like criticism; it's a faint expression of concern. How do you go about communicating to people, "I really have to know what you think, because once we step outside with a case or with a program, nobody is going to give us any mercy, so I have to know on the inside whether we're going the right way"? How do you create that?

There are a few things. First of all, I'm not sure that I am that successful in this respect. You never know. You conduct meetings and you hear different thoughts, but you're never sure that they put the criticism roughly enough in front of your face. So it's always an open question. I really try to encourage people to say their real thoughts in meetings. I call on them if they're quiet and try to hear what they have to say. In very big cases where we are going ahead, especially with enforcement cases, we would try to build a mock team with the specific mission of finding where we are wrong. Find the problems, find the loopholes, find where we will fail. That is their assignment, so they're looking just to find where we're wrong. This usually brings a very good discussion. They get into their assignment, they are doing it very well, and they make our life very hard.

In a similar sense, how do you solicit views from outside the agency about how you're doing, about whether you've got it right?

I don't need to solicit that.

It comes your way anyway.

Exactly. The business community is not shy at all. They know how to express their opinions. They come in. We usually do not refuse to meet anyone, unless there are very exceptional circumstances. Anyone who wants a meeting receives a meeting. We want to hear everyone on every issue, and indeed we dedicate a lot of time to it. In cases where we are conducting an enforcement or in cases where we come up with a new regulation or a new guideline, we will always conduct a formal hearing. When I entered the office, I was concerned that when we opened up a guideline or a new regulation to a hearing, we would not get enough responses from the public, from the business community. So we brought in incentives to make them respond, and there was a lot of improvement. In conferences that we conduct, we do not allow people who did not file responses to our hearings to be active participants in the panels. We usually invite people who did participate in a hearing to a roundtable or an internal discussion with us. We try to give incentives to the business community to come in and to bring their thoughts.

Let me ask you a closing question. You're speaking with the person who someday is going to succeed you and they're approaching the beginning of their term. What advice do you give them about getting off to a good start?

As I said before, you should not be pressured. A head of the Competition Authority should be on the one hand not anti-business. It's wrong to come into this position with an anti-business attitude. I think the Competition Authority cannot allow itself to have an anti-business attitude. By the same token, I think it should not try to please the business community. It should be able to confront it. It should be able to be persistent and to go through with its decisions. I think this tension is the essence of being a good competition authority.

Frédéric Jenny*

OECD Competition Committee, Chairman (1994-2023)

You have had a broad range of experience as a competition enforcement official, as a judge, as a head of large international networks that are responsible for the formulation of ideas about what competition agencies should do, and you have had extensive experience as an advisor to competition authorities. As a way of beginning the conversation, I would like to ask you to give us a bit of a tour through your career in competition law, the experiences that have shaped your perspective about what makes a good agency, how agencies work – what, in other words, has brought you down the path of competition law to where you stand today?

That is a long story, but also it may be a separate issue than what makes good leaders because I may have been drawn to the field even though I did not myself qualify to be a good leader. But let's go back to what was most important that drew me to competition. It's a combination of two things. One of them is sheer luck or events that took place that I had no control over or no anticipation of.

One of them was the fact that when I went to the United States to study, I was sponsored by my university, a French university, that wanted me to come back and teach at the university. I wanted to study economics. They wanted me to study business because I'm a professor at a business school, and they finally relented on the agreement that I would study something that I could teach in a business school. This is why I looked at microeconomics and then applied microeconomics because I thought that this was something that could conceivably be used in a business school. This is one of the elements.

---

* Interview conducted on 30 July 2019.

The second element was the University of Chicago, very clearly for 3 reasons. One of them was that the teaching is excellent. The second one was that it gave me a sense of the fact that law and economics are very, very closely related. You cannot have a good economic system if you don't have a system of law that will support the economy, and certainly competition law is a good example of this. This was quite developed in the teaching in Chicago at the time. I was there for a year and after that switched to Harvard for various reasons, but not because I was dissatisfied with the University of Chicago. I was quite happy.

You loved the weather so much, the winters.

I didn't like the weather, but I particularly liked Milton Friedman, to be honest. I thought that he was – and this is the second point – the most effective teacher, with the ability to transform an analytical thought into something which is policy-oriented and can be used and be concrete. There again, I think this is something which is quite important for competition law, to move away from abstraction and to try to apply and to understand. As a teacher he would challenge and would make the most outrageous statements and challenge students. In fact – this has nothing to do with microeconomics; it was monetary policy – a lot of students had already taken the course and already passed the exam, and they were coming back to try to find a fault in his logic, so it was like a sport. But it was very much based on exchange and questions and answers but trying to give you a sense of how theory can be applied, used in real life.

Anchoring it in a vivid way that is readily accessible.

That is right. So, law and economics, policy and theory, those were two really important intellectual inputs for me at the University of Chicago, which I think have kept all through. After that I became an economics professor, but I was of the mind that a professor has to practice, and therefore I have always had some kind of activity outside of teaching because I thought this would enrich the teaching on the one hand and also deepen my understanding of what I was teaching in fact.

Then I came back to France at a time when there was the beginning of a change in mentality, moving a little bit away from price controls, regulation of the economy, toward a slightly more open system. It turned out that we had a prime minister who was himself an economist. We knew each other. He asked me to be the staff member in charge, the aide to the minister of finance, to push the first competition law in France, which was a competition law that created not only the institution but also the procedure for controlling mergers. So I did this, which was very interesting because I got into the political world, which I knew nothing about.

After that, I went back to the United States, taught, and then went back to France. I started in the institution which had been created through this law, which was the Autorité de la concurrence, first as a case officer – my best years, which were the most interesting I think. I was dealing with cases and trying to find the logic. Each case I thought was like a little film, a different reality, and I was very interested in getting into those different realities. Then I became the general counsel of the Authority and then the vice president of the Authority.

At the same time, I developed fairly early on an international interest through the Organisation for Economic Cooperation and Development (OECD) and after that through the World Trade Organization (WTO).

What brought you into the OECD, which has been in a way one of your main professional homes?

The fact that I thought that the French system had to closely keep benchmarks; and the fact that the OECD was providing this, that this was the place where already at the time it was a small set of people, but the best thinking on competition was going on with people who had experience that we could benefit from, so I was very early on interested in this. Second, the fact that I had been studying in the United States and in France, so I was international in that way. I think it is really the benchmarking which was the important aspect for me of this. Then, there was a third phase where I finally personally was able to achieve the synthesis between law and economics because I became a judge on the French Supreme Court. Joining the Court as a judge, not as an economist for the Court but as a judge, and interacting with judges was one of the most interesting and challenging experiences of my life.

This makes you distinctive in our field, Fred. I can't think of others who have this broad range of experience crossing the disciplinary lines and synthesizing them in a professional capacity in the same way you do.

Yes. I don't know if I'm distinctive, but I'm very sorry that when my time was up on the Court I couldn't find an economist to replace me because they thought it would be too challenging for them. It was the one experience, but the positive aspect of this experience was that toward the end of the 8 years the Chief Justice said, "You know, we didn't know how it was going to turn out, but we like having somebody who has an economic background. We think it enriches the discussion."

Would the appointed officials have been willing to take another economist, or was it hard to find another economist who would rise to the challenge?

The Chief Justice said, "We would like you to have a successor. We know that by law you cannot continue. Would you help us identify a suitable successor?" I knew it would have to be a senior economist with a microeconomic background because for contract law, for regulation, that is what you need. I pretty much knew all of them in France. I went to see every one of them, and I said, "I'm on the Court." They said, "Yeah, that's fantastic. You do a great job." I said, "Well, good, because I'm leaving the Court, and the Court is looking for another economist." And everybody said, "Not me.", because the real reason is that all those senior economists didn't want to go back to school. They had a very comfortable life, usually a good practice as a consultant, and they thought it was too challenging to do it. So that is it. From that point of view, at least in France, I was unique.

But what was interesting was the fact that the judges, besides the technicalities, really liked the idea that on many different cases, not necessarily competition cases, I was able to say, "Okay, aside from the legal technicalities, this is what it means. This is how it's going to change the incentive. This is how some transactions are going to be in the future if you go in that direction, if you go in this direction." At least, civil law judges are not used to thinking in terms of the external impact of the judgment. And they thought that it was great that somebody was able to tell them that over and beyond the particular case there was a different meaning to what they were doing. I think that is why we got along well.

So you had many teaching opportunities in a way inside the Court.

Yes. As a matter of fact, even more than what you said. I've always done economic training for judges, but it was very difficult for a long period of time because, for all kinds of reasons, judges don't like to be trained or everybody wants to train them. That creates a problem. But the day I became a judge on the Supreme Court, everybody came to my courses, which were exactly the same as the ones

I had given previously; but, because I was not threatening anymore, I was not a threat, I was one of them, so it was all right. That question of trust was quite important. Afterward I went back to – not really back because I never stopped chairing the Competition Committee of the OECD – teaching.

In what year did you start the position as chair of the committee at OECD? It has been 25 years now, right?

Yes, a long time ago. It's not 25 years – it's 25 times one year. There is the yearly election. Thanks to it I never stopped doing this for the same reason. It brings oxygen, it brings new ideas, it brings new issues, and I was able to use this both in my teaching and also in what I was doing on the Court as long as I was on the Court. So I kept on doing this and doing some consulting, particularly in Eastern European countries, which were trying to set up institutions. So, the teaching, the OECD, and the technical assistance I would say is pretty much what I do.

It's an astonishing tour through a life's work. All of these experiences have given you a remarkable perspective on how agencies operate, how they're structured, what they do, concepts as well as institutional design. I would like you to reflect on what you have seen from these different perspectives as someone who has worked inside of an authority, as a judge, as a teacher, as an advisor, and as the head of the network that has had such an extraordinary impact on the way in which nations think, this remarkable comparative perspective. I would like you to think for a moment about the appointment of new agency leadership. If you look at all these experiences and you're thinking about what makes for a good appointee, what kind of background makes for a good agency head?

My first thought is that there is no unique solution. But first of all, you have to look at whether we're talking about an established agency that wants to move forward or you are, as I was at the beginning of the Conseil, leading an institution which is in a fairly hostile environment, the purpose of which is not well-understood by most people and most politicians, and which may have resource problems as well. The qualities that you need for the head of such an institution are probably different. Depending on whether you're a startup or a well-established institution. Depending on whether there is a culture of – well, there is never a culture of competition, but there is a real understanding and kind of a consensus on the value of competition or if there is none, also makes a difference. Depending on whether you're talking about a small group of people, if it's under-resourced or if it's normally resourced. So there are all kinds of dimensions that I think are quite important and mean that the leader that you want is not necessarily good.

When I worked as a staff member for the minister preparing the competition bill in France, I went in there very naïvely assuming that you want to have a minister who understands the topic that she is going to talk about, which was not the case of the minister I was working with. She was very charming, she had all kinds of qualities, but not one of understanding what the issues were that we're talking about. I came slowly but surely to the view that what you need a minister to do is to be good at making political deals, and he has staff people who are supposed to provide the technical backup. Certainly in France, whenever you put a teacher as the head of Ministry of Education or a judge as head of the Ministry of Justice, it's a catastrophe because they have very strong views about what they want to do, and they completely forget that they're in a position where you're requested to in fact cut political deals, which is different.

Now, there are cases, if we come back to competition agencies, where particularly at the beginning when you set up an agency and the choice is between someone who is not really all that knowledgeable about competition but who is very forceful, very well-connected to the political elite and has a lot of influence and is able to establish the institution as a strong institution, well-resourced, that may be more desirable than sometimes somebody who is more technically apt in terms of competition but doesn't have the kind of influence that is necessary to build up the institution to something which is going to survive over time. That is why I'm saying one has to look at the environment to decide what kind of good leader you need to have.

Second, why are people interested in competition? For those people who are interested in competition, they're interested in competition because they have an idea – which may come from economic analysis – that a more competitive world is a world which is more open, where there are more opportunities, and which leads to better allocation of resources and increased quality. All these are very generous intellectual ideas. So I think you need to have somebody in an institution who is inspirational, somebody who can convey the fact that we are not just technicians applying a technique to particular problems. We are here because there is a fundamental purpose behind this which should inform the way we interpret the law and the way we try to develop it. At least in France, there are very few people who have – or at least there were at the time – this background, one, because law and economics were quite separate, and two, because competition was not very developed in university curricula. So, the idea of being able to transmit the fact that we are part of a project which has a technical application that we're going to promote but for a purpose which is a generous purpose and a purpose which is useful to society, I think it's very important to be able to convey that because it makes people proud of what they're doing and willing to try to give the best of their abilities for the purpose because they see the meaning of it.

The third thing, again this was because my first experience was with a young institution. I was following each and every case. I knew the case nearly as well as the staff who were doing the work, and I could discuss it with them and, I don't know, offer them directions that they could/should explore, and they enjoyed this interaction because they were a bit intimidated themselves because they didn't have much experience. So, at the beginning it's very useful to be able to be involved in the case and to have a dialogue and to show the staff that they are not alone at sea and ready to drown. So, inspiration, ability to involve yourself in the substantive matter, possibly the fact that you have good connections when you really try to set up the institution.

Fourth – but this is more because I was on the board of the Office of Fair Trading (OFT) for 8 years, an ability to make people work together, in particular lawyers and economists, to integrate the two. I think the ability to make the lawyers understand what the issues are in competition and how we look at things and vice versa is crucial to the success of an institution because this is going to be the security, meaning that the most important cases are not necessarily to be disasters when they are reviewed by courts, which is very important to establish the institution and to protect it against criticism, which is necessary again to come from the business community or others or people who are aggravated by its decisions.

The final thing is a great communicator. That is in all of the countries where competition law is relatively new – and this is most of the countries in the world – you need to have somebody who is able to explain to the lay people, to the press, to academia, and to politicians what this is all about. If somebody is technically very good but not a good communicator, it's not going to work, at least not in the long run. So, in terms of leaders that is what I would say.

Then there is the question for more advanced institutions to know where you want to go, to know which areas of the law you want to explore, which advances you are trying to make, and therefore which cases you should take and where you should set your priorities. I think that this is the second step. It's for an institution which is already well-established but needs to be managed. For this you need somebody who understands the substance, who knows the jurisprudence very well, somebody who is quite knowledgeable and is able to clearly discuss about priorities and the strategy that should be followed by the institution.

I know that my answer is a bit complicated, but as I said I don't think there is a unique answer to the question of what is a good leader, what is the most appropriate leader for an institution at one point in time.

I think the emphasis that you place on identifying the place of the institution in the life cycle of its history makes a lot of sense that you want perhaps a different set of skills and that the ideal appointee in the first 5 years might not be the ideal appointee for the second 20 years.

Absolutely. For example, I have done some work both for the European Commission and the ADRB in Eastern Europe in countries that were formerly in the Soviet bloc, and I have seen cases. For example, if I compare Georgia and Ukraine, Georgia is much less advanced than Ukraine on the competition dimension, and Georgia has a former minister of finance I think as the head of the institution. He's not particularly technically a competition person. He's more of a general maybe microeconomic person, but he's very well-connected, and if anybody can help the institution establish itself, it is someone who has a good relationship with the central government. In Ukraine, where we are now – there has been a longer tradition – there is now somebody who is a lawyer by origin and has worked in the private sector and understands business, and he is much more able to herd the institution in the direction of becoming a really efficient institution. I'm not passing judgment on the two, but I'm explaining why the difference in perspective of who is the leader should be related to the local circumstances of the institution.

Would you say if we're thinking about characteristics that might be helpful in either context, newer authority, older authority, one thing you point to is some degree of understanding of the political context, of how the political process functions, the place of the agency in a larger political environment, what might be called broader political awareness, that would be a valuable attribute I gather from what you're saying?

I think very much at the beginning, when you start the system. I think it becomes less important as the situation is stabilized and the institution is more accepted. But I think it's always interesting for an institution, for example, to understand what politicians or what people feel would be the benefit of competition and to be able to understand when it is that some interesting cases are not going to resonate at all with the people either because they're going to seem to be unfair or because they are going to seem to be irrelevant. So, some awareness of the environment is very useful at all stages. But I don't want to say that the heads of agencies should follow political trends. That is not what I meant; I meant more an intelligence of the environment.

I would think part of that environment is the intersection of both economic developments and basic knowledge of the economy, economic forces as they intermingle with political forces that sometimes respond to those. It's the awareness that the environment we're speaking of has an economic and a political dimension.

Right, that is why I would say – and this is working against my own profession – a pure academic is not necessarily the best person. Maybe he knows more about competition than anybody else, but in terms of a leader of an institution it might not necessarily be the best person.

Not that we have to come up with a list of names today, but I share your intuition that the supreme academic expert who spent decades studying the field, preparing papers, doing presentations, in a number of instances falls on her face when she is in the leadership role.

If I can recall one personal experience, one of the very difficult tasks of an executive of a competition authority is how to terminate an investigation. You have a case, and the staff comes to you and says, "Well, we think this is the theory of harm that is under this case. We don't quite have all the evidence. Could we have another 3 months to investigate this and that?" After 3 months, they come back to you, and it's the same story: "Well, we found things, but it's not all." At some point you have to say, "This is it." First of all, it's not necessarily a very good use of our resources to keep on digging in this one case when we could take other cases, and second, maybe you have looked enough that what you could find would only be marginally interesting or marginally change the outcome of the case. Academics would tend to keep on looking by coming up with new ideas or new angles, and they would have a hard time giving up.

An executive of an authority must manage their resources and must be able to make those calls, and to make them acceptable to the staff, which is the most difficult part. That requires a little bit of psychology.

To explain to them why we are going to put this on the side; that you did your best job.

That is right, and that it's not a failure. It's just a fact that maybe the case was not the best case that we should have chosen in the first place, or maybe the evidence is not entirely there. You did your best job. But it is difficult to explain to people.

Is it helpful for potential candidates to have had some role in which they had management experience, where they had to deal with perhaps personnel management, personnel, the human relations department ingredients of the job, a little bit about what a budget is and how you think about resources, and just the experience of being the focal point of attention?

At one level, it's always better to have more experience when you get the job. Is it absolutely necessary? I think it would be desirable, particularly I would say the human management part of it because you need to have a team and work with a team, and the team is the resource of the institution, the brains of the team. You want to manage this asset really well, and this requires psychology, this requires empathy, this requires also procedures, so experience there is useful.

On the budgetary side I think it can be useful if you have already had to manage the budget of a public institution. Whether it would be useful to have business experience of managing a budget, maybe a little bit, but I don't think that this is the most important part. Communication is very important. Because advocacy is absolutely crucial, and this requires the ability to translate what is a very technical field into things that people can be interested in. So it means that others, the chief executive or whoever he hires for his communication department, has to be somebody who really understands how to translate what is basically a scientific truth into something which is of importance to people.

I'm thinking in part – if we were the screening committee that we're talking to candidates and we're looking through résumés and talking with the candidate about background, we would be looking for this dimension of communications capability, too, not someone who runs away from a reporter or a camera.

An enormous amount is in the packaging of why we did this, why are we moving this way. Why is competition good? It is painful in the short term, but it is good. I would say that based on my experience one of the most important things is once you are in the job is to try to make sure that people don't fall asleep, don't repeat the same case over and over again, and are willing to move to a different theory of harm, don't always try to frame the thing in something that they know, one; and two, that people don't become dogmatic by applying automatic reasonings without really thinking about the reality of each case. If staff has had a very successful case, there is a natural tendency on its part to go back to this case whatever the evidence is or whatever. So it's a constant struggle to say, "Okay, forget about this past case. Maybe this one has specificities that are important that we should look at and require a definite approach." I have found that this is in fact quite important work to do and quite significant because otherwise you end up having very dogmatic, literally cutting-and-pasting decisions which lose their relevance really. You're just applying a rule automatically, and it doesn't mean anything to you. It doesn't mean anything to anyone, and it becomes mindless.

In a number of ways you're identifying aspects of the topic of how you manage effectively once you have the job, too. This seems to be a very important consideration as well. How does leadership avoid the possibility that the agency would become stale or repetitive or dogmatic in these ways? How do you ensure that your perspective is refreshed, that you challenge assumptions, that you avoid a tendency simply to walk through the same paths that you have taken before?

I think that this is an important function of institutions like the International Competition Network (ICN), like the OECD, UNCTAD. What happens in those institutions is you compare it first of all to other competition authorities who may have either a different point of view or maybe interests in different issues or who may be toying with different theories of harm. It forces you to think about if it works well, why it is that you have done things the way you have done them, and maybe how you could improve in your way of looking at those cases.

To be honest, having been the chair of the Competition Committee for a while, one of the things that I fear most in the Committee is that delegates will come and just explain what they have done. Then the question comes up, "Okay, fine. This is how you looked at this case. What would have been the alternative, and why didn't you choose the alternative?" Then the answer is, "This is what we did."

They give you a book report instead of a book review.

That is right. I think the reasons why competition authorities meet together so often and talk about cases as often is partly to stimulate each other and to force each other to acquire new ideas: "This jurisprudence or this case in this other country, that is interesting. Maybe we should look at this." It's an exchange of experience. Being open to the rest of the competition community is usually important to avoid the risk that you were mentioning.

One theme of your work at OECD and in other settings has been a hazard of talking to other competition agencies, that that itself produces an element of insularity and potential detachment from larger developments. How does top leadership go about ensuring that – considering your early point about the larger environment in which you operate – you are aware of changes taking place that challenge the assumptions that underpin your system and bear directly upon your effectiveness as an institution?

This is partly why we have several international institutions which at first sight might look like being duplicated but are not. The ICN is very much focused on competition authorities talking to each other and exchanging good practices, exchanging experience on what they do. The OECD, because it is an intergovernmental body that looks at all the spectrum of economic policy. There is pressure in the OECD to take up horizontal topics – competition and environmental regulation; what is the relationship? The natural reaction of a competition authority may be to say, "Well, at home I don't deal with this." Yes, but at OECD, because we cover all this field, we have to look at what the possible interactions are, and so we are going to have whoever is in charge of the environmental dimension come and talk to us. We did this for corruption; we did this for trade; we did this for consumers. I think that this is more particularly the function of OECD to try to put competition policy, of which competition law enforcement is a part, into a broader perspective of growth, development, and interaction with other economic policy dimensions. I think it's good that the networks are differentiated like this because they bring different things and complementary things to the institutions.

The point you mentioned in your personal biographical tour was how important your comparative perspective was and how that became part of your own life from an early stage. These mechanisms make it possible to engage the work of other institutions in thinking about what you do yourself. Could I point to a tension that I think an agency head faces, which is you're appointed to lead your agency, and if you wanted to, you could probably be outside your own country every day of the week. There are lots of networks. There are bilaterals; there are regional events; conferences; seminars. How does an agency head go about deciding how much time I spend at my desk, which in some sense is where I am evaluated and graded – it is where my staff pays attention to whether I'm there and what I'm doing – but also give myself a chance to refresh my knowledge and my perspective by engaging in other authorities?

One dimension is the following. It doesn't have to be the leader of the institution or the head of the institution who is always present in all those meetings. I think those meetings are important, but first of all in many institutions you have a set of commissioners. Those commissioners are part of the institution, and you also have a team of senior staff members. So I think being a team member there and trying to manage your team in such a way that the weight of travel and time can be divided among them, and making sure that whatever wisdom is gotten from it is brought back to the institution, for example, by having systematic reporting, either in writing or orally is one way.

Then, after that you also, of course, have to ask your question, "Do I want to go to this cartel workshop? Is it really important for us given the kind of issues that we face, or should we rather keep our resources to go to an abuse of dominance workshop because this is more relevant?" So you may prioritize. I'm a bit resistant to the idea that it's only the head of the institution who should be present always in all those meetings because I think that – as a matter of fact, at OECD I really like we ask for many contributions, and many delegations bring the staff who have written the contribution to the debate, and I think that this is a very effective way not only to reward to people, to say, "You've done a good job, you have a paper, so now you're going to explain it," but also to diffuse within the institution the common wisdom of those meetings.

Another point that you mentioned earlier involves your perspective when you come to the agency about what you want to do. How important is it as a new appointee to have the agency have a plan, to at least have thought through why do I want this job, not simply the personal recognition, the personal advancement? How important is it for that appointee to come to the job with at least a basic initial hypothesis about what they want to do and how they want to go about it?

I think personally it's tremendously important, which is different from saying that this is the way things develop in many countries. We know many countries where being the head of an institution like a competition institution is a reward for services rendered in other fields, and whether he has a plan, whether he has an idea or not is not the issue. The issue is whether you exceed.

It is also true that some people who were rewarded in this way became interested in competition. If competition has a great talent, it is infectious. Once you put your foot on the issue of competition, you can't let go. I do remember that there was a time when the Japan Fair Trade Commission (JFTC), for example, would usually have a diplomat who was especially assigned to international relations because that is the way things were done in Japan, and a lot of those diplomats had absolutely no idea what competition was all about. Several of them became so interested in the issue that when they went back to the public service and served as ambassadors they thought they were terribly bored compared to the intellectual stimulation they had seen in the competition discussions. So, even if you appoint somebody who doesn't have a plan, sometimes they reveal themselves to have a plan.

But it's quite important for the staff to know that whoever is going to become the next leader is not somebody who has just been chosen because the powers that be have decided that he should be rewarded but somebody who is able to come and say, "Look, we are going to try to do something together, and this is what I want to try to do" – it could be to beef up the institution; it could be to deepen the interpretation of the law; it could be to change the law, but to have a plan to which everybody can adhere to. As the field becomes more professional, as competition authorities become more experienced, and as their standing increases, I think there are fewer and fewer cases where people just have no interest in competition end up being the heads of competition institutions. Slowly but surely one realizes that it's important to have an institution that has a direction and the quality – I'm not talking about the quality of the people but the technical quality of interest in competition tends to increase among the leaders of competition authorities, and I think that this is a healthy development.

Although I think one thing that we see in a number of different environments – academic institutions; international networks – is more attention to the question of how you actually formulate a strategy, how you choose priorities, how you select projects. I think what public administration specialists and political scientists would regard as obvious ingredients of good policy making are being integrated more into discussions about what competition agencies should do, too.

But there is also an issue of political legitimacy. When you have an institution which is led by somebody who has no particular interest or relationship to competition, the message that is sent is that the decisions are going to be made by people who have not been chosen to be board members but are the staff really because the board members are really not adequate to control them. This does a lot of damage to the standing of the institution, and it creates a resistance to the development of competition law and the spirit of competition, so I think that it is also in the interest of the people who appoint heads of competition to try to match the particular skills of the candidates to the job of being head of a competition agency and not the head of any agency.

I can mention one other consideration in this excellent set of ideas you have been giving us, which is building the team. What kind of team do you want to have advising you most directly, possibly your own cabinet if that is how your agency is structured, but heads of unit? What should you be thinking about aside from, say, technical capability, in selecting people who are going to advise you directly, who are going to be responsible for senior leadership positions in the agency, building that team?

To me building the team meant that whenever we had discussions I always wanted the case officers to be involved. Of course, people were overseeing their work technically, but I never wanted to cut out the staff people from the important decisions because, after all, they are the ones who are through their mental activity and their energy going to implement things. So I think it was very useful to have a very wide dialogue. As a matter of fact, we instituted something at the Competition Authority in France. I don't know whether it's still going on because, of course, the institution has grown, and there are sometimes impossibilities which are material impossibilities. But one morning a week we had a meeting of everybody from the board members to the most recent staff talking about the issues that we faced, whether it was cases or whether it was advocacy or whether it was policy issues that we wanted to explore, and we had this general discussion.

How large were you when you did that?

We were up to 40. If you have several 100 people, you can't do it. But there may be other ways to do it.

I think it is an interesting advantage for a smaller agency that you can do this.

That is right. In fact, the staff members were gratified to be part of this discussion. And they were able to bring from their experience things that made sense to the leadership. So I thought very much that this was a good way to start. When the agency becomes very big, clearly it's not feasible anymore, but there may be a way to have sector-by-sector or type of issue-by-type of issue meetings. Of paramount importance to me is to have the whole range of people participating in the discussion.

You underscore such an important point, which is internally to create awareness of what your aims are, what you're doing, what you're thinking, to build morale by providing that contact but also to ensure that people know.

I also think that it makes a big difference when it's relatively clear that lots of people in the agency have had at least a say in the definition of where those objectives, those priorities, are. It doesn't mean that they will be followed, but at least there has been a general airing of the issues. Obviously, the board of the OFT was a little bit of an institution like that, where a lot of the staff members would come and explain their ideas, and the board would listen to them and have a dialogue.

In fact, at first I was wondering whether the staff members were really willing to come to the board or whether it was a pain in the neck for them because the board members would raise questions, but all the signals I got were that, no, no, they loved it because they loved to know what was in the mind or could be in the mind of, and they liked to be able to maybe not influence but at least give their opinion. I think that this dialogue part is crucially important within the institution, involving everybody in the discussion, maybe not in the decision making but at least in the discussion of the issues.

I want to close with the last question, and you can either focus on something you've mentioned already or bring something else into focus. Let's say I'm about to start the job; I've been appointed; my first week is coming up. What would you tell me about how to get started, to get off to a good start in my job?

Take a case and read it from top to bottom, from the beginning to the end. To then have a discussion with the people who dealt with it. What difficulties did they have? Why was the case chosen? What does it mean? What happened then at the court level? Understanding the fundamental issues behind enforcement. That is one thing. But I would start with this because I think that cases are usually important. Then, study probably the history of the institution and how good it has been at doing some things, for example, advocacy, or maybe how it has failed, and then try to possibly have a dialogue with the people who were there before on what they think they did well, what they think didn't work as well and why. A third thing, go around, come to OECD, go to the ICN, to try to see what other institutions are talking about, what are the difficulties that they face. If you have those 3 things, at least from the technical point of view, you start having a view of what the issues are and where you want to put your priorities. Maybe it is in having a better relationship with the court or maybe it's prioritizing more important cases from a social point of view or maybe it's forcing the staff to be more efficient.

I think that simultaneously I would advise you to go and talk to as many people as possible outside the competition authority, in the business community, in government, or for example with the Ministry of Economic Affairs or Industry; just to get their views. What do they think of this institution? What do they think of competition? Do they have prevention? Are they open? That gives you a second set of references. I think those two, inside reference and outside reference, are crucially important to understand the environment.

Francis Kariuki[*]

Competition Authority of Kenya, Director-General (2013-2023)

You are the Director-General of the Competition Authority of Kenya (CAK). The Kenyan experience is so important to us because it is not only one of the most important competition authorities in Africa; you can make a strong case that it is the anchor tenant for competition policy on the eastern coast of Africa. But you can go farther than that, to point to the large number of jurisdictions that study the Kenyan experience as an exemplar of how to build a new system and to build it effectively. You have been in the midst of that process of development. It's a wonderful example for getting started with a new regime, and your own contributions to that effort have been significant day-in and day-out. What was your professional path into competition law and the Competition Authority of Kenya?

My first degree was in economics and business studies. Immediately after I completed my first degree I was employed in the National Treasury in the then Monopolies and Price Department. Competition used to be regulated under the National Treasury. I was not based at the headquarters. I was pushed to a far satellite office outside Nairobi, which is about 200 kilometers from Nairobi. It's a cosmopolitan community. They are Kalenjins and Kikuyus, but at least in Kenya most people speak both English and Swahili. When I went there, it was tough. It was my first job. I was 22 years old and a case handler, so when I went to the rural satellite station, I didn't like the career because it's a remote town. I had not been inducted; I had just been told "go and work." So I met people who used to be in the price control regime. They didn't appreciate this new policy shape, the paradigm of competition regulation. By good luck the then-head of the Department, the Commissioner, visited the office. The lady

* Interview conducted on 21 May 2019.

gave me some opportunity to discuss my career growth and expectations with her. After 6 months I was brought back to the headquarters in Nairobi. I was given an opportunity, which I took up and expressed my career ambitions.

When I came to Nairobi, I was put into a division which was dealing with mergers. To be honest, the lady – Commissioner Sarah – was good to me. However, I also learned from her how not to do some things. From the time I was employed, we wanted to make the Department autonomous, a state agency. But we were just talking within our floor because we didn't have networks within the National Treasury or in the other government departments and policymakers who would drive this agenda. I noticed that the message was not going outside. It made me realize that the message needs to go outside your boardroom if you want to make it move. Secondly, the Department was somehow not aligned to the economic agenda of the country back then, so it was just in the periphery. In terms of the budget, after all the other departments had been allocated, whatever was remaining was allocated to the Monopolies and Price Department. This was another issue I realized.

I said "I'm not going to stay here. I'm going to change my career path." But 5 years down the line I was still in the Department because the Kenyan Economy was not doing very well and there was less job mobility. I can say it's an act of God – maybe that is why I'm here – but I did not move. For 5 years I said, "Let me end my career at the top of competition regulation in Kenya." So I decided to search for a course that could change me and to be exceptional in terms of competition regulation. I got a course, an MSc in competition and economic regulation, in one of the leading schools in London. I went and I did an MSc in economic regulation and competition. Coming back, the government gave me an opportunity to serve in a task force which was reviewing the competition law. I became the secretary to that task force.

You were the rapporteur.

Yes, I was given a chance. We traveled around the world and across the continent. We went to Zambia to learn about consumer protection. We went to South Africa to learn about institutional development and how they came up with their law. We went to London, which was then the Office of Fair Trading (OFT), the Competition Tribunal and the Monopolies Commission. We also went to Indonesia to learn about advocacy. So we collected and collated information across the whole world. Being the rapporteur, I was the interface between the team and the other persons we were meeting.

The task force completed the work, and by then also the Competition Policy Regulation had been anchored under the Economic Recovery Strategy document of the government, so it became part and parcel of driving the economic recovery strategy in Kenya. It was very clear in regard to the strategies that the government was going to ensure that we build a credible competition authority. When the task force was completed, my then-boss's contract came to an end and we had our report with a draft bill. At that time I was 36 years old, and was the one who had to take up the mantle.

There are some people I would like to recognize. The then Permanent Secretary of National Treasury; he's the current head of the Public Service in Kenya; and also the current President of Kenya; he was the Deputy Prime Minister and the Minister for Finance back then. The best thing is that they were real good economists, and they saw where we are moving as a country that needed effective regulators. So I took up the report and presented the bill, and there was a lot of support from the 2 people. Those are people I respect. We took the bill and it went through Parliament, but by the time it became law we had about 5 ministers who had been transited. But at least each and every minister came, and we convinced the minister.

We created the Competition Authority with the position of Director-General, who is appointed by the Board of Directors and vetted by the Parliament. I was the first Director-General of the Competition Authority of Kenya.

I'm fascinated by the connections you draw from your earlier experiences. I take it that one useful form of preparation was your previous experience in the civil service, which taught you about how the civil service operated, and the chance to watch other leaders, other senior managers, do their job and to take lessons from that.

Yes, being in the service gave me the networks I required. It gave me the opportunities I required. It gave me the funds to train me in London, which is very expensive. Those are 3 key things I will always cherish. But also, it taught me that an opportunity in government comes once. If you don't pick it up, it will disappear. Also, when you're driving an agenda and are aligning it to the economic agenda of the country, people will listen to you. You need to identify the champions within the system who you walk with.

It's sometimes said, maybe often said, that agencies should be autonomous, apart from the political process. But I think you're underscoring how you have to have a connection to the political process; you have to understand the larger aims of government, you have to understand the larger environment in which you're working, and draw connections between your program and those other aims and objectives.

I totally agree that agencies should be autonomous, but it's functional autonomy. When you're making a decision you should not be influenced by the government or by anyone else. It is what is highlighted within the law. However, a competition agency is a cogwheel in the government machinery. You are driving the agenda of the government in power, and that agenda is broad. For example, in Kenya, currently we have the "big four" agenda: build decent houses; affordable healthcare; manufacturing industry; food security. How do you align your authority's agenda toward that agenda, because even funding from the government will be based on those programs? When I'm taking a position in regard to healthcare that is my decision. But this decision should be based on research so that I can convince them why I arrived at that decision, and I require that budget from them so that I can do the research and inform them. That is the kind of relationship I see between our authority and the government.

The distinction you draw is so important; that is, for an agency head to realize in what respect the autonomy is important – as you call it, a "functional" autonomy – but to realize that you are one part, you are one wheel in the larger machine, and your effectiveness, your legitimacy, your ability to obtain resources, and to be seen as a valuable part of the larger society is so closely tied to your ability to see the larger themes and aims and show how you contribute. In a way, a good leader as you're describing it is a bit of a political scientist as well as, say, a good economist or a good lawyer.

I believe a good leader is a person who should have a vision. I don't look at my shoes when I'm walking; I look ahead. I look at my shoes when I stumble on something, and I believe that is what a good leader should do. Secondly, you should always communicate this vision to your team, the people who are following, and this will highlight the mission.

Tell me, when you became the DG, what was your vision at the time? You're now the Director-General, an extremely significant position for the success of the Competition Authority, for the CAK; what was your vision at the time coming in? Again, I think it's so helpful that you've underscored that your ability to lead is going to depend on your capacity to define a vision, not just to be happy to have the big office. What was your vision going in?

I asked myself: Why did we become an autonomous state agency away from the mainstream Government Service? State agencies in Kenya are created so that they can have more efficiency, effectiveness and flexibility when making decisions, because the government realizes there is a lot of bureaucracy within the civil service. The first time I was handed over the letter, I thought about how I am going to make this organization different from the department I was working in; how we would make it efficient, effective, and flexible to deal with any emerging market dynamics which are coming up. So the first thing was to have an organizational structure. You don't wake up and decide about the organizational structure; you have to have a job evaluation in terms of the optimal number and also the structure itself. So you hire a consultant with whom you are totally aligned and who appreciates your mandate.

From there we came up with a strategic plan. The strategic plan and the organizational structure were aligned. We started populating the organizational structure progressively because we were not just given money. It was progressive. So we identified the key areas to populate first. The first change is to create a culture very different from the usual civil service; the second to have a strategic plan; and the third to communicate to your team about your vision and what you want. But it is not just communicating and saying what you want, but communicating both orally and action-wise. I would arrive at the office at this hour and leave at this hour, and they would see you are doing it. You also need to inculcate performance contracting and performance management systems in all your decisions. That is what has created a wheel which can even move when I am not there.

My vision was not about building a chair for myself. I know I would be judged when I leave the organization – "Did he leave a legacy? Did he leave an organization which can progress without him?" I'm the captain now. The captain of a plane is not judged positively just because it's at cruising speed. It's when you land at the Dulles Airport in Washington safely. We're at a cruising altitude. I have not taken my people to where I'm supposed to take them. After I take them and I depart the equipment, that is when people should say, "Francis did this for the organization." That is my wish.

A couple of wonderful points you've raised here. Can we talk a bit about how you shaped the organization to suit your purpose, the crucial aim of having an organizational structure that is suited to the aims that you want to carry out? What kinds of changes did you bring about to create a distinctive form of public administration, something different perhaps than what the country would have been accustomed to? Can you tell us a bit about how you did that?

One thing is the recruitment and the placement policy. Whom do you bring onboard? There are some regrets I have sometimes, that we laid too much emphasis on educational background. But experience has taught me that there are some professions, and when you look at an attitude of someone, that is a key driver of a good employee. So we had a very good recruitment and placement policy.

There were some staff who had come from the civil service. We had to send them back to the civil service because they couldn't enter into the Competition Authority because of the culture I needed. I needed to start an organization with zero culture and build a culture as we progressed. What do I mean by "zero culture"? I didn't want a culture of the people who had come from the civil service to be entrenched. We moved from the civil service because it didn't have a good culture, and the government accepted that. Also, I didn't have a culture of people coming from outside who could not understand public policy management. So I needed to bring these two and blend that culture within the CAK to have our own culture. My vision was to start from ground zero culture. We would create an organization culture because the culture of an organization is what pushes the organization to the next level or takes the organization to the lower level. So there are people who came from the civil service. I think we were about 25. We ensured we did a placement. They were interviewed afresh, and 8 of them were the only ones who joined the CAK. We had an approved establishment of 72, so we had a carte blanche to bring onboard 72 minus 8. Some of them would come from other government agencies, the corporate and others freshly from the universities. So we had this boiling pot, we were making our food, and we had to come up with our own CAK culture, where efficiency is the main driver of everything. So there was a large opportunity of creating and placing new blood in the organization.

Really starting a new model of public administration in the country.

We also have a board of directors. I would say that the first board of directors was under the leadership of David Ong'olo – a man I respect a lot and who has shown me that you can have a great impact without talking much, but with a lot of humility. We had a board which had cross-cutting professions. It was a mix of accountants, financial experts, economists; and, therefore, they could bring this kind of collegiate thinking within the organization. That thinking ensured that the management came up with decisions which are very well-thought; and, therefore, decisions which are research-based. The other culture which I wanted to create is a culture of transparency and accountability. You should be able to explain any decision you make to outsiders as well as to your colleagues. As a leader, you have to make a decision whether it pleases you or not; and, when it doesn't please you, you provide the reason: "I'm rejecting this because of reason 1, 2, 3, 4."

First you solicit their views, you want them to tell you what they think; but then you do have the mandate to decide, so you have to choose; but then to explain the reason that you've chosen a particular course.

All the decisions in the Authority start from the bottom. They come up to the top. There are many decisions I reject, but I reject them with reasons, and I give the other view, which sometimes has been good and some other times maybe not. But you know senior managers always look at two things which is a challenge I have experienced. One is the resources; they are just thinking about resources and the processes. Secondly, they have the challenge that they are not able to tell their juniors "no," because maybe these are the stars in their departments, they are the ones who do their cases, so they have formed some kind of formal interconnectivity. But you're not building that staff member. You have to tell them that there is a wider perspective to whatever you are doing, and if we all do not follow these rules we might not be able to achieve what we want to achieve. So as a leader you have to be decisive and also transparent in how you are making decisions.

You were describing before the importance of communicating your aims internally. How are you doing that with your managers and your staff? What steps do you take to explain on a regular basis what you're trying to achieve? You've mentioned part of it; you tell people why we're going ahead or why we're not going to take that path and you explain to them what your thinking was there. Other things you do to perform this vital function of communicating your vision, your strategy, regularly throughout your organization?

The first thing when you're in the Authority is that you are given the key documents of the Authority and inducted. Then, possibly, when you join the organization, even if you're an intern of 3 months, the DG always creates 3 minutes or 4 minutes. So I meet them; and I call them by name. That has helped tremendously.

I'm guessing you know the names of your entire team and you address them by name. So they're not simply an anonymous mass; they are your colleagues.

Yes, I operate with not an open-door policy, a no-door policy. And I have created a chance that when an intern comes, whether they're in the university, let them come and see me before 7:00 in the morning. Why do I say before 7:00 in the morning? I create time to work, but also I show them the culture of working. You have to be dedicated.

We also communicate; we usually have quarterly meetings with all the staff. It's called the "DG's High Tea." We have it in the boardroom. There is nothing we're not discussing. Maybe somebody has come from the ABA meeting and they tell us what transpired there. And then we just have some tea. Also people can raise issues in regard to the social welfare of the employees. So that is another way of communicating. We also have quarterly DG circulars in regard to the happenings within the organization. In terms of management, we have an Executive Committee, which meets every month to review what the Management Committee does, which focuses on the technical work, and then the Executive Committee focuses on the strategic plan achievements. That is how we communicate. Maybe somebody will even be tweeting about this interview to the staff, and this is what the DG is talking about.

My guess is that this conversation we're having would be good for your staff, too, for your team, because this is such a wonderful way of capturing what you're seeking to do and how you're going about it.

Yes, sure, and there are so many other ways of communicating. You might want to communicate a certain message, but you think that they might not listen to you; so you may get those tapes that relate to what you're thinking and play them to them. Or think if there is somebody who may come and drive your agenda; and this person could just come to Nairobi and talk to the board members. That is a way of communicating what the DG thinks. Even the board itself will not listen to me a lot, so I tell them to call somebody who has your own vision or who understands your vision and talk to the Board, and that is how they'll appreciate it.

It is also a dimension of communications that you mentioned earlier, not just the communications internally to convey your aims, to explain to people why they are working hard, what the point of it is, but also the outward communications that you mentioned. Can you speak a bit about that, your efforts to reach audiences outside the walls of the CAK?

We have a list of stakeholders whom we have classified. For example, who is at the top there? It's the Parliament. How do you deal with them? We have crafted different kinds of messages and decided how we need to craft the messages to them. We have also classified who is required to talk to which stakeholder. If it's Parliament, that is Code Red. That is the DG – so me. If we have other stakeholders, we might have them meet with the directors and also the managers. And what am I doing? I listen to the people outside to know whether the Authority is on the right track, rather than listening to my managers, who may lie to me about how good I am so that they can get favors.

Mention a bit about how you do that. How do you listen? Whom do you talk to? Through what ways do you absorb this external impression of how the CAK is doing?

One is that we have lawyers with whom we deal at legal firms. They are the head of the Regulatory Unit within the legal firms. I create some time to have lunch with them or breakfast with them. I ask them, "Tell me how we are doing. Do you think we are working within your timelines? What is the view of your clients with regard to our products?" Also, I always ask them, "In this department, which officer can you recognize as efficient, listening to what the stakeholders want?" Now it's even managing my succession plan from outside there. That is my intel and how I communicate, especially with the legal officers.

Then, we also have stakeholders within the government. I always create time to meet with my mother ministry, the Policy Ministry – the National Treasury – to have some chat with my minister over some time in regard to, "Oh, I see some kind of government policy on consolidating banks, or coming up with some laws, or even the budget policy paper." I create time and I give my thoughts – not as official thoughts, but just chatting. He is getting information from me and I'm getting information from him. Just courtesy calls with the sector regulators, which I would say is maybe one of my regrets, and I will discuss later. Also I have colleagues and we discuss: "I am seeing these kinds of regulations which are coming up. We need to give some opinion in regard to them. What are your thoughts in regard to when you are coming up with these regulations so that we don't start writing back and forth, so that when we are writing we are informing the process rather than fighting the process?" That is how we get intel.

Also, in Parliament there are specific committees that have clerks, and we are in constant touch with them and they always tell us before we are summoned,

"We are writing a letter in regard to this." And you tell them, "That letter you're writing, even if we come there, we are not going to add any value." Maybe you align your letter based on this. So you're not refusing to go, but you are telling them to be sure that our interactions should be a value addition, not just for the cameras. I think that has really worked.

The important role you've mentioned several times in building networks outside the agency – you're emphasizing in such a helpful way the necessity to be effective, of understanding this collection of relationships, to develop them, and to make sure that you situate yourself in a larger framework of policy making, social debate, and discussion, that you realize you have a strong interconnection to a wide variety of other features of both the government and the larger society, to have that awareness.

Sure, competition agencies have quite a wide scope of mandate and powers. Don't use those powers to bully others. I would rather use the powers to carry along the others for the common good of the organization or the country. That has been my approach. It's not an issue of "This is the Competition Authority talking." We are all working for the same objective of the Kenyan citizenry. I want to show people that our way is to work together and walk together.

You have become one of the leaders of the larger international community. So many countries that are starting out look to Kenya for guidance about how to work, not simply in Africa, but in the larger community of new systems. You offer in a generous way your observations about policy in a collection of different forums, including the one we are attending this week in Washington, the American Bar Association Annual Spring Meeting of the Section of Antitrust Law. All of these activities require a lot of effort on your part. Yet, you also are the Director-General of the Competition Authority of Kenya. Your desk is in Nairobi. How do you resolve the competing demands on your time to learn and contribute to this international community but at the same time, in a sense, do what you're demanded to do in your position in Nairobi for the Competition Authority? Your domestic role and your international role, how do you resolve the demands on your time there?

It's quite a demanding schedule. But we always prioritize the things we want to deal with as an organization, and when we prioritize we have also categorized what the DG is supposed to attend to. For example, right now in Kenya, the DG is focusing on data, online platforms, and artificial intelligence (AI). Any forum which is discussing that, is the DG's, because we don't have a policy in regard to how to move forward, but I need to understand it so that when my technical people are advising me, I'm already on top of things.

So you choose venues and activities that assist you based on a priority process that you've established: "This is the area I want to focus on and I will structure my international activities to enable me to advance that program." Not simply accepting invitations, "That looks interesting, that one," but with a purpose.

The program and the interests of the organization go first. I'm not simply accepting invitations. Also, the DG has to be accompanied by another person who is involved in that policy, so that when the DG is not there, that person can take over the mantle and progress the agenda. Another question is about what is currently happening in Nairobi. We have very able directors where the work is progressing, unless some things which statutorily I cannot delegate. But, as we know, technology has really helped things. So that is how we balance.

Again, that is part of your effort as a leader, to encourage the development of good managers, good deputies, the leadership team, the management team, so that they can do their jobs well, not simply when you are attending an international event of this kind, but also that in the day when you do something else and there is a new DG, that the program continues to advance. To have that process of succession, the transmission of knowledge and responsibility is consciously in your mind as you develop your own program.

You develop your own program. Also, when you come back after leaving managers in charge, you are able to identify your successor based on how they managed when you were not there. But the other issue is that also within the Authority we ensure to make sure people understand no one is indispensable. Nobody does not go on leave because the moment you stop going on annual leave it just shows that the organization cannot move without you. And that is a bad signal. You have to go on your leave, leave the others to take charge, and then come back and progress.

You have to regenerate yourself, your spirit, your thoughts. You need to be restored. But the deeper message – that no one is indispensable and we are building an institution, we are not building a cult of personality – is a crucial concept as well. In so many ways you pointed to how your responsibility as a leader is not simply to address this specific matter of the day or the week, but this eye on how to create an organization, a framework, a management team, a culture, that will progress, develop, and become still richer when I'm not here.

If I can close with a general question to you – when the day comes that the successor is identified and you sit down for a chat and give tips, what reminders do you give them, saying: "These are things I've done that I think are worth emulating. Here are things that I might do differently." What do you offer by way of guidance in that conversation about the future, based on what you've learned?

I think one thing I would have done differently is related to the Board of Commissioners – which we call a Board of Directors. It is appointed after every 3 years. I'm on my second Board of Commissioners and I'm going to my third Board of Commissioners. The mistake I made is when the first Board was appointed, we didn't give them rigorous induction in terms of competition policy. We also didn't do it with the new Board. What I have seen is that the stakeholders out there may not appreciate the thinking of the Authority in terms of the decisions. The different Boards could have been approaching issues differently, because what happens is that the DG takes both papers, and then the decision is taken by the Board. The first Board was seeking information. Some, unfortunately, just seek for the stakeholders, and they can tell you, "We are not approving because we don't get information." When the first Board left the second Board was seeking for totally different purposes, which may not be related to the case. I'm not casting aspersions, but I thought that I should be doing it differently, by giving them a very rigorous induction in competition assessment and public interest. That is something I will tell my successor. The other issue is that I talk very comfortably about coming up with an organizational structure and populating the organization. I'm an economist.

It's a good way to make a living. It's okay, but there is still time for you to go to law school, Francis. [Laughter]

I'm in law school, when talking to you. [Laughter] I may be biased as an economist – and also maybe due to our historical attachment to the Monopolies Department, which was generally focusing on mergers – so we thought that maybe economists are the main drivers of a competition agency. I later came to realize they should be sitting at the back when the lawyers are driving. Sorry. [Laughter]

But, as we progress toward hard enforcement of cartels, I feel that we need to increase the number of lawyers because these are cases which require a lot of observation of due process when we are dealing with them. Economists have no time for due process; it's just numbers. But in terms of cartels, the due process is very key, going to the magistrate to get a warrant, whatever laws you need to respect. So I feel we need to progressively increase the number of lawyers within the agency.

The other regret I have is that when we started recruiting, we had this notion that it's only people who have worked for some years who can work within the Authority. We retained some people who, when I compare them with the young people who have come onboard, I always quietly in my corner ask, "Why the hell did I retain this guy instead of getting this?" Those are some of the regrets I have.

Bruno Lasserre*

French Competition Authority, President (2004-2016)

Your appointment as Vice President of the Conseil d'État in France began the later stage of a remarkable career in economic policy regulation and public administration. A major focus of that career before coming to the Conseil d'État has been competition law and policy. From 2004 to 2009, you were President of the Conseil de la concurrence and from 2009 to 2016, you led its successor institution, the Autorité de la concurrence. In both capacities you helped build an elite competition law system, one that is greatly respected at home and deeply influential abroad. When I was Chair of the Federal Trade Commission on many occasions I turned to you for advice about how to lead an agency, and it is delightful for me today to be able to continue that conversation [...] You were my finest teacher. I would like to start about how you came to the field of competition law, that is if you could reflect for a few moments on what influences in your life, what occasions brought you into the field of competition law?

To be very frank, I didn't discover competition at University but much later, by chance, when I was first appointed as the regulator of the telecom industry in the 90's. It is during this period that I discovered the virtues of competition, because I was responsible for driving a very important reform, opening up telecom to competition, creating a new independent regulatory body and privatizating France Telecom, the main public telecom operator. Quickly, I got really interested in what competition can drive as potential and beneficial effects for our economy but at the same time, I was struck by the fact that in France, maybe more than elsewhere, the benefits of competition need to be explained. It is something which is not given: you

* Interview conducted on 17 July 2019.

have to explain all the day why competition is important, what benefits it can bring. So I discovered competition, but also the necessity to develop education and pedagogy about it.

One of your signature contributions to the field, both in France and abroad, has been an underscoring of the role of what you called the competition pedagogy. And dealing with what you described once as the schizophrenia that individual citizens have: we love competition when we go to buy products and services, but as employees, we are not so sure. And to make that an essential element of what a public official must do, is to make the case daily.

Yes, exactly. It's like everybody has different parts in one's brain, and the role of the regulator or the enforcer, as far as we talk about pedagogy, is to reconcile these different parts of the brain, as consumers, as employees and as citizens interested in political and economic debate.

Perhaps, at a time when in many parts of our societies, there is so much turmoil, so much discontent with the way in which the economy works, the political environment stands, the urgency to bring this message home to individual citizens, not at a high level of abstraction but at a level they can apprehend, is ever more important.

You are very right, especially in a time where populism is more and more accepted, but also in a time where the way to do politics and competition gets more and more complex while people ask for simpler and simpler answers. But competition doesn't bring simple answers, it is not like that. If you start from equilibrium A which is suboptimal, everybody understands that there could be maybe a better equilibrium to build, but most of the people are still satisfied with the *status quo*. Then you explain that you have to shake that up because competition will build a new equilibrium, which would be more beneficial for everybody, but getting from equilibrium A to equilibrium B is always very difficult because it will necessarily cause some disorder. To change your equilibrium, you have to destroy, you have to shake up some things. One of the problems is that politicians are very sensitive to short-term instability because even if they understand that things will get better in the long term, they fear that the benefits will only be for their successors. That's the difficulty of pedagogy about competition: accepting a short-term disorder to build on the long-term a better equilibrium.

In your role of competition official or the regulator in telecom, in your role as a teacher, how did you convey this message persuasively? You described the state of mind of the elected official exactly right: "I am aware of the short-term effects of disruption, they are disturbing to my citizens, and then they are disturbing to me, but I have to build faith in a better future that the instability would be worth it". How did you find it most effective to convey that message?

Governments in France were never that easy with competition. They were explaining reforms which intended to drive more competition in such and such sectors not because of the economic benefits it could bring to citizens or companies, but because of the legal constraints coming from Brussels. They would say: "Well, we have the best public service in the world, efficient, cheap, modern, etc.", and never explain to the public that things could get even better with a little more competition.

So people ask, "Well, why do you change that if it is so performing?" "Ah… we have to change it because Brussels asked for it". Even though Brussels, the Council of Ministers, that's you and your colleagues from other member States! "Oh, yes but we can't escape that, there is a legal constraint to do so". And the way competition was explained was like that: "we are very satisfied with what we have today in France but we have to disrupt that because Brussels asked us to do it." And the question people were asking was then, logically: "Why is Brussels changing a well-doing system?" That amounted to transferring the unpopularity of the reforms from Paris to Brussels without ever trying to explain how private individual consumers and companies would be better off with a more competitive, open system.

That responsibility fell on the regulator to explain that, even if Brussels didn't exist, competition would still be useful to modernize our economy, to open new spaces for innovation, to get chances for new companies to get into the market, to get more choice for consumers and so on. That is all the more delicate that we had to cope with the fact that sometimes, the consumer prefers to be unhappy with the existing system, in which he has very few choices, rather than investing actively in choosing and taking risks. Sometimes, people prefer to be out of the picture, criticizing the system, "I am not happy, bad service, high prices", rather than investing positively in being an actor of its own success. Competition needs a consumer more engaged, more active, willing to invest oneself in studying the different options which are open and so on. You have to explain that.

Do you see things in France better today in this respect than they were, say, 15 years ago?

Yes, much better. I think competition is praised more and more from a consumer point of view. There has been a huge progress, and when we made polls about how competition is perceived in France, the results were not so far from those which have been collected in, for example, the UK, Germany or the Netherlands. Now, when you ask the French why competition is important, you would expect an answer about having better prices, better choice: but what's interesting is that answer number 1 is that it drives companies to be better, to be more efficient, to enhance services, to develop innovation, that it's a driver for efficiency. The argument about prices, quality and more choices only comes in second. And when you ask the French about why we need a competition agency, a competition enforcer, what seems the most important to them is to feel that they have an arbiter that protects small companies against big ones. They see the enforcer as bringing equality of chances between small companies and big players.

The crucial function of teaching pedagogy is something that agency leaders have to keep in mind and, to do justice, you suggest to make the case daily of why this is important. If I could look backward again a bit more and anticipate the moment when you came to the Conseil de la concurrence and then later to the Autorité, when you look at the whole span of your career's experiences before that, which experiences best prepared you for your role in the competition authorities?

First, my years as the telecom regulator. I spent nearly 10 years in that position, so I learnt a lot. But I also learnt a lot from the Conseil d'État, which I am heading now, because this institution is a real school of independence and collegial discussion. You must learn to act independently. And there are collegial panels for every decision and advice we make, so you understand how to manage collegiality in order to draw the best from the different points of view around the table. And I think it's very important, when you manage a collegial institution, to invite the college, the panel, to confront positions and to take the best of it. That experience prepared me for my years at the Conseil and then Autorité de la concurrence [...].

You have the experience of being the head of a significant regulatory body, and everything that comes from substance and process of that, the experience of being in this house, the Conseil d'État with its remarkable overview of public administration, policymaking, economic policy, administrative policy in France; being part of a collegiate environment both as a manager and as a substantive policy analyst and a student of the political and economic environment in the country, you took the right courses.

You are right. Though, the regret I have is missing a strong economic knowledge, even though I was very keen on developing economic reasoning and working with economists. But I did not have the chance to be educated in economics, and I always regretted it [...]. I loved working with economists very much. Our experiences were very complementary. The economists help you to develop analysis, to analyze a situation, for example the pro or anti-competitive effects of such or such strategy. But then you have to decide, and I think the legal background you receive in the Conseil d'État provides you with an ability to opt, to decide because all the life here is about choosing an option: it always finally gets to saying yes or no [...] You can start by saying "well, it's complex, it depends", but then you have to decide. I have been very lucky to benefit from this remarkable help of the economists to analyze very subtly a situation which is much more complex than you guess at first. But then, not being shy to decide and to say yes or no is something else for which I feel I was prepared.

If we had just taken your career in the telecom regulator, you could have taken the rest of your career off given what that did for France, given the transformation that set in motion but, of course, you have had subsequent careers. And as we have been saying today in competition policy, there came a point where France undertook a basic restructuring of its regime. A dramatic upgrade that, I think, created the foundation for a better future. It wasn't easy both to gain approval for it, to put it in place. You were in the midst of that process. Could you spend a bit of time talking about how that happened, how did it come about and what was it like putting the new institution on its feet?

To be very frank, it has been a miracle. We have been very lucky. In fact, I had the chance to be appointed in a sort of independent expert committee set up by former President Sarkozy. Because he had many ideas to modernize our economy, to boost innovation and growth and create new opportunities, he decided to set up a commission with 40 people, 40 experts, not only French but also some foreigners. The commission was led by Jacques Attali, an economist who had been Advisor to President Mitterrand. I had the chance to be there with Mario Monti, who was a member of the Attali Committee. Mario Monti and I decided that among the agenda we should discuss, there should be some space for giving more importance to competition policy and giving more space to change the institutional design. In France, we were late compared with many other countries but especially Southern European countries like Spain, Portugal, Italy who made that reform before.

Nobody supported us, though. The companies, businesses were especially happy to deal with the minister when they were discussing a merger. It's easier to discuss with a minister – different kinds of arguments can be put on the table – than negotiating with an independent agency. Consumer organizations, that was not their top priority. Lawyers on their side were very cautious: « we will see who will be the winner but let's not take any risk ». The problem was to get support from allies, but we couldn't identify friends or allies! So with Mario Monti, first, we had to convince the other members of the committee, which has not been so difficult, and then we had to convince political people. So I spent a lot of time in meetings with the political teams of President Sarkozy, the Prime Minister, and the Minister for Economic Affairs. I used very simple arguments that were easily understood and, I believe, welcomed.

First, simplicity: the organization we had in view was to be much more readable, much simpler. Second, efficiency: we had to merge because the split was not understandable anymore. The new system would produce efficiency gains. The third argument was about strategic influence. I said: "if we have a weak system in France, which doesn't produce confidence, decisions will be taken in Brussels"… At the time, Brussels used not to refer mergers back to France because it was not confident in the ability of France to do it impartially. These arguments were listened to, and I remember very well, in January 2008, President Sarkozy said yes to the reform. It was a big surprise. Christine Lagarde was at that time Minister for Economic Affairs, she was also very surprised. So she rushed to Mario Monti and me and said something like: "You plotted and you succeeded in your plot". I said, "No, no, it's not a plot, and I am sure you will be very happy with the results". Finally she understood that there were good reasons to do it, but it still resembles a real miracle to me.

So the window opened up.

Yes, and I am not sure that it would have kept open indefinitely. It was in January 2008. In September, Lehman Brothers collapsed and the financial crisis broke out: I am not sure that 8 months later, we would have received the same positive welcome from political people in France […].

Interesting how it's a mix of both preparation and a bit of luck, a bit of good fortune. But to be ready for the opportunity, to see the opportunity, this is something that you, Commissioner Monti, your colleagues, saw: a path, and without reflecting on how things could be better, I don't think you could have offered the vision about how to proceed.

I don't know but you are exactly right saying that it's a mix of anticipation, preparation and luck. That's the truth. There was still some skepticism at the beginning: were we going to succeed in taking up new responsibilities; were we culturally, psychologically ready to do so? There were some fears, and the first months after the reform was enacted were critical to show that we were ready.

What did you do to meet that challenge? That is, now you have this larger community watching you, there are some who think you are going to fall on your face, you have taken on too much. Maybe those who were opponents want you to fall on your face.

First of all, I was very clear in saying that we would first be judged and evaluated on mergers. We had to be reactive, to be inventive and show that we could deal successfully with mergers, which from now on had to be notified to us. That was a challenge because just before, we were only advisors in the Phase 2, mergers were discretionally transmitted to us by the minister [...]. We had to exercise this new power. Time was of essence. We had to show that we could be reactive and that we were not too "court-minded", but ready to receive company people in order to discuss pragmatically. We had to show that we could be inventive in terms of remedies, in terms of the way we could solve competition issues raised by those mergers. I think what was also very important was to be predictable. So the first priority in terms of mergers was to publish soft law and to show that we were not breaking the rules set up by the Commission and the minister's practices. There was a real need for continuity. That was very important at that time.

This strikes me as so interesting, how you and your colleagues saw immediately how you had to establish the credibility and perceived effectiveness of the new regime. You saw it was going to be merger control, and you masked your efforts to make that work.

Yes, because we were sometimes seen as anti-business. We had imposed huge fines in the past, so people thought that we would be against any merger. The fear was real. We had to prove that this was not the case, that we would deal impartially with mergers, that we truly believed that reaching a critical mass, gaining efficiencies was sometimes natural and positive. We had to encourage that while sorting out the good deals and the bad deals.

When you look at the experience since 2009 and, of course, you are building on good work that was done before, but this willingness to undertake a major upgrade with all the uncertainties involved, I think in retrospect has been so well justified. You have seen the continuing ascent of the French system to the point of not just being another entity in the room but being at the elite table [...] Merger control was part of it, what else did you do with your colleagues to build the profile, the effectiveness, the stature of the Autorité?

Two things. First, advocacy. The Conseil de la concurrence, and that was the difference with the new Autorité, had not the right to do advocacy by its own initiative. We had to be asked to give advice but we couldn't launch market studies or decide which subject would be important for consumers or innovation or the French economy. So the big, big change was the possibility now, like in the UK or in Germany, to decide by ourselves, to build up our own agenda and to choose, to select our subjects for advocacy. We decided to select subjects which were very important for daily life: spare parts for automobiles, railways, medicines, food products and so on. So we were very keen in selecting issues, which were identified as key issues for French people and French politics. That has represented quite a change to explain that we could improve the daily life of French consumers and bring new opportunities.

Second, soft law. I was impressed by the experience of the European Commission, and I understood very early that one of the things which was important was predictability. The question was not if we were fair or harsh or too severe, the question was "are you predictable?". Can a senior advisor or a general counsel predict what you will decide on such and such matter? The condition to be more predictable was to publish soft law and to engage ourselves in describing how we will deal with such and such situation, under which procedural rules and under which substantive rules. What was very new is that we developed in France very intensive soft law not only for new tools such as leniency, direct settlements, commitments but also on fines, which was something very strange and unknown in France. The Autorité was for the first time very prescriptive, very detailed about the method it would use to impose proportionate but deterrent fines. That was something, I think, which helped a lot.

This had a major impact in France but I think a consequence of the fusion is that it assisted in giving France a larger, more powerful voice in international affairs within the context of the European Competition Network but I think globally as well. And you played a key role in that taking place, your engagement in the ECN, in the international networks, the work extensively that France has done with emerging market economies in Africa, for example, was this a deliberate part of your strategy as well coming into the role of the new authority?

Sure, but we were helped by this huge dynamism driven by institutional reforms. We were on the upswing, and we used to see our future as very promising. It helps a lot. It also helped that we were not that different from other competition agencies. You can be persuasive and convincing only if you look like the others. It's more difficult if you are too different. The fact that we are organized like the others helped us to take part of the club and to influence its members. Maybe the third reason is that there was still a French specificity in that we still have no discretion to select our cases. In France, there is a long established tradition that you have to investigate all the cases which are brought to you and not able to select them under a discretionary appreciation. It can be a burden, but at the same time, it has been a fantastic chance. We took bold decisions or made important discoveries, which were not granted at the beginning. We investigated cases which at first seemed a bit risky. And at the end, we found them very promising and very helpful. So surprisingly, the fact that we couldn't spend hours wondering "is it the good case, is it the best case, should we investigate that case?", it helped us to take risks. It transformed a sort of drawback into an opportunity.

I would like to finish by giving you a chance to reflect on what you would tell a younger Bruno who is about ready to embark upon this type of career? The kind of advice that you would want to give someone who is coming into this role as a competition agency head, to alert them to what's good and what's difficult about the job. If I can start about what's enjoyable and what's exciting, what gave you the most satisfaction professionally and personally from your time as the head of the two agencies that you led?

What gave me a lot of pleasure was when I met companies, startups which, in fact, took opportunities from spaces we opened to competition. I really enjoyed seeing young people take investment risks after we strengthened competition on such or such market. It was incredibly rewarding to feel that we had provided new opportunities for their businesses. To feel that I helped young people, because competition is about helping young people against entrenched people, it is about giving opportunities to younger innovative people and encouraging them to take their responsibilities.

I also enjoyed feeling that we effectively changed the way the French benefit from different services. I can take the example of coach long-distance transportation: that was an advocacy exercise by the competition authority and now young people take that coach and are very happy about that. It was, at the origin, an idea from the competition authority and I tried to convince President Hollande and Emmanuel Macron, who was at the time Minister for Economy, to follow that idea. This is also incredibly rewarding.

So what's important, of course, is to be independent. I often say that you have not to be weak with the powerful people and strong with the weak people, but just the other way around. What is also important is the pedagogy. Explanation is of essence and one should maybe spend as much time on the decision that must sound, solid, robust, as on rewriting the press release and explain not only about the importance of the fine but also why, for example, a cartel is damaging economy, why a cartel can be very dangerous for the trust people put on the economy. So the way you talk to journalists about a story, about a case is very important; of course you are tempted to talk about the sensational, the importance of the fine, 200 million or 300 million, but you should do more than just that [...]. The question that matters most is not how much but why. Why the way these companies behaved is bad for the economy, why we want them to act differently. The story is sometimes much more important than the result.

You said the good things, the opportunities to make a difference, to see a better future and then to see it realized in many ways, all good reasons to do this. As a caution to the new agency head, what would you say are the hardest parts of the job, the most difficult?

Maybe loneliness: you are often very lonely and that's why I was so keen on meeting with my colleagues, sometimes sharing this sense of unpopularity or loneliness. Sometimes I felt that I was like an acrobat that, day after day, show after show, had to prove his skill and his legitimacy. And many people expect you to fail. You have to prove every day, at each exercise, that you are able to do it again and be successful.

There is not always a net underneath you either.

Exactly. So you must not be afraid of that. This is not an old institution like this one – the Conseil d'État – which is occupying Republican temples with centuries and centuries of existence. You are very fresh, very new, very fragile and under constant pressure. When the *dompteur*, who tames wild animals, enters the room, he is seen as powerful and deterrent. On the contrary, the acrobat looks fragile and has to count on his own skill.

And the skill based on all of these experiences, the touch. In a number of ways, you are on stage the whole time, you are on stage inside of your building. Probably the staff notices what color tie you wear. If you wear the same tie twice a week, aha, Lasserre is wearing the same tie. Outside the building, you are on stage all the time, the press follows your words, the bar, like criminologist, looks at every phrase and tries to figure out what you meant. That kind of a continuing observation can be glaring at times. How did you cope with the spotlight, how did you keep for yourself time to refresh your knowledge? How did you cope with that fact of being onstage all the time?

Well, on stage all the time, not really. In fact, I was not so well known. Maybe in the business community or by some journalists, but not in daily life. So it allowed me to keep space for tranquility and anonymity. Fortunately, that changed a bit. What I loved in my previous life was traveling like you do, and, in fact, I used to make a lot of long, long travels abroad. That was a time when we were not troubled by mobile phones or computers and it allowed me to read, to think and so on.

You have been collecting a number of observations for the potential head of an agency. Anything else that comes to mind that you would tell them, things that you knew when you stepped out of the Autorité that would have been good to know perhaps more clearly on the first day, anything else that you would tell the new head of an agency: "Think about this as you do your job"?

Of course, management is very important. Though it was not that difficult to attract good people, because we had a good reputation that allowed us to recruit bright and motivated people. The most difficult thing for a small agency – Autorité de la concurrence is less than 200 people – is to keep those bright and motivated people. It is to incentivize them to stay. We are in a very competitive world and when they get well known, their peers have the temptation to approach them from outside. There are law firms, economy consultancy firms which, from this point of view, compete very strongly with us. So you have to juggle everyday with the need not only to attract but convince people to stay with you in the future. And it needs pedagogy as well, even if you can't promise everybody that they will be at the top at the end…

> It is a testament to how effective the continuing improvement and continuing renewal of the system has been that people want to poach your people. It is a bad sign if nobody wants your people [...] So many have come to want your people to present you with a problem that is difficult but in a sense wonderful too. It's a testament to how well things have gone with the demand you continue to replenish.

And what is very rewarding is the incredible network composed of people who have been in the Autorité de la concurrence and are now scattered in many streams of the political environment. I remember you were at the Autorité and together we share so many memories. We created a huge and incredibly strong network of ex people with the Autorité.

Norman Manoim*

South African Competition Tribunal, Chairperson (2009-2019)

You are the head of the Competition Tribunal of South Africa since 2009 and have served with that body since its inception in 1999. You have had a panoramic view of the development of the competition regime in South Africa, which is regarded as being one of the modern success stories in the 100 or so agencies or systems created since the late 1980s. To begin, we would like to explore the path that you took to the Tribunal. What was the collection of experiences that led you into the Tribunal and now to the head of the institution?

It's a very unlikely path because I started off my career as a human rights lawyer, so until 1994, with the democratic transition in South Africa, I was a human rights lawyer dealing with state power. After the transition I was, as it were, out of work as a human rights lawyer and I needed to reconfigure my career. A lot of my contemporaries at the time said, "We need to start worrying about private power in this economy, and hence an interest in antitrust law." I knew nothing about the topic, but it sounded very sexy, and we liked the romantic story of the American Sherman Act and the breaking up of Standard Oil. That appealed to us at the time because the South African economy was incredibly concentrated, largely in the hands of traditional white firms, and that was a major social problem. So antitrust started off as a project to deal with the private power problem and was a compromise between people who wanted to nationalize all the industries and those who wanted markets to work but to work more fairly. That is how, almost by accident, I got into this area. My first involvement was to work on drafting the legislation from day one, without any experience whatsoever. But as they say, "In the kingdom of the blind, the one-eyed man is king."

---

* Interview conducted on 26 August 2019.

Your involvement in the drafting process began about when?

That was about 1998. Fortunately, we were able to call upon a number of people for their expertise and ideas. I remember you making some submissions to us, and we had a number of people both internationally and locally who helped contribute to the draft. It was done in a hurry, as all government projects are; they have got to be done overnight. So it took about a year to get the thing from the conception stage into legislation, and then we got the institutions going on the 1st of September in 1999.

You joined the Tribunal. Could you describe those institutions for a moment as it's a several-tiered mechanism?

Yes, what we had before was what was called the Competition Board, and it was an administrative board of people who did both the investigation and made the decisions, but the decisions were recommendations to a Cabinet minister, who would then choose to implement them or not. I recall serving briefly on this body and being called into some meetings. They were like boards of directors meetings, so you would walk in and out during a hearing, and it didn't matter. We realized that this was very, very deficient and that we needed to have a proper set of institutions. We divided it into 3 institutions. There is the Competition Commission, which is the prosecutor/investigator or policeman of the system; the Tribunal, which is the court of first instance of the institution; and then there is a Competition Appeal Court to hear appeals from us on the record.

That mechanism reflected the assessment of experience internationally and was designed crucially to provide assurance that the prosecutor/investigator would not also be the decision maker.

The new Act gave it considerably greater powers than had been before. For instance, the first-time notification of mergers was compulsory, and the business community was up in arms. They were very worried about this and said, "Look, this has never happened before, and these guys have got so much power. What's going to happen to us?" I think the fact that there were these 3 separate institutions – each with their own budgets, their own institutions and own accountability – gave some assurance that the system would be fair.

Have you ever had any experience acting as a decision maker in a judicial capacity, or even in a dispute-resolution capacity? Has this been part of your background at all?

Not really. I had been a litigant in the courts, so I had sat at different sides of the room, but not in the middle, and it's a very different experience when you sit in the middle. You've got to listen to both sides of the case and you realize it's actually easier to be on one side of the case and to take a view because you can look at the facts that favor you and largely ignore those that don't. But when you sit in the middle and you've got to weigh up both of them, it's a different mindset, and it is a huge challenge. The most difficult part of the job is to write a decision and to write it coherently, in a way that people who read the thing can understand why you got from A to B.

Was part of the thinking that went through your work that "We are not simply technicians deciding specific issues, but we are speaking to a much larger audience and we have to ground our observations in language and concepts that our society will grasp?"

That is the challenge. I don't know if we've always met that challenge. In a sense, we say to each other, "A reasonably intelligent person who is not vested in competition law or economics can read this thing and understand why you made the decision you made." It's very challenging in this area to keep translating the economics into something vaguely intelligible.

I would guess that in thinking about the experiences that make an adjudicator effective, the work you had done before – it's a different field – had nonetheless given you a deep appreciation for the history, the political science, the economics, the social dimension of the new nation. Your work in the drafting process joined up with your experience as an advocate doing human rights work probably gave you a deeper appreciation for why South Africa had this law and what it was meant to do.

It does give one a background. Often I find that people who have just done commercial law, have done contracts or tax or something like that, find getting into competition law quite difficult because then they find looking at a more purposive interpretation of the law quite difficult, and they find taking context into account, instead of just looking very closely at the text and getting the answer, is a difficult thing. I felt that having done human rights work gave you an appreciation of context. Even though it was a very different context to antitrust law, it was a way of thinking that made it easier to get into this area. Also, I think what was useful in the drafting process was just going through the various debates, why we've chosen to put this into the legislation and why we've chosen to leave something out.

And, of course, as a judge, when debates occur about what did they intend, is this part of the law or what was the purpose of this, it's nice to be able to raise your hand and say, "I was there."

Yes. Except on occasions when people say, "We realize that this clause is unintelligible, but our best guess is that it means that...," and I sit back very quietly and pretend I had nothing to do with it.

Do they ever look at you and say, "We're not talking about you, Your Honor. It must have been the others"?

It has now taken so long that people have forgotten. I remember my predecessor, David Lewis, said "This is aimed at you" when that kind of argument was raised.

My impression in watching the work of the Tribunal from the beginning is that the government made a determined effort to see that the membership of that Tribunal indeed had exceptional skills, which was a certifying mark of the Tribunal.

I think a body like ours would only work if we can offer expertise. If it was simply there just to hear cases and people had no background, that would offer no value. Then a junior case manager in the Competition Commission would know more about the subject and have to sit there and listen to somebody who had no idea what was going on, and that I think would be bad for the system. The challenge, however, is to keep people because they serve fixed terms and then move on to other things. You need to regularly get new talent that you can put into the system.

Without going colleague by colleague through the history of the institution, do you have some general observations about what mix of experiences enriches the work of the Tribunal? What backgrounds, what capabilities, make the ensemble more effective? What is the number of members in the Tribunal at full strength and do you have the capacity to meet as a plenum if you choose in individual cases?

The first is that, unlike a court, we have a mixture of lawyers and economists, and the Act allows that. So we've always had 3 or 4 economists who have been part of the Tribunal, and that has been quite helpful. At full strength we have 11 people. When we hear cases we sit as three-person panels. Hence the Tribunal. We've always got to sit at 3.

The background would be more lawyers and economists; it has been that. I suppose I ideally look for people who have legally had some commercial experience or had some adjudicating experience and economists who have specialized in industrial economics or microeconomics. We haven't always got that skill on day one, but I think the way it has worked is that there have always been a number of people onboard who have had some experience, so when the new blood comes in they can actually sit on a panel with 2 other people who have had some experience, and they get experience over time. Because you're not guaranteed in a small country with a small skills base that you're going to have that skill level from day one. Most of us actually had to learn it in the beginning.

It would be my impression, but would you say that there has been the development of a fairly strong collective memory because of yourself and because of other colleagues who have served for a long time?

Yes. And because we have developed case law and jurisprudence. If a new person is facing a problem, there is now a body of 20 years of case law to deal with that, so they're not alone.

Can you tell me something about how you develop a sense of common purpose and understanding among the members of the Tribunal? What formal and informal ways do you take to build a common understanding of the issues, to share thoughts about solving problems, and to share thoughts about how to resolve specific issues? How do you deliberate in the broad sense?

We often try to meet before we decide a case to discuss it and say, "Look, what are the issues here? What do we have to look at?" Once we have heard the case, we will then meet again and try to look at how we resolve that. There are people who come from different places in trying to look at these issues, so it's a matter of debate and discussion to see if you can come up with a common view. In fact, over the years we've had no more than 2 or 3 dissents, I think, in all the time we've been there, so usually we've been able to, as it were, develop a common approach. We also get training done, and as you know – you've done some training for us – we've called people in from the outside, outside experts, to run training. In that way there is a lot of discussion of some of the issues and, hopefully, developing a common approach.

One thing I have found most impressive in the way in which you examine your work. You think about the way ahead, you engage collectively – sometimes with outside observers – in a deep discussion of individual matters to explore technical details but also broader policy directions as a group.

We have had after-the-fact case analysis and saying, "Well, was this the right approach? Did we explain what we meant? We might have come to the right outcome, but did we explain how we got there?"

You have the formal framework that you were instrumental in developing in the legislation. You have 3 distinctive institutions. One of the most important things I suspect is to define in practical terms your relationship with the Commission and the role that you play in the development of the law. What was the initial conception among the members about our role in dealing with the Commission, and how has that developed over time?

Initially, it wasn't clear what the boundaries were between the institutions, and gradually, it has become much clearer. I think everybody in the institutions understands the separation and we understand that for public perception that separation is important. So, if the Commission is bringing cases and is investigating, they don't tell us anything about it. If the Commission wants to interact with us about a case, they only do so in the presence of the other parties to the case. That has been very, very important for everybody to understand and I think it's respected. We haven't had any problems in that regard. Sometimes there is interaction more generally about whether the system as a whole is working. It's not case-specific, but there might be an interaction with the leadership of the Commission about bottlenecks in the system; and if so, why is that the case? You might say, "Why do these cases seem to be taking too long to come from you guys?" and they might say to us, "Look, decisions are coming too late from you guys." So there will be a frank discussion about that, but it's never a case-specific discussion.

Do you find that in writing opinions part of your work is thinking about the attitude that you adopt? How would you describe your attitude in looking at decisions or prosecutions or complaints that come from the Commission? Is it one of some deference in principle or is there no deference in the process? Are you simply deciding matters that come to you, or in some way are you assisting in pointing the direction toward how the system might develop more effectively over time?

I think it's context-specific. If the Commission has after long, bitter litigation reached a settlement with the parties, I think we will defer to them on that largely, unless something looks shockingly disproportionate to what it should be. In that regard, we show some degree of deference. I would also have a degree of sympathy with the Commission's task, which is a more difficult one than ours. I think the difference between us and, say, an ordinary court which is not a specialized court and has no interest in the way the institutions function, is that we want to see the system work. If the system fails, then the public is failed.

I've seen from some parts of the world in some instances a consequence of creating a special tribunal means that the tribunal has to make sure whether they want to run the agency or whether they want to be judges or do both. But it seems as though you have a clear understanding of what in that range of possibilities your job is.

I think we have so far. Of course, that is not a guarantee going forward. Maybe other people will show a different attitude and send the wrong messages to the Commission who are always dissatisfied, who always think they're smarter than the people at the Commission. I think there is a danger of institutional arrogance and one wants to avoid that.

If you take your initial assumptions and understandings from 1998 and 1999 and you look at the way the institution has developed today, does anything in that evolution surprise you in a good way or maybe surprise you – is that quite fulfilling your expectations? If you take your early expectations and match them to what you see now over time, what are your impressions?

I think that we never knew how busy we would be because the Competition Board, our predecessor, didn't have that many either merger cases or anticompetitive practice cases. We were surprised by many things. We then went to a compulsory merger notification system, and we've been a bit overwhelmed by the number of mergers that have come through the door, even though we tweak the notification thresholds from time to time. Once we introduced the leniency system, the door just opened and cases – particularly cartel cases – flew in, and that caught us completely by surprise. We just didn't expect that they would be out there.

We had a conception that we would be breaking up the traditional conglomerates that existed in the South African economy. I think of Anglo American, which at that time was the biggest conglomerate in the economy; it has never had a case against it in the entire 20 years. Instead, the cases had been brought against other firms or firms we would never have seen in the time. Our preconceptions about what we would be doing and who we would be up against turned out to be wrong, and we turned out to be – I think our first merger prohibition involved people who sold furniture. They would never have been on our radar screen beforehand. But also the volume caught us by surprise. We were certainly too small from our side, and I think the Commission was also too small in terms of resources, to face what we had.

Perhaps you can mention what access you have to clerks and to référendaires. What resources in addition to yourselves can you bring to bear on individual cases?

We have good resources. We have the equivalent of judge's clerks. Each panel that hears a case will have at least one judge's clerk. They're a mixture of young lawyers and young economists who help us out, and it's an invaluable resource.

In the routine resolution of disputes, what are some of the greatest challenges you face in actually hearing cases, taking evidence, and resolving disputes? Again, this was all new when you began, but what have been the most difficult elements, of actually conducting the proceedings, taking and evaluating the evidence, and reaching decisions?

I think the hardest have been procedural challenges. Because the system is driven by lawyers, lawyers like to look for a good procedural point rather than dealing with the merits. So there has been a sense of frustration that it takes a long time to get to the merits of the case. Once you get to the merits of the case, you're then dealing with interesting stuff, and it gets sorted out. But there is a continuous need to deal with these procedural challenges: Is the Commission's case clear enough to the other side; has there been proper discovery – and all sorts of other South Africa-specific problems that we've created for ourselves in how we've designed our procedure. That has involved years of litigation, which has slowed down cases and has been very, very frustrating, but it was seemingly unavoidable.

Do you detect progress over time in starting to resolve some issues in a way that is clear enough to the parties to realize what is not really worth the time anymore? At the beginning of the system you usually have a number of what might be called new issues, and until they're clearly resolved, they will continue to be litigated. Are you seeing some progress in basically taking those questions off the table?

We've progressed in the sense that we take some off the table, and new ones emerge. One of the things that has been useful, and we do it in the system, is meetings with parties – we call them "pre-hearings" in our system – which are informal meetings of the parties to a matter, and you call everybody into a room, and you say, "What are the procedural issues we've got to sort out?" We find that if you get everybody in the room, you can get much better cooperation out of people than if you deal with them through writing angry letters to one another and not sorting things out. But once people are in a room, they want to appear cooperatively in front of you. I think those things are signs of how to manage a lot of the, as it were, small headaches in a case so that you can actually get to the merits.

Preliminary hearings are informal meetings without a court reporter, so it's off the record in a sense. But it's a way to resolve issues without prejudice to any party for what they might say. You might prod people by hinting that they could be wasting everyone's time with a particular theory about the case. So, you might say to a party, "You've got 3 different defenses now; are you going to rely on all of them?

Thinking of innovations that other tribunals might use, this is a noteworthy one. I should ask at this point, is there a framework in which you and other similarly situated tribunals – maybe some that have comparable traits in South Africa but maybe globally – can meet to discuss your own special needs and to share observations about techniques like this?

I think there can be. I know, for instance, that in the United Kingdom the Competition Appeal Tribunal (CAT) is using very similar methods of meeting with the parties and trying to resolve issues. We've had discussions with them. But I think wider discussions would be very useful in this.

Competition cases and major mergers can seem dauntingly complex – lots of evidence; the parties bring in experts, everyone has an expert to say it's either flat or it's round; lots of competing views about the world; and, I suppose, a desire in some instances to bring in all the evidence that exists on the planet. How have you gone about trying to manage the litigation of these matters in a way that permits decisions in a generally timely manner, in a way that approaches the best result possible?

One is an appreciation that if you give lawyers enough space, they will fill any volume that they can occupy. There is no upward boundary. So we try to manage and impose time limits on people. We have this chess clock rule that comes from arbitration, where you meet the parties in these pre-hearings and say, "How much time do you think you're going to need?" and then you allocate that time to the party and you hold them to it. That forces people to get the job done in the time that has been allocated. We have found that to be a very useful discipline. We started off doing that in merger cases because there everybody and the merging parties had an incentive to get the job done expeditiously. Then we started applying it to cartel cases and into abuse cases. So that is from the disciplined time point of view.

With regard to economic evidence, which we find takes the most time in the system, economists' reports – bless them – can be 100 pages long. Those are the executive summaries. We now ask these people to use the hot tub system, which basically is having the experts sit and testify simultaneously. We start off by saying to them, "Look, meet informally amongst yourselves and agree on the major issues on which you can agree on or don't agree on. Then, when you come to the hearing, we'll go through the areas that you don't agree on, each of you can do a brief input on that and you can have a debate amongst yourselves about that particular issue. We'll throw in some questions. The lawyers are going to sit in the back of the room; they're not going to get involved in that." We go through that, and when we feel that they have debated the issue sufficiently, we move on to the next topic.

That has mostly worked, but it doesn't always work. Sometimes the personalities of the economists are not conducive to that kind of thing; you may have one very aggressive personality and on the other side one fairly passive one, so there is a bit of an imbalance; or it may be a very experienced person and a very junior person on the other side. So we don't always think it's going to work, and sometimes if we don't think it'll work, we won't do it that way. But it's starting to get acceptance. It has certainly cut down on the time and shortened the issues.

Have the efforts to confine the duration of proceedings been challenged in court, or is this a step that parties regard as being generally sensible – "We see a benefit in having a decision in a timely way, too, so we're going to accept it"?

The first time we did it, it did get challenged, interestingly enough, by our minister, who was an intervenor in the merger. This was a merger of a South African company and a US company, and we had limited time, so his legal team felt that their time had been limited too much and they challenged it. But the appeal court said it was okay. It was a slightly grudging admission that it was okay, but they said it was okay, and it hasn't been challenged since. One has to use the pre-hearing to get parties to buy-in to that, and that is important. So, if somebody wants an excessive amount of time, you need to say, "Well, justify why you should have more time than we think should be the case." I think there was an acceptance of the system. There is a reasonable approach to estimating time. Sometimes we will end up slightly short, but then we will give people a bit more time if we think it's helpful to resolve the case.

If you look at the role of the judge or the Tribunal, one view is that as a judge, you're never speaking in the courtroom, but you mostly write texts of opinions where you speak; and you do not spend a great deal of time outside of those contexts talking about what you do, how you do it, or what you've done. I think a more common approach is to have some engagement with the outside world, such as attending this conference at the International Competition Network in Cartagena this week, but in other settings as well. Can you say a bit about the role that you and your colleagues have defined for yourselves in engagement with the larger environment beyond the room in which you make decisions?

It's a difficult issue as to knowing that boundary. In the beginning, when the system was young, we were quite conservative about that and we would virtually say nothing and refer to "read our opinions." We sort of adhered to that when we were asked to comment on a specific case. Firstly, because it's a joint effort of 3 people, what I say in a particular case may not be the view of my 2 colleagues. So we were very careful about saying anything further than in the reasons. But we will speak more generally about the system. Why are people concerned about cartels? Why do mergers need to be notified? What is the public interest in the South African system, a very hot topic always? Why do we have that? How do we ground that? At a fairly general level, we think we do actually have a duty to educate the public. What are the institutions? How do they work? Why is this job important? Why does it have meaning? At that level we would see ourselves saying something. The Commission can obviously say much more than we can. They can talk about particular cases, why they take on certain things, and so they have got a much more important advocacy role. We have got a smaller one, but I think it's still an important one.

I imagine something that has reflected in your own use of your time is that there have to be opportunities for the Tribunal members to expand their body of knowledge, to engage in other activities that expose them in more depth to the features of the system in which they operate and the substantive material.

Yes, absolutely.

As you look back – I think you've described for us a number of things that have unmistakably been successful in the evolution of the system – if you had to identify areas where the system can continue the healthy improvement that it has throughout its 20 years, what would you like to do better?

I would like to have done it faster. That is my biggest regret about the system, is how slow cases take. It's not entirely the problem of our institution, but I think that we could have created more pressure on the litigants to get moving. And we ourselves, because we've been capacity-constrained, could have written decisions more quickly than we did, and perhaps shorter than we did. Mea culpa on my part. I've fallen down on both length of time and length of decisions. If I had to redo it again, I would like to have seen greater speed and greater conciseness and showing that the system can deliver in time. Including the parties who are actually facing a case on the wrong side of the Commission. I can see them in the back of the room when they hear there is another court postponement, exasperated, almost, saying, "Why doesn't this thing get finished?" I have empathy for that kind of frustration. Really, if it's going to go badly for you at the end of day or not, you want to resolve it.

I suspect there may not be a systematic way of looking at this. But is there a rough average – and, of course, it would depend on the case – period of time from the last day of proceedings to the issuance of an opinion? Do you track that over time?

We track that depending on what kind of case it is. For all mergers we have a period of 20 business days for giving the reasons in those types of cases. At the other end, at the wrong end of a complex case – say, an abuse case, a sort of 100-page opinion type case – we would look at 6 months from the end of the hearing as our target. Do we always hit those targets? Unfortunately not.

This is another area where benchmarking across systems would be very informative, both to look at specialized tribunals but other appellate-like bodies, or even trial-type bodies, to get a sense of what human beings tend to be able to do given the constraints they face. But it's a way of setting a target for what we might do better and find out how they got to that point. I think this kind of tracking has been a very healthy ingredient in the process.

Absolutely. And we reported on that very early in our system. Parliament always wants you to report on targets. We said to them, "Look, we can't report on how many mergers we prohibit or how much we fine. We are not fundraising for the treasury. But what we can report on as an independent institution is efficiency.

So what we will do is come up with targets that reflect our efficiency: once the case is with us how quickly do we get it on the road, and how quickly do we get our decisions out, and what are useful targets. That we will report to you."

I would like to turn to a last question for you to think about. Let's say Norman's term comes to an end at some point, and there comes a time when new appointees come on the board, and certainly a new chair comes on the board, on the Tribunal. Do you have advice for them about what to do – how to get started; how to work with their colleagues; how, in other words, to do the job well? Anything that you didn't know on day one that they should know?

I think it's a really interesting situation which is different from an agency. In an agency you have a head of the agency who is the boss of the institution and people are the employees of the agency. When you are in a body like the Tribunal, which I think is like being on any judicial bench, you've got people who have been appointed not by me but by the political process. They are not your employees. That creates an interesting tension within the institution; how do you assert some kind of leadership over the institution when you can't say, "Well, you're going tomorrow; take your files." So that is difficult. It's a personality in one way, but I think it's about experience in the system and talking to people through issues, and saying, "Okay, I see you're thinking that way about the case; but if you go that way, how would you give reasons for it?" Often when I've had a colleague who I think is going in a strange direction, I'll say, "Well, that is an interesting point, but you better justify that. We've never done it in that way. Why are we going to go – how will you explain that now if you were going to reflect on that?" The person will probably come back in a day or two and say, "You know, I've given it some thought again, and maybe that is not the way to go, in that particular way."

I would assume that as part of one's existing personality, and perhaps some element of change, that it's certainly important in your capacity to be a good listener and to have patience in discussing matters with colleagues.

Yes, absolutely. There are times when you are under pressure and you can be a little short with colleagues. That is often a mistake, and you've got to walk back from that. But it is important to have that, to allow people to reflect and to see through it and have more discussion. It may take longer to get to a resolution. But at the end of the day, I also say to people, "Look, you're free to disagree with the other 2 people on the panel. You think they're wrong and you want to express your own opinion, you're welcome to do so, but you must put those opinions down. The public are entitled to know why you differed with the other people and what it was based on. The majority will write this thing first. You can have a look at it. Read that opinion and say, 'Look, I disagree with that and that approach and this is my view,' and you're free to do that." Sometimes that is the way to deal with a situation where there may be differences and tension.

Would you say it's worth an additional investment of time to have discussion and persuasion for the sake of getting the complete consensus that speaks with one voice for the body?

There is always an interesting debate as to how useful dissents are in a particular body. We're not the highest court, we're not the Supreme Court, so, in a sense, they may be more meaningful there than they are in a body like ours. So there is always the danger if we have continual dissents that people will say, "We're not quite sure where this body goes. Every time we bring this particular case there is a dissent. Lawyers can't advise their clients." So it is useful to try to get that if you can, but it's not always going to be achieved.

One thing we haven't mentioned is that indeed you work in a hierarchy in which you're not the last word. You do have to think about framing decisions, and just more generally behaving in a way that increases confidence in what it is you've done in the eyes of a reviewing Tribunal, which is not going to simply take what you have to say at face value and put a stamp on it.

Yes, that is right. Certainly, there have been differences between our body and the court on a number of issues, which have been interesting in themselves.

Last, are you happy, generally speaking, with the choices you made in 1998 and 1999 in drafting the law with respect to this institutional configuration?

Yes, absolutely. I think that one thing I'm certain of is that it's the right institutional configuration. I think it has worked. We weren't sure in the beginning, but I think it worked over time.

Andreas Mundt*

Bundeskartellamt,
President (2009-Present)

You have been the President of the Bundeskartellamt in Germany since 2009. You have served in a variety of public policy capacities during your professional career, and have achieved extraordinary distinction as the head of the institution where you now work. I would like to start by asking you to think about the path that led you to your current position in the Bundeskartellamt. If you think about the experiences you had professionally, your work experience, education, what experiences gave you the best preparation to do the job that you do now?

I think it's the variety of jobs that I've had and of posts that I had to occupy. I started my career in the Ministry of Economics. I spent almost 2 years in the Ministry at a time that was quite turbulent in Germany because it was right after the reunification of the two parts, so everything was new. Everyone who had worked on the new law for the "New Länder" was an expert after six weeks, which meant that you had to accompany the minister traveling to the "New Länder," to Dresden and Leipzig. This meant that from the start as a very young professional in the Ministry of Economics, I gained a lot of experience that I would not have gained if I hadn't been working in this area.

To give you an example, it took us to the city of Magdeburg, and the Minister, Mr. Möllemann, was giving a speech there, and we were in an old cinema. I was the expert for the return of real estate in the "New Länder," and he wanted to talk about the economy and how to provide help. It turned out that in this cinema there were around 400 people that had bought some real estate

---

* Interview conducted on 5 August 2019.

and wanted to know if they had to give it back. I was sitting there. I had been in the Ministry for six weeks. The Minister said, "Ah, for that question we brought an expert." All of a sudden, I had to stand up in that cinema and give a speech and say something. That is a type of experience that normally you cannot gain in a ministry. So these two years were extremely helpful.

How old were you when you were in the spotlight?

I was thirty, and I had just started my career.

That's a very powerful initial introduction.

Yes, that was a powerful initiation, most of all because I didn't know anything about this. Everyone had told me, "Oh, you will be sitting in a room; there will be some people who have some questions for you." But it was different. It turned out to be different. That was an exciting time. I then moved on to the Liberal Parliamentary Group, and I worked there for almost nine years. I was doing work on labor law, social law, and so on. There you have a lot of contact, of course, with quite high-ranking people. I still remember I entered the room for the first time, and Hans-Dietrich Genscher was sitting there, together with Graf Lambsdorff and other very renowned personalities of German politics, and from one day to another you were working for these people. I did that for eight years. In Parliament you can really learn a lot. The third stage was working at the Bundeskartellamt. The government had moved to Berlin. I worked for the Bundeskartellamt in various positions. I started as a rapporteur, went on to international competition matters, became head of the general policy division. Then came the day when they needed a new president because our president had moved on to the Ministry.

All of these three stages were extremely helpful in learning what it takes if you want to have the responsibility for such an agency. I think this is a huge step, being in the very end the only one who has the responsibility vis-à-vis the Ministry, vis-à-vis the public domain, and vis-à-vis policymakers. I think that is the best preparation. If you know all of these areas at least a little bit, you know how they will react, you know what it takes. For me it was extremely helpful that I had been working in all these areas. There you learn what you need, at least you hope so.

Several themes that come from your comments strike me as very important and have broad, universal significance for many agencies. You gained, I sense, a very good understanding of the broader economic context of Germany, its larger geographic and economic context, specific issues, the policymaking demands that ministers and parliamentarians both face. It's an excellent introduction to the political science of the nation, and this provides crucial context for you in what you do today.

Absolutely. I think this is where you gain the skills you need. What you do not learn, of course, is how to manage an agency. In this regard I was in a very favorable position when I was head of the general policy division because I had accompanied Ulf Böge, my predecessor, for some time, and I was someone who, in my capacity as head of general policy, did not only look at general policy. I was also very interested in things like how to hire people, whom to hire, all these things that the general department does in fact. So I was very interested in the Bundeskartellamt overall and not only my tasks. Then, of course, I also had the chance to accompany Bernhard Heitzer, my predecessor as President, and I was already deeply involved in many of these questions. That helps a lot, of course, when you come into the position to do it yourself.

So it's a tremendous advantage also to have been in the agency that you are now going to head.

Yes. I also could have moved on to another agency because it was not so much about learning how to deal with the Bundeskartellamt; it was about how to manage an agency. If it had taken me to another agency, I could have benefited a lot from what I had learned from my predecessors and what I had learned in previous jobs.

You learn about how to deal with personnel issues; you get a sense, as you said, of budgeting and resource allocation; you learn the basic sets of rules and procedures that public institutions live by. And having the opportunity to work side by side with the head of the institution – with Ulf, with Dr. Heitzer, with both – that gives you the chance vicariously to see what this job really demands.

Yes, and then you have a chance to develop your own style because everyone would lead the Bundeskartellamt differently. It's a question of personality. Then you have the time. But that only happens once you have actually gotten into that position, and you have a good opportunity to lead the agency because, luckily enough, maybe you have the skills and maybe you have learned enough to do the job.

I realize that within the Bundeskartellamt authority is distributed in a very fundamental way to the decision-making chambers. You don't decide which cases to bring. You don't decide how to bring them. That is dedicated to the chambers, so in one sense you do not directly decide what the Bundeskartellamt shall do. But you do have responsibility for speaking to larger policy issues, to spell out a vision perhaps of what the institution might accomplish. When you came into the position of President, did you have in some form a list of things you wanted to do? What were your ambitions for the Bundeskartellamt when you arrived on the day that your mandate became effective?

Of course you have ideas, you've been watching what others have been doing over time, and then you have a chance to rethink: "Would I do it the same way, or would I do it differently?" Of course you have some ideas. You always do. On the other hand, being in that position is quite different from not being in that position.

What's different about it?

The difference is that you are the one who has the responsibility. If something goes wrong, you get the call. It's not someone else who gets the call; it's you. You are accountable to the Ministry, accountable to policymakers, to the business community. Everyone is blaming you if it goes wrong, and if it goes well it rarely happens that people say you've done a good job. That is the key difference, the sole responsibility for what is happening in the Bundeskartellamt. That is the huge difference. I think nobody who doesn't have that responsibility can imagine what it's like. You have to experience it before you really can relate to this sentiment.

Is that sometimes a lonely job?

No, no, no. It's not a lonely job.

Is it intimidating in some ways?

No, it's not intimidating. It's not lonely. I have a lot of highly skilled colleagues who support me. I'm not someone who's sitting in his room making a lonely decision. I listen to people a lot. I listen a lot, and then I try to take the right decision, and when I take it, I hope that I have listened to everyone whom I should listen to. That doesn't make you lonely, I think.

On that, can you talk a bit about your philosophy and a bit more about how you take decisions, what kind of consultation you go through before you reach the point at which you're ready to decide yourself?

It's mainly discussions with many people. Of course, there's a very intensive dialogue with my Vice President, Konrad Ost. There's an intensive dialogue with the head of general policy. When it comes to cases, you have a very intensive exchange with the heads of the competition units, those who decide on the cases; and that's vice versa, it's a give and take. In the very end, when you take a decision, you should have listened to all of these people. When it comes to changes at the Bundeskartellamt, structural, organizational, in my experience you are very well-advised to listen to those who are ultimately subject to these decisions to make sure that the decisions work well in practice. I'm a hands-on man, I always want to know: "will this work in practice?", and not "what would theoretically be the best thing to do?". By the way, this also applies to the International Competition Network (ICN). I always want to know what works best in practice. I think I'm really someone who listens, and then I take a decision, and I hope it's well-founded.

Inside the house, what kind of methods do you use to communicate to the larger staff of the institution to lay out what you feel to be the goals for the institution, to obtain feedback from the entire body that you have? You're not a tiny agency; you're a substantial organization. What do you do to stay in touch with those people from the engine room up to the bridge of the ship? What do you do to communicate your views, to talk to them, to bring the entire team in a particular direction?

We have various fora where we meet. I meet with all the heads of the decision divisions, with all the heads of the Bundeskartellamt's units. We also have smaller circles where we debate. Sometimes we have a long debate about cases, about organizational issues, about general policy to find a line within the house. There, you learn a lot. There, you really get to hear from everyone around the table what the problems are. We are a very informal authority. Normally, if someone says, "My door is always open," you can never speak to them; at least that's my experience. I try to do that differently. I never say that "my door is always open," but I hope it is open. We have very informal exchanges, and I think that is maybe a bit different than in many other authorities. Whenever something is at stake, they give me a call, they come in, and we discuss the issue.

If I'm a case handler and I want to talk to you, how do I do that?

If you're a case handler and you want to talk to me, there are several ways to do this. You can give me a call and ask me if you can talk to me. That happens rarely because this means you are skipping one level, the head of your decision division. So normally, it's the head of the decision division who gives me that call. But if it is a personal matter or something else, people come to me or to Konrad Ost.

Or I just have an idea about what we can do better, maybe it's a matter of organization practice, and I just want to meet the President.

I think that is a case where the door has to be open. You receive an email, you meet people at the agency and they say, "Do you have five minutes?" I know the people who work for us very well. I do hope that I'm a person who is easy to approach. But there is no institutionalized way of doing this. We also meet twice a year with the entire staff to discuss things. At irregular intervals, I have breakfast with the agency's junior staff members to inform them about career chances and to discuss all kinds of things. So there are quite many mechanisms.

And many of these, as you said, are things you choose. These are part of your personality.

Sure. That's what I believe in. That is why I say everyone has to find their own way of doing this. Maybe I do it in a quite personal manner.

When you came and you mentioned that indeed you had been thinking about things that you wanted to do before you became the President, what general directions did you want to take the agency in? What did you want to add to the mix? Of course, you have a well-established program. If you were a commercial enterprise, you have successful products, and no new manager would decide not to produce them, but you might decide to do variants; you might decide to add something else. In general terms, what did you want to do in the time ahead for you?

One thing was that I wanted to do more economics. The Bundeskartellamt was said to be lagging behind a little bit in terms of economics for some time. I did not think this was true. What I thought is that there is not enough visibility for economics. Mr. Heitzer, my predecessor, had already started doing that. He had set up a stand-alone unit dealing with economic issues. So that already existed as a nucleus. But what I did pretty fast was to have more resources assigned to this task because I really wanted this unit to give good advice to the decision units on economic issues. Be that in a merger case or an abuse case, we received elaborate expertise on economics, and we had to make sure we were in a position to assess this properly. That was the strongest wish I had when I became President, to do more in terms of economics.

The digital economy is another big topic. Today, we have a digital economy unit within our general policy division, we can look back at successful enforcement in the digital sector, and agencies as well as policy makers around the world are very active in this area. But I remember very well how it all started: as a first step I established a think tank and we did extensive and pioneering groundwork. This means that I had to dedicate resources and – difficult to imagine today – convince colleagues that we need to focus on digital issues. I believe that this is an essential role of a head of agency, to identify the topics of the future at an early stage and go for them.

Another thing was that I thought we needed more teamwork. With regard to important cases we should be able to have more people working on each specific case.

May I ask what you had to do to create the flexibility to move your resources in the direction that you wanted?

That was not only a question of flexibility; it was a question of resources. If you want to build up a team, you have to have the people for that team. That was a very important feature, but approval on this had to come from outside. We needed more staff. That was another thing. I talked to policymakers. I went to Parliament, to the Ministry, and said, "Listen, if you want us to do good work, you have to invest. It's as easy as that." We were lucky enough that we received that support. People understood that. We received staff. But this is an ongoing process, and we still need new staff. Meanwhile, the Bundeskartellamt has been given new competences and responsibilities. This concerns the application of extended abuse control rules regarding digital companies, consumer protection, the Competition Register for Public Procurement, which has been in full operation since June 2022. And the list goes on. Also, the integration of new staff needs to be well organized. There was a time when there were around thirty people coming in all at the same time. That was very demanding. To give you an example, when we moved from Berlin to Bonn in 1999, we arrived in Bonn with 220 people and today we count up to a bit more than 400. I am confident that we will further increase our staff numbers over the next one or two years if everything goes well. There is some growth, and we could convince policymakers through our work that this would be a good investment.

Another thing was that I thought we needed more legal advice from those who represented the Bundeskartellamt before the courts every day because they were the ones who knew best what the courts want. You only know that very well if you have been representing an agency before the courts a couple of times. This is an area we expanded, too. If you want to put it this way, we increased coordination and mutual support between the units within the agency.

There is a great deal of discussion in academic literature and public discussion about the importance of autonomy for a competition agency in making decisions, certainly deciding how to use its powers to prosecute and to investigate. Sometimes those decisions are taken to suggest that the agency should be in some way aloof from the political process, separate from it, no routine interaction with ministers, with parliamentarians. Yet, your experience sheds light on how that routine interaction isn't simply optional but perhaps is vital to the effectiveness of the agency. I take it that this engagement with the larger environment is indispensable to what you do.

Of course. We are not a political body. Everybody knows that. We are an independent agency, but we are embedded in a political context. That is very clear. You need to be in contact with the policymakers, with the stakeholders. You need to know what is going on, what are their demands, even though you are an independent agency. I'll give you an example. When this issue of digitalization came up many years ago, of course our intention to do something in this area was met by the demand from policymakers that we do something in this area. You're not well-advised to take up everything that is coming from the political arena – that's not the point – but to ignore everything that is going on in the political arena, that's not the point either. So you have to find a balance in what you want to do and what you are expected to do. I think we always hit that balance very well. But in order to know that, you have to have an eye and an ear in the political arena and you have to talk to these people and know what is going on.

They're not doing the talking.

They're not doing the contacts in the political sphere. That is me, and I'm kind of a transmission mechanism between what is going on in Berlin and what is going on in Bonn, carrying to Bonn what I hear in Berlin, carrying to Berlin what we do in Bonn, and explaining what we are doing in Bonn. From my perspective, the worst you could do is believe that independence means you are in a kind of bubble and have nothing to do with the rest of the world.

You also have to listen to what is happening in the business community. Not in the sense of doing what the business community wants you to do, but you have to know at least what their demands are, what is seen as a deficiency, and then you can make up your mind: is it a deficiency, and do I have to take action; or maybe it's just an interest-driven complaint in which case I do not have to do anything? In any case you have to know what's going on, and this is why I think it's so important to listen, listen, listen, and to judge for yourself what is interest-driven and what is something that you need to fix.

If I can turn to your ongoing conversation with political leaders, tell me more about how that takes place. Do you have a regular habit of going to specific officials with responsibility for oversight? Do they seek you out? Are there formal mechanisms by which you routinely interact? Can you tell me more about the way in which you carry out your conversation with what I'll just generally describe as the political decision-makers?

That is purely demand-driven. There is, of course, some routine with the Economics Ministry. There's a unit that is in charge of competition law, and you know these people very well. There's a close exchange. Also, formalized in a certain way, the general policy division meets at regular intervals with the unit that is in charge of competition law. I know the Secretary of State of course, I know the head of the division that is in charge of competition policy, but we do not have any institutionalized talks. We meet irregularly, but that is an intensive exchange.

They know how to get in touch with you.

Of course. For the time being, the contacts are very intensive because of the latest amendment of the German competition law. And sometimes, of course, you need to be in touch with the budget people, with those in Parliament who are in charge of your budget, to explain that you need an extra budget, you need some more resources, you need staff, and so on. These contacts are not really institutionalized, but they take place frequently.

You mentioned before that you are the public face of the agency; you are the person onstage now with the spotlight focused on you. One element in that spotlight, the illumination is the media, and in many different settings you are the person speaking to journalists, broadcast organizations, any number of others. Was that a difficult adjustment for you, going into the role of being the spokesperson on that scale, where people watch everything you do, they listen to everything you say, they probably keep track of what color tie you're wearing every day of the week? What's it like being onstage in that way, and how do you deal with the responsibility for being the voice of the authority?

That is a twofold issue. On the one hand, I like doing that. That is maybe because I'm not a very formal person. If I give a speech in front of many people and make a mistake, I just say, "Oh, sorry, I just made a mistake. I should have said it differently." Even with the media, when I said something and I was not right, I would stop and say, "Oh, no, forget about that. We have to do it differently." That helped me a lot. I like talking to the media. On the other hand, I was very much aware, of course, that your word and what you say has a different weight if you have a certain position. If you speak on behalf of an important agency, you have to take care of what you say and, even more, how you say it. You have to be very much aware – and that was my greatest fear, and still is my fear sometimes – that sometimes it even materializes that you say something very correctly and very clearly, but someone who has a certain interest in this matter interprets your words in a way that is simply incorrect, but a media person will do that on purpose.

Have you seen a way to address that, or is that just a cost of doing business?

That's the cost of doing business. You cannot go to a newspaper and say, "Listen, don't do that again." They know what they have done. They know that you are not happy. Nevertheless, they did it. It doesn't make sense to make this an issue. You can only hope it works better next time.

I'm gathering that with the frequency with which you do speak in public, the many occasions in which you speak to a larger audience, maybe a smaller one, individual journalists, that collectively an accurate impression of what you're trying to convey one hopes comes across.

Of course. I think this is a very important job that I do, given the enormous power that a competition agency has – you can prohibit a merger, maybe an important merger; you can impose fines amounting to hundreds of millions of euros.

Yes, you can do things that hurt.

You cannot do that – and here I quote Philip Lowe – "like a cat that comes out of the bush from time to time". These kinds of powers need an underlying foundation and they need explanation. You shouldn't surprise people; they should expect that you do certain things from time to time. They only expect itxif you communicate your task and communicate what you do, why you do it, and how you do it. This is why talking to the media is really important for the acceptance of our work. I always say I don't do that for my own sake or for anybody's sake. I really do that to explain our work and in order to sleep well once we take a decision. And I sleep well before the day we announce it to the public because I know the public will in the best case say, "Well done"; in the worst case, they say, "Ah, here they go again." But what they should never say is, "Which agency? Why? Why is this happening? Where did this come from? Who is this?" That is not the way to do it.

As you're suggesting, the process of communicating your themes, your expectations, your program, goes on every day, and it has to be reinforced all the time that you're engaged in a continuing discussion about what you're doing, and engaging your colleagues, who also appear in different settings, to communicate collectively repeatedly the message about what you want to do.

Yes, that is very important. It also doesn't make sense to give an interview once a year and that's it. I have the aim to regularly raise awareness, through cases if possible. That is the best basis to gain the audience. But also by giving interviews on specific competition policy issues, being part of the conference circus, giving speeches to the business community as well and explaining what we do and why we do it. Generally speaking, what I'm striving for is kind of a general presence – not so much in the media, but a general presence in the mind of our stakeholders – by repeatedly talking through the media or being present at conferences, giving speeches and so on.

What's the hardest part of the job for you?

The hardest part of the job is that it is a lot of work. I think my way of leading an agency includes a lot of work. You can't steer an agency by saying, "You, do this, and you, do that." That doesn't work at all at the Bundeskartellamt. You have to convince people. It's persuasion. It's about having good arguments. It's about knowing the case. It's about knowing where you want to go. I think that's a hard part of the job. But I also think that this is very fruitful because it's an exchange of views between me, the general policy division, the legal department, and the decision divisions, always respecting the independence of the decision divisions, and in the very end, if feasible, we come to a good decision.

You have to explain it.

Yes. As I said, you can't tell anybody what to do. We have decision divisions who reach their decisions like a court, with a chairman and two rapporteurs.

They're quite proud of that responsibility.

They are proud of this responsibility. I would never interfere with it, but I want to be heard and I want to have an opportunity to introduce my arguments if necessary. It's not about taking the lead but about making the best possible decision. That's maybe the hardest part of the job, trying to lead through convincing people, through persuasion, through having good arguments. But, as I said, we have many cases every year, and for that you have to know and do a lot of stuff.

In a difficult schedule, which includes this element of preparation, engagement, discussion, how do you take time for yourself to restore your energy, to renew yourself, to read? Instead of facing the next event, addressing the next crisis, being the fire department where the alarm goes off and the truck goes out, how do you keep time to rejuvenate your own spirit and to restore your intellectual capital?

That is a difficult part as well. It's probably the same for everyone in that kind of job. You are permanently on-air and there's very little time for absorbing. I'm German, and I like sitting in a car. I'll tell you why. For example, when I go from Bonn to Paris for an Organisation for Economic Cooperation and Development (OECD) meeting, I sit in a car for six hours. It's the perfect time to absorb. You can read; you can think. Creating these kinds of islands during the day is very important. Friday afternoon is a good time for that as well – not that there's nobody in the office; there are still very many people – but there's a sense of calming down before the weekend.

Do your colleagues sense on Friday afternoon that Andreas is reading, Friday afternoon's not the best time to walk in and say, "I want to talk about" –

I would say it's the other way around. They know I'm sitting in my office reading and they think this could be the perfect time.

Perfect time to come in.

That happens, of course. Some are better at this than others. But then I take my time to do this. I know a judge who says of himself, "I have so little time;

I always tell everybody I don't have time." I do it exactly the other way round because I never have time. You never have time in that job. Where should it come from?

If you do, something's wrong.

I say, "Yes, of course I have time and of course we should discuss this issue; maybe not at this very moment, but we should definitely discuss this." It is difficult to find these islands of silence where you really have the time to reflect on something. It also happens when you're on holiday, on vacation. It's not that you don't think about these things when you're somewhere else. What I enjoy very, very much is the debate with the people around me because usually we develop ideas together. Sometimes it's you who gives the impulse. I think this is the key issue of leadership, to try to anticipate where to go, what to do, what is going to happen, how to react. I often do that in discussions with my people and we try to develop a good idea together.

My next-to-last question deals with another complication in your life. This would be a difficult job if it just involved Germany, and if Germany was in isolation and you were only doing things related to work specifically within your own office. But you do more. You've been the Chair of the International Competition Network (ICN) Steering Committee for several years. As part of the ICN responsibility you go to lots of events outside of Germany. You participate in lots of conferences. You go to the OECD meetings. There's the European Competition Network. I suspect if you wanted to let your calendar run wild, you could be out of the office every day of the week – and, of course, you don't do that – but how do you manage these two lives? In a sense they're integrated, they're related, but the people of Germany to some extent pay you to be at your desk and doing your job in Bonn. How do you manage to combine this contribution to the larger international world with the very demanding job you have in Bonn?

You always have one first priority, and that is to run an agency. That is always the top priority. That is the most important issue. The international work is also ranking extremely high. It matters a lot how we cooperate worldwide and how we communicate. And I like working internationally. I headed the international unit of the Bundeskartellamt for a couple of years. I like the exchange with my colleagues and the international community. But I always try to keep the balance between Bonn and the world. There are some events that I participate in. Of course, the ICN is extremely important; for me, the annual conference is the most important conference of the year – except for my own conference that we host in Berlin every two years. In 2022, we combined both conferences. But to be frank, when I'm at an ICN annual conference, I always have the feeling, well, this is your conference, and you're in charge of everything, and everyone else seems to be of the same opinion. Sometimes the Wi-Fi doesn't work, and there were representatives, delegates, who came to me and said, "Andreas, the Wi-Fi is not working." I said to them, "Well, I'm very happy about your trust in me, but I really cannot help you." So, you have your priorities. There is the ICN conference. There are the OECD meetings in Paris that are held two times a year. There are the meetings of the Directors General at the European level in Brussels where we meet two times a year. That is the workload you are dealing with every year. You are right, if I wanted, I could travel 365 days a year. That wouldn't work. And I also have to give speeches in Germany, which is not an international task, but also keeps you away from your office.

I give a lot of speeches in Germany. So it's really a question of priorities, but you never know which kind of invitation is coming in. A conference you usually attend can all of a sudden become uninteresting if the right people are not there, if the topics are not interesting, and then you might decide not to attend and go somewhere else instead. What is difficult is long-distance traveling. Paris is easier, it's one or two days; we can go there easily. The same is true for Brussels or Berlin. Sometimes I start in the morning and after lunch I'm back in my office. Such issues also play a decisive role. But I would say I travel much less than many people think.

Has this international engagement made a difference in how you think about your own agency and what you do?

Sure. I learn very, very much. To give you an example, when I joined the agency back in 2000, my predecessor, Ulf Böge, went to an OECD meeting that was about leniency and leniency programs. With him was the head of our general policy division, and Mr. Böge asked him, "Why don't we make a contribution here?" The head of the general policy division said, "Because we don't have a leniency program." I have always liked that story because you see how much you can learn. You go to a conference and somebody says, "Well, we do it this way." I go home and I ask people, "Are we doing this?" And they say, "Well, we have just started." No one ever says, "No"; it's always, "We have just started." Then you can drive it forward. There are so many good ideas out there.

There are a lot of smart people around the world working on this.

Absolutely. What is important to me as well is that it's not only me who is traveling. For every bigger event, for example in Brussels, we take care that one or two staff members attend the event. It's very important that I learn about what is going on, but sometimes it's maybe even more important that case handlers and the heads of our decision divisions know what is going on. This is very important because otherwise – well, in Germany we say, "You are stewing in your own juice". This could be a delicious stew, but some ingredients from the outside might make it even better. There's so much to learn. It is not wasted time, it's about learning things, and this is work I can only recommend to everyone.

Final question for you: you're talking to your successor and they ask, "What should I know starting out?" What would you tell them?

That is a very difficult question because if everything works well, I still have a long time to go, so I rarely think about my successor. What I would do is I would try to make two things clear. First, the Bundeskartellamt is a wonderful agency. Why is this so? This is because the people are independent, and this gives all staff members an enormous intrinsic motivation to achieve things. This, you must understand, you must have trust in them, trust them to do it right, and I trust my people to do it right. To convey to my successor this feeling, this trust in the agency, might be one of the most important issues because I believe that if you want people to deliver good work, you have only one chance, and that is motivation, motivation, motivation. That is the only way it works. I try to be motivating, but that means that you leave responsibility with these people.

My second advice would be to keep in mind how important it is to stay in touch with the stakeholders. When I say stakeholders I am not only referring to the Ministry, not only to Parliament. It is equally important to be in contact with and to explain things to the business community and to the broader public. This would be my very serious advice: don't stay in your office and think we're so good that nothing can go wrong. If you're good, you need to explain it to the outside world; and if something goes wrong, you have to explain that, too. But do explain and communicate. That would be my second advice because I think these are the key pillars on which my work relies. Whether or not your successor will follow your advice, you never know. As I said, everyone does it differently.

I would say that a new appointee who took those two things to heart – understand the culture and the basic DNA of the institution they're coming into; don't stay in your office; and recognize your responsibility virtually every day of the week.

If I may add to that, sitting in the ICN Steering Group and steering the ICN sometimes feels very much like steering the Bundeskartellamt and sitting in front of these self-reliant heads of our decision divisions. At the ICN, you also have a group of people, self-reliant heads of agencies. The difference is not so huge.

Maureen Ohlhausen*

US Federal Trade Commission, Commissioner (2012-2018) & Acting Chairperson (2017-2018)

You were the acting chair of the Federal Trade Commission from 2017 to 2018. Along with that, you also were a member of the Federal Trade Commission from 2012 to 2018, you also held a host of different positions within the agency in the general counsel's office: attorney advisor to Commissioner Orson Swindle, the Director of the Office of Policy Planning, and before that, one of the principal administrators in that office. In short, you have seen the ship of the Federal Trade Commission from the engine room all the way up to the bridge. We're delighted to have you with us today. To begin with, we're very much interested in what knowledge you can bring to the subject of how to be a member of an agency in a key leadership position. I would like to take you to the time when you became a member of the board, the commission. What experiences in your life prepared you for that position, to come to the agency, to be a member of the college of 5 that oversees the operations of the commission?

There are 2 types of experiences that I had which really helped me prepare. The first one was when I worked at the US Court of Appeals for the DC Circuit, as a staff attorney and as a law clerk to Judge David Sentelle. As an appellate court, it is typically a multi-member body working in three-judge

* Interview conducted on 21 November 2018.

panels. Working in that repeat play situation, where the judge may agree or disagree with his or her colleagues on a particular decision, but then has to move on to the next matter. That dynamic was very important to me.

At the Federal Trade Commission, as you mentioned, I had a host of different jobs. I was in the general counsel's office and I was an attorney advisor to a Commissioner. Especially being the head of the Office of Policy Planning helped me for my future work as a Commissioner. There, I went from reviewing other people's work, to being responsible for coming up with ideas for where the Federal Trade Commission should be going in new areas. These may involve new industry knowledge that we needed, new legal doctrines to get up to speed on, or where we wanted to make changes in the law, like the state action doctrine or Noerr-Pennington doctrine, or technological changes like online commerce, issues like that.

In those jobs, I had to figure out what was the agency's power; what kind of contacts did it need to understand the new issues; how did we get the knowledge and perform the research that we needed to do; and how to do it in a way that would get bipartisan agreement at the FTC. Finally, how to get a useful product out of it at the end, typically, a report; a brief or an advocacy filing. I think those two sets of experiences are really crucial for me.

The Policy of Planning Office had a specific mandate within the agency to do that, looking over the horizon to anticipate new developments, didn't it?

Exactly. It was a job that had no inbox. There weren't matters walking in the door that you had to deal with. You had to come up with the ideas of where we should be going as an agency. For example, we did all the competition advocacy work, but there were new areas that were being developed, such as telemedicine. For that, I had to get a handle on licensing for people, like nurse practitioners, who might be performing the telemedicine services. It also involved things like online sales of goods, such as contact lenses. Another issue that was very important had to do with the convergence of our communication systems. I was the head of the internet access task force and looked at the issues as formerly separate areas of competition, such as cable systems, telephone systems, online, all started converging and competing with each other. In question were the right responses for competition law and consumer protection law.

How did you and your office start to focus on what now or popularly discussed is the digital economy, the new information economy? You were there very early. You were there not quite 20 years ago, but in the early part of the previous decade. What led you into that area as a key area of concern?

The FTC has a long history of looking at competition problems that are arising because of out of date regulations or regulatory responses from competitors and it had previously looked at taxicab regulations and optometric sales. Building on that and looking at how the new economy of online sales was causing the same kind of disruptions that the commission had paid attention to in the past. Very early on in our tenure, we talked to folks who were paying attention to this as an overarching development in the economy, not just in a single industry. They called it disintermediation, which was a long word, but the idea was that the traditional middlemen were being disrupted and pushed out and challenged. They would have to compete harder and they were looking for regulatory responses to fend off those new forms of competition.

How does an agency do best in finding out what is going on out there? That is these are changes, the common critique, a regulatory agency of competition agencies that you're riding along in a bicycle. The world is going by you in a formula one racer, things are happening so fast that the agencies are looking backward. How do you stay abreast of developments? What do you do to stay in a position to know what is going on?

It takes real effort. You can't just talk to the same old characters that you talk to all the time, the echo chamber of people who are just your friends and the people of your little community at the Federal Trade Commission, or even in the antitrust community. You have to reach out and talk to people in the technology space. I did a lot of just going to events, calling people.

Do you go to events that are outside the field of vision of the traditional competition policy? Do you go to events that are not antitrust meetings or conferences? Where do you go beyond this?

Yes, you go outside of that box. The other thing that I did was pay attention to developments as a consumer myself and how I was experiencing the world. I have children who are in their 20s and early 30s. I would talk to them and ask "How do you engage in commerce? How do you get information?" I would call up people and say "Hey, would you like to have coffee? I'm interested in what you're doing." This way I built a contact base. I remember once going out for coffee with someone who was at a trade association. I hadn't brought my notebook with me. He gave me so many good ideas and so many names of people that I should be talking to. I was scribbling it down on the back of a paper menu. It was invaluable because he pointed me towards a great source of information. I reached out to people who are both sides of these issues, and got much more immersed in it. That is how I had to do it over and over again. It doesn't always show up on your doorstep. The other thing is, once you do that, once you start talking to people and they know you're interested, they will come to you. Some of the great opportunities arose that way, for example, in the work that we did in the state action doctrine.

When I started looking at these issues about a new delivery system for healthcare, we found out that there was an issue going on with dental hygienists in South Carolina, and that the state legislature wanted to expand dental healthcare access to poor school children. The legislature had rescinded the law that required that a dentist had to be on site for cleanings and screenings. It applied for each treatment where hygienists go to a school, do an evaluation, clean the children's teeth and give them a sealant or a fluoride treatment. The dental hygienists were then the ones who were going to be doing these treatments. The dental board didn't like that the legislature had opened this up for a competition through a change in law. The dentists had an emergency regulation that put the law back into place. The hygienists came to us saying that this is a problem. They approached us because they knew that I was the one in the Office of Policy Planning who was looking into expanding healthcare access. We were able to bring a case, which eventually settled, but then, once people knew we were interested in this area, that led to the North Carolina dental case involving tooth cleaning. That went all the way up to the Supreme Court.

We would say a very successful outcome for the Federal Trade Commission.

A very successful outcome. When we did our workshop in 2001 about online competition, we examined different industry segments: contact lenses, caskets, and real estate was one of them. That signaled to people we were interested in this issue. As these anti-competitive things were happening in those markets, people reached out to us. That led to future enforcement actions from the FTC as well.

These are long-term investments, are they not? This is the life cycle between the first commitment to do work in this area and the litigation successes.

Yes, for many years. Over a decade for some of these matters. I worked on the task force to clarify the State Action Doctrine, do the research, write a report for the commission, look for the kind of cases that would generate the kinds of legal issues that then could move through the courts. Ultimately, this work resulted in 2 Supreme Court victories clarifying it. Then, as the Acting Chairman, I tried to put into action what the Supreme Court had done in these cases to further enforcement actions that are now, again, working their way through the courts. It's an iterative cycle, but you have to lay down the intellectual foundation, and then find the right cases to apply it to. Then, win those cases or lose them and then win them eventually, one hopes, on appeal.

It seems to me that a crucial part of the life cycle that you're describing is one where you have to take a long-term view, you have to be willing to make major investments at the beginning of that life cycle. The good things that happened later on, all built upon the accumulation of effort that reaches back quite away.

That's absolutely right. I always told my staff "We're playing the long game here. This is not a short-term, dip-in and hope for a quick outcome. Just make a splash and then move on without some follow on." I would always say "We need to start with the end in mind." Not that we prejudge any particular cases, but what is the goal that we're trying to achieve? It's always better outcomes for consumers, but what are the competition problems that we're seeing that we need to solve? Then, work backwards from there. How do we get there? Obviously, you have to change the law or clarify the law. There are different ways to do that. We have to lay that foundation first, but one of the things that I always recommended was "Start with the end in mind and then work backwards from there."

How do you coax the agency to make that long-term commitment that is certainly in Washington, maybe in other cities, the long-term is maybe a month away. The very long-term is 6 months. Indeterminately long project is one year. There are a lot of pressures, cultural, political, personal, and otherwise that press you to look for things that create good ribbon-cutting ceremonies, but without necessarily doing enough to build the road that's going to go with the ribbon-cutting. How do you persuade the institution to make the investment that will yield good results over the longer term?

The way I did it, when I was the head of the Office of Policy Planning, which was a small office. We had 5 attorneys working directly for me and one admin. I assembled teams from throughout the agency. The way I did that was by explaining why it would be beneficial to those parts of the agencies. For the economists, I explained that this could spin off really interesting economic research that they could get published. For the litigators I said "This may lead to cases where you will win." That's really how I did it. I made the case to other parts within the agency about why it would be in their interest. Even once I became a Commissioner and the Acting Chairman, I still had to explain why this is good for competition, good for consumers. Once you have developed a good reputation from being able to deliver on these things, then it makes it a lot easier. Once you've had a few appellate victories in the cases, once you've brought that makes it easier. For example, in the online wine sales issue, we did a report on that topic that the Supreme Court cited extensively.

These were restrictions that individual states imposed on the shipment of wine across borders using internet-based sales.

That's right. This grew out of our disintermediation through an internet online sales project. It was an issue where we couldn't bring the case directly because these were state laws, not actions by private actors, and they were not subject to federal antitrust oversight. So what we did was create the research to show what their impact was on competition and on consumers. We did research about what prices were in states that had these restrictions versus those that didn't have these restrictions, and documented the value of online shipping, in quality, in variety, in price for consumers. Then, the other issue here involved concerns that online sales would facilitate underage drinking. We did research in a state that allowed online wine sales and asked "Do you have this problem?" They said they didn't and we compiled their answers into a report. The issue came up before the Supreme Court on a dormant commerce clause challenge, and when the Supreme Court was deciding the matter, they said the restrictions on online interstate wine sales discriminated against interstate commerce, but then had to decide if such discrimination is necessary to protect consumers. It drew on our report and came out in favor of more competition.

I think the court cited your report over 20 times.

Yes. When you have something like this happening you can explain "Here is the type of policy work and research that we're doing, even if it doesn't itself result in a case, here is how it can move the law along, or the policy, or regulation, to help consumers." That is a powerful argument for continuing to invest in those kinds of projects.

There are a lot of discussions about how important an advocacy function is to the effectiveness of the competition agency. I take it from what you're saying that a crucial foundation to be effective as an advocate is to do your homework. That it works best if it's based on this research platform that you've developed over time [...] You don't get anywhere by just saying, "Competition is good."

No, it is so superficial that way. You have to offer something more, you have to offer expertise and knowledge, whether it's research the agency has done, or research of the agency that has drawn upon what others have done. I think that is so often what makes the difference, what tips the balance for regulators who are trying to make these hard decisions about what is the right approach to take.

There is a huge discussion today about what competition policy can do for small businesses. What it can do for people suffering from economic disadvantage. Am I right that a significant number of the matters that you worked on in the advocacy capacity is the Director of the Office of Policy Planning, as one of the senior managers before that, that the beneficiaries of many of these initiatives happen to be small enterprises, medium-sized enterprises, end consumers who are people with lesser means and lesser advantage?

Absolutely. I think that that was something very important to creating the support for the programs that we were doing. Big companies can often invest in creating this kind of information or research, or campaign for their interests. Public choice theory teaches us that anti-competitive regulatory outcomes are most likely when the benefit from the anti-competitive regulation is concentrated and the downside, the negatives or costs are diffused. How do you have a unified voice? How do you get that viewpoint out there for small business, for individuals? We've done things for people who are on the bottom end of the economic ladder and they're trying to take that first step. When I was the Acting Chairman, the economic liberty task force that I founded was based on that idea of letting the little guy into the economy. These regulations, particularly state occupational licensing, have run wild, and it is really hurting this part of our population. Veterans who want to start a business, hair braiders, florists. I mean, it's just a small town people.

People not knocked up by wealthy venture capitalists tossing billions at them to get started.

Exactly. That is really, really important because those voices are not being recognized in the regulatory discussion. To have an agency like the Federal Trade Commission through our advocacy function and through our enforcement function, we can possibly have a hook into antitrust enforcement and I think helps rebalance the debate.

I wonder whether competition agencies have focused enough on making clear to outside audiences that this is a major dividend from a good advocacy program. That this connection with ordinary citizens is an important product of what a good advocacy program can do.

It's very tempting just to focus on the big cases, the big merger or the big enforcement action. Those are important and you should do a good job with them. Any competition agency needs to get those right. But doing those alone leaves something out of the equation, which is the value of competition to having a dynamic economy for small entrepreneurs, for mom-and-pop kind of businesses, for the individual who is just trying to start a small business. Whether it's hair braiding, horse massage or teeth whitening, these are all the first step on the economic ladder. We should be paying attention to those things too, not just the big cases that grab the headlines.

The day comes when you get the call. The question is are you interested in being considered to be nominated, to be a member of the Federal Trade Commission? Happily, that process works its way in a successful way. Good outcome, you get the nomination, you're confirmed, you take office. What changes for you when you become a member of the board as opposed to an adviser to a member of the board, the senior manager, what is different about becoming a member of the board itself?

The first thing that I had to do as a Commissioner, after all this hoopla, everybody leaves and you get the first matter on your desk. The first thing for me was to sign a civil investigative demand, which is basically the administrative version of a subpoena. I said to myself "I'm here asking an American citizen to provide information under penalty of law because I'm signing my name to this." I found that was an enormous responsibility.

For the compulsory process requests a member of the commission does sign the instrument?

Yes, exactly. That's what I found over and over again in every decision that I had to make. I felt the responsibility of the office, where under the power of the US federal government, I am saying "You 2 companies cannot merge," or "You have to stop your behavior," or "You have to pay a lot of money and change what you're doing." I found that moving from being someone who recommends that others take action to being the one who's actually taking the action, was a big responsibility. I felt that burden, an obligation to try my hardest to get it right.

Being part of a college is different from being the single administrator who heads the institution. Those are different experiences. You mentioned the time you had as a law clerk for the US Court of Appeals for the District of Columbia, watching panels, working for an individual member of that court, seeing how the court deliberates, seeing how it works. How important is it if you're going to be appointed to be on a board to have had some experience either being on another tribunal of that kind or watching firsthand how the board works? How important do you think it is being an effective member of the board that you have an initial understanding of how that is a different world with different demands?

For me, it was an experience that I found invaluable, that I had seen the court in action and then understood how it worked at the FTC. As I said, it's a repeat game. You have all these decisions to make with the same people. When I was in the advocacy office, I would remind my staff, "We have to go back to that well every day." How you treat other people is important. I thought it was important to be clear about where I thought things should go and where I didn't agree and to suggest where there was common ground and try to move towards that common ground. Not just say "No. You'll never get my vote." Or "No" without being clear about where the lines were for me, but to try to work constructively to find where there could be agreement.

I think that is a very important part of being effective on a multi-member body. Particularly, for most of my time at the Commission, and I was a Commissioner for 6 years. I was in the majority at the commission for about 4 months of that entire time. How do you operate in that situation? Even as the Acting Chairman, it was just myself and my colleague Terrell McSweeney.

The two of you?

The two of us, one Republican and one Democrat. My experience of being a Commissioner in the minority party for most of my tenure was very helpful for me because I had some experience in operating that kind of system. It helped me be effective in operating by saying, "Here's where I think we can reach agreement and I won't move the goalposts." Continually moving the goalposts makes it hard for people to deal with. I had my firm lines that I wouldn't cross, but people understood where they were and why.

When you disagreed, how did you communicate that? That is to be a good colleague, is there a way to disagree with your colleagues that is more palatable and effective than others?

I think for one thing just being very clear about where the lines were and why, why the lines were there. How I interpreted cases and what was influencing my decisions so that they could understand. If there was room to reach an agreement, we could. Certainly, the fact that we are in this repeating environment means it was very important to be respectful to people. I always appreciated when people treated me that way. That was an important part of my experience.

I assume, talk to the other person privately individually to say "Here is what I'm thinking", instead of letting them read about it in the newspaper.

Yes. I think it's important to build that trust. When people had said to me, "How have you been an effective Commissioner when you're not in the majority?" I said, "It's all about trust." That's another way to build trust with people.

Is it difficult to be a subsidiary member of the board that is – The chair is the chief operating officer, the others are Commissioners. Only one of these people has the word chairman in their name. Is there something frustrating or limiting about being basically a Commissioner as opposed to the chair? Something that you have to anticipate and to come to grips with over your time in the office?

There can be. You need to think carefully about how you can make a contribution. If your view is, all I do is vote on things, thumbs up, thumbs down, and you're not influencing what those things are that are coming before you or what they look like, I would find that frustrating. The way I addressed it was to try to engage to shape the outcomes. I call it moving the needle. I remember early on in my tenure, someone asked me, "You're a Republican in a Democratic administration. Are you writing a lot of dissents?" I said,

"Well, when you're dissenting, you're not winning." I prefer to not have to dissent because I would find that winning. My focus is on how to engage with others to get to that point. One of the things that I tried to do also was lay down a public framework for how I approached issues. I did a lot of speeches and law review articles. I did independent research on my own on a number of topics, such as intellectual property protection and the FTC's administrative litigation process.

The administration and management of the agency.

Right. I thought that was a kind of contribution that I could make that would shape outcomes to where I wanted things to go. I thought it was also incumbent on me to provide that input. If I want to have the influence and the impact, I need it to work to make it happen. I didn't have the power to force it to happen. Having run the advocacy program at the FTC, it always made me think about how to persuade other people. You persuade them by having the research, getting in at the right time, and building trust. It works whether you're trying to influence people in the States or other parts of the government or whether you're trying to work with your colleagues and staff at the agency.

I take it that you would say it is a benefit to have been at the same agency before; to give you a better feel for how the institution works, or its culture and moods are.

Yes. For me it is very much a benefit. Also, how to lay out the principals and the framework for where I thought things should go. For me that was very much based on a knowledge of the agency's underlying statute, its history, its jurisdiction, where it fit in the bigger US government structure and the relationship between the federal government and the State government, and internationally too.

In January 2017 you get another call. This one says, "You're going to be the Acting Chairman of the Federal Trade Commission." It's a job that you have for almost a year and a half. A long period of time.

Yes, longest ever Acting Chairman by far. [laughs]

Going back to the glorious beginning, 1915 when the FTC opens for business. What's different as you go from being a member of the board to being again the leading face of the Federal Trade Commission, to being the chief operating officer, to being the person who is indeed the head of the agency? What changes for you?

I joked to my staff that "Oh, no, now everything is my fault." Right? Something goes wrong or computers are down, or there is a government shutdown, whatever. You're responsible for everything. One thing I did, even though it was unprecedented for an Acting Chairman to do, is that I brought in my own acting bureau directors, which I was very glad to have done.

Why did you do that?

I got along very well with the previous administration's bureau directors and there wasn't any conflict. But I thought it was very important for me to signal a new approach and a new vision, and to have people who were consistent with that vision. I brought in people who were compatible with my views and who wanted to make the kinds of changes that I wanted to make. I thought that worked well. That allowed me to help shape things almost immediately. I mean, mergers still walk in the door and the investigations that were there continued, but I made some changes in our process, particularly on the consumer protection side. Changing the focus of some of our cases and having my own bureau leadership in place was very helpful in that regard. Though, as I said, I had very good relations with the previous staff.

In that job you are on stage all the time. Inside the building people watch you all the time. They watch where you are, where you're going. They closely follow everything you do. Certainly, the outside world does too. There is intense coverage of what you do. Is that a bit oppressive?

It's a big responsibility. You've taken this responsibility, as I said, to the American public, but now you're responsible for being the leader of about 1,200 people. I took over in a time that I think had unprecedented uncertainty. There was a new administration that hadn't been anticipated to have won the election. There was so much uncertainty about who would ultimately be the permanent head of the agency, about appointments, all of those things. I felt it was very important to step forward to show to staff, we are going to keep forging ahead, we're not going to stop enforcing competition law or consumer protection law. I have a vision. I want you to be a part of it. Here are the things I want to do. I had a positive agenda that I articulated very, very early and continued all along. I think it was very important not to sit back and wait because it would have been a very unfortunate thing for American consumers, I think, and for the agency's morale.

If you drift for 15, 16 months.

Yes, exactly. The cases that we brought have really stood up well to scrutiny. We've won a number in court. We've had successful merger challenges. We've had a whole host of consumer protection cases. Actually, on the competition front, we tied a 20-year high for enforcement. That was a very important message to send. Also, as I said, I made changes in some of FTC's processes to make it clearer, less burdensome to legitimate business. I think it was important to continue to move ahead. I was confident during that time period.

What was the hardest thing about the job? Maybe you've been describing it now, but the things that caused you to stay awake the most at night, the things that caused you the greatest routine concern? Maybe not anxiety, but what was the hardest thing about being the Acting Chairman of the Federal Trade Commission?

I think the hardest thing for me was I was really operating without a net. I was the Acting Chairman. I didn't have a majority.

As you said before, there were two of you. On the board of 5, you had 3 vacancies and it was you and your colleague Terrell McSweeny.

Right. The longer you've gone on as the acting chair, it's not like your power gets stronger. I mean, it gets stronger in some ways because as you achieve and you win cases and you make decisions that turn out to be right, I think that helps, but the longer you've gone on the more it becomes clear that someone else was going to be taking over the steering wheel. I think that was a challenge to continue to make those hard decisions and forge ahead, and to define my program, to achieve, to get resources, to get support, both from within and without the agency. I wanted staff to continue to be engaged in what we were doing and not look over my shoulder, asking if somebody else is going to come in a few months and this work will all fall by the wayside. I had that support, I had that engagement from staff. I worked very hard with my colleague to reach common ground. To be very clear, on the few times we disagreed we would articulate why she came to one decision and I came to another, and then we would move ahead, to not have it be a mystery. Sometimes we're going to be in a different place, but the process is still working. It worked out well, but I think unlike a normal chairman, who would come in and would be given other Commissioners to support them and have gotten the blessing of the new administration, I, for my 15 month-period, had to operate without a net. I feel good about keeping the agency moving ahead and tying previous records for enforcement activity.

After your other experiences and watching how the agency works, were you ready for the intensity of activity for how fast the treadmill works out, how all the demands to speak, to talk to media representatives, to talk with legislators and others? It is an intense experience.

I was ready for that actually for several reasons. It is intense but I had responsibility for being the point person on things previously. When I was head of the Office of Policy Planning, I had testified in front of Congress a couple times. I was on the forefront of a lot of issues. Then, as a Commissioner, I took it upon myself to speak and publish, and to be the public face on a lot of issues. I had interacted a lot with Congress. People knew who I was. When you talk about when I got that phone call to come and interview to be a Commissioner, you kind of hope you get through and nobody pays much attention to you. A friend of mine who used to run the Office of Congressional Relations at the FTC said, "Don't look at it that way. This is your opportunity to build relationships with these people because you'll need those relationships down the road. There will be things that you need, or they want from you, or questions they have about what you're doing, and you should have built those relationships already." When I was just a Commissioner, I worked on that. I think there is a good saying which is, "You fix your roof when the sun is shining". I had built on both sides of the aisle relationships with people in Congress. When I became the chair and the focus was much more on me, I wasn't starting from scratch on any of those things.

There is a lot of talk about how agencies have to be independent and think about how they take decisions, about how to use their powers. From what you're saying, I take it that can't mean that you are aloof from elected officials, that you are simply distant from them. What is the right relationship between the leadership of the agency and the elected officials let, say, in the legislature or in the executive branch?

Congress defines our authority and provides us the resources that we need, the budget to do our work. Being an independent agency, in my view, doesn't mean that you are somehow up on a mountaintop and there is no influence over you in any of those things because that's not what our representative democracy is about. We are all beholden to the American public. In my view, what being an independent agency means is that our enforcement decision making, our choices in particular cases are based on the facts and the law before us, the economics and that's how we decide. We're not part of the administration in that. As a Commissioner of the Federal Trade Commission, you can't be removed except for a good cause. You are somewhat insulated but the head of any of the cabinet agencies can be removed at will by the president because they're directly accountable to the administration. As an independent agency, you're one step removed from that. I do think it's important. You're spending American taxpayer dollars, you're affecting American interests, business interests, consumer interests. You have to be accountable. Part of being accountable is not that you're dictated to, but that you have to be transparent about what you're doing and why you're doing it, and accountable for the money that you spend in the cases that you bring, and the cases that you don't bring.

We have oversight hearings. One of the things that I tried to do also during my time as the Acting Chairman, was to be a real resource to other agencies and work with them. I did a workshop with Scott Gottlieb from the FDA, looking at what are some of the government barriers to more competition in the pharmaceutical space.

I did a workshop jointly with the Department of Transportation about autonomous vehicles. I did joint work with the Small Business Administration about the needs for small businesses to protect themselves through cybersecurity threats and scams. I worked a lot with the Department of Labor on the economic liberty work, with the Department of Defense on veterans issues. I thought it was important to be part of the bigger US government response to the concerns that the American public has.

You're talking to your successors in the future. You've had an experience that gives you a tremendous firsthand view of how the agency works. What do you know on the last day that you wish you'd known on the first day that you'd want to pass along to your successor?

Well, I would say a couple of things. I would say that with the onslaught of everyday work, of all the responsibilities that you have of just running a big organization, and the cases that walk in the door, the demands on your time, that it's very important if there are outcomes that you want to achieve that you start with those in mind and you work backwards from there. For example, I wanted to do the economic liberty task force and I announced that right off the bat. We set it up, and we did it. There was a report that came out on my last day at the commission about license portability to allow people to carry their occupation license from state to state with them. I also brought cases focusing on abuse of government processes as well as policy work. You don't just do a hearing and say, "Well, that is the end of it." It's about what you do with what you learn from that hearing. How do you put that into something useful that has a shelf life and how do you operationalize it? I would say start with the end in mind and work backwards.

Another really important thing is that sometimes people who reach a successful position only bring people like themselves. You have to have a lot of self-knowledge to say, I don't need a team of people who are just like me. I need a team of people who complement me because they are stronger in areas where I'm weaker. We have to have some self-knowledge to understand what those areas are. Certainly, as the head of the agency that is very, very important as you are putting together your advisors and your senior staff. You can't be knowledgeable about everything: Congress and economics, antitrust law and the international situation, and privacy law. You can know a lot about them, but you can't be an expert in each so you need to think about how to bring those complementary skills together in your team.

To have a program in mind on day one, to know yourself, and to surround yourself with people who complement your skills, to listen to them.

Yes, I've always told my staff, "Your job is easy when you tell me what I want to hear, but you're a lot more valuable to me when you tell me what I don't want to hear." When you are the Chairman, it's hard to get people to tell you what you don't want to hear.

John Pecman*

Competition Bureau of Canada, Commissioner (2013-2018)

You were the Commissioner for Competition in the Competition Bureau of Canada from 2013–2018 and before that had a long and distinguished career in public service, including in competition law. You are now the Senior Business Advisor to the Fasken law firm in Ottawa, Canada. I would like to begin by having you describe a bit about the path that took you to the position of Commissioner and to reflect on the traits, the characteristics, in an individual who is well-positioned, to handle the leadership task best.

My path was an unusual one, I must say, to the extent that my wife has called me a "black swan," in that I began working at the Competition Bureau as a case handler right out of school. I obtained my master's degree in economics, and one of my professors was a former Director at the Bureau, and he taught competition law and policy. I signed up for his course. I was very interested in the topic. He had a pipeline for interviews for students, and I was very fortunate to have been hired. I started as a case handler and worked as a case handler for, I believe, 18 years or so before moving up the ranks to management, helping lead the organization at the front lines, if you will, and then up into the executive ranks near the back end of my career. Then, as luck or fortune would have it, there was the sudden departure of Commissioner Aitken, and I was asked to be the interim Commissioner for a period of time. When I was asked to take on the role, I never contemplated actually keeping it, but after I did the work for a while, I said, "Well, I think I have some value to bring."

---

* Interview conducted on 1 April 2019.

How long was the interim period?

For me it was 8 months. About 2 or 3 months in, after having started to sail the boat or steer the ship, thinking I could add to the value of our organization – help "build the brand," as you like to put it, Bill – I put my name in the ring. This is a political appointment. I was apolitical. I was an insider, a career staffer. I was appointed, so the first career staffer as Commissioner as well as the first non-lawyer. I'm an economist by training, so it was a first on many fronts. I think over the course of the years I've worked for many Commissioners. I had 7, I believe, that I emulated and watched very carefully in terms of what worked and what didn't work. You accumulate that knowledge over time. Obviously, being a career staffer I understood the organization and I knew the people. So I focused more on the direction, creating a vision, and then implementing some changes to make us better, to make us work as a team as opposed to a siloed organization which was firewalled against the business and legal community. Knocking down those walls was one of the primary objectives I had as Commissioner.

What was the adjustment like going from being a member of the professional staff to being a senior manager to now sitting in that wonderful office that looks out over the gorgeous river and the city, being the Commissioner? How did that change things for you?

For me it was very difficult. The transition from case handler to manager created a lot of anxiety for me, to the extent that I was actually sick for a short period of time, because I was giving up control over my case files. When you build a case, you understand it backwards and forwards; you know the witnesses; you know the issues. Then, as you move up the ranks, you have to give up that control and rely on your team, and you don't know the facts as well even though you're advancing them, you're advocating for them, and you're responsible for them. As a result, giving up that control of a case handler was, I think, the most challenging part about moving into the management ranks. Then, the transition from management to the executive was not that much different, because by then you've learned to give up total control of a file, to work with your team, to make sure you have the right people around you, and to lead implementation going through the enforcement process. To me letting go of the mastery of the case and trusting your team was the biggest adjustment to leadership.

Clearly, I moved up the organization together with peers and was able to rely upon them and their support. Without their support it would be a bit more difficult when your own teammates don't really respect you and give you permission to lead. A lot of my time would have been spent on earning their respect. Over my career at the Bureau, I had a lot of support from the Bureau team and when I became the leader of the organization I was able to make significant changes in the organization because of that support.

You must have approached the appointment both as interim but then as the Commissioner with a fair amount of confidence that you had watched others do this; you had observed what the job takes. I'm guessing there weren't that many surprises for you in moving into the position – or were there?

I think it goes both ways. Because I knew the business and I knew the people, it wasn't as difficult as it would have been for someone who was unfamiliar with the organization who might have to spend months, maybe years, to understand how the place works. So I was ready to implement significant changes right away. The challenge was actually implementing the change and having people move along with you, particularly when you're an interim appointment. Most interim leaders are cautious because they don't want to make a policy change or directional change knowing that they don't have the job full-time and do not want to seriously disrupt the organization.

Your staff may look at you a bit differently, saying: "Well, let's see how long he's going to be here."

Absolutely. But there were some immediate changes I had to make given where we were. Our organization had drifted in terms of shrinking its approach to the application of competition law and promotion. My immediate response was to take back the organization to a more horizontal and holistic approach to delivering our work as opposed to just being an enforcement litigator, which is what we had become when I took over as interim. So I immediately restored some work on advocacy, which had shut down. I delegated inquiry commencement powers from my office on day one. On the enforcement side, I wanted us to use our formal tools to collect information as opposed to relying on voluntary returns because, in my view, companies are strategic; they're not going to voluntarily hand you incriminating evidence. Unfortunately, we had drifted to just asking on a voluntary basis for information for some of our civil inquiries. I announced early going forward that we would be using our formal tools during all formal inquiries, which was a bit of a shock to the outside world. The staff loved it because we would be using the tools that Parliament had bestowed upon us to conduct our investigations.

There were a number of little things. I talked about more cooperation and collaboration with our stakeholders as opposed to just conducting our investigations and not engaging with them. Also I advocated for more transparency in our enforcement work. In my interim period we published a bulletin on transparency and announced a desire to provide more enforcement guidance: whether it be through enforcement guidelines or position statements following an investigation – whether we proceeded with the investigation or closed it. The position statements were to be issued mainly for the more significant investigative files because issuing them for the hundreds of cases you have in the pipeline would be very resource-draining. In sum, we did put out more guidance during my interim stage.

This vision of a more open, transparent, and collaborative organization, was the model that I presented to the Selection Board for the Commissioner position. Obviously, they liked it. I was appointed, and I carried on with that approach when I became Commissioner. So there wasn't a significant change following my appointment as Commissioner from my Interim period. In those early days, whenever I met with the management team, I shared my vision for the organization, and then made changes incrementally because significant, meaningful change can't happen overnight.

So, very important in coming into the job – instead of simply saying, "I'm glad to have it" to say "There is something I want to do with it". Having that defined in your mind the moment that you sit down at the desk was valuable for defining the program.

It was an opportunity to bring some change that I thought was much needed, having spent almost 30 years in the organization and seeing that we had moved away from some best practices that we had. Some previous Commissioners were big on advocacy or very concerned about corporate compliance and issues of putting out bulletins and being transparent, and those had for some reason evaporated under other leaders who didn't share that approach. Being able to restore some of the better practices was important to me. It was something I could bring during the interim period, as I said, and then when I became Commissioner was able to proceed with that more fully. So it was very important.

Were you able in the interim period or over time to shape your own team of, I would say, closest advisors, senior managers? Did you have some ability to assemble the group that is going to be your sounding board, to be your most important immediate link to the organization?

Moving staff out of their positions in government, and even at the executive level is difficult because of entrenched employee rights. There is case law supporting the employees who do wish to move from their position, you can't force them. Often you inherit your team from the previous Commissioner. But over time people move. If they're not sharing the vision or want to do something else or they can see roadblocks in their career, they inevitably move on. Initially, I did not have my team, I just inherited the team that was there, but over time I was able to bring in a senior management team that I trusted, that were always brighter than me. [Laughter]

My aim was always to raise the average IQ of the office, and I did that.

One of the concerns raised by the legal community about my appointment was that I was not a lawyer. They seemed to be protective of their profession. I don't know why this was an issue otherwise. Yes, protecting their monopoly I suppose. In response, I surrounded myself with a lot of legal talent on my senior management team and in my office to give some comfort to the legal community that I was receiving good legal advice within the organization, before I turned to my Department of Justice lawyers who provide the Commissioner legal advice in a more formal way.

I think part of what you're suggesting is that you build a team that complements your own strengths. You have your own experience, your own ability, and you surround yourself with people who fill out a larger profile.

And I've been blessed with my senior management team, good people such as Matthew Boswell, Jeanne Pratt, Vicki Eatrides. Many of them I had worked with for years, and we had developed a good trust relationship. Any one of them could have been the leader of the agency and will be future leaders of the organization.

Matthew Boswell is now the Commissioner, after an interim period now the Commissioner.

Matthew and I worked closely for more than 7 years, I know him well. Matthew is a natural leader with the right experience and ability to mobilize people to take the Bureau to the next level.

What did you learn as a case handler, then a middle and senior manager about how you wanted to do the job when you became the Commissioner? You had the special experience of joining the ship in the engine room, putting coal in the boilers, and gradually moving up a few decks until you're on the bridge. What did you learn from the engine room and in the other positions about how to behave, act, and lead as the Commissioner?

An important lesson I learned while a case handler, which many trained in economics have trouble with, is the knowledge that enforcement cases can only advance when there is supporting evidence, not just an economic theory of harm. As a case handler you put your life and soul into a file. You work hard, you build the file collecting documentary evidence and witness testimony, and you're very active internally promoting and moving the case through the approval process to either take enforcement action or to resolve a competitive problem. Having enforcement files stagnating ultimately demoralizes the team. So making quicker decisions as the cases move through the internal system I believe is important not only to keep morale high but to placate external stakeholders as well.

Even if they're not perfect decisions, to decide.

Just to make a decision, a decision moves things one way or the other. But in making those decisions, I also learned, because case handlers have so much passion for their files, at times they can have blinders on focusing on the inculpatory evidence and minimizing the exculpatory evidence. There is possible confirmation bias to look out for as a leader. Once a file is assigned to a case handler, the management tendency is to support their team, and so there needs to be a hard look at the file, a critical analysis, by a third party outside the case team before any action is taken.

And committing so much of your personality and your emotional and intellectual energy into building a file. You're not doing it for the money.

Absolutely not. Case handlers do not receive a bonus for advancing cases. These unintended consequences of bias can arise because there is so much commitment to the path, not fully absorbed and contemplated. As Commissioner, before reviewing a case for decision, I would ensure that I had special advisors who were third parties to the case team, to play devil's advocate who would kick the tires of the file.

Some of the worst meetings, I think, for staff were with me while Commissioner because I too would ask the hard questions in front of their peers and managers about their recommendations on cases. Now, I didn't like to do that, but I had to do it for the sake of the organization. I wanted to ensure that we had a file that was worthy of investment, whether it be litigation or negotiating a settlement and that needed to be acted upon. We therefore institutionalize a forum so there would be an opportunity for the case team to debate the issues with the decision maker. These Commissioner briefing meetings were difficult for staff because the leader is questioning them in front of the entire case team and challenging some of their conclusions or lack of evidence, if you will. I believe these sort of introspection meetings for files were an important step to improving our case selection.

I sense that you conveyed that to them; you said: "I have no special interest in misery or torment for its own sake. I'm doing this to make sure that when we step outside and have to be in the court or some other forum that there are no surprises and we're ready to go."

Yes and I tried to do it very respectfully, understanding what efforts case handlers had gone through to bring the investigation to the commissioner approval stage. I tried to be careful on how I framed the questions, more open-ended than closed, to start a dialogue; and then, ultimately, if I didn't support the recommendation I explained why to them. I did that very rarely because we have such a good team and the process is so refined there are very few files where the case team recommendations were not acted upon.

You have a lot of quality control built into it.

It's already there for the most part through the reporting lines within the organization. But on occasion you don't agree with the direction, and, as the leader you're accountable, and there are some discretionary issues that you put into the decision process that the staff don't because they're focusing on their file. Leaders need to take a broader perspective and need to consider intersections with other government policies and objectives. For example, public interest considerations for domestic investment and employment when deciding on how to tackle a problematic merger.

It was important to me, knowing how disappointed staff would be with any decision that did not support their recommendation, to have a word with them to explain the reasoning behind my decision. They may not be entirely happy, but at least you communicated why and there is no remaining mystery.

I think they respect you for that. The importance of communication, to spell out why, to make sure they have a chance to offer their own views, but ultimately you can point to – I assume you get a document that says, "You're it, you're the Commissioner" – the document on the wall and say, "That says that I have to decide."

The buck stops here. [Laughter]

"I want the value of what you have to say, and I don't want you to pull your punches in telling me, but I have to decide ultimately. That is my job."

Right. I was a big believer in a horizontal approach to decision making as opposed to a command-and-control approach to advancing files. So we established through a realignment during my tenure a committee called the Major Enforcement and Advocacy Committee, led by one of my senior executives, who would do that review of the file and make a recommendation to me about whether we should be investing to go to a formal stage or moving to litigation where we're going to spend significant resources.

That process was extremely effective for 2 reasons. It institutionalizes the devil's advocate process because you have others to review a file who are outside the case team. It also involves your senior managers in decision making. They're giving you a recommendation. We set it up so I had a veto right, but 99 percent of the time I just went ahead with the recommendation, having seen the analysis and all the issues that were debated. I thought that was helpful to show that this is not just about the Commissioner, this is a team approach, we're all involved in this. I also established other similar horizontal committees comprised of Bureau managers.

As I said, I think it's important that you delegate as a leader and not take it all on yourself. Otherwise I think you risk losing your organization's support along the way because there is not always going to be alignment which can quickly become a wedge which can really hurt team morale.

An important lesson that you point to here is that you want to devise organizational methods that give you a way to test evidence and ideas strongly, to make sure that you have a clear-headed view of what your opponents will say on the outside – there are no uncontested layups in this field – and, again, that you're doing all the testing inside that you see can succeed on the outside.

You want any case that you may go to litigation with to have gone through the internal testing process that will be as rigorous as going through the courts and the questions you'll face from the defense. I always thought the most difficult act was to get a file through your organization, and, once it has done that, you can stand up to just about any cross-examination or attack on your approach and what you've done.

It's so important to a new leader, or even someone who's in the job, to keep in mind your precept, which is to make sure people understand why we're doing this, that the point is to be successful when we do meet the other challenges, in the way that a coach or a trainer for an athletic team explains to the team: "This is why we're practicing so hard."

Of course, agencies are often judged by their successes before the courts. When an agency loses many of their files, there is a question of the quality of that organization and the quality of the decision making. Often the matters that go before the courts are the difficult ones; the ones that are obvious are settled. Therefore success or failure before the courts in a contested matter can be an unfair way to judge an enforcement agency. As a result, you want to make sure that you're a bit risk-averse before pulling the litigation trigger. For the cases you actually bring forward you want to make sure there is a strong likelihood of success as opposed to the ones that, "You know, we're likely going to lose this; but there may be some good case law." I think there is a hesitancy of leaders today, given how agencies are judged, to take those matters which only will build the case law.

There is, and it's a news coverage environment where if you lose one it's a grave setback, you lose two it's a catastrophe, and you lose three and it's oblivion.

They're looking for your head.

How did you go about defining your appetite for risk or the management team's appetite for risk? Again, I'm John Pecman decades ago, I'm working on the file, and I want to know in what instances this institution's going to back me up. I want to know how far to the edge to go. How did you define for your team what the Bureau's appetite for risk-taking was?

Case handlers always felt that their case was the number-one priority for the organization. They did not compare them to other files. I understood that mentality. When we ultimately had these risks discussions on whether to settle or to fight, believe it or not, one of the most important considerations was your budget. Without funds you cannot litigate. Litigating is so expensive, between the experts and hiring counsel and the process, and litigation goes on for years.

So the first question is: what is our pot of resources to litigate versus resolving it and having a solution that may not be perfect – but the economy can go on and the practice may have stopped, but we didn't get the administrative monetary penalty, we didn't get the grand deterrence that we wanted; we just resolved the issue. That is the balance you make. I think budget is first of all. Do you have the right horses to fight? Is the team capable of going through that very long and arduous process? Can we bring in the right counsel to build a team that is going to be successful at the end? I think that was an important consideration.

Then, of course, is it something the public cares about? If it's some widget or some chemical going into a final product, the public is going to say, "Why is the organization, the government, spending all its money litigating for a product that is sort of input that people don't see or understand?". "What are you doing? You're so obtuse. And what are you fighting over, a potential increase of prices by 1 or 2 percent? I mean, come on." So it has to be something that is significant, an egregious act, something the consumer cares about – "Put it at the top (of your priorities), put it at the top."

My preference always was to resolve outside of litigation. I was very proud of the fact that we engaged with the Bar and our Competition Tribunal, our court process, to come up with a mediation process to limit potential litigation during my tenure.

Can you tell me a bit about how the mediation process worked?

Following an investigation and the filing of an application to the Tribunal to challenge a merger or other anti-competitive conduct, the case management of this file by the Tribunal now includes a mandatory mediation session to see if a resolution can be reached early in the litigation. I believe in 2 of the 3 cases that we brought forward since this mediation process was implemented it actually worked. A settlement was reached because of the mediation led by the Tribunal. This result, I believe, is both a good thing and a bad thing for the Tribunal because they're always looking for files to develop case law. There are some mixed feelings. But in terms of resolving matters and implementing change that is going to benefit the economy, I think it's the ideal solution. Where 2 parties can't agree, I believe you will ultimately go to the courts to resolve the dispute. Where one can get to the fix more quickly, I believe that is often the better route to take.

You pointed before to several firsts with your appointment. The staff member progresses through the institution and ultimately receives the appointment, and that is a fairly powerful signal to your staff, to the institution itself. But to be the first economist to be the head of the Bureau in a long line of impressive and distinguished appointments – How were you able to use your background as an economist to add something new to the mix of what the agency did and to its culture, to bring this part of your own experience and personality to the management and guidance of the Bureau?

Economic analysis, the analytics, is the foundation to all the antitrust cases, so economics plays a key role in the entire enforcement process. In some jurisdictions economic units have equal voice with the legal side in case disposition. In others they don't; they're sort of just part of the case team. Sound economic analysis is an important piece to advance a case file, but economists are not often equal partners in cases or in the development of the direction of an organization for that matter. Many antitrust agencies around the world are led by economists by training such as Commissioner Vestager in Europe and Rod Sims in Australia. In Canada, because our competition law requires that competitive harm be quantified for the purpose of challenging a merger, I have publicly stated that economists are antitrust "Rockstars". What I think as an economist – I don't want to be derogatory, but I think lawyers have a way of thinking that is very structured. It's: "We have the law. Does the law apply?" It's more what I call "in a box," very careful. I'm not trying to disparage it, but that is often the thinking pattern of many of the lawyers. Whereas I think economists are more prepared to experiment, think about other policy implications, and just bring a different approach to tackling the same matter as opposed to just pure application of the law using this cookie cutter "is it in or is it out?" I think as an economist – it's not an exact science so we can be more creative – I think we often bring more creativity to files and to policy development. Our training also pushes us to go beyond competition policy when considering a difficult antitrust issue and also to look at economic policy more generally. For example, where does competition policy fit into the country's industrial policy? Where does it fit in the overall government economic scheme? Being able to align our work with the government direction was a fresh approach I tried to bring to the Bureau.

This change was not entirely welcomed by the legal and business community because they thought the Bureau would become political as opposed to an independent enforcement agency. But we're not becoming political. The goal was to become more relevant to government (and by extension the public) by saying: "Here's how we can support your policy."

What happens if you become irrelevant to government?

If one believes their antitrust agency is underfunded (which the Bureau was), you'll receive even fewer resources in the future and you may see your policy get changed if your operations do not align with government priorities. The recent action by DG COMP to block a merger in the railway sector in Europe is reflective of what can happen when the politicians aren't happy.

Alstom/Siemens, yes.

Yes that is the case. It is an example where the politicians were not happy with the strict competition law approach to an important transaction for the economy. So it's a tough question. It was very difficult. I thought Commissioner Vestager did an amazing job standing up for competition. But, you know, when government's not happy with the actions of the agency they will make changes. So you do have to keep an eye on the big picture. It's part of your discretion as the head of agency. I'm not saying you must take the government's industrial policy into the final decision, but you certainly need to be aware of it so you can effectively respond to the political pushback.

It's again an interesting point, that you need the autonomy to make important decisions about how to use your power without having an elected official, for example, saying, "John Pecman is my friend, leave him alone," or "John Pecman is my enemy, attack him." You need that autonomy, but you need to be accountable ultimately to a process and to be effective you have to have a conversation with the elected officials, and I think you're underscoring how important that part of the job is. The awareness of the larger environment is important to doing your job.

It is so true, not only to deal with the politicians but also to deal with the public. It's still the case today – notwithstanding that antitrust is sexy again – that the vast majority of the public have no idea what antitrust is or what it does and how it fits into government. So it's incumbent upon competition authorities to use outreach and to explain in simple terms what the organization is trying to accomplish and why it's important for the economy and for jobs and all the things that politicians care about. I just think there needs to be more work by agencies on marketing.

We were looking at investing more heavily into the public communications area, but because of our budget restraints – it's expensive; it takes time; it takes planning, and you need to get your people out interacting with the public and you have to have a systematic approach to it all. It's not just a one-off. Currently, it is the major case files that catch the attention of the public. Let's say it's a price-fixing case for gasoline. People care about their gasoline. Outside of the weather in Canada, people talk about the price of gas on a regular basis.

So when you have a file in that domain you attract the public's attention, and that is an opportunity to communicate the importance of the work we do. But it doesn't happen every day, it happens maybe once a decade, and for the most part you're just under the radar of the public. As a result, you get forgotten by government, you don't receive the proper funding. At least, that is the situation in Canada.

Compared to a number of others, your resources are decidedly modest, given the mandate – competition, consumer, other things, too. It's a lot to do with, I would say as an outsider, not a lot of money.

That is true. Canada is a bit more tolerant of concentration than the United States, for example, and so competition policy is not the highest priority, the thinking being bigger firms can compete better internationally. So our merger review process has been set up that way. "Less is better," in terms of intervention by the Bureau, I think has been the historical approach by the Canadian government. Canada has an efficiency defence in merger review that has been applied by the courts and the Bureau to save anti-competitive mergers for example. Changing that mindset requires advocacy, it requires outreach, and those are the 2 areas that we were trying to build up during my administration. But your priority is always on your urgent enforcement files. At the end of the day you have to slow down the important advocacy work. It's a zero-sum game.

What kind of adjustment was it for you to now be in this larger spotlight – from being well-known inside the Bureau to being the face of the agency? In the interim period, during the appointment itself, you are now the face of the Competition Bureau with the bar, elected officials, public journalists, advocacy groups, and others. How does that change your life, to be onstage all the time?

It is so different than being a case officer, in that you are accountable for any issue that may arise in the organization (administrative, enforcement or policy) and you need to be able to converse about any policy matter or issue that affects your organization while anything you say will be held against you and the entire organization. There is so much more responsibility as the head of the agency than worrying about the outcome of your case file. You have to be briefed frequently on what is going on within the Bureau and relevant external stakeholders to be prepared for a question by your team, by the press or by a stakeholder, (whether it be the bar or a politician) on what you're doing and why you're doing it. So you have to stay on top of a lot of moving pieces. The requirement to keep your head up all the time is to me the most significant difference between being a leader of an organization and being a case handler who primarily works head-down on their investigations.

Also, when you're speaking to the bar or the public, it's necessary to message where you're headed with the organization and your priorities. That is why it is so important to establish a vision of what you're trying to accomplish with the organization. When speaking with the public, one needs to regularly build in a narrative that fits the strategic direction of the organization.

In the news environment now, where you might get 15 or 20 minutes to contribute to the narrative – not a day, not "I'll think about it over the evening" – but the blogs, the tweeting, it's off to the races, and if you're not putting an oar in the water quickly, you're left behind.

It is vital to work closely with the communications team. Good speechwriters, staff who are very knowledgeable about social media and how to use it are key today. Today's communication is in sound bites. The goal is to capture the public attention and then attach the more substantive portion of the message to the sound bite. Making antitrust interesting and easy to understand is a constant challenge. The case handlers and lawyers don't always see eye to eye with each other. Whether it's through animation, through a catchy title, everyone's fighting for the eyeballs and the ears of the public, everyone's fighting for it, so your message has to stand out and be relevant to the public.

One of the catchy titles we've had recently was "Bread Price-Fixing Investigation in Canada." There was an alleged ten-year price fixing in the supply of people's bread, a main staple, something that people really care about. We had the public's attention for a while and took advantage of it to educate the public about who we were, about the offence of price-fixing and how it was investigated as well as explaining our immunity program. News is the reporting of important events and we were fortunate to have had one with the bread price-fixing case.

One of the distinctive characteristics of the Canadian experience is its extraordinary contribution to the development of international standards, international networks, bilateral relationships, multilateral relationships, and global relationships, but with the construction of a policy infrastructure that will improve the development of policy in a world where there are over 130 country jurisdictions that do competition law now. Canada is a large country with a small population, small resources, but in a completely disproportionate way Canada has affected the development of global standards, I think, as a trusted partner, as a thoughtful partner. When you go back to your budget, though, and you go back to your role inside the country, I suspect someone might say: "Why are we doing all this? Why are we building the International Competition Network (ICN)? Why are we making this contribution to the larger global pool?" Is there a tension between your role as the head of the Competition Bureau of Canada – that is, of Canada – and the larger international role that Canada has played so successfully? How do you decide how much to devote to each?

A very good question, Bill. Konrad von Finckenstein, one of my Commissioners and one of the founding members of the ICN, warned me. The international multilateral fora, the bilateral relationships, it's all very intoxicating, and you could spend all your time in that area, and then at the end of the day you'll have to look at what are your outputs and what are your results from all that international engagement and bridge building, which Canada has done well not only in the competition field but in many other arenas, including our good work on the consumer protection side of our business, cooperating on investigations and sharing best practices bilaterally and multilaterally through such fora as ICPEN and the OECD.

I think Canada has a very global perspective of markets and recognizes the importance of trade, notwithstanding the barriers we have within our own country to competition, so regulators prioritize working collaboratively with our international counterparts. In today's global economy, agencies must work closely with their international partners to effectively combat cross border anti-competitive conduct. Building bridges and trust with other agencies are essential. How best to do it? In Canada, we contribute to the development of the international standards through leadership in multi-lateral fora, we develop relationships on a bilateral basis through agreements and through shared practices, through cooperation with joint and parallel investigations, by sharing our knowledge- providing technical assistance, by remaining open to sharing information which is a challenge when working with other jurisdictions and partners. Without the legal authority and the trust, sharing of confidential case information just won't happen, and your cross-border cases will not be managed efficiently. You may then have disparate outcomes from your international counterpart; with businesses very upset with the enforcement process because of the duplicative regulatory burden and the uncertainty.

I believe the allocation of an agency's resources to the international advocacy business should roughly equate to the percentage of cross-border enforcement cases you handle in a given year. That would be the order of magnitude.

With the limited resources, you also have to pick and choose which multilateral fora you're going to support and which relationships you're going to build because there are so many. How we at the Competition Bureau tried to align our decision making on resources was to consider "where our government is looking to develop stronger trade ties" because any trade deal can be undermined by lack of an effective competition law and policy in one jurisdiction. For example, Canada recently entered into the Trans-Pacific Partnership Free Trade Initiative (TPP) with the Association of Southeast Asian Nations (ASEAN) community. During the trade negotiation period, the Bureau prioritized building bridges with the ASEAN community. As Canada was interested in increasing trade with the signatory countries, it was important that the rules of the game for competition policy between trading partners would be similar and, we anticipated that there would be future cross-border cases between us on account of the increased trade.

This was how we prioritized our emerging international relationships when assessing requests for technical assistance and developing bilateral relationships. Similar principles were applied to prioritizing multilateral fora participation to get the biggest bang for the buck because there are just so many options [...]

I think a point you suggest here is the significance of the personal engagement in building these links. How much do those relationships matter?

In my view, we are in a people-to-people business. You have to get out of your office to develop relationships. You're not going to build a relationship over the phone. It's the key rational for international travel. You actually have to meet with people, engage with them to build their trust. It can be over breakfast, dinner or just drinks to talk about our families, our political issues at home or whatever to get to know your counterpart. It really establishes a trust at the top that disseminates down through your organization because your team is watching, and they develop similar linkages with others in the Authority. A bond is built, and this bond building is key to, I believe, international engagement. I like to think Canada does a good job at it. We like people and we're friendly. We like to say "sorry" a lot, eh? [Laughter]

Canada has a uniquely significant constructive role in building these relationships, and thank goodness it has seen this as a priority.

I've been very proud to carry that torch forward and carry on in the tradition of Sheridan Scott and Konrad von Finckenstein, former Chairs of the ICN, and other Commissioners, such as Cal Goldman, who continues to carry that torch internationally at the OECD and the ICN.

Let me ask you a finishing question. I am your prospective successor, one of the many extraordinary economists or lawyers in Canada who might be candidates to be the Commissioner, and I think I am going to get the job, it's coming my way. A few suggestions you have for me as I approach this appointment? What should I think about?

I think number 1 is making sure you have the right team around you – Absolutely first priority. The right team is a team that will share your vision, so you need to communicate that to your organization and have a conversation with your leadership and talk about that vision; and, if there is significant divergence, you want to think about bringing someone else in, because you will not be able to implement your plan where there are people who are not prepared to make changes. There will be roadblocks and they'll slow you down. You just won't accomplish as much as you would like. So that is my number one piece of advice.

Number 2 is keep an eye on those resources and always advocate with the government because they are stretched with so many asks for resources. You need to continue to show your value, what you can bring to the public and to the economy, and try to get a hearing with government so that competition policy is seen as a priority. Another big challenge, huge challenge.

Then, of course, delegate, be horizontal, don't be a command-and-control, knock down the walls, try to be as transparent as possible, so that you become a trusted agency with your team and with your stakeholders. I think that is so important.

I would underscore one other thing that is implicit in everything you've said: have clearly in mind what you want to do with this job, what is that vision.

Absolutely develop that vision. Presumably, the candidate would have articulated that to the decision makers for the hire. But the vision is important. Are you just going to be a caretaker? Are you going to carry on with your predecessor's vision or just focus on taking cases to the courts? Enjoying the experience as agent head, as opposed to trying to improve the brand and improve the organization. The whole concept of continuous improvement is one core value that I think most good leaders have. They strive to improve the good work that has already been built upon within an organization.

Eduardo Perez Motta*

Mexican Antitrust Authority, Chairman (2004-2013)

You are the former President of what was then the Federal Competition Commission (Comisión Federal de Competencia) in Mexico, now known as Comisión Federal de Competencia Económica (COFECE). You held this position for 10 years, from 2004-2013. You are the former Chair of the Steering Committee of the International Competition Network (ICN), where you played a vital role in the continuing development of a network that has become a crucial part of the process by which competition authorities speak to each other, develop an understanding of what each is doing, and achieve agreement on what standards ought to be developed in substance and process. You are currently a partner in a law & economics consultancy. You bring a wealth of experience to this area, and it's impossible to tell the story of competition law in the 21st century without including a chapter on you. Could get us started by talking a bit about the career path that led you into competition law and to think perhaps a bit about what kinds of background and experience are valuable in assuming the role as the head of a competition authority?

Basically, I can divide my professional career into 3 areas. I started in the academy. I was a professor in 2 major universities in Mexico. I was a full-time professor, and then I was a part-time professor for many years in microeconomics and international trade. Then, I became a member of the government, and in that second part of my professional life, I worked on international trade, international negotiations and international trade policy in Mexico. I participated in the North America Free Trade Agreement (NAFTA), and was responsible of the Mexican Trade office to the European Union when we negotiated the FTA with the European Union. I also participated in Latin American negotiations. Finally,

* Interview conducted on 15 April 2019.

I was Ambassador in the World Trade Organization (WTO), so I was involved in the multilateral side of the negotiations. In my third area of professional work, I became Chairman of the Competition Authority in Mexico.

I think there is one element that goes across all these experiences, and that is the interest and the privilege to try to understand and to work in market competition, how markets could function more effectively to improve the welfare of consumers and the welfare of producers of wealth, to open opportunities to producers to participate in any market, and to give the possibilities for consumers to choose the best prices, the best quality products and the best services: that is the virtue of competition. So, markets in a competition environment are the main source of innovation and that is something that has been behind everything I have done from academics and the government, and this is something that I'm doing today as a practitioner in economic regulation and competition.

All of these experiences before going to the Authority gave you deep exposure to the economy in Mexico, the role of Mexico's economy in global affairs, some of the political science about how policy is shaped, and trade as a quintessential example of that process; and a deep understanding of international relations, too, by virtue of your time in Geneva and your time working on the negotiation of trade agreements.

Yes, I totally agree with you. Trade in Mexico has been the most important source of competition that is the most important engine of efficiency and growth.

In other words, you were a student of political science, economics, international affairs, before you set foot in the Competition Agency.

Yes. Actually, my formation is in economics, but my life experience has been related to political economy and international affairs. That exposure gives you the best position to work in competition enforcement, that is a complement of the domestic economy, in order to position your industry to be successful in the global economy.

What was the most difficult part of the transition to becoming now the head of the Competition Authority? What stood out in your mind?

The first element was to understand the legal framework of the competition law, so the enforcement part. I knew the analytics, the basic principles of why markets should function in a competitive environment, and believed, and still believe, that is the best outcome that we can have in order to improve the efficiency and innovation in our economy, to improve the welfare of the community in general, and even to improve the economic equality and to give better opportunities to low-income people as well. Competition goes very much in line with that. When I became head of the Competition Authority, the first challenge was to understand the legal part of that, to see how that applies to enforce competition law and to define the best competition advocacy. That's not an easy issue, especially when you are not a lawyer, and I started to work with lawyers all the time, and I still work with lawyers all the time.

There's still time for you to go to law school, too, if you'd like.

Actually, at some point in time, when I was chairing the Antitrust Authority, I spoke with a good friend who I highly respect professionally and is a former Minister of the Supreme Court, and precisely asked him what kind of law courses he suggested I should take in order to complement my academic background. What you say is absolutely correct: economists working in the application of laws or counseling companies on this matter have to understand the basics of the legal framework in which they work. Let me just finish with an anecdote. When I was a student in Mexico, in my bachelor's degree, the Dean of the university (ITAM) where I was studying at the time said: "You economists have to understand law. You have to understand the legal framework in the area where you are working. That's going to be very important for you." At that time I was taking some law courses, specifically constitutional law, and I said, "I don't see any relationship between law and economics." Many years later, when I became Director-General of International Trade Policy and I received the legal framework I had to apply at that moment, I started reading that, and I said: "My God! I cannot even understand what they mean by that." I understand the economic effects of tariffs, tariff barriers and antidumping, but I did not know the legal fundamentals and procedures to apply those instruments. So I began to try to understand law and to start talking systematically with lawyers. I remember making a telephone call to the former head of the university, and I said, "You might not remember when you told me that I should learn law in order to better apply my knowledge in economics and to be able to design public policy. Now, I understand why you suggested that I understand law to apply economics; you were absolutely correct." After that day, I always have had a very close exchange all the time with lawyers and I have a high respect for good lawyers. Good lawyers are disciplined in the way they articulate all their arguments to be consistent with the legal framework in which they are working.

One thing you built that was a matter of great distinction globally is a team around you that could assist in this process but help you formulate your program. These are individuals who have become globally famous, but they were part of the Eduardo Pérez Motta team. How did you go about building the team to help you put your program in place and to complement your own skills?

I think that's a crucial element and I appreciate that question. In any professional task, you have to always start by building a very good team, that is a key factor to do a good job and to be able to build or consolidate institutions. In order to have a good team you have to delegate responsibilities and you need to trust and respect them. You need to hear them and make them understand that we are all part of the team. You need cracks but they have to understand that they are part of a team. You need to trust them and sometimes be open to hear and respect arguments although you might not coincide. That was the culture in the Antitrust Authority I had the privilege to lead. We knew that only working as a group we could grow. You grow along with your team, and your team is part of yourself in that case. That has always been the case. You have to make the people in that team understand that they have to play for the shirt they have, and they have to understand the importance of doing that.

When you entered the agency what were your objectives? That is to say, "What do I want to do with this job?" What were your main points?

It was clearly to consolidate an institution that started more than 10 years before and had been led by persons that I truly respect such as Santiago Levy and Fernando Sanchez Ugarte. I have always thought that if you want to make a difference in your work, it has to be in building and consolidating institutions. That's the only thing that stays, and the main difference between countries which are in the developing process and countries which are already developed; the value and the strength of their institutions. I always have in mind the book by Daron Acemoglu and James Robinson: "Why Nations Fail".

There is a clear importance to having inclusive institutions to promote economic development. That makes a major difference. If you want markets to function, you need institutions to be sure that they are going to work well with stable and predictable pro-competitive regulations. Any economic system needs institutions to correctly apply and interpret the legal framework. That offers certainty to economic players. Markets need strong, stable and credible institutions that apply regulations in order to work properly and efficiently. Companies and consumers always make long term decisions that need stable frameworks and stable law and law application by institutions.

To go back to your question, that was the main objective, how to continue the consolidation of a crucial institution: The Antitrust Agency. The institution already existed. The institution started at the beginning of the 1990s, actually with the discussion that we had with the United States in our free trade agreement, what was called NAFTA. We didn't have any competition law at that time, so it was strange to have a free trade agreement with the United States and Canada, with the 2 countries that have the oldest and the greatest experience in competition in order to have well-functioning markets, and not having that in Mexico. When Jaime Serra was the Minister of Trade, Santiago Levy and his team designed the Economic Competition Law that, at that time, was a state-of-the-art. The Antitrust Authority (CFC at that time) was designed with a structure inspired by the FTC from the US. The Antitrust Agencyk, as an institution, started to learn how to apply the competition law, how to enforce competition, and how to advocate competition. So, my objective was precisely to find the ways to start the consolidation of that institution. I really wanted to see this institution have the strength that you can see today in COFECE.

When you established your broad goal for yourself and you started observing the operation of the predecessor agency, which became COFECE, what specific things did you say, "This is how I accomplish this end; here are the steps I'm going to take to build that institution"? What kinds of initiatives became part of your program?

I think there were 2 elements important in that task. One was to decide on the team you were going to work with. There were many people with very high human capital levels, with a lot of experience, already in the institution, and you needed to respect that and to take that advantage. That was very important because that is part of the game of building an institution: to respect the human capital that is there. At the same time, you needed to invite additional highly qualified and honest team players, as well as to make a clear diagnostic of your instruments vis-à-vis the best international competition practices. An active participation in the ICN was also important.

When you came in, is this a message you communicated to them?

Yes. Obviously, you start by introducing and inviting some additional people who add value to the people who were there already. I knew the former head of the Competition Authority and the original head, Santiago Levy and Fernando Sánchez Ugarte, and I had a lot of respect for them. I tried to continue the work that they did very, very well. Additionally, we needed to modify the law at that time. We needed to put the law in line with the best international practices. The law already had some interpretations from the Mexican Supreme Court that basically needed to be corrected or changed. I'm not sure if you needed to give a lot of strength to regulatory issues in the US, but I think in countries like Mexico, regulatory decisions that could come from other areas of the Executive Branch, from the Congress, or even from some administrative decisions from other regulators, need to consider the importance of protecting competition and increasing the efficiency in those markets. You needed greater strength for the Competition Authority, and that was part of the changes in the law, increasing the sanctions and giving more regulatory instruments to the Antitrust Authority. That was in the 2006 reform.

Then we had a reform in 2011, which made changes in the Law that we couldn't obtain in the first round in 2006. I have to recognize that any change in the Antitrust Law in any country is a major challenge, and Mexico is obviously not the exception. Mexico has a very concentrated economy, there are business executives with a strong political power, on the other side of the coin, you have a society that needs to be conscious of the importance of well-functioning markets. As part of the Antitrust Authority, we actively participated also in the Constitutional Reform of 2013 that gave full autonomy to the Antitrust Agency and created COFECE. That is something most people do not know. We worked behind the scenes because we were invited by the opposition parties in the Pact of Mexico. That was a major step to make a crucial improvement in the institutional design of the Agency. The Law Reforms were a major challenge to consolidate the institution. This is the first time I make public that we were behind the most important components of the Competition Constitutional Reform that among other elements introduced constitutional autonomy to the Agency, like the Central Bank. The appointment of Commissioners became technically and not politically based. I would say that maintaining and improving the human capital of the agency and promoting the reforms in the legal framework were crucial.

And, number three, obviously you needed to start important cases. We needed to set priorities, given that our resources were not enough to do all the investigations we wanted. The priorities at that time were basically 4 sectors, which are network sectors that were going to be concentrated in any case, because they operate with strong economies of scale and network. They needed to have the best regulation in order to generate efficiency because they have an impact on the productivity of all the other sectors in the economy. I am referring to the financial sector, energy, telecommunications, and transport. In my view, those were the basic platforms of productivity and competitiveness of the country, so if you wanted to be successful in your export experience, in your export orientation, you needed to have a very good platform of competitiveness, and that was important elements to promote efficiency and competition in those sectors.

It's so important to the well-being of an agency to define those aims and to say, "We can't do anything. Where can we make the biggest difference?" and you pick these vital infrastructure areas that have huge multiplier effects throughout the economy.

Exactly. It was efficient to intervene, so we started to make market studies in those sectors. We started investigations that we could start *ex officio*. Let me tell you that there were also additional elements, which were sectors that had an important social impact. In a country like Mexico, that is crucial. You have to put a lot of emphasis on how to improve the living standards of a great part of the population [...]. The lack of competition in industries that supply basic consumption products is important and the Antitrust Agency needed to act there. We also made market studies in industries whose products represent a high proportion of the expenditure of low-income population.

I'd like to turn your attention to another point that you've mentioned, which is this remarkable experience in Mexico in starting from what in many ways if it were an automobile, it was a relatively weakly powered automobile at the beginning – not real powerful sanctions, an automobile that the government kept somewhat close to itself. But what has happened since, starting from the early 1990s? You have this gradual progression with upgrades periodically, and, come the end of your mandate, you go to the Congress with a bold program for reform, which gives the new institution, COFECE, extraordinary stature compared to the earliest days of competition law. How did you go about persuading the Congress that it is time to do this? How did you develop a conversation with elected officials and say, "It is time," and what made your request persuasive to them? In short, how did you do that?

The story that ended with the Constitutional reform of 2013 started with the first reform of the Antitrust Law that took place in 2006 and with another reform in 2011. At that time, we had developed excellent communication with all the major political parties represented in the Congress, regardless if they represented the party in power or opposition parties. The message was clear: the best way to open an inclusive participation of consumers and members of the business community in the market place and to improve the productivity and innovation needed to insert Mexico in the global economy was through markets free of anticompetitive conducts and gifted with a procompetitive regulatory framework. Lawmakers were already convinced that a strong and independent Antitrust Authority was needed with a state-of-the-art competition law. In 2013, a new government was starting, and that new government had a very efficient strategy to start a set of reforms in different sectors. They developed what they called the "Pact for Mexico," so all parties got together and started to discuss how to design reforms to increase productivity in the country. That is how the reforms in Competition, Telecommunications, Energy and Education took place. A group of members of the Antitrust Authority team were invited by key participants of the Pact of Mexico to inject their experience in the efficient functioning of markets. That exercise created the critical mass on the Congress to make important changes in the Constitution. We were able to complement many changes that we had started in the reforms of 2006 and 2011. With that reform, the Competition Authority obtained autonomy embedded in the Constitution.

Today, the independence of the Competition Authority in Mexico is as strong as the independence of the Mexican Central Bank. The selection of commissioners is based on experience and technical legal and economic knowledge, there are specialized courts in antitrust and telecommunications, there is a separation of the technical staff that deals with investigations and the Board of Commissioners. Together with a visionary group of members of the political parties, we were able to create the basis of the stronger and professional institution that we now call COFECE. The team of COFECE maintains a high level or human capital of a superb technical staff and highly talented group of Commissioners. It is embedded directly in the Constitution, which is something unique. It's something that you don't see anywhere.

Very few. This is extraordinary compared to other institutions. It's remarkable to have that stature right in the constitution.

Absolutely. The fact that all these elements are embedded in the Constitution gives stability to the Institution and an important element of legal certainty to the economic players either in the demand or the supply side of the market. I have to confess that there might be some countries that don't even need to have that legal autonomy in their antitrust authorities. That is the case in those jurisdictions where there is a government culture of respect of the technical and independent application of the Antitrust Law by the agency responsible to enforce it. I remember having a discussion with some – I'm not going to give names – heads of authorities of some Nordic countries in Europe, and they told me in a meeting of the Organization for Economic Cooperation and Development (OECD): "Why are you advocating for autonomy and independence in such a strong way? We don't feel that we need that. We already have respect of our decisions by the Executive Branch and our autonomy does not need to be in the Constitution." I personally think that we are in a very different situation in Mexico.

That's good, and was made by the team we had in our institution. If you don't need the Constitutional Autonomy, that's fine. But the reality of my country is different. I think that Constitutional autonomy protects the technical nature of competition law enforcement and offers the Antitrust Agency greater stability. But autonomy and independence needs to go hand in hand with responsibilities that the enforcement agency needs to comply with. Obviously, autonomy will have to go with transparency of decisions, with a lot of information exchanged with the players and with the Congress. You have to have accountability at the same time as independence. You have to show results and a responsible use of your instruments.

But that was part of your program, too, during your mandate.

Yes, that was part of that. All the time we were also fighting for that transparency and we discussed with the Congress to inject more accountability obligations to the Agency. I remember that in 2006 and 2011 we discussed with the Congress the possibility of having an appointment from the president and a ratification from the Senate, and also some legal obligation to inform the Congress, and so on. I remember the Executive Branch at that time went to the Supreme Court and basically said, "Well, because of the legal division in Mexico, if this is not in the constitution" – because at that time it was not included as a constitutional change – "the Supreme Court ruled that those actions were not constitutionally consistent and should not be applied." The Supreme Court agreed with the Executive Branch that those reports should not be in the Law because they represented a contradiction with the Constitution. In 2013, given that it was a constitutional law reform, that was not a problem. So now, there is a report to the Congress that COFECE has to provide, and the Presidential appointment of Commissioners needs to be ratified by a qualified majority of the Senate. The appointment of Commissioners has to go through a process that limits the political motive to nominate Commissioners and is quite unique in Mexico vis-à-vis other jurisdictions. First, there is an *ad hoc* commission that is formed by the central bank, by the head of the Statistics Institute, both constitutional autonomous institutions. They make a public call to anybody who wants to be Commissioner, and then they make a C.V. review, and after that, they take an exam. After the exam, they pick 5 names, which are the highest grades on the exam, and the president can choose one from that group only. Then, it has to be ratified by two-thirds of the Senate. It's a high threshold that assures you of the technical quality of Commissioners. That binds the process of appointments to be technical and not political. That supports the technical principles of decisions.

But to me, it's impressive the combination of features that are built into the reforms: "Yes, we want more autonomy, but we want a mechanism that provides assurances that the people exercising that authority are high quality, and we commit ourselves to being accountable for our policy choices. We explain more of what we've done. We issue reports, we give speeches, we appear before legislative groups, so we are accountable for how we are using this authority, too."

That is very important. The third element of that reform, which was very important, was to create specialized courts in the judiciary in competition and telecommunications. It gives legal certainty to the players, to companies. If you appeal a decision, your case is going to be analyzed and judged by persons who are experts not only in the legal framework but also in economics, so they know both areas. They decide faster; the decisions have a much higher quality. That, combined with the fact that even with the support of the FTC and with some European authorities, our judges have been trained by other judges, judges from here in the US and judges from Europe [...].

In some agencies in the world, a single individual is the head of the agency. Others have a college. The agencies that you and I each worked for – the FTC in the United States, the Competition Authority in Mexico – was a college. What did you find to be the special challenges or needs associated with being the head of a college, one member of the college? How does that change your approach to governance?

That is a very important question. In Mexico, we are not accustomed to have colleges in the administrative agencies. You have to learn how to deal with a college. I had never done that before. Even after the 9 years that I spent in the Antitrust Authority, I would say that I still have things to learn about how to deal and how to work together with a college, and together with some legal instruments that the head of the agency has vis-à-vis the other part of the Board, and that is not easy. Sometimes you have a lot of trade-offs. Sometimes you need to make market studies, and this is going to be part of the success of having good regulation in that market, and the college discussion obviously gives the richness of the plurality but also the complexity of having to discuss a resolution with many members. In my case, the Law at the time gave the Chair the faculty to make and publish market studies and to react to anticompetitive Law projects in the Congress. It sometimes risks the quality of the resolutions of the agency because finally the resolution or the decision is the result of a very strong and complicated discussion. In that discussion, in those tradeoffs, the decision becomes not as high quality, if you would like to put it that way, but it has the benefit of the plural elements that you need, and that is useful in this kind of agencies. It's a complicated issue. You have to learn to work with a group of equals, taking decisions as a group with each person sometimes having a different interpretation of the cases. In the end, I think it is an important challenge, and it goes very well in line with what you would like to have to give also some certainty to the economic players.

Suppose I'm a new appointee and, like you in this position, I've never worked in a college before. I'm new, but I'm going to become the President of COFECE. Do you have some specific suggestions or tips about how I keep my colleagues happy, my fellow college members? What should I think of doing in order to maintain a spirit of common cause? How do I maintain their goodwill?

I don't know if I am the best person to answer that question because, as I said before, I think there are things that I would do differently today. But I learned.

Today, the mechanism of selection of Commissioners reduces the possible political motivation of the appointments and might simplify a bit the difficult process of internal coordination and the variability of criteria and finally the good environment in the college. As long as you can, as a chairman or as president of the institution, you have to make each and every Commissioner the owner of the final outcome. I think that is one of the most difficult but important challenges in order to have the majority of the people happy with the outcome. You will not always have all of the people happy because I don't believe consensus is the best way to deal with these issues. That doesn't mean you are doing well.

Sometimes, if you wait for everyone to be happy, you do nothing.

Look at the WTO. The WTO is a consensus-building. In my opinion that has been one of the reasons why the organization is impeded to move forward. Obviously, in the WTO you have 160-something countries, and that's a completely different issue. But here you have 7 people today, 7 persons, and it's a complicated task. But I think it's worth it to try it. The fact that you work in good faith and you really work as a team with the people who are taking decisions is something that is going to add value in the quality of the decision. Let me repeat that I might not be the best person to do that because it was difficult for me to maintain the best environment in the Plenum. I had to work sometimes with different groups depending on the cases. Then you have to have a minimum critical mass to have a majority decision, and that makes some people unhappy. In order to deal with the timing required by the Law, with the fact that you have to make decisions in an efficient way, sometimes you are going to make some people unhappy.

But I think that suggestion about the importance of talking to your colleagues, trying to build this sense of common ownership, and spending lots of time with them – I found that I spent lots of time telling them how brilliant they were in individual conversations, that they're doing a great job. But to be aware that this is a different environment than if you are simply the head, and you have to take account of the importance of getting – with a total college of 7, a magic number of 4.

I think that the current Chairwoman of COFECE, Alejandra Palacios, has worked seriously to have a good environment in the Plenum and that is perceived by practitioners. That sends a good signal of the strength of the Commission. The new mechanism of selection of Commissioners makes that exercise of coordination more attainable.

For me, with 5, the magic number was 3.

For me it was 3 as well, because we were 5 when I was in the Commission. But today it's 7. It multiplies the complication of the decisions. For every person you have. But something that I have to recognize – and I do it gladly – is that I feel, at least from outside, that the environment of the plenum of COFECE from outside looks very positive, very well-managed. So I have to make a very sincere recognition to Alejandra Palacios Prieto, the new head of the Competition Authority.

To develop the package of reforms and to build support, you had to have a continuing conversation with the Congress. How important is it for the head of the Agency to have at the same time autonomy to decide but also a link, a channel of communication, to preserve both?

I think it is very important to protect the independence of your work and open a good and trustable channel of communication with the Congress and the different parties of the Congress. When you really spend time explaining, discussing, and communicating with people from the Congress, you start realizing that the ideologies and the principles that move the different parties can converge in the end, and they converge in the public interest of the people they are defending and representing. If you are able to build your argument giving preponderance to the well-being of people, which is basically the end of the enforcement and competition advocacy, you can work with all of them.

This was the case. We had a few reforms with almost unanimity, with almost consensus, and for me it was one of the most interesting experiences to work and to communicate constantly with the Congress in order to promote these reforms. So I think it goes beyond ideology. I speak especially about the current government. I think that as soon as this new government, which is much more oriented to the poor people, realizes that well-functioning and competitive markets are an instrument that should be behind public policy to protect the low income people, the Executive Branch could take the advantage of a professional Antitrust Institution. We will see. As long as members of this new government understand that the combination of well-functioning markets, competition instead of regulation – and in some cases you will need to regulate in order to promote more competitive outcomes – but if you have well-functioning markets, you can concentrate in the equality or in improved opportunities of the majority of people in my country, in Mexico. I think

– I hope – that is taking place. I saw, for instance, just recently, participation of the Mexican president, Lopez Obrador, in the financial convention with all the banks in Mexico basically saying, "Competition is better than overregulating. In some cases, you will have to regulate to promote more competition or to avoid the difficulty of new members to enter into those markets." But, for me, that speech was very well taken because basically it goes very much in line with what you would need, markets that generate opportunities for companies and for consumers, and goes very much in line with your social objectives and with your social projects, and the fight against corruption. The best way to fight against corruption is to promote transparent and procompetitive decisions in infrastructure and government procurement. We are still in time to see how the new government proceeds and uses markets as a powerful instrument to attain different objectives of economic policy. But I hope it will go very much in that line. Actually, the new government recognizes the competition through trade as a very important source of benefits for our country, so they are very much in line with respecting the international trade agreements that we have already signed.

You built a career in part around trade. You are an international person with an international orientation, the trade agreements negotiations and then several years in Geneva as Ambassador to the WTO for Mexico. You're interested in international affairs, but now you're at the Competition Agency, and I ask as an outsider: "Why is Mexico so deeply involved in all these international matters? Don't we have enough things to do at home? And here is the president, who has become part of this International Competition Network and he's the Chair of the Steering Committee." Why was international so important to you as a part of what you did?

I think it is important for Mexican society in general, not only for me, to be inserted in the Global Economy. I think we have to understand that we are part of a global economy and we have to benefit from what others have already learned from their experience. You have to use international experience to develop best international practices. You have to apply competition policy in your own domestic markets, specially for nontradeable goods and services that are not necessarily disciplined by international trade. Sometimes, when you look at where we are lacking in competitiveness, it has to do with the nontradeable services sectors, where you need local, domestic competition enforcement and competition policy. And, as we say in Mexico, you're not going to discover the "warm water." You should use the best experiences, the best practices abroad, and I think we have to understand that to be part of the International Competition Network (ICN), and even to be an active participant and the Chairman of the ICN Steering Group, is important. It's a good sign you send internally to the Congress, to the Executive Branch, that you can play there. But in order to play there, you have to understand the importance of respecting and using what has been learned abroad. That's important.

Was the engagement with international organizations valuable for Mexico in pursuing its own reforms and building the system?

Without any doubt. Just in the case of competition law, as I was saying, the fact that we were negotiating the free trade agreement was precisely what generated the pressure and the need to build a new competition law and an Antitrust Agency. The design of the competition law used the best international practices as an essential input. We, in Mexico, used the OECD input to design the original Competition Law in 1992, and we used the design of the FTC as a reference to build our own agency. And we used the best practices in Europe because we are an administrative legal system (French type), which is different from the legal system you have in the United States or in the United Kingdom. So that was important. All the reforms that we made afterwards – 2006, 2011, 2013 – were all inspired by the best international practices, so we were basically building our legal framework and its reforms from the experience of matured agencies. I think this is the moment to also think about what should be the next step for organizations like the ICN.

Perhaps you could close out our conversation with your thoughts about what those next steps should be. What do we do next?

I think this is a good moment to start reflecting on what should be the next step for the ICN. This is something that I discussed yesterday in an FTC hearing in which I was invited to participate. Let me first, very briefly, start with the diagnosis that I consider very clear: we are facing an international movement which goes very much on the nationalistic and populist side. Countries of different latitudes are looking inside instead to consolidate their global integration. When you look at some mergers that have not been approved, because of political pressures in Europe and in some other countries as well, attempts to influence decisions of the Antitrust Authorities by the Trump Administration and some publicly critical positioning of the Mexican President against the Antitrust Agency; this is also happening in other jurisdictions. There is a growing lack of confidence in well-functioning markets and a reconsideration of sound market-oriented policies. I think that, in those circumstances, we need to avoid the idea of national champions, the idea of making your domestic consumers pay in order to have domestic big companies without the pressure and without the dynamics of international competition. This is something that we have to consider today and it's a reality that we all have to face.

For me, one way to start thinking about facing that reality is to make a reflection on what should be the role of the ICN in the international arena to defend well designed procompetitive market oriented policies. The ICN has been maybe one of the most successful networks, a "soft law" very efficient network, a virtual network, but maybe questions like: should we build an international organization? A more, let's say, not virtual but with some permanent secretariat, to defend some basic principles, to monitor, and to generate not only best international practices but to go a little bit farther with some sort of obligations from the members? The members will decide if they want to be members or not of the ICN as an international organization. The ICN started with 15 members at its origins; now they have more than 130 members. My impression is that the ICN should have a more active presence and defense of markets to improve the wellbeing of citizens and to be the source of innovation. We need a strong organization with greater international presence. If the network of almost all competition authorities does not defend markets and open international trade presence, who will do it?

The transition of the ICN to a more formal international organization is a tough discussion, but in my opinion, this is a good time to start that discussion. Maybe you decide that the best way is to maintain the way the ICN is working, that's fine – I mean, if the end of the discussion is to go back or to stay where you are or to modify some elements of what you are doing, that's fine. Constructive discussion and dialogue are going to be worthwhile. My point is that this is a good moment to do that reflection, the international situation deserves an organization with a strong voice to advocate for open markets that are the essence of the incentives to innovate and to continue the process of competitive market disruptions that create wealth in the global economy. The ICN Steering Group could assemble an *ad hoc* commission to reflect on the future of the ICN that itself has been a very successful network.

James Rill*

US Department of Justice, Assistant Attorney General for Antitrust (1989-1992)

I have the wonderful opportunity to talk with one of the most distinguished leaders in our field, and that's Jim Rill. A challenge that engravers have when they prepare the plaque that goes in the Hall of Fame is that they only have a limited amount of space. So what are they going to say about Jim? They'll have to mention that he was the Assistant Attorney General for Antitrust in the U.S. Department of Justice and served there for several years. They will mention that he is the Former Chair of the American Bar Association's Section of Antitrust Law. They will mention that he co-chaired the International Competition Policy Advisory Committee (ICPAC), which was convened by Assistant Attorney General Joel Klein in 1997; and, among other things, it was the true catalyst for the formation of what became the International Competition Network (ICN). Jim, you had a number of distinguished positions in private practice and are currently a Partner with Baker Botts. My aim in talking with you is to give successors to your position and other leaders around the world insights in what it takes to be a successful head of an agency. Let's, first reflect for a moment on your thoughts as you went into the Division, and watching numerous agencies over time, what characteristics or background provide the best possible preparation for someone stepping into a position of such significance in public service.

Well, a somewhat unusual situation is that I had actually been 30 years in private practice in the antitrust field and had just come off as Chair of the Antitrust Section of the American Bar Association. So, if I didn't know a lot of antitrust, I certainly was exposed to a lot of antitrust. And I had managed to have a fairly varied career in managing to deal with mergers and unilateral conduct issues. I broke my teeth on the Robinson-Patman Act. That explains, I think, what was

* Interview conducted on 3 May 2019.

extremely valuable to me, not one necessarily that could be replicated by everyone taking that position, but for my purposes, from my experience, it was extremely valuable. Interestingly enough with respect to the Antitrust Division, one area that I had not practiced a great deal in was criminal antitrust enforcement. A lot of what the Department of Justice does is criminal antitrust enforcement. So, when I was approached by the person who was doing Transition for Justice under Boyden Gray, who was doing transition for the whole United States for President-Elect George H. W. Bush, there had been a suggestion that I be made Chairman of the Federal Trade Commission. I said, "That's probably not a good idea. We're a small firm and we're just getting underway." He said, "No, we agree with you, you shouldn't be Chairman of the Federal Trade Commission." I said, "Thanks a lot. By the way, I figured that one out for myself." He said, "We want to make you Assistant Attorney General." Well, I went through this whole business of small firm and getting underway, getting started, and I said – the guy's name was Mike Uhlmann – I said, "Mike, I'm going to be honest with you. I haven't done a lot of criminal antitrust work. I've had some grand jury experience, but I've not tried any criminal cases, haven't played any out." He said, "That's all right. You can pick it up." I said, "Okay. Well, but I'm not sure I can really do it." He said, "Do me a favor, send me over your curriculum vitae and we'll use it to compare with the people being sent over by presidential personnel and to see if it works." Well, I wasn't born yesterday. I knew the minute that I sent my CV I was in play. I turned to my wife Betsy and I said, "What do you think?" She said, "It's a government job. You won't have to work that hard." [Laughter] I only disabused her of that later.

Others value teaching, which can be obviously of great help. Government service can be a great value. The only government service I had was two years in the Army. But I think government service can be a great experience base for a job like Head of the Antitrust Division.

And you had been a manager at this startup enterprise, your firm.

I was the head of the practice group and on the executive committee, and so forth and so on, at a firm. So, yes, I have had some management experience with that.

And all the experience in the professional startup, the American Bar Association, your counseling work, it made you an astute student of the two agencies and how the system worked, so that you were no stranger to the organizations or the people who were there.

Strangely, though, I had actually done a fair amount of work before the Department of Justice, but more work really before the Federal Trade Commission.

With the Robinson-Patman beginning.

Yes, when Earl Kintner was Chairman of the Commission. I had done that. I realized early on that I needed the "hothouse course" on criminal enforcement. I got in touch with Judy Whalley, who was the career Deputy Assistant Attorney General, who had been head of the Chicago Office and Joe Widmar, who was head of operations and with Gary Spratling, who was head of the West Coast field office. I pulled them all together and I said, "Okay, what's on the table? What are the considerations? What's your evidentiary base for bringing a criminal case? Do you need corroboration; what level of corroboration do you need? How do you proceed in it? And how can I be of help as well as support you, and you can support me?" We spent a lot of time together going through all of that.

What did you have in mind when you approached the position, you went through the selection process, confirmation? What were your aims in coming to the Division? What did you want to do?

This is now taking me back to really early 1989. About this time there was some question as to whether enforcement, particularly in the merger area, had been fully effective. And one of the problems was the states of the United States were taking a more aggressive role and beginning to more or less occupy the field. I thought we really needed national leadership, particularly in merger policy.

So, my objective was to promote a more vigorous and rational – I'm not saying it was irrational before – strong merger enforcement program at the DOJ. I was concerned with some of the doctrinal issues that were coming down. One case cleared a merger because of the entry, without any further analysis – "it's cheap to buy a trash truck, so therefore the merger is okay." That's not really a particularly articulate analysis on which to reach a decision. I wanted to do something particularly in the entry area to clarify the standard. So the real principal objective that I had in mind at the early stage was to develop a more coherent, and I would say somewhat more aggressive position – not for the sake of bringing cases. It doesn't matter how many planes take off; it matters how many land. I keep that in mind.

But there was an important element in the sense of enhancing the credibility of the institution.

That was a problem. We actually developed a very good working relationship with the states that was encouraged by Dick Thornburgh, who was the Attorney General, who had been a two-term governor of Pennsylvania. He was totally prepared to work with the states, and in fact promoted, directed, the establishment of the Joint Working Group that the Federal Trade Commission and DOJ put together with State Assistant Attorneys General for Antitrust, which I think is still working today. That produced, I think, a very good working relationship that served both sides, all antitrust.

I want to come back to some of the substantive programs that you've already touched on. In those early days in 1989 coming in, what was the biggest adjustment for you going from long experience in private institutions into a public agency at the highest level, into a large and complex department, a major part of it of course the Antitrust Division? What were the big adjustments that you went through in making this transition?

It was really broadening the management scope and broadening the decision-making process. My law firm, Collier, Shannon, Rill & Scott, had 75 lawyers. The Antitrust Division had 500. There was an adjustment to delegation with the deputies. I was blessed with a really good set of deputies: Mike Boudin, who's now a judge in the First Circuit, for example; Judy Whalley, who had wonderful experience both in criminal and civil antitrust enforcement; Alison Smith, a politically very sensible person out of Texas; and Bobby Willig, the Deputy Assistant Attorney General for Economics. I don't think he ever thought he was the deputy, but he sure thought he was a general. [Laughter] And he was excellent. He was superb.

And I take it that certainly one thing that a leader has to think about very carefully is building that team, which you built very successfully.

A lot of people like to put out the cliché that they don't like meetings. I like meetings, and I like to have a regular meeting at least three days a week with the front-office staff, the deputies and the special assistants in the front office. We usually had them around 7:30 in the morning, which drove Joe Widmar crazy. Bobby was okay because he had probably stayed up all night; he was a nighttime worker – and worked; I don't mean he did anything but work – to review everything that was going on. I also had regular calls with the field officers, who played a major role, particularly in criminal antitrust enforcement.

I mentioned Gary Spratling, who was head of the West Coast office, who was particularly noteworthy in that area. I told Joe Widmar "I don't want these calls to be social events. I want to know what the people are doing. I want to know what are the big cases that are pending, and I want to hear about them in substance. If the calls go on for an hour or two, that's fine with me". I think the field officers – it was initially a shock, but I think they liked it; they liked the idea that the AAG really wanted to hear what they were doing and play a key role.

Keep a connection to the program, yes.

I think that – I'm told – stimulated a lot of morale at the Division, to hear "Here's what we're doing." I'm not saying the other prior AAGs didn't have the same thing, but for me it was an ideal way to reach out and find out what's going on in the guts of the Division and in the field offices as well as, of course, the Washington-based sections. I think it was very important to have a career Deputy in Judy. There were some in the White House personnel office who said, "Why do you need a career Deputy?" I said, "Well, if you don't have a career Deputy, for one thing you're going to be doing a lot of learning curve stuff you wouldn't otherwise have to do and you're probably going to endanger the morale of the Division."

It's the memory that you have that runs through the organization.

Absolutely. As I say, Judy had been head of the Chicago office and she had a wealth of knowledge, and was widely respected within the Division. So I was very well served by the deputies. The surprising thing – maybe not so surprising – is that I was able to select them all. There were suggestions from the White House in one case, that was fine, but otherwise I was able to pick the deputies, and that was very, very helpful.

In so many ways – and you referred to one of them – you built important bridges throughout your time in the Department: the bridge to the states, to take a relationship that was in disrepair and enhance that. But in so many other areas. There's the remarkable set of events in 1989, near 30 years ago: the Berlin Wall comes down and the Soviet Union unravels, the Warsaw Pact is dissolved, and there is now suddenly a new world of international affairs than existed before; it's the first year of the European Union's Merger Regulation; and it's time to come back and look at mergers again, too. And you built a relationship with the Federal Trade Commission that leads to the government's first Joint Merger Guidelines. How did this all come about?

Well, it came about because it was not only desirable, it was necessary, essential. Janet Steiger was the incoming Chairman of the Federal Trade Commission. She had many outstanding skills. One of her particular skills was really being a manager and having objective views and really marvelous people skills. And she knew how to deal with me. [Laughter] I knew that we needed to build something together. As you may recall, the first set of Merger Guidelines put out by Bill Baxter were only DOJ Guidelines.

I think Jim Miller said something like, "Well, we're going to enforce the law, not pay any attention to these Guidelines." Maybe it's because he wasn't given any advance notice. I don't know what the background is. But they were not joint Guidelines. Two objectives: (1) to be sure that they are joint guidelines; and (2) to try and minimize, if possible, the objection that might come to the Guidelines from either the states, for example, or the Hill. Remember, during the entire time, the three-plus years, that I was AAG, the other party controlled both the House and Senate, and it was necessary to establish comity and a working relationship. I actually had a very good relationship with Senator Metzenbaum. I think the people on the fifth floor, the AG's Office, were a little suspicious of me for that, but it was necessary to have that. And then, on the international side –

This is Howard Metzenbaum, who was – was he the Chair of the Judiciary Antitrust Subcommittee?

Subcommittee Chairman, yes. Internationally, really, I had done some international work, but it wasn't one of my major focuses in private practice. I was very well served by the head of our International Section, Chuck Stark, who was very well thought of, particularly in Europe but everywhere; knew everything there was to know about international antitrust law, knew just a wealth of information; and also a guy with tremendously good people skills.

So I was very well served. Well, I got a call one day from Leon Brittan who said he'd like to talk to me. So I said, "Chuck, who's Leon Brittan?" He said, "He's the Commissioner for Competition, Sir Leon Brittan to you, the Commissioner for Competition for the EC." I said, "So I guess we should meet with him then." Well, we became friends. Leon came in and said he wanted to create more or less a formal agreement, whereby, even though Party A would have jurisdiction, if Party B had more of an interest Party A would step aside, waive jurisdiction, and let Party B handle the case. I said, "Sir Leon, if I go to Congress with this suggestion that we're going to surrender even where we have jurisdiction, there will probably be an impeachment filed the next day. Can we back off and do something else?" That's how we developed, instead, the Antitrust Working Agreement with the EC, which was signed in September 1991.

That was a breakthrough agreement, and it was one in which both DOJ and FTC participated as equal partners on the U.S. side, and Leon Brittan and his staff participated very actively – Claus-Dieter Ehlermann, who was the Director General at the time for what was then called DG IV or DG COMP – met four or five times to thrash it out.

We developed this notion of positive comity under which if an activity was occurring in Jurisdiction B that had an economic effect in Jurisdiction A, not necessarily through imports into Jurisdiction A but broadly into Jurisdiction A, Jurisdiction A could request Jurisdiction B to take enforcement action since the conduct was taking place in their territory. For positive comity, the effect would also of course have to be in Jurisdiction B as well as Jurisdiction A.

It could be an effective way not only for resource management, but also an effective way for comity: rather than for Jurisdiction A necessarily to have to – which they reserve the right to do – go plunging in and taking the case over, let Jurisdiction B have the opportunity to handle the case. That was worked into the 1991 agreement. I don't know how long or how often it has been enforced, but I think putting it in the agreement has paid good dividends.

In so many ways. You built, and certainly led the development with others, an infrastructure under which policy still travels today: the development of the continuing, evolving framework for the U.S.–European Union relationship; the framework for the relationship with the Federal Trade Commission in which you engaged the Commission in the preparation of the Guidelines; and the role in international affairs. The development of the Guidelines is a highlight of policymaking. None of these directly involved cases. They are not the events that provide you a ribbon-cutting ceremony and you can say, "Look at the trophy I've just brought home." But, if you think of all the ways in which policy today still uses these roads – enhanced, but still travels over these roads – it has to be a source of satisfaction to realize that you were in so many ways the architect of that infrastructure.

Well, nobody does it alone. When you mentioned each of these issues – the Merger Guidelines, you can't underestimate the work of Janet Steiger to keep that process going, to keep her four colleagues on script, which didn't – actually we had one dissent from the Guidelines. But to keep that going and to keep it moving, I cannot understate the value she had there. At the same time, internally I can't understate the value that Bobby Willig and Paul Denis brought to that effort. Bobby was innovative, creative, understood what we wanted to do with the entry aspect of mergers, worked this whole notion of unilateral effects into the Guidelines. It might have been a little bit overdone. We may have gotten more than we asked for there, but it was innovative and proper. Paul was the scrivener for all of us. We'd work until 7:00 or 8:00 on the Guidelines and then I'd go home and they'd go out to dinner and work until 2:00 or 3:00 in the morning on the Guidelines. So, as I said, nobody can do it alone. And during this whole period I kept the states briefed on what we were doing, giving them drafts, so forth. Then, when the time came, April of 1992, where we'd reached agreement with the Federal Trade Commission.

Bill Barr said "We're in an election year. What's going to be the reaction in the Senate and the House on this?" So, I went down to see Senator Metzenbaum. We had a good relationship. He said that we were putting elements in the Guidelines that made for a more rigorous analysis, I think, than had been before. A more in-depth analysis into the competitive effects aspect, or what probable competitive effects – I'm probably going into too much detail – but some thought that it made the work harder for the Division. I told the staff, when they expressed concern, "I said, 'We've lost three out of four cases,' and you think I'm going to make it harder by making this more realistic? Come on!" Well, Senator Metzenbaum's reaction was, "Jim, are you making this too tough for yourself?" But I said, "No, Senator, I'm making it easier for myself because now we'll give the courts a better, if you will, pathway to reaching a rational decision on mergers."

It did happen. So, I said, "I certainly think it's going to be a positive for enforcement." Well, his being a Democrat, we're not in the same party – I'm not saying Democrat versus Republican – but he had the seat and blessed it right away. He said, "This is a very interesting step and I'm certainly going to keep an eye on it." So I went back to the Attorney General and I said, "Senator Metzenbaum's okay." He said, "No, he said he's going to keep an eye on it." I said, "General, that's a victory." [Laughter] He said, "I guess you're right."

I underscore a couple of things here that, again, I think a successor would reflect on well: the importance of building the team, the general manager who assembles the best possible people, because you can't succeed without people like Bob and Paul, Judy, the entire ensemble. That's one of your key functions, is to bring that team in and let them prosper.

Don't forget Mike Boudin while you're talking about the team, who was very well thought of at the staff level and a remarkable person, too.

And in so many ways part of what you did is building trainworks with a durable life. All of these involved investments in activities that in many ways would not generate observable benefits that you would realize during your tenure. This was an investment in the future. This is an act of faith in creating structures that will have enduring value, even though on the day that you leave and go back to private life there aren't obvious immediate results from this process. That creates a standard that people feel, I think, over time they should emulate.

We didn't know what the reaction was going to be in the courts to the Merger Guidelines. I remember at one of these ABA functions Judge Thomas Penfield Jackson was asked, "What about these Guidelines coming out?" His reaction was, "Well, we'll view those as a government statement against interest." [Laughter] Fortunately, the 1992 Guidelines have been generally accepted in the courts. I think – I don't know – we'll see how the 2010 Guidelines work out. There was definite room for modification and improvement. But I've noticed in litigating the cases, the government still sticks pretty close to the 1992 Guidelines in presenting them to the Court, because they're something they're familiar with.

And to look at many judicial decisions that, of course, always acknowledge "these don't bind us but this is an impressive way to think about the problem."

They have generally been accepted. I have to add one quick anecdote on the 1992 Guidelines, and I don't want to take up too much time on it. On April 1, Janet called and said, "I've got the votes at the Commission. We can get them out today." I said, "Janet, hold it one day. We don't want the 'April Fool's Guidelines.'" [Laughter]

As you left, was there unfinished business that you wish you had been able to get to?

My favorite case, which was ultimately brought under Mark Gidley, who was Acting AAG towards the end of the Bush Administration – I left in May-June of 1992, and the Airline Tariff Publishing case was ready to go. I was ready to go on it. I think that the airlines were pretty sure where I was coming out on it, and they were doing their best to see if they could spin it out, and they succeeded. I went to the Attorney General before I left and I said, "They may want to see you on this. If they do, it's a good case and here's why." Ultimately, as I say, the case was brought under Mark Gidley, but we did a lot to keep it going. One of my regrets is I didn't get the case out under my watch. It's one of my favorite cases.

This was a major contribution to enforcement policy dealing with the interaction of competitors using high-tech interaction. Today, we talk so much about artificial intelligence, algorithms. This is an antecedent on the kinds of issues that we face today.

High-tech in a smoke-filled room. That was great. I also wanted to terminate a decree, the so-called Financial Interest and Syndication Decree, which I felt had utterly no – if it ever had any residual consumer welfare effect, that had long since gone with the advent of cable television. This was the prohibition against networks owning the rerun rights to sitcoms, which is where most of the money is. Of course, the Hollywood producers were strongly against my terminating the decree. The networks were definitely in favor of termination. We didn't end up really being able to do it during the time I was there, but Anne Bingaman, to her credit, ended up terminating that decree.

It finally toppled.

Yes. But those are kind of minor things that I would rather have gotten done during the time I was there on the enforcement front.

Regarding the international world that we've touched on a bit: you had a pivotal role in establishing the technical assistance program that the Federal Trade Commission and the Department of Justice pursue jointly, the remarkable set of developments that those of us of a certain age could not have imagined easily. And in your life after the Department you keep a major hand in public policy with the International Competition Policy Advisory Committee (ICPAC), which you mentioned at the beginning being a key accomplishment – with others, as you say; you co-chaired the committee – leads to ICN. At what point were you convinced that this had to be a major focus of attention by U.S. policymakers?

We had a whole set of hearings with the ICPAC. In one set of hearings we had literally half-a-dozen leading heads of enforcement agencies around the world – from the EC, from European States, from Canada, Japan. As the story unfolds, there was so much going on – I had just come off of the Japanese talks, the Structural Impediments Initiative talks – that had global ramifications, that the activity in one country not only substantively, immediately, but from the standpoint of doctrinal policy ramifications cannot be isolated within one jurisdiction. The idea of fomenting a mechanism for greater cooperation became more and more evident to me and to others who were interested in and working on the area. I have to give huge credit to Joel Klein, who was instrumental in establishing the ICPAC, with Janet Reno, who was then the Attorney General. I think that the members of the committee – I mean it was a working committee for the most part; people really put time in. The head of Merck [Raymond V. Gilmartin] spent an awful lot of time concerned with this; the head of Allegheny Steel [Richard P. Simmons] spent a lot of time working on it; Eleanor Fox spent a great deal of time contributing to it. John Dunlop, who had been Secretary of Labor, also spent a great deal of time on it. It was a totally nongovernmental committee, academics as well as businessmen and practitioners, that just, I think, worked beautifully.

And an exceptional Secretariat.

I was going to get to the really critically important one, who was of course Merit Janow, who teaches at Columbia.

The Dean of the Foreign Affairs Program.

Right. She was Executive Director of the committee, and she as much as I had the notion of what we called the "global forum," to get it started. We had general agreement among the committee members that it was a good idea and we recommended it. It lay there for a while, until Merit and I – I don't know how much time we've got – we went to Joel and said, "You need to give this a push." He said, "Well, what about the September Fordham program?" "We said that's too late. We have an election year." This was going on 2000. So, he said, "Okay, I'll do it at the Tenth Anniversary of the European Merger".

In Brussels, he addressed the meeting and he recommended this. Mario Monti, who was the Commissioner for Competition, was taken somewhat by surprise, but the next day he endorsed it. That gave it a shot, gave it a good start. Another shot in the arm was at the very beginning of 2001, at a conference at Ditchley Park, which was a wartime location for Churchill to meet, and brought together the heads of about ten different agencies. At that time, I think, Doug Melamed was Acting AAG, or maybe John Nannes. But that gave it a start. Then, what really gave it a final start was DOJ and FTC pushing this, and particularly you and Tim Muris working with Charles James, as the new leadership of the agencies took over – putting this on, getting the project started, I would say, as a priority, which you were able to do in September of 2001. Adjacent to the Fordham Conference. I think the ICN has served a tremendously valuable purpose.

The guidance documents of the ICN are marvelous. The work that has been done, I think, in many respects by both agencies – and a lot of credit goes to Randy Tritell and the people who set up the FTC international shop – has been terrific. The problem we need to face now is some level of accountability – not necessarily a report card, but some means of assessing whether the jurisdictions are really paying any attention to the guidance documents.

For example, in process we want to know, let's have more transparency as to what's going on. When you go to the OECD meetings, you need to have a country review: "Do you do transparency?" – well, nobody's going to say, "No we don't do transparency, they say we do transparency. Next question." I think this is an effort that current Assistant Attorney General Makan Delrahim had in mind in trying to establish some multilateral framework. There seems to be some progress in that area now. It looks like there's a two-track effort that will take into account ICN. Much stronger steps – we'll have to see how it works out – towards assessing accountability. I think that is the next crying need in international enforcement.

In carrying things forward.

To see if the guidance documents are really being adhered to. And we don't want to have trade-type sanctions, I don't think, for countries that don't adhere necessarily to the guidance documents, but the reputational effect of calling a country out for transgressing against global standards of process or substance can have an effect. I think that's the next step, and that there's a crying need for that step, and a crying need for the agencies, FTC and DOJ, to work together in that direction. I'm not sure how effective that's been, frankly.

I think the spirit with which you helped develop the relationship during your time at the Department was an extraordinary step ahead, whether it's the work you did with Janet Steiger, the FTC Chair, the work internationally, the Guidelines – so many ways. And, in the narrow sense, you didn't have to do that. If you were a purely parochial government official, you could have brushed that aside. But you had to take the step to cross the boundary in a global way.

Do not underestimate the role of Janet in all of this. She was huge. It didn't make any sense to me to have Guidelines that one agency followed and the other agency had its own standard. Why not have the same standard? You've got to have the same standard in the merger area. And she agreed and made it work. She had to deal with four colleagues. All I had to do was deal with an Attorney General. [Laughter]

The same thing is true internationally. You can't have two voices. There is one United States. I appreciate the notion, being an alumnus of DOJ, that there are certain things that the DOJ has in the way of being a member of the Executive Branch that gives it a certain, if not priority, at least more of a particular institutional structural role than the FTC. But the FTC's part of our government, too, and the input the FTC can have, is substantial. I mean, the agreement with the European Union and the other enforcement working agreements have been joint. If they can do that jointly, why can't we do other things jointly? Like make this next step towards accountability. I would like to see more support from the FTC for Makan's notion of a multilateral framework and perhaps more communication from the other way on what the objectives are and how that can best be achieved.

I want to close our conversation with a couple of reflections on key points you've mentioned. The awareness of the larger environment outside of one's own institution and the formation of partnerships to improve, the development of the right team to do the job, the investment in the framework that's going to carry policy forward in so many ways. A final observation about what you've done: when we look at all the structures, the part of the bridge where you see the names of those who were involved in the design – the road, the rail line, the port – all the infrastructure we depend on in this area, look how much of it has your name on it.

Not alone. Never alone.

Never alone. But it's striking how often the same guy show up again and again because of this forward-looking investment, and not a day goes by when we do not travel over those roads.

I appreciate that, Bill, but no man's an island.

No man is an island, but real leadership involves the commitment to do this. On behalf of Concurrences, I'm enormously grateful for you sharing this. And may the spirit continue to motivate others who hold these jobs, Jim.

Barbara Rosenberg[*]

Brazil's Secretariat of Economic Law of the Ministry of Justice, Senior Manager (2003-2005)

You were a crucial participant in the development of Brazil's highly successful competition system. You were a senior manager at the Secretariat of Economic Law of the Ministry of Justice (SDE), at a time before Brazil carried out the fusion that put together the current configuration, due to a set of very ambitious reforms in which you had a hand, too, in the formulation of policy. You are one of an extraordinary collection of young Brazilian professionals who played a fundamental role in the establishment of what has become, by all acknowledgement, the most successful of the Latin American agencies and, by any global standard or measurement, certainly one of the very best by any standard across the board. I would like to begin with a little bit of a biographical journey. Could you describe a bit about what brought you into the competition policymaking world?

I started working a little bit in competition in a practical way. I didn't have it at school because at the time there was no competition law in Brazil. It was just being approved in Congress but had not been enforced. There was a little bit of competition work at the firm I was working at, and I was also doing other areas.

I should add now that you, since leaving the public enforcement role, head the Barbosa Müssnich & Aragão (BMA) competition law practice in São Paulo and Rio.

That's right. Basically, at that time I was doing merger and acquisition, intellectual property work, a little bit of other things, but I was always interested in the topic. I joined a PhD program at the university where I graduated

* Interview conducted on 10 May 2019.

where I was already looking into competition and IP – that was my topic of interest – and I had the luck of going to UC Berkeley. It was great. They had an intellectually very interesting program on IP and antitrust, so I had the chance to develop. That was a very early topic in Brazil, I would say, in those times. But really, it was something more of an academic interest rather than a practical possibility to work with because of what we basically had in Brazil. CADE already existed, SDE as well, but they were not as relevant, and, honestly, I never really thought about going to an agency at that point. I had the chance to work in a law firm after, where I was not working with competition because they thought that there wouldn't be enough competition work in Brazil to do in that area.

When I came back – I was supposed to stay longer in New York working for this firm – to São Paulo, it was to conclude my PhD studies. Then, on January 1st or 2nd, I received a call from Daniel Goldberg, who had just been invited to be the Superintendent at SDE, which was the competition agency within the Ministry of Justice. At first, he asked me if I knew somebody to suggest joining him as his deputy at the Authority. I gave him the 10 names of people who, I thought, could work with him. He said, "No, I think you would be the right name."

Then, it's interesting, because I ended up going to competition and shifting. I would never have thought at the beginning that it was very thrilling. At that time, I never thought of being an enforcer, much less becoming an antitrust enforcer, even though I had had the chance to study that quite deeply and had the chance to work with that a bit. I also had spent some time at the World Trade Organization (WTO) and also had the chance to deal with competition issues at that time, more on a theoretical point – there was a big discussion about our trade competition agreement in that context. But, basically, that was the big challenge and I think that was probably one of the best decisions I made without being that sure.

The way I answered was probably not the most obvious way of answering. Normally, people go to the Authority because they already have had a long-standing reputation in the specific field. I was somewhat young, but I had been studying that, and I was sure I wanted to do the right thing. Then we had a very challenging time, and we can talk about that later. But just about the career, I think the way I entered was somehow a coincidence of a number of facts. I had great admiration of Daniel, great admiration of the Ministry of Justice at that time. I never had any political links. It was really a technical job. I had to move to Brazil and leave my life back in New York, where I was supposed to move [...] Nowadays I don't see myself doing anything else. But there were a number of small coincidences that led me to competition.

But at that point, you did bring with you as a beginning an academic foundation that was truly superior. Were you working on your PhD at that time?

I concluded my PhD in 2004, so one year and a half after, I was there. I basically had done all my research by then, and what we call in Brazil "qualifications", so I had already well defined the studies; and I really had the chance to take advantage of the studies I did in Berkeley as well for collecting data and material, being updated on the discussions on the topic, and so on.

One reaction that an outsider – and certainly something that has impressed many of us – is that when you look at the leadership group that you were part of – Danny Goldberg; Mariana Tavares de Araújo, with whom we'll be speaking as well in this book – when you look across the front office of the relevant institutions, they're really young by international standards. An initial reaction would be How can that work? Yet, it was enormously successful and, I think by any measure, Brazil ascended during this period. How did that happen? Did all of you feel overwhelmed by this? Did you have collectively a clear idea of where you wanted to go? How did you make this work in Brazil? [...]

Being young puts you in a situation where it can be very challenging but also very interesting, because it was the beginning of a new government, everybody was very thrilled about possible changes. There was this idea of choosing what would be our goals. I think that, being very young, the first thing I learned when I got there was that it was a very different world from what I was used to, living in São Paulo or living in New York, and working in a law firm. You have very limited resources. You have to choose your goals very clearly. I think that when you are young, probably that's the main challenge you have, because you want to do everything, and you cannot clearly admit that you might not be able to do it. But I think the successful outcome of that was we had very strong support from the Minister himself. He gave total independence. He relied on the goals that we chose. At that time the fact was that fighting cartels was the one thing we were obliged to do. That was something that was established in the law. Brazil had had the law at that time for 9 years. Included in the law for 2 years were the leniency program and the possibility of dawn raids and so on. It hadn't been enforced. At that time, if you asked me what the success of the program was – and there were a number of other young people – that was shocking, not only probably for other jurisdictions but also within Brazil – I think that it was possible to admit that we needed to choose one big goal, and that was basically what we did.

How did you choose that one? What was the process that led you to say, "It's going to be cartels first"?

I think I should really give credit to Danny for this. It was a great choice. He had been talking with the then Minister of Justice, Márcio Thomaz Bastos, who was a very well-known criminal attorney at that time, a very great guy, too. I think the decision had to do a lot with the type of work that SDE could do. At some point, Brazil had 3 authorities: one within the Ministry of Justice; an authority within the Ministry of Economy; and then CADE, which was also a tribunal. Because of the power that SDE had, it was the agency that could assert it, that would do more of the legal work, and the economic work could be done by the Secretariat for Economic Monitoring (SEAE). Clearly, it was kind of natural that SDE would devote more resources to cartels and SEAE could devote more resources to merger cases because of the type of people who were at the agencies. What is interesting is that I remember, at that time, the agencies were duplicating a lot of work. Then, basically, in deciding an opinion on a merger, it came to SDE, which did the second review, then it went to the tribunal, it also had the opinion of the general attorney's office and the prosecutor, and then the commissioners and so on. I remember the day Danny told me, "Okay, so now you have to choose one case. We have to have this one case." Because everything had to do also with the advocacy of showing how important it would be to fight cartels.

Going back to your question, it was probably a choice when Daniel joined and he looked at what would be the best scope. We actually talked a lot. We tried to structure that in a manner so that would work. But we really had an issue of resources. I remember the day he came into my office – I was at my desk, trying to understand everything that was going on there, knowing we had a very good team there, and actually that was great because people were very excited about the possibility. At the beginning, they were probably skeptical as well. We were probably younger than most of the team working there. But I remember the day he came in and said, "Okay, you should choose one case that should be our case to make the anti-cartel program start. So we should think about doing an investigation, a dawn raid, to receive information there, and then you will go forward with the case. But we will never go out for a search or make really a case." I told Danny, "I have two problems. I don't have enough resources to do that and

I don't know how to do on investigation as such. I've read all the books" – I mean all the books I hadn't read by then, I probably read in 2 months all the books I could ever read – "but you never really learn how to do an investigation."

Reading a cookbook as opposed to actually cooking.

Exactly. That's the big difference and a big challenge. And honestly, there is not sometimes a book of – I don't know, how to mix the eggs, and sometimes if you don't do that in a proper way, it will not work. That's not written. And then it was hard to say, "Okay, but how do I do an investigation?" That's not written in any book. Who do you talk to? How do you choose the evidence? I never learned how to investigate.

When you show up at the office and knock on the door, what do you say? What do you do when they say, "Go away"?

Yes, and where to go – well, all of those questions. I think it was also a very good thing that we were able to cooperate with other agencies. At that time, basically what we said was, "We know antitrust, competition; we don't know how to investigate. The federal police know how to investigate. We should see how we can exchange experience with them and with the public prosecutors to work together."

Also, what we did in terms of resources, which was also key at that time, was to make sure that we would focus on cartels and SEAE would focus on mergers. I am mentioning that because the key challenge you have when you are an enforcer is, as I said before, to choose one goal and, because you have limited resources, you would not be able to do everything you would like for all the time. I can look back and see all the things we could have done better. But I think one thing we did right was to choose one thing. We were not trying to be the best reviewer of a merger and the anti-cartel enforcer.

I think this is such a crucial lesson for not just new agencies but the oldest of the agencies, is how important it is to define what it is you intend to do, to have a clear-headed process for making those choices and looking ahead and asking, "What can we do now that will stick, that will work over time?" How vital that is. If it were a ship or a commercial airliner, "Where are we going?" as opposed to saying, "We're going to go to the West Coast of North America" – Which city? Where? What you do shapes everything.

That's the whole thing. I think it's important for whatever work you are doing. You have to make choices, and especially if you are talking about less-mature agencies, where you have fewer resources and less experience. I think in that sense Brazil had a good push from other agencies in Latin America. We should say that the United States, through the International Competition Network (ICN) and also the European Commission – and then, again, we had tons of help through the ICN, through the Organisation for Economic Co-operation and Development (OECD), the United Nations Conference on Trade and Development (UNCTAD), and a number of other agencies – and people like you, Bill, and a number of other people – that were very instrumental in being very generous to share the experiences of other jurisdictions. Honestly, that's something I didn't mention but I should have said. I talked about Danny and Márcio Thomaz Bastos, but we talked to so many people. Something I really did was talk to everyone, talk to enforcers, talk to practitioners, trying to hear, trying to learn – "What can you share with us? What's your experience on this and that? What worked? What did not work?" We were open to receiving criticism. It was a big change for the business community, as you might appreciate, it was a big change for practitioners as well, because we changed the way we were dealing with a number of investigations. I think that, in that sense, talking to other enforcers at that time was key, especially for developing jurisdictions. When we drafted our leniency program, I remember calling Scott Hammond [then Head of the Criminal Unit of the U.S. Department of Justice] to talk specifically about our leniency application program. He said, "Okay, but how does your marker system work?" I said, "Sorry, I don't know what a marker is." This is just an example. Whoever works with competition will know how key it is to have a marker system; that is, to go to the authority and make sure you have your place in line.

We never thought about that. We never thought that we could have to run to get the first place in line, for instance, or that you would have to be very careful about not producing written documents. I could give you tons of examples. There are many things. I think, in that sense, it was very important. The ICN material produced was very helpful and instrumental for us.

Another thing that helped me as an enforcer was to know that we didn't know anything, that we really needed to learn – in that case maybe more, obviously, because we were really learning from scratch. But whoever joins an authority, even if they have practiced for many years, they have to learn a number of other things that they never really had to deal with. So, at the end of the day, I think you have to be very modest and understand that it's a very different approach to things. I think being young makes it easier because you admit that you don't know everything, right? That helped me.

Your point about how being open to learning and never stopping that process applies to all of us. The danger that can occur as you become more experienced is that you forget to learn. You become more rigid and inflexible. That is such an important point for leadership. Also, your observation about how, in a number of settings, having a younger person, who has no firm and rigid assumptions about how the world works, is more likely to approach it with open eyes and a broader willingness to absorb what's good.

Absolutely. As you were speaking, I was recalling the whole thing about leniency. Culturally speaking, that was terribly seen in Brazil at that time. And probably, if I were 45, as I am now, at that time and I had never seen that before – because nowadays that has really become a reality; collaboration, cooperation is now a triviality, spread throughout the government nowadays for different areas – I would say, "Well, I'm not going to rely on leniency because that's something that I would not be open to deal with." I remember we invited one professor to come and talk about leniency. His speech was about how unconstitutional, immoral and unethical that would be. That was a big shock. We should have talked to him before inviting him [...] When you're young it's easier, but I think if you are an enforcer, if you are becoming an enforcer, you have to think about a number of things from a different perspective. I probably had the inverse challenge because I started to be an antitrust specialist as an enforcer rather than starting as a practitioner. So when I went to private practice, I also had to change a lot of the things in my mindset because I was used to seeing things from another perspective.

For many of us who went from a public agency to another setting, it takes a while before you stop referring to what the government is doing as "we are doing, this is what we are doing," and you are reminded it's not "we" anymore. I think it's also interesting to think about the wider range of backgrounds or preparations that would be useful to coming into an agency. As you reflect on your own experience, I think you've given us a good idea about why a new, fresh perspective, a young team, can be very valuable – and, by the way, it was a smart team, too. These were accomplished people who had wisdom that usually is acquired much later in life, which was a great advantage. But as you think now about what you would like to see in a leader, reflecting on your experience, other characteristics that you think would be valuable for someone who's going to be appointed, say, to the head of CADE – or the National Institute for the Defense of Free Competition and the Protection of Intellectual Property (INDECOPI) in Peru; or the Fiscalía Nacional Económica, FNE) [National Economic Prosecutor's Office] – what are the kinds of experiences that put you in a good position to do that job well?

That's really a key question. This week the OECD launched the Brazil Peer Review Report. Frédéric Jenny was down in Brazil and he pushed very hard. It is something that I feel very comfortable to rely on him for, given who he is. He pushed very hard on the technical capacity and having somebody from the area that is prepared. I am going to develop a bit of what that means.

I think we would start by saying that it needs to be a technical appointment. That's the first thing that is key in a jurisdiction. I think that the way the appointment happens cannot be only a political one, with no background. The key thing, here, is what the background needs to be. I'm maybe even more open than other people could be on this point. Actually, I'm coming from a meeting with a current Securities and Exchange Commissioner who was saying how interesting it is that there is a Commissioner with a business background and the type of questions he can ask in the context of a case being reviewed.

So I think it's important that it's somebody who has enough background on law, economics, business, or something that is related to the day-to-day work. I think it cannot be just a politician or somebody who is there to do politics. I'm not saying that antitrust is not linked to politics, but I think that when you are doing a technical job, having studied, having enough background on the matter, is key, even if you're not necessarily an antitrust professor or lawyer or economist.

We can look at a lot of examples of effective leaders who came in without a competition law background at all, but I take it we're thinking about someone who knows in a basic way a good deal about the economy; someone who, even though he's not strictly the product of a political process, knows something about the politics of the country and the larger environment.

You have to. And you have to negotiate. It's a key point. At the end of the day, you are doing antitrust, but you are not out of the rest of the world. Sometimes, you like to think that, right? that We can solve many things from antitrust. I think antitrust is a key part of our economy, but there are a number of other things that are also key, we need to be independent and ready to have some fights. It's never easy. If you want to follow something that is not necessarily the best decision or the best outcome, that is a problem.

You need courage. If you are coming just with a political – and political in a very broad sense – mandate of "you have to go this way or that way," that is something that is really bad for the outcome at the end of the day. You definitely have to have courage. And I think you really need to be open to hear. You have to hear, learn, pay attention, talk to people, and be ready to try to make the best decision. I always have a very hard time thinking there is a right decision on anything – I mean you have many economic theories – but you have to make sure that you are making the best decision you can for that purpose.

And I think it is important to be aware that competition is one of the things among a number of things, so you must also look from different perspectives at how this affects the other areas that are directly interrelated. I'm not talking at all about non-antitrust issues deciding antitrust issues but knowing that your decision affects a number of other things outside. You cannot think that data privacy is not related to, for instance, antitrust, even though I'm not saying you are going to decide something because of how this would affect employment or how this would affect other areas. In this sense, CADE has been historically very antitrust-limited. We don't have public interest being brought into antitrust decisions. I think that's right from an antitrust perspective. But you cannot think that a decision can be made without seeing everything that is around. Again, at the end it all goes back to the same point: learning, being open to understand, seeing the different perspectives. I think that, the more you can be open to hear different views, the better chances you have to make the right decision.

How do you create an environment inside the institution that promotes that openness and that kind of debate? How do you do that? Is it with your own immediate team of advisors? Is it through some process of decision-making internally? How do you create that openness and that willingness to challenge assumptions so that when you step outside you've thought about the problem correctly?

That's a very good question that I never thought about before. I think we were, to some extent, lucky in the time we were there. We maybe made the right decisions, being able to have people with different backgrounds. I think different backgrounds and different perspectives are very important. In Brazil we do have very limited resources, very limited availability to hire people at the end of the day. That is indeed a problem. I am very keen on thinking about how diversity generally speaking can bring different perspectives on different things because of different backgrounds. Here, diversity can really be taken in a very broad way. I think that, to the extent you are able to bring people to the agency with different perspectives – in that sense, I have a different view than some of my colleagues in relation to "revolving door," for instance – I think that it's positive. In Brazil, we had that more in the past. It has been happening much less in recent years. I think that only helps.

It's a continuing debate globally about how fast the door revolves, what happens when you go out back into the private world.

You have to be very careful about how to deal with that, but I think that is one of the points that could bring additional perspectives. And then, again, something we had at that time were people from private practice, people who had been in the government for a while, people with different backgrounds. We also had, because of antitrust having to deal with different industries, people from different areas. I think you have to be open a lot to also hear the business community and practitioners. We were very much open. I remember this being a process as an enforcer. As we were coming from private practice, I think it helped that we were not active antitrust practitioners, so we did not necessarily have debates directly with those people at that time. Danny and I had some practice, but we were not regular antitrust practitioners at the Authority. I think that at the beginning, some of the people who were already there, the case handlers and so on, were a bit like, "Oh, those guys are coming here to try to deceive us or try to tell us something different."

"I'm going to hold on to my wallet when they walk in."

That's pretty much it. What we tried to show to them was being open to hear their arguments was key – and not because you are coming from private practice, but just because in the same way we should hear the perspectives of other governmental agencies and from other people. It was important to understand their points. It was amazing to see how they were gradually opened on that point.

Do you have thoughts about how to carry out as an agency head that kind of engagement today? How do you reach out to and speak with this community of practitioners, business leaders, public advocacy groups, or others? How do you go about engaging with them in a way that gives you the benefit of what they know but preserves the reality and appearance that you are taking the decisions and that you are not simply attached to them in some way? How do you structure that relationship?

That is a key question, especially if you are coming from private practice, because you do not want to be seen as somebody who is doing their job. So it's hard. I think that talking through the different bar groups, doing that in a more institutional way, is something that helps a lot. We see how the Agency can engage – in Brazil for instance, through Instituto Brasileiro de Estudos de Concorrência, Consumo e Comércio Internacional (IBRAC) [Brazilian Institute of Studies on Competition, Consumer Affairs and International Trade], as it would be here through the American Bar Association Section of Antitrust Law – on ways of having a more institutional conversation rather than "I'm close to that lawyer, or businessman, or in-house counsel." That is something that could help. And I think that trying to build up confidence from one side to another. Sometimes, when you, as an enforcer, recognize some of the private practitioners' arguments, when you are going to say, "Here you are right but here you are not," it means that you are open to that. If you reject everything, or if they just attack you – because that's another point, sometimes we also see the private practitioners merely attacking the authorities rather than trying to do that. Trying to find a good balance, and sometimes trying to do that not in a personalized way but rather through different ways, is good. I think in that way, for instance, the conversations through nongovernment advisers (NGAs) at the ICN have been instrumental for that.

And one thing that I see also working, and I find it interesting, is sometimes even talking to practitioners in other jurisdictions, seeing different perspectives. In the same way Brazil relied a lot on more developed jurisdictions, Brazil also played and is playing – I hear that a lot from my enforcement colleagues today – how key they have been in helping other developing antitrust agencies within Latin America.

I think the impact of Brazil throughout the continent – I would argue throughout the hemisphere – is extraordinary, and that the reason that Latin America is probably the most exciting arena today for newer authorities – whether it's Chile, Mexico, Brazil, Colombia, the renaissance in Argentina, Peru – is happening in so many ways because Brazil is the exemplar.

I think you're right. Maybe we started before. Sometimes, talking to Brazil is closer to their reality. Even though, as I mentioned, it was very useful to have the examples of other more developed jurisdictions – I mean if the programs already existed, why not try to take advantage? – but, of course, you had to topicalize them to our reality. We are, for instance, a civil law country, which has very different approaches to law than a common law country. But at the same time, the reality was different. If we compare the structure of the Brazilian Agency vis-à-vis the Latin American agencies, they are closer. So sometimes the challenges of an enforcer in Latin America are more similar. Some things are global, as you were mentioning, and some things can affect any jurisdiction. Some others really can be more related to the realities. I think the whole thing about the reliability on the agencies in developing countries is something that has been changing over time, the whole thing about risks of corruption and independence.

Just to go back to the point on leniency I mentioned before, I remember one of the big challenges we had as enforcers at that time was: how do we get credibility from the business community so that we would now get somebody confessing a crime and we would not prosecute them? That seems so obvious in the United States, but at that time it was not –

That doesn't happen on day one, though.

Exactly. So how do you build up that reputation? I think that also has to do with being ready to – I mean you cannot be too greedy. So, again, you need to choose your goals, you need to choose what you are going to do, and you have to know that if somebody applies for leniency and the leniency is dropped, of course you are not going to go after that case because you want to get others. If not, "Oh, this would have been my chance to go after that." Again, that might sound obvious, but when you don't have cases, people can get a bit confused about what the goal would be.

Let's talk about the merger and the fundamental structural reforms that took place in Brazil. One thing that all of you did as leaders was to reflect upon the existing framework and spend a lot of time thinking about how it could be better. What brought all of you to say "In order to succeed in the future, we need a better platform. We need to streamline the platform. We have to clarify areas of responsibility. We have to eliminate redundancies"? The reaction in most systems – and I think human beings tend to be about the same around the world – part of our DNA is very protective of what we have. Government agencies do not willingly step forward and say, "I want to surrender authority." But all of you worked together across agencies to devise a proposal that has put Brazil in a much better position to function effectively in the years ahead. How did that happen as leaders to do this?

This project started even before we joined. I remember Gesner Oliveira, who had been the president of CADE, talking about this already. And then, over the years, Daniel, and Elizabeth Farina; and the whole process was completed by Vinicius Carvalho I would say maybe 15 years after. The bill was approved in 2011 and the discussions started at the end of 1997.

The key point was probably to have the true will of doing something. I think if you really want to get something approved you have to know that you are going to have to lose some power specifically to gain a broader power. That was the key challenge that we had at that time. It was important at that point to have strong political support because you would have to choose which of the ministries CADE would have to be linked to. But I think that, as an enforcer, you have to be willing to have one goal and to lose some things on the way. You are going to have to make some concessions in some ways, but at the end, you are going to be able to have the best system. We weren't totally sure at that time, at least during the 3 years I was very much engaged in that discussion, that that would be the best way. I remember spending nights with Mariana, Danny, and a number of CADE's Commissioners discussing what would be the best format, if having one single agency would be good, what if we had one system that had the superintendents, and then you had one person trying to really clean what was easier and could go through, but then this person would have too much power [...] So we kept discussing it. It was interesting, because at some point we said, "Okay, but when Danny is the superintendent" – and Danny said, "I do not want to be the superintendent. I'm leaving" – in fact, he left like 10 years before. This is to go back to the point of saying that people had to think institutionally; they didn't have to think about themselves.

It's got to be a car that does not just depend on who the driver is.

That's the key point. And people discuss. They have to be very open that what people wanted was to have this approved. At the end of the day, if you ask me what I think is the most important thing of CADE during those years – and I heard a lot at the beginning of this year about what will happen at CADE with the new government – my answer to everyone was that I think at this point CADE has achieved such an institutional position that it would be very hard to have a huge shift. If you ask me, "Can you guarantee me that no Commissioner would be a political appointee?" I cannot guarantee anything [...] I think that if CADE shifted the way it deals with things, this would really not be viewed well. It's something where there would be some type of outside control and people saying, "There is something strange going on there."

But I think all of you had a role in building a custom, a norm, a standard, that said, "We are investing in an institution that will endure and function well, and it doesn't just depend on us."

That's exactly right, and I remember hearing that from the Ministry Márcio Thomaz Bastos. Probably the first time I talked to him, he said the big challenge he had at the Ministry of Justice, as the head of the SDE, was to transform Brazil from a country of laws into a country of institutions. I think we planted the legal seeds and what we could, and that over the years, all the other appointments at the different CADE authorities have been taking that into account.

It creates an example in Brazil, and in other countries, that affects public administration outside of the competition mechanism. If you create a framework that shows that this can work this way, you provide an example that others can think about.

I agree. And, honestly, I think that was probably true for CADE, not only about the institution itself but also, just to give an example, the whole antitrust enforcement program, to some extent, was taken into account in the development of the anticorruption law. And the agencies exchanged a lot – I was not there anymore for a while when this happened, but from talking a lot to Carlos Ragazzo, the Superintendent at the time the new CADE was set up, and to the new people who were there – they mentioned how instrumental they were also to the new anticorruption law and so on. So the idea is to spread good practice, spread what has worked, what has not worked, and I think good practice should make more good practice at the end of the day. And be ready to say some of the things we really cannot deal with, some of the things the next enforcers will have to do.

I'm really taken by the spirit of the young team that began this, whose only aim was to get better and not just worried about themselves – that is, "what's the best result for our country, and we are open-minded about how to do that, and our aim is to keep improving." How to import that spirit into old and new agencies alike is quite a challenge, but I think it's what makes the Brazilian experience such a good case to study, because that happened.

I think good things improve, and I think over the years – I mean we have been lucky with different appointments and different people handling the things.

Maybe some luck and skill, too. Last question for you: I'm a new appointee to the senior leadership of CADE and I want your advice about how to do this job well. What can I do to be really effective? I'm assuming that I have the background, the technical expertise, and the spirit that you described. I know a lot about the economy; I know a lot about what's affecting the competition process; I understand the governance and the culture, history, politics of Brazil. I'm well prepared that way. What do you tell me? What advice do you have for me? What did Rosenberg and her colleagues learn about how to do this?

The first thing I would tell you is get there and in the first 15 days or a month – depending on sometimes you get there and there are too many urgent things for you to do that – but take advantage to understand how the system works at the government. You might have the greatest experience at a university or at a law firm, but it's a totally different world. Talk to people. Hear people. I think really having the chance to understand the cases they have been looking at, what they are doing.

What people inside learned.

Inside and outside.

Talk to your predecessors perhaps.

Talk to your predecessors. Definitely that's a good point. That's something I did actually when I joined. I had the chance to talk and they were very generous in talking to us. Talk to predecessors. Talk to practitioners. Hear the people inside. When I say "talk," it's more hear than talk.

Listen.

That's probably the best thing I would say. I think after hearing a lot – and that goes back to your question on Brazil "why cartels?" – we talked to quite a few people, we learned, we heard, and we said, "Okay, this is what we can do the best among tons of things that needed to be done." And choose one priority, one or two priorities. If you have 10 things to conclude, you will probably not be able to do any of them. But if you are able to get 2, up to 3, at the end, then you feel –

Champagne for everybody.

That's exactly it. It's great when you are able to look back and think again, I'm sure we made tons of mistakes and could have done many things better, and that's part of the learning process.

We are human beings.

But I think that it's nice when you look back and say, "I did my little contribution to something that I think is important to the country," and I want you to leave with that feeling when you leave the Authority.

Your metaphor, "plant seeds, grow trees."

Yes. And at the end of the day it will be good for everybody. You are going to feel good, and when you leave you are going to keep contributing to that as well. I feel like that's the tree that I keep watering.

Sheridan Scott*

Competition Bureau of Canada, Commissioner of Competition (2004-2009)

You are the former Commissioner of the Competition Bureau of Canada and the former Chair of the Steering Group of the International Competition Network (ICN). You went to the Bureau, you served as the Commissioner for 5 years, from 2004 to 2009. During that period, for 2 years, you were the Chair of the ICN Steering Committee. When you go back to the time when you're entering the bureau, what experiences in your professional life best prepared you for the assignment of being Commissioner?

I spent half my life in the private sector and half in the public sector. In all aspects of that, I was engaged at some point in economic regulation, and I felt that was very important in preparing me because I was always interested in economic regulation. I began as a staff lawyer at the Canadian Radio-television and Telecommunications Commission (CRTC), when I was young and inexperienced, and had the pleasure of working on files both in telecommunications and broadcasting, particularly cable TV, which was very heavily regulated at the time. The telecom market was opening up, and it was an exciting time, and I got to sit in on the big hearing into long-distance competition.

Interestingly enough, in Canada long-distance competition didn't come about by way of government policy; it was the result of an application of a company asking to interconnect to Bell Canada's telecommunications system. So, it was done as an application and a hearing, and I was fortunate enough to be one of the CRTC staff lawyers. I became very intrigued with this idea of how you open up a market successfully to competition, a market that had been a monopoly for so long. That whetted my appetite for competition issues.

---

* Interview conducted on 27 March 2019.

Then, I went off to the Canadian Broadcasting Corporation (CBC), Canada's public broadcaster, for 2 years. That, again, was an area where a public broadcaster competed against private broadcasters, raising different sorts of questions.

Next, I went to Bell Canada, Canada's largest telecommunications company, and was responsible for getting Bell into the broadcasting business, something that was prohibited at the time by policy and by law. Legislation had to be changed to allow Bell Canada to hold a broadcasting license. I then moved on to become Chief Regulatory Officer at Bell, and had to deal with the opening up of all sorts of telecommunications markets. The rate base rate-of-return regulation was changing and local service was becoming competitive. When I was Chief Regulatory Officer, I was responsible not just for the CRTC but also for the Competition Bureau and the Copyright Board. So, when the job came up as Commissioner, I thought, "Why not apply for that? It looks like the next natural step in my evolution." That's when I became Commissioner in 2004.

You've touched on a number of things that, I think, point us to thinking about the sorts of background that provide good preparation for the job. If you think more generally about the selection process – suppose you're in the position on a board advising the government about to pick the next Sheridan Scott, or the future leader in the mold of very successful leadership that the Bureau has had – what kinds of experiences would you regard as must-have elements? What would you be looking for on that board to pick the leader of the Bureau, the nice-to-have elements?

First and foremost, you have to have a sense of your own basic values. I think that is extremely important in leadership: what are my values as compared to somebody else's? These are the values that are going to inspire the people who work for you. They're going to cause you to move in a particular direction. They're going to inform you of all of your actions. So, trying to understand what is it that makes this person tick, what are their values, is a very important thing. Everyone who has led the Bureau is very different. They have different types of backgrounds. At one point, we thought you should be a lawyer in order to lead the Bureau, but John Pecman left that myth in the dust. It's possible to be an economist as well and lead an organization successfully. So, I think: a sense of value; a sense of priorities: do I have a sense of the direction I want to move and the priorities I will set?

One of the huge difficulties I found of running an organization was the lack of resources. There are never enough resources to go around. So, one of the hardest things to do as the leader is to decide how you're going to allocate those resources, and what are you going to use them for. I think those are very important things to look at.

As for your background, you can come from very, very many backgrounds, as we've seen over the years. In my own case, I felt I brought a strength in the legal area. I think that can be very, very important. You're constantly called upon to analyze issues, to weigh evidence, to determine what you think is correct and what is not. But I also felt my management experience was very valuable. You forget sometimes, when you're picked as the head of an organization, that you're not just there to select cases. You're there to lead an organization, and to lead an organization, one of the most important things are the human resources that you're leading. I think it was Jack Welch from General Electric (GE) who said that he spent something like a third of his time engaged in managing his resources because they were his ticket to success. I felt that was very important for me, to have management experience.

If you've never managed anything before it's a shock.

I think that's one of the biggest shocks when you come from somewhere else and you haven't been in the Bureau or some other large organization. All of a sudden, you're going to these meetings all day that relate to the allocation of resources, the priorities, all sorts of things that are quite far from industrial organization (IO) economics and from competition law.

And you have several good candidates, but you have to pick one.

You have to pick one. And how do you weigh that? How do you, as a manager, say, "I think this person would fit in"? How to pick the right person, quite frankly, that is more easily said than done. Jim Collins wrote a great book, called "Good to Great: Why Some Companies Make the Leap…And Others Don't", and speaks about getting the "right people on the bus." By that, you don't mean people who are like you, who have your personality; it's people who share your values, values being quite a large concept rather than a small one. So, you're having people who share your basic values but can go in all sorts of different directions because they have different personalities, different skill sets. What you're trying to get is to fill out your organization. What are your strengths? What are your weaknesses? How do you fill out your organization? For example, in my case

I felt I brought quite strong management skills to the Bureau because I had been a manager in a private organization, but I didn't have formal economics training. I hadn't taken many economic classes as an undergraduate. I felt it was extremely important to have a good grasp on economics in doing –

I think you absorbed a lot in the course of your position.

For sure, and I was very interested in economic regulation. But in terms of running cases, understanding how to actually do the econometrics that you might want to underlie some of your cases, I couldn't do that work, and knew that I needed to have a very strong person in that position. So I developed the position of Chief Economist – we didn't have one at the time – and I scoured the country to find the best possible Chief Economist who could come and work at the Bureau. And again, that is a huge challenge to attract people from outside to come inside and do government service if that hasn't been their background, and have them move from some part of Canada to Ottawa. It may not be as attractive as moving to Washington, so that was a challenge. I worked very hard on attracting one of the best IO people in the country and had the pleasure of having Lilla Csorgo working with me for several years, who I could rely on 100 percent because she filled out my team. She was excellent, she devoted herself 110 percent to the work of the Bureau. I could always rely on that, and I felt it sort of filled me out so I didn't have to be the economist.

If you were the general manager of a sports franchise, you played the crucial role of getting the players, especially for these key positions.

Getting the people on the bus, making sure you have the right people who can help you in your task, analyzing what we need to do: "where am I strong, where am I weak, and how can I reinforce the strength of the team around me?"

I gather that in the work you did with this legislation, as you mentioned, there were a number of key initiatives that had to have given you a broad, important awareness of the political science of the nation and how that atmosphere affects the development of policy.

I think that is another very difficult transition to make if you haven't had that experience. When I was at Bell Canada, I appeared quite regularly before parliamentary committees, so I wasn't hugely intimidated by that. But I must say my experience appearing as a business leader was quite different from my experience appearing as the head of a government organization. The questions are different, the attitude is different, how they view your role is different, the type of information they want to elicit is different. That is a challenging part of the job, there is no doubt about it. You're leading a large organization, an important organization, a public organization, and having a good sense of the political dynamics of how that works is key, meanwhile understanding that you have to retain your independence as a competition regulator, because that is another very important aspect of our work, maintain our independence.

But you need to have a conversation with the political officials.

Absolutely, and know how to have that interaction with political officials – and not just political officials, elected officials who would sit around parliamentary committee tables, but also other members of the public service, because you engage with your colleagues in other parts of the public service quite regularly. I think if you don't do that, you do it at your peril. I think it's extremely important for the Bureau to have the ability to connect into the public service, even though, as I said it, remains independent in its decision-making abilities about cases and whatnot.

If you go back to the time that the selection process was unfolding, and you're asked the questions: "Ms. Scott, why do you want this job? What do you want to do with it? What are your aims? Where do you want to take the Bureau?" – do you remember what you said?

I'll come back to that specific question. What I do remember is that I drew up a plan. Coming from the private sector, you always have a hundred-day plan for your first hundred days in a new job, and, believe it or not, I had a little book that was my hundred-day plan. It had what I was going to do for human resources (HR), what I was going to do on the international front, and what I was going to do in some of the cases I was getting ready for. A hundred days into my job I laughed at myself because I thought: "What was I thinking? How could I possibly get this done in one hundred days?" Because managing in government is much more challenging than in the private sector. You have fewer levers and you have a little less flexibility. To get back to your question, when I sat before, one of the things that fit into my little book of a hundred days was continuing to open up the Bureau. Konrad von Finckenstein, who was my predecessor, had begun that before me.

The Bureau came from criminal roots. For a long time, all aspects of competition law were criminal, and this was ridiculous because it was very difficult to see through a lot of cases where judges were unwilling to convict to a criminal standard. So, the Bureau had remained quite secretive during that time period – obviously, when you're engaged in criminal enforcement – and it had begun to open up through Konrad. But, even when I arrived, I felt the Bureau should be more engaged at advocating on behalf of what it was doing, and that was part of the work that I saw that I could do.

I also thought that, as a person with business experience, I could bring a targeted and disciplined selection of cases and enforcement activities and whatnot that were specifically connected with the economy and how they would have the greatest impact on Canada's economy. I thought the selection process of cases was very important. And then, I felt that Canada had played a role on the international stage and wanted to continue that work, and I was privileged to be able to continue it, both through the Organization for Economic Cooperation and Development (OECD) and the ICN.

You mentioned before the types of adjustments that are involved in going into this public leadership position, and the importance of choosing priorities. I think if you benchmark the Bureau with its peer organizations around the world, one would find that on the spectrum of resourcing, it lags behind others in expenditure per citizen, regardless of the measure you want to use. The Bureau is expected to do a lot – competition, consumer protection, a number of different regulatory tasks – with what I would call "modest" outlays from the treasury. How did you go about choosing priorities?

Of course, the mergers you have no choice about. They come, they go, and, depending on a given year, you may be spending more or less resources in that, depending on the merger activity.

Cartel activity was driven, in part, through immunity applicants. I would say one of the changes I made there was to try to shift the focus more toward domestic cartels. There was so much interest in the cartels' international plan, and I often found that the international work was covering many of the cartels that touched Canada as well. So, we tried to focus and staff up our offices a little bit more in the region so we could focus on domestic cartels, and we were successful both in bid-rigging and also with finding cartels at the retail gas pump because of some of those efforts.

Where you're really exercising the discretion relates to consumer protection, misleading advertising and your advocacy work. In consumer protection and false and misleading advertising, we attempted to theme things, so we were trying to accomplish something in particular, and you could try to measure your progress. We picked health, for example, and we would try to look at misleading health claims, on the Internet in particular, and then work with our partners, like the Federal Trade Commission (FTC), on a regular basis, and also the Australian Competition and Consumer Commission (ACCC) – to say, "Let's attack false and misleading complaints about diabetes, for example, around the world and go after all the scammers."

So, it was in bringing together outside resources and focusing that I tried to use them in a more successful way. And also by having certain themes that we were trying to attack, health being one of them, telecommunications being another one that we were looking at, and several others that would guide our work.

If you're speaking to someone who's contemplating the appointment, who's coming to the agency in this key leadership position – as you say, it's an adjustment to become the head of a public institution, even though you've had excellent preparation in a number of different ways – what would you tell your successor are going to be the hardest adjustments that you have to make? Things to be ready for that will come at you in a way that confronts you with challenges you might not have really faced in your life before this?

Obviously, it would depend on their background. It's totally different to come from the private sector into the public sector without any public-sector experience. I would say one of the most challenging things for private-sector people is the time. You can't do things as quickly, things take time, so don't let it bother you if you don't get it done in a hundred days.

What stretches out the time?

Process, and fairly so. I understand that when you're subject to public scrutiny, there are more procedural requirements. And besides, the government is a big machine. It can't just go like that. In hiring, for example: I came from a world where if you wanted someone, you hired them, that's it. That's very different in government, how you go through the process of hiring. It's also very different how you go through the process of acquiring services. You have to go through certain competitive processes – and I don't criticize the government for that, I understand – but when you're coming from the private sector, that's quite an adjustment to make. In terms of working within a hierarchy, that's a bit of a challenge too for a lot of people coming from the outside. Also, being in the public eye is something that is quite challenging. If you're coming from public service, of course, those are significantly less relevant. But one of the challenges of being the leader of an organization is that you are alone, you are the decision maker. No more passing the buck: "Oh, those crazy managers, who knows what they're up to?"

You are the Commissioner, not a Commissioner.

The commissioner, that is right. And, because we have a Commissioner without a commission in Canada, there aren't even other commissioners that you can look at. You are the one and only Commissioner who is making the decision.

There were times, when I was at the Federal Trade Commission, when I thought that having 5 was 4 too many. But you were the Commissioner.

That creates its own problems. Maybe you don't have to worry about the process of negotiating with your colleagues and seeing if you can find common ground, but you have other issues, which are that you are alone.

Did that loneliness bear upon you? Did you feel that?

It did.

Was that a bit unsettling to realize it is my choice and it's a choice about things that matter?

And it's a choice about things that are going to affect other people's lives, both inside and outside. One of the things I recall is a very early meeting of senior managers, where people said, "Okay, what are your priorities?" I said: "You know what? I'm not going to tell you. I may have my priorities, but if I tell you my priorities and tell you what to do, you may not work on the weekends and evenings because you want to get them done. But if they're your priorities, you will work on weekends and you will work in the evenings to get them done. So I want you to tell me what your priorities are. We will discuss them and we will have joint, shared priorities that we are doing as a team." Because I lacked my 4 other commissioners that you had, I felt it was a way that I could get buy-in because I think that's extremely important. As the Commissioner, you set the tone for the values of the organization, even though it is very hard to influence corporate culture. When you're passing through these organizations as the head, you're only there for a mandate, and it's difficult to change culture. But everyone does take their cue from you. They look up and see what sort of person you are and they know what they can get away with. I think that's quite important. You have to tell people what the general direction is, and once you've all decided on strategic priorities, then you should give them the rope to go and do that work.

Did you have advisors, your senior leaders, others, people who worked in the front office, people you could turn to say, "We're going to have a chat" at the right time, "close the door, and tell me what you think"? Did you have people who you could rely on to say: "Here are the ideas. Here's what I think. I think these are better than those. This is why," who would give you not a challenge in a harsh sense or a hostile sense, but to say, "I want you to think more about this because I think this is not the best path"?

Absolutely, yes. I had a chief of staff. That role was very important. I had several chiefs of staff over my time at the Bureau. But that was a critical role for me – not just their own perspective of the direction, but they were often the sounding board for other people inside the Bureau who were troubled, and the message would filter up that way. I thought that was extremely valuable.

I had a couple of positions. I had a legal advisor and a chief economist, who all had one-on-one relationships, so those 3 people were very important to me, obviously. I also, again borrowing from my private sector experience, instituted an employee survey, and I took that very seriously, as it was taken at Bell Canada when I was there. We would administer this survey once a year, and we could compare the results then to counterpart organizations in the public sector and the private sector, but we focused on the public sector, to see where there were deviances that we should pay attention to.

You did this each year so you could look at the evolution?

Its evolution. Again, the idea being you would have teams in each section that would try to decide what steps could be taken to address the shortcomings that were identified. Sometimes there are shortcomings that you don't really care about because they don't feed into employee satisfaction. You know, everyone thinks they should have more information; everyone thinks they should have more holidays; everyone thinks they should be paid more. So those aren't really determining factors. That's why you benchmark against other organizations, and you can see where you deviate from a standard that is expected in an organization that's functioning well. So I did that, and I got some useful feedback that way.

This idea of having a regular survey where you try to identify concerns, areas of satisfaction, areas for improvement, is a very healthy way.

And then people aren't worried that if they criticize the boss there might be repercussions. That's one of the problems with speaking truth to power, is people do worry a little bit about that. This gets back to the truth and values. If people believe there will be negative consequences to speaking out, they won't speak out. So you have to address that through your culture that you're trying to create inside your organization.

Another thing I did that I found useful – and I borrowed shamelessly from the U. S. Department of Justice (DOJ) on this one – is they did a moot of big cases. They did something they called "red team/blue team," we called "red team/green team." It was to stop the case or green-light the case. We would have two teams, and I would try to put people who didn't agree with that side of the argument on the team, so they would be arguing against their true beliefs. Then I would hear the arguments, and I would go around the table and have the young officers tell me what they liked and what they didn't like. You had a huge amount of honesty in that discussion with those young people observing this and saying what they thought had worked and what had not worked, and where there was strength and weakness in the arguments. So that was another way of getting indirect feedback on some of the cases that I was working on that I might not otherwise get.

And a good way to make sure that, at the point at which you have to go into court, when you have to justify what you're doing – maybe you don't win all the time, but there are fewer surprises.

There are fewer surprises, that is exactly right, and that was a large measure of why we did it. Not so that we would know the outcome, but no surprises [...]

When you're on the bridge of the ship, you've talked about a couple of ways to stay in touch with the people who are in the engine room. Are there other things you did to get to know what the people who are doing the work in the operating groups? What they feel, what they think, other steps you took?

Once a month I had birthday breakfasts, so everyone born in that month was invited to come and have breakfast with me. We would go around the table. I would sometimes have topics that people were chatting about. At the time, my executive assistant was a smoker, and she would be in the smoking line outside the building. She picked up the best information for me standing in the smoking line. She would come up and say: "You know what they're all chatting about? They're chatting about this." So I would try to introduce these topics and get feedback. And no managers were invited to these meetings. It was only at the working level that they would be invited. So that was useful, although there's always a bit of an intimidation factor. You are the boss, and so people are a bit worried about that.

They are talking to God.

Yes, and you have to recognize that. When you're a leader, you can't assume that people are contemplating you as their buddy in the next office.

They don't automatically go from "Commissioner" to "Sheridan, how are you today?"

To buddy, exactly. But this was relaxing, and I think people thought it useful, and I used to get very good feedback about the birthday breakfasts. Another thing I liked to do – and probably should have done more – is walk the floors and go around, stop by, and say, "So, what are you working on?" Even a half-hour a day. I think that is an excellent practice, and I should have done that more. If I did get memos from staff that I liked, I would go to their office and tell them that. I remember one of my staff told me "I almost had a heart attack" when I turned up at his office. I just thought "I'd come and discuss your memo." To try to have a direct conversation as opposed to talking through supervisors, where there's sometimes a broken telephone, I thought was a good practice as well.

I've heard in some of our interviews a very similar technique, just drop in and say thank you. Sometimes, it's a note or a card that says "thank you" if they're in a regional office, or a phone call. And, of course, there's the initial sense of worry – "My God!" But just to say "thank you."

I used to try to visit the regional offices, and that would present its own challenges because Canada's a big country, not population-wise but certainly geographically-wise, and we had 5 regional offices. So, I would try to get there. Again, I did a better job with respect to some rather than others because those people can feel a bit disengaged, and we were trying to have them do particular work for us. We were trying to get them to focus on these domestic cartels, which was not always easy, so I liked to reinforce the work that they were doing in that area.

You mentioned the spotlight before. You are the Commissioner. Internally, you are the leader in the institution; externally you're the face of the agency. You have legislators, you have ministers, you've got the bar, you've got business leaders, you have citizens groups, you have academics. Was it an adjustment to be in the spotlight with people listening to every word, watching every gesture, every adjustment? Was that a big change?

I didn't find it was a huge change, maybe because I was a bit used to that from Bell, where I was a relatively senior person, although it's not a public persona. That said, the Commissioner isn't really a public persona in Canada. Sometimes, the heads of commissions around the world have leaders who are quite well-known. Allan Fels, from ACCC, comes to mind.

Allan Fels was for a long time the head of the Australian Competition and Consumer Commission.

The third-most-recognized person in Australia, apparently, when he was the head of the ACCC. The Commissioner doesn't have that sort of persona in Canada. But you're absolutely right that in the circles that care about this, you are a very noticeable person. Again, that comes back to knowing who you are yourself, not pretending to be someone else, knowing your own values, and that's how you can deal with people. You are who you are. That allowed me, anyway, to deal with parliamentarians, who can be quite aggressive, business leaders, who can be very, very aggressive, members of the bar, who can be excellent at advocating for their clients. For sure, it's a stressful existence. But I think, again, if you have a very good sense of who you are, of your values and what you're trying to accomplish, you can contextualize your actions much more easily, and it makes it easier to deal with people in that way.

And that goes back to having these life experiences that you referred to before the appointment where you reflect on who you are. You don't take the job just to have the job, you take the job with a purpose in mind.

If you're a person with certain attributes that could accomplish something that is within your realm of knowledge and experience, it's quite important to believe you have a set of skills that you can bring to bear on the task, and that will help advance it. I think that brings personal satisfaction, and it can continue to motivate you through work.

Ultimately, nobody expects you to know everything, and to bring to bear on the job the things that you do know.

That you do know. Malcolm Gladwell talked about that in one of his books, about how the happiest people are those who know the job to be done, have the skills to do it, and are given the opportunity to bring their skills to bear. In a job as complex as leading the Competition Bureau, you can of course supplement your own skills with other people, and jointly you will be able to accomplish the goals that you set.

I want to turn to the other dimension of the job, which was such an important part of your tenure: your role in the world with international competition and consumer affairs. Among other things, you were the Chair of the Steering Committee of the International Competition Network, an association of competition agencies around the world, and you were one of many Canadian officials, including Konrad, your predecessor, who played an indispensable role in the establishment of this institution and its work over time. What led you to make this a top commitment for yourself?

That's a really good question. After I said yes, I thought: "What have I done? I have a day job." Because it was a commitment. The ICN was a commitment. And I had several conversations with people. Some people approached me and asked if I would be interested in putting my hand up when we knew we were going to lose the previous chair, who was no longer going to be the head of the competition agency. I've always been interested in international things from my childhood. I was fascinated with reading French off the back of the cereal boxes as a kid in Vancouver. And I went on to learn – at some point in my life I have spoken one of seven languages. So I've always had an interest in international things, in other countries, and also in different cultures and how people do things differently around the world, but how in the end we're human beings and we share many, many values, and we do things in a very similar way.

So I thought the ICN was sort of an interesting microcosm of that, these different countries, these different cultures, but all wanting to advance the interests of competition law and policy. I was always intrigued by the ICN. I always thought it was an amazing organization. I was a member of the Steering Committee. I stepped into the shoes of Konrad, who was already on the Steering Committee, so I was lucky in that context. But when I thought: could I make a difference to this organization? Could I lead it?, I thought: "You know, I have a background of international interests that could help me, and I also, at that point, had a sense of where I thought the organization should go".

I felt that the ICN was reaching an inflection point, if you wish. It was maturing in a very interesting way. It had begun with 15 agencies, all like-minded generally speaking, but as I came into the Bureau and progressed through the early days, I could see the ICN changing with its growth, to 60 agencies. I think it was by the time I took over at the Steering Group. This was a critical mass of people who were not necessarily like-minded. They had different experiences, different economies, different legal frameworks. It was a very different group, and until then, in the early days, they had sort of been sidelined. They were there to listen to the wisdom of the 15 founders of this organization.

The great established members, yes, yes.

Yes, and they were to sit and listen and take notes. I felt that time was over. It was no longer time to take notes. It was time for them to move into the center and become part of the guiding minds of the organization. That was a challenge, and I saw that as being really what happened during my 2 years in the Steering Group, with changes in the organization to accommodate the integration of a greater variety of economies and countries.

As you said, it's a very demanding position, and you can't do it in a casual manner and be effective. Does it create tension with your job at home, your full-time job, the job that Canadians turn to and say, "What are you doing for us?"

Absolutely. And it's your colleagues, also, saying, "Oh, so it's more important for you to be in Paris 3 times a year?" You say: "I'm working, I'm working. I can't help it." But you would go to Paris for the OECD meeting, and you would be working day and night, and you wouldn't be visiting the Eiffel Tower.

It's a decathlon, and when you're done, you're exhausted.

Exactly. But I understand that when you're looking from the outside it does look very appealing. And for the ICN, again, I felt it was important to travel, to reinforce this message that the ICN-recommended practices should be the standard in accordance with which competition laws around the world are judged; and you may choose to deviate, but this is the standard you should measure yourself against. So I did take time from my day job to go to 2 countries in particular, India and Chile, where I was quite active, trying to explain what the ICN was doing and why we felt that in the merger area in particular, we thought we were the gold standard that the world should measure merger legislation against.

You've given us so much to think about and so many thoughtful reflections on what a new person could do. I'll ask you one last question. Now, you know a lot that maybe you didn't fully know on the first day. Here comes your successor. Any other advice you'd give them about how to start, how to get the job done?

Patience. Rome wasn't built in a day. Personally, I found it very difficult to understand that it is not going to get done immediately. So you're going to have to pick priorities and be bloody-minded about them. Because people are not all going to agree with you, and there will be different barriers as you go in different directions. It can come from anywhere. So, don't worry if it's not getting done overnight. Be bloody-minded about the specific goals you set yourself. And then find some time for yourself. That's probably the hardest, to find time for yourself. My children had left home by the time I took this job, and I remember saying to my husband at the time, "I wouldn't put my name forward if my kids were still at home." I found this a demanding job in terms of 24/7, and the international travel component, too. So, just personally, because I don't have the superwoman capabilities that might allow you to do that, I felt that was important, and I had to think about exercise, reading, outside reading, which I find important. I used to go in Sunday morning, put my feet up on my desk, look at that beautiful view down the Gatineau River, think "I am the luckiest human being in the world that I get to come here", and just read stuff that I found was sort of interesting related to the Competition Act, and that was my form of relaxation.

We're enormously grateful to you for doing this, and I think a new leader, a prospective leader, who takes this to heart, is going to be so much better off and do their job well. You served with such distinction, and so many of the things you do live on very well in the lives of your successors and others outside of Canada who were able to observe your work and to be your colleague for a long time. Thank you.

Thank you for inviting me. And you were my personal inspiration. I stole so many great ideas from you shamelessly. I thank you for that.

Jacques Steenbergen*

Belgian Competition Authority, President (2013-2023)

As the President of the Belgian Competition Authority, you have a variety of experiences that you draw on in formulating law and policy. As a practitioner, as an academic, you have come to the field with a collection of different experiences and stand as a deeply respected leader across the field of competition law at home and abroad. I would like to begin by asking about what your path into the Competition Authority was and, as you think about it, to think what sorts of background tend to provide good preparation to perform this kind of role.

There is no "one fits all." There is no ideal path. There are many who come to a job like mine and do well. My path – I started as a young academic, and I wrote my PhD thesis on legal remedies and ailing industries. That was in the 1970s, and the more I wrote, the more ailing industries there were. At the end, I found it rather depressing. So my idea was that one should be able to do more positive things. It is very important that there are remedies for those who suffer in the case of an ailing industry, but industrial policy is perhaps a more proactive approach, and in a market economy we see competition policy and competition law as the default regulation of a market economy.

I hope nobody is too shocked when I consider competition law and policy a type of regulation, and even as industrial policy. But that is how I basically see the relation between free enterprise and government. We developed this view with the then Minister as a kind of step-by-step approach. When you have the impression that something doesn't work well in a market, first, you try to see whether the consumers or the relevant stakeholders really

* Interview conducted on 17 May 2019.

know what their possibilities are. Sometimes you just have to improve their information. And if they're well-informed and the market still doesn't work as stakeholders are entitled to expect, competition law being the default regulation, you examine whether operators restricted competition in infringement of competition law. And if you cannot find any, you may have to go for more specific regulation.

You also sometimes have to look at *ex ante* regulation when you have to admit that on a case-by-case basis it will take too long before you can give the necessary guidance to the market and to have a sufficient legal basis for adequate disciplinary action. It may also be that you see that existing regulation is anti-competitive.

My background was economic law. I came to competition law, as a research and teaching assistant, and starting at the Bar. Then, I had the privilege and great pleasure to have been the Legal Secretary – you would say the first law clerk – to the President of the Court of Justice in Luxembourg, and there I was immersed in what is now EU law. Coming back from Luxembourg was – if only because my own field had narrowed to some extent – logical that I would go on in a practice focusing on EU and competition law. That is basically how I became a practitioner in this field. On that path I had the invaluable privilege of being formed by prof. Walter van Gerven, my PhD director, prof. Pierre van Ommeslaghe, my 'patron' at the Bar, and of course prof. Josse Mertens de Wilmars, then President of the Court. Before going to Luxembourg, I was in charge of the course in competition law at Leuven University. I started with about 8 students, if I remember well, in the late 1970s and I ended with about 130. The law had changed; the students had changed. I was no longer teaching in Dutch but in English, to (for about 50-percent) an international group of students.

What a great illustration of how things change.

There are a lot of coincidences in somebody's career. And you have to be lucky. I have been very lucky to have been given this opportunity to go to Luxembourg, then to work in a firm where we did interesting things, not only with regard to the legal practice in the field but also in the development of an international firm. Then the next step: why and when did I go into public service? There, I'm afraid I just have to say that I was approaching the then age limit in my firm, and I decided that there were still more interesting things to do. I had been closely involved in redrafting the Competition Act, and as they say in French, "*l'appétit vient en mangeant*": when you're involved, you start liking it. I usually get to like the things I do. I really enjoyed my time in private practice, I enjoyed my time in academia (there, I am now also retired but still involved), and I thoroughly enjoy what I'm doing now. Is that the path? No, it's my path.

It seems there are some general observations we could draw from that path. That is, whatever path you take – the broad knowledge of the economy, the understanding of how an economy functions, how the economy functions in the region, in the jurisdiction – that was part of the knowledge you brought with you.

To be an efficient competition authority, it is important to understand the economy. But I think it's even more important that you understand how businesses work. The micro is at least as important as having an understanding of the macro. The fact that, as a private practitioner, I was involved in – and that was a privilege – the preparation of business plans, in the development of strategies of some international groups, in discussing the possibility of transactions that never took place. It made me understand what makes them tick. Business is a very personal business, but it also made me understand what drives them, the interests, so not just the personal side of it, but the real business side. It doesn't necessarily have to be the president, but you need among the decision makers of a competition authority people who understand business. You also need people who have more of a helicopter view, who are used to thinking about the impact of what others are doing and what you're doing yourself and balancing them out to try to come to a good outcome.

Yes, I think that's such an important point that, however you obtain it, the knowledge of how business works, what motivates them. And, again, it doesn't just have to be the leader, you can accumulate an ensemble of observers, but the helicopter view you describe as well.

I have seen authorities work very well with a chairperson who was really not a competition law expert, and I have seen authorities work well where he or she was a competition law expert. Did one function better than the other? Well, if you have insufficient technical knowledge of competition law, you must make sure that you're surrounded by some people who do, and when you are not an economist, please make sure that you have a few good ones around you. A good one does not only mean a good economist, just like a lawyer is not necessarily good in this job when he is only a good lawyer; he or she must be able to understand the others and talk to them because otherwise you have just a juxtaposition of expertise. But that doesn't yet make an authority.

No, and I share the same impression that you can have good outcomes both ways, the competition specialists or no such background, but your observation about complementing your own skills and abilities with others who bring other things to the process, too.

Then you must make sure that your profiling to the outside world is consistent with a person's abilities and specialities. You cannot expect to have the respect of what is usually a highly specialized group of stakeholders if you're not seen as one of them. But again, you can be one of them in many different ways. However, if you do not have a certain degree of expertise, you will not really be listened to. My feeling is that it is – I'm not saying more important in a small authority or in a smaller jurisdiction than in a larger one – certainly very important in the international field when you come from a small jurisdiction, because why otherwise would they listen to you if there's nothing for them in the conversation?

As you were saying, that expertise can take many forms. It can be from a variety of disciplines, but a genuine connection to the field.

Yes, so that you know when parties are trying to play up to you, or when they have a genuine concern.

Yes, and that is such an important observation for someone coming to this and thinking: what will I have to do to be seen as effective to this larger audience that now will watch very carefully everything I do?

There are also some elements in the profile of persons you need that depend very much on the type of authority. My authority has a strict distinction between the investigation and prosecution service and the service, or the role of the President chairing the competition college that takes the final decisions and who is also the person who represents the Authority internationally. If you do not have that strict distinction, I think that the pure management qualities of the head are more important than in my case, because I'm not even allowed to manage the major part of the core activity, namely the investigations. In my case, or in an authority like ours, it's probably more important that you know how to respect the roles of the others and not overplay your own hand. So that's a different set of requirements, and those are really dependent on the design of your own authority.

I think the distinction across authorities about whether you are the head of the college that takes decisions and other functions are delegated –

It was not so in the first part of my career in the competition authority. The present BCA with the Colleges has really changed the way I need to look at my colleagues.

If you look at the earlier role, where the management function is more important, does it help to have been a manager in some other capacity before you do that?

I'm sure. Did I have that experience? Well, I had managed a team in a law firm and I had helped to manage a law firm in its internationalization. That doesn't necessarily make you a real manager. That makes you perhaps a little bit more of a leader, but certainly not necessarily more of a hands-on manager.

What was the adjustment going from the world of the law firm, the academy, into public service? What changed for you?

Much less than people think. Of course, I often got that question after I made the transition. You deal with the same issues in what is your core business, competition policy, and competition law enforcement. You may be on the other side of the table, but there is not that much difference between the two sides or their toolboxes. When I was advising companies, I tried to figure out what the authority was going to do. Now I try to figure out what the Court of Appeal might think of it. When you're advising companies, you try to figure out what the decision, the policy, will be. Now I try to figure out what the decision should be. From an intellectual process point of view, that's not very different. I think there is a real difference in types of legal thinking and arguing between being a litigator and being an advisor or a decision maker. A litigator must also try to figure out what is likely to work, but then you argue starting from a position you have to defend. An advisor must figure out what will work, but he can still hope to shape the position of his client. That was basically my case at a firm where I was not really a litigator, more an advisor – I did some litigation but not much. And for an academic it's also the same. The only times I really had to coach people in thinking as a litigator was when I was coaching moot court participants, but not when I was lecturing, having discussions where you usually discuss more policy and decision making than positions.

You are, as you said, externally the face of the institution in so many ways. What is the experience of being in the larger spotlight, onstage? You're the representative in so many international fora and you're onstage as the face of the institution in your own country. What is it like to play that role?

First, you must make sure that you're not the only face. It's very important, and I'm very lucky, I think, that our Prosecutor General, and our Chief Economist, also have international visibility. They acquired visibility in the European Network. You should never be the only face. If an authority is seen as a one-man shop, it is not a real institution. So you have to institutionalize your institution. When it was restructured, that was, I think, a part of my job. I think we now have several faces.

And you encouraged them to play the larger role.

Of course. Also for the more junior colleagues to write, to be in panels, to represent the authority in working parties and advisory committees. Apart from that, I had been in the field for so long that I can't really recall what you really do to get there. What I have seen more is what is likely to make it work. First, I think people must see that you know something about it. We discussed that already. Second, you must make sure that you do not overplay your hand. You should not try to have the last word on everything. You should know when there is sufficient likelihood that you bring added value. Now, added value in our types of discussions can be because your market is particularly affected by an issue. That obviously gives you additional credibility. It also makes it natural that you speak out. That is one thing.

On issues, it is very important that you know your colleagues. That doesn't necessarily mean that we are personal friends of the type that go on holiday together, but as a team of heads, and also in a larger sense with teams of the European Commission and our colleagues, you must know people. You must appreciate people, and you cannot appreciate them if you don't really know them a bit better. Then you feel when they expect something and who has specific experience with what. One of the experiences, not necessarily of me as President of the Competition Authority but of the European Competition Network (ECN) in general, is that over the years we developed a common experience and a kind of team spirit. It was not always the same authority that was the first to develop experience, knowledge and skills on certain issues. Some had more opportunities because they had more cases and received more questions than others. You have to know them. In conclusion: have something to say, only say something when you have something to say, and really help to make the group work as a group.

To understand how success is measured in the success of the larger group, the team instead of individual enhancement, is a custom or culture that is so important to build. And the European Competition Network (ECN) has been rather good at it. This was an important component of the modernization program in January 2003.

I joined the ECN in 2007, so there was already a couple of years of experience. I think what was really key was the realization that the Commission could never take up a sufficient number of cases. When they "decentralized," as it was called, the enforcement by allowing also the national authorities to decide on exemptions under Article 101(3) – sorry if I get more technical. It meant that the Commission was no longer, as it had been perceived by some, rightly or wrongly, inclined to try to get everything. It no longer – at least, I have never experienced that a few years later, as I said – saw the national competition authorities as a kind of less-welcome competitors. On the contrary, when they decentralized, and abandoned the idea of the mandatory notifications for exemptions that came with it, we moved indeed to self-assessment, and we moved really to a genuine network. That went smoothly but progressively.

By now, as you know, more than 80 percent of all EU law enforcement decisions are taken by national authorities. That doesn't even mean more than 80 percent of all decisions on competition law; no, you have to add to that the ones taken under their domestic competition laws. Has that changed the balance of power? Not necessarily. That has meant that we are, as I often say, a "network industry." Yes, the Commission is *primus inter pares*, and yes, the most leading decisions tend to be Commission decisions, but I don't think I can recall a decision of the BCA in the last few years without referring also to a national authority. So you take the lead from EU case law, you look then at EU decision practice, but you also look at what your colleagues are doing, at least to the extent that you can understand the language. That is, I think, the key factor that made the ECN a success, the realization that we can only deal with what might become a sufficient number of cases if we do it collectively.

You underscore an important role of the agency leadership in the modern world, certainly in Europe among the Member States but in the larger arena as well, the important role you play not only as an official inside your own nation but the increasingly important international dimension of what you do as a Member State.

Certainly European. When we have discussions in the OECD or in the International Competition Network (ICN) on international cooperation, we usually have to say that our cross-border cooperation out of a jurisdiction like Belgium is essentially within the ECN, not so much with third countries. Now, we have had a couple of times the pleasure of working together with the US authorities. And yes, we do also work with European non-Member State authorities, but that is just a very small fraction of the number of cases in which we have cross-border contact.

I very much like what I might call "guidelines" or "suggestions" for an official about how to contribute in these other arenas. Know your subject. Speak to your subject. You don't have to know everything or speak beyond your subject. I think it's a way of engaging in these arenas. To follow the Steenbergen suggestions on this means that when you do intervene, when you do engage, people put down their electronic devices and they'll listen to you, they'll pay attention, because they know that there's something worth listening to.

That's the goal.

Yes, and that's a very good suggestion for all of us in a number of different settings, enormously helpful. I want to turn to one other question. It's a more general question, looking ahead. But imagine I'm a new appointee. Perhaps, after September in this year when you complete your mandate, I'm a Belgian official, appointee, I'm going to step into your shoes; or at an earlier time, before you assumed this role as the head of the tribunal, I was going to follow in your footsteps there. I'm about to begin and we're having a conversation about the future. What should I know about how to play this role? What would you tell me about what to think about?

When you come in, listen. Listen to the people. When you come from the outside into a public service environment, you tend to be looked at somewhat as an extra-terrestrial. And you may also feel a little bit like an extra-terrestrial. Listen. Make them understand that the way you look at them and at the issues you jointly have to deal with is not all that different. That's how I think it should start. Understand the dynamics in your team. In the end, you may prefer them to be different, but you're not going to change them if you didn't understand them in the first place. Know who they are, what they are. I think that's how you have to start. See where the complementarities are. As we discussed before, there is not one ideal profile, and most profiles require compensation by the input of others. So know who you can go to, who you can rely on. That's, I think, how it works out. To listen and to learn from people who have been there for longer. Never to one person, because people may have very different views on how an institution works, even though they've both been in it for some time.

I'll quote a famous journal article, "Many Views of the Cathedral," about what it looks like to do that, and, I imagine, to talk to those who have been there, who have done this.

Yes, but then – and now I'm going to be talking about myself inevitably – it gets delicate. You should be available, really available, but you should not be the ghost behind the scenes or, even worse, in the corridor. So you have to feel, How far can I go? What is welcome?

So your presence does not hover like a specter in the background as everything happens. On that, when thinking about future steps, I would mention again your observation that your aim is not to make this a one-man shop, that you want to nurture and develop the presence.

That is, let's say, institutionally easier when you have a separation of powers, because then it is more obvious that there are several players. It's probably even more important if you have a more hierarchical, fully integrated authority.

I think it avoids what one political scientist has called "the tyranny of individual charisma," with the suggestion that "I am the only person who can really do this, and without me the foundations will shake."

Charisma never survives tyranny in my experience. It's the dead end of charisma.

It's the building of a foundation and an institution that will endure because of these qualities.

And then, you have to regularly question what you're doing, how you're doing it. That's not, in my experience, the difficult part. You usually have enough stakeholders who are inclined to remind you of what they would like you to do differently. There again, every jurisdiction, every environment, has its own mechanisms. For us, we have e.g. the annual conference organized by the main Belgian competition law review, and that starts with a kind of survey of the previous year by a well-known practitioner, and, with what he says and the questions you get from the audience, you have a very good feel of the way the wind is blowing.

So you have no shortage of feedback.

I think we have feedback. Whether you have enough, that's a bit difficult to know. Sometimes you have to be much more specific. For instance, we organized one-half year ago an audit of our forensic IT practices and instruments. That's not something you can easily get in sufficient detail in a general setting like a conference. Then, sometimes you need to go to the experts and ask for an audit.

It has been a notable part of the Belgian experience that this periodic revisiting of the system has been a healthy process. In a jurisdiction that makes a point of thinking every 5 to 7 years, we have to think about updates. It's like in IT you have big updates and smaller ones or a collection of small ones, and sometimes you need to install something entirely, a major system makeover.

We've always had this duality, ever since 1993, but the way we organized it has changed significantly over time. Bringing the two components into a single autonomous authority was, from an institutional point of view, a significant change, which also changed the dynamics between us and the political world.

Could say a word about how that process began, what was the inspiration for it, and then how was the actual reconfiguration designed?

It was all, I understand, decided in a meeting that lasted less than 30 minutes between the heads of staff of the Vice prime ministers because they could not reach a political consensus on a restructuring that increased the powers with a person who would still be part of the civil service, the then Director General job. There had been proposals to isolate this Director General as much as possible from any possible input and impact from politics or the other parts of the ministry. But nothing was enough, even when they had gone so far that they started to wonder whether they would ever find somebody who was willing to do that. The solution was making it an autonomous authority when you do not have these worries. It is the option that was taken. We received, I think, 4 days to transform the bill from a significant upgrade of an existing institution to setting up a new authority. That's why it came and how it came, a bit of improvisation.

It's impressive how Belgium and a number of other jurisdictions have devoted so much attention in the modern era to framework and structure, and this is a great example of that.

These developments in different authorities were often very different. If you look at, for instance, the Netherlands and Spain, it was more an exercise of bringing different authorities into the same institution. That has not yet been an issue with us. For us, it was more repositioning the competition authority as a competition authority.

The attentiveness to possibilities for improvement and the pursuit of changes again are characteristic, I think, of a healthy system [...] To pick one point that we've touched upon here now, when you come in the door, listen, learn, and observe. You can make changes, but know what you're changing first. Very good advice.

But then make changes when necessary. And well-informed.

Mariana Tavares de Araujo[*]

Brazil's Secretariat of Economic Law of the Ministry of Justice, Deputy (2001-2006) & Head of Competition Department (2006-2010)

You have 9 years of experience in the Brazilian government, several of those years at the top of the Brazilian agency responsible for enforcement in the Brazilian competition system. You played a crucial role in helping formulate a program earlier in this decade to accomplish a major transformation of the Brazilian system, which took an already effective and renowned system and put it on still a better platform for the future, with the consequence of making Brazil simply one of the best competition systems in the world. This makes you a leader in the formulation and policy in Latin America, and a tremendous exemplar of how a good system can be developed. You are currently a partner with the Levy & Salomão law firm in Brazil. I would like to start by taking you back to your path into the field of competition law. Can you tell us a bit about how you got there? I would like to ask also along those lines of thinking about the kinds of experiences that were very good preparation for you when you come into the competition area and your thoughts about the sorts of background that a leader might best have in entering the field.

My career path, I think, was in some ways quite unusual. I started off right after graduation at a biotech firm. The head of the firm was a medical doctor with a PhD in genetics. He introduced DNA paternity testing in Brazil and he was hired as an expert in all paternity lawsuits and some horrific criminal cases. I was his liaison with the courts, also a garden variety of legal issues involved in the

* Interview conducted on 4 June 2019.

work of the lab. I did that for a number of years. Fun work, but been there, done that. So I decided to do my LLM. I came to Georgetown, took Steve Salop's classes, and decided I wanted to be an antitrust lawyer. I was here in D.C., and I was introduced to the head of one of the former competition agencies, which you also know very well, Claudio Considera and to Paulo Correa, his deputy at the time, both at the Secretariat for Economic Monitoring (SEAE) at the Ministry of Finance.

There were 3 institutions at the time that had a major role in the Brazilian system.

Yes, and SEAE was very active then. They were primarily in charge of merger review, but Paulo and Claudio were also excited about cartel work. They were very enthusiastic about what was going on in Brazil, also with respect to antitrust. We had price controls until the middle of the 1990s. That was mid-2001, so things were picking up. They invited me when I finished my LLM to come and work for the agency. I didn't think twice about it. It was a great way to start practicing antitrust. So I went. But to tell you the truth, when I accepted I didn't realize that it was going to be a 9-year project. I thought it was a one-year thing, maybe a couple-of-year thing. But then I became involved in different fronts, having growing responsibilities.

Actually, as you said, there are 3 agencies. I worked for SEAE for a year. At some point the government changed and Daniel Goldberg and Barbara Rosenberg went to work for the Secretariat of Economic Law at the Ministry of Justice, the other agency – the SDE. They invited me to come and work with them. I was Barbara's deputy. They were really focused on cartel enforcement, and that was the SDE's project. I was Barbara's deputy for a few years. Then Barbara left and I became head of the Competition Department. Then Daniel left at the end of 2006 and I became the head of the SDE. So that is where I started.

For all of you this is an exciting time. It's a remarkable team, in part, because you are all so young coming into these jobs. When you became head of SDE how old were you?

I was 36.

I think Barbara and Daniel were both in their 20s.

Exactly. Everyone was in their late 20s, early 30s at that time. It was great. I really enjoyed working at SEAE, but when I joined the SDE it was as if we were on a mission. Cartel enforcement had to happen. Paulo and Claudio were doing what they could, but at that point at the SDE – and I think that was made the difference and what made the team successful – they realized that it would not be possible to achieve deterrence doing it alone, that we needed partners, and getting closer to the criminal authorities was key. And it was and it became effective because of that.

But I think, leaving the substance apart, what made it special was, as you said, the enthusiasm about it and the fact that there was a plan in place. We knew it was going to happen. It wasn't always easy, but we knew we were trying to accomplish something important there.

Before you become the head, you have the opportunity to observe the work of Barbara and of Danny. Does that give you a better sense of how you want to leave the agency, after watching their work at close hand, having a senior responsibility yourself?

I think that was certainly key. Effective leaders have different backgrounds. I don't think there is one way of doing it right. But for me it was very important having held different positions, having been at another agency and then going through different positions before I became the head of the agency. I could watch them making decisions. And helping build the strategy was very helpful for me.

Also, studying more and learning more about antitrust served me. But knowing how the government worked, learning how the government worked, and knowing the people, knowing policy, politics, and the challenges of how to get a project in place, whom to call, how to get a budget – that made my life much easier once I became the head of the agency.

What are some of the distinctive features of working in a public agency? Previously you'd been with a private institution. Now you're back with a private institution. What are the features of the government culture that a leader has to be attentive to, that you have to understand in order to work well in that environment?

Without a strong team in place you'll be able to do little, and for that you have to be able to recruit and retain good people. At law firms pay is flexible, so that can be a tool. That flexibility does not exist in public service. But you had the opportunity to show, if you believe in it of course, that you're doing the good for society. If you are able to pass that on to your team, I think they'll likely stay around. That is one aspect of it. The other aspect of it is that a career in government can become very boring if you're always doing the same thing. I think it's important that the team feels that they're going somewhere, that they're progressing professionally, that they're learning what they are doing, and of course that they are doing something important. How the leader organizes the agency can make a huge difference. So strategic planning, prioritizing, and making sure that everyone is aware of that makes an important difference, too.

This is a key advice for a leader to keep in mind. Can you tell us some more about how you worked with your team, with the employees in the agency? How did you go about communicating the sense of purpose and making clear what your aims are in order that you could inspire them to pursue the goals, but also to maintain that additional motivation to do well? How did you inspire or motivate your team to do their best?

I was able to inspire and motivate because I was very inspired and motivated about what I was doing. I thought that was important. I think if you don't believe what you're doing is important, you will likely not be able to excite and communicate that to others. I was convinced that what I was doing was important and I was able to communicate that well because of that. But we weren't that big of a team, so we talked a lot. We had weekly meetings and we discussed every project. And I listened, I paid attention to what they had to say, because some of the case handlers – and many of them are still with the Conselho Administrativo de Defesa Econômica (CADE) [Administrative Council for Economic Defense] today – were already around, they were studying hard, and they had a lot to contribute. I think I inspired them because I was inspired, but I also listened and I made sure that they participated in putting together that project.

On a personal level – and I think this applies to a law firm as well – I feel that everyone works very hard, these projects can be very stressful, things go wrong. As the head of the agency, you plan to do a dawn raid and you go to court and you don't get a warrant. What do you do? You have to go back and plan again. Then who do you call? You call the prosecutors. Are you going to try it again administratively? Things will go wrong and you'll go through stress. But if you're around people who like what they're doing, who you like, who like you, and where there is a trust-based environment, things will get lighter. I think this personal aspect of it, of people liking to be together and trusting each other, makes a huge difference.

So you invested a significant part of your time in the consultation with your people.

Absolutely. I think these weekly meetings were very important and very productive. Sometimes they were forty-minute meetings and they sometimes were 2-hour meetings. We discussed every project in our pipeline. It was also an opportunity for people to tell others about their results and to exchange views and experiences. I thought it was useful as a learning experience for the younger members of the team, and it kept us together.

And as you mentioned, I think a major contribution that you made with your colleagues – you didn't do this alone, but you were such a key participant in this – is that it's striking that so many of your more junior people have stayed in the system and continued to contribute to it. That adds a vital element of memory and experience to make everybody more effective.

Yes, absolutely. This was something that, together with Barbara and Daniel – Arthur Badin was then the President of CADE – was a priority. Then Ana Paula Martinez came in and it became also a priority for us. We knew that without a government career, even if it were just a government career in antitrust, making sure that people stayed within CADE, that if we were going to leave, then things could go to where they were. So people had to stay. Heads of agencies come and go, but if you have a strong career where people are experienced and held different positions, you are on a good path to becoming a strong enforcer. We paid a lot of attention to that. So there was training, there was recruiting of government officials from the government career, making sure there was a budget, first, to be able to attract the case handlers. It's interesting – and this was very challenging – that in the budget of the SDE there was a specific budget for conferences, for dawn raids, for paper, but it didn't cover personnel. This came from the Ministry of Planning. So "Let's not spend, let's save money in, let's say, international trips and bring in more people" – you couldn't do that. The way around it was to make sure that whenever the government recruited for the government careers that part of these officials were assigned to the agency.

Were you able to do some recruitment directly from universities because at this time you're seeing the development of a strong academic infrastructure related to competition law? Did you have the ability to go into the universities, to graduate programs, and say, "Join us"?

We did that as well. It was a two-way process. One side was we got the government to allocate some of the officials who went into a government career and came and worked with us. Those who came and worked with us were trained. We engaged one of the Fundação Getúlio Vargas to provide training to those new case handlers. The way the government works, you have these officials who are part of the government career and others that you hire. But there are a limited number of these. These limited number of officials we brought, exactly as you suggest, were people from academia. Because they were excited about what the project was, they were willing to come to Brasilia for not as much as they would earn if they were working at an economic consultancy or at a law firm. But they were there because they wanted to be part of the project.

And it seems as though, as an outsider, you've had a lot of success in creating what we could call a "buzz" about being in the competition field, in the public enforcement mechanism, that part of your identity was an exciting place to work, a place you can make a difference. Am I right about that?

That is exactly how it felt. I'm very proud of that. I think part of it was because we enjoyed working with each other so much, too. Of course we thought the project was important. We were a great team together, all of us and the people who came and joined us. There was this buzz about the project and because we were excited being there together.

You've given us lots of good insights into how you work inside the house with your people, building a team, creating a sense of mission, and defining priorities. Part of your role as the head of an institution, when you ascend to the top leadership position, is you become the face of the institution for the outside, for the bar, for the media, for nongovernmental organizations, for international organizations. You are the force and the face of the institution outside. What was the adjustment like standing in the spotlight, on the stage now, where in a sense everything you do is observed and watched by all these communities? Was that much of a change?

Interesting. I think it wasn't so much for me because I was there at the agency, I had been at the agency for some years before that happened. So it was a natural process. I already knew the people. I had already participated in International Competition Network (ICN) projects, in Organisation for Economic Co-operation and Development (OECD) projects. I had participated in International Bar Association (IBA) and American Bar Association (ABA) conferences and projects. I knew my counterparts at other agencies, and foreign lawyers too. So when I was in the spotlight it didn't feel awkward. Because I knew all these people, I had several people who I considered friends of the agency to rely on. For me it was very lucky because I think it was an easy transition.

Did you have a way in dealing with outsiders to get at least informal feedback on how you were doing?

I did that a lot. If I were to give a tip to a successor, listen to friends of the agency. They will tell you if there is something that needs change. They will tell you if something that seems great from the inside perspective of the agency actually can backfire for one or another reason. Friends of the agency you have inside the agency of course as well as outside the agency in Brazil and outside the country. That was very, very helpful.

I'm imagining that inside the house, too, with your team you had a way to turn to people and say, "I want you to tell me what you think, even if you disagree with me. I have to make a decision at some point. That is my job, my responsibility." I gather that you tried to create a culture internally in which people, as you were saying before, told you what they thought.

Absolutely. I think that is something that you teach by example. If people know that you're frank with them and they're complimenting them when their work is great but you're saying, "Look, there is room for improvement here," or "Let's go back and if you need help, let me help you through with that," but you're also someone relaxed, fun to be around, they will behave the same with you. And if you ask, "What do you think?" they'll tell you, "Umm, don't go that way."

There is room for improvement.

Yes, exactly. If you are open to criticism and if you're open with the people from your team and what you think about them, and they feel you're their colleague not a dictator, then I think they'll come and tell you if you're wrong. That can be extremely useful. That can save you a lot of trouble.

So both from the inside and the outside you're listening, you're attempting to get a full range of views, again realizing that you are the person who ultimately has to make choices.

Yes. I think listening and telling people what you think is a critical part of reaching the right decision. You're not going to ask for anyone's advice; you know who to ask and about what to ask. But you have to be willing to listen and to do something about what you hear, because it's not just pretending you're listening; you have to actually have been listening to improve your decision-making process.

In speaking to the bar and speaking to news organizations, what aspects of the communication proved to be important? What do you have to tell them? What do you have to explain in formulating your plan for laying out your program? How did you go about doing that?

Part of what we were doing while we were in government involved change at some level, and change in an area that wasn't entirely known. So one key aspect of what we did was refer all these people who you mentioned, all the stakeholders and the media, to international best practices and tell them: "Look, we're not making this up. We may be being creative on how to approach this because Brazil has a unique system, so if we're going to do cartel enforcement, we need to cooperate with the prosecutors, but cartel enforcement is not no news." "We want to introduce a new law and we need a premerger review. This is not something we are coming up with. Look at the ICN Recommended Practices about that." So referring the stakeholders, including the media, to international best practices was an aspect of it.

And being willing to sit down and explain. I went to every conference that I was invited to and I was willing to answer questions. I sat down with the media several times – all the time actually. Also, we spent a good part of our resources on outreach initiatives to make sure that everyone understood what we were doing.

And then I gather that drawing upon international organizations and the work they were doing was helpful to you in building your program and carrying suggested changes forward.

We wouldn't have been able to do it without the ICN, the OECD, the more mature agencies; and with people like you and like Scott Hammond and John Fingleton, who were willing to come down and meet with the prosecutors, meet with our Congress officials, and refer all of them to the materials that were prepared by the international organizations. I think that it wouldn't have happened without that.

One of the most important things that you did – which I think again is part of the culture of the Brazilian system and an important practice that other jurisdictions should take into account – is that you were engaged in a continuing process of improvement, of reform. You got major upgrades to the system that you've been referring to before, including one that again you pointed to, a major restructuring of the framework itself, a redesign of the enforcement mechanism, the addition of a premerger notification-and-review process, criminalization of certain serious offenses. What in part is striking is that you got 3 distinct organizations to collaborate in a measure that involved some transfers of authority. My experience is that government agencies when confronted with the possibility of giving anything up fight more ferociously with each other than they do with the private sector enforcing the law. Yet, the group of you joined arms, formed common cause, and formulated a program that took a successful system and made it still better. How did that come about? Where did you get the capacity, the willingness, the commitment, for all of you to come up with the reform package?

An important element of it is trust, I think. When the discussion about changing the law started, I was still at the Ministry of Finance, SEAE, where the draft bill started to be prepared. The first discussions about the draft bill started at the Ministry of Finance with Claudio and Paulo and Kélvia Albuquerque. Then, I moved to the Ministry of Justice at the SDE. We became close. The 2 agencies were committed to that process. Then Arthur Badin, who was Chief of Staff and who took the lead in the great part of the discussion within the SDE, then became President of CADE. Elizabeth Farina, who was President before Badin, was also very committed to that process. I think the fact that we all perceived that as being critical, that, without that, Brazil would not become a lead enforcer. But it was also thanks to the fact that we were friends. We worked together on different projects and were exchanging views on what was important. Through that we became friends, and we're friends today.

Seeking improvements, where the aim of your work is to improve, to build institutions that will be effective and not just build monuments to oneself becomes – I would say part of the character of the Brazilian competition system is the result of this. That is a striking accomplishment. But the role of the development of the personal relationships, the fact that you had worked in 2 institutions, that you have the movement that you mentioned from one to another to another, meant that there was, I guess, a level of common understanding.

Yes, exactly, and I think that made it easier to have difficult conversations. But it also helped in a way where we shared the burden. It was a very long process, it took a decade to get it done, and it felt like Sisyphus – that you rolled the rock up the hill and then down it comes and then you pass it on to someone else, then the rock goes up again and when it comes down you pass it on to someone else, but you pass it on to people who believe that the same goal should be accomplished and whom you trust.

Is there something that happened that finally made it possible, an event or a series of events, to push the rock up over the top? This was a long growth that you referred to, a decade-long commitment. Did something happen that enabled you to cover that last distance to the summit and push the rock over?

I think the draft at some point incorporated views from as many stakeholders as possible. That was certainly critical. But I think it was the commitment of Fernando Furlan and Vinicius Carvalho that at the very last mile made it happen. I think that was very important. The way they approached the right people meant that they were willing to advocate for that. I think they deserve a lot of credit for that.

As an outsider, this kind of impression can be completely wrong, and you should tell me if I am. But I have the sense that part of what you built is a continuing bond between those who work still inside the public enforcement arena, those who are the alumni of that system on the outside and working in different capacities, that you have a connection, a shared sense of purpose – not necessarily agreement on everything to be done, with the wisdom of every matter chosen – but you have in Brazil a shared sense of purpose on both sides that contributes to the effectiveness of the system. Am I right about that?

I share your view about that. I think when you see how the Instituto Brasileiro de Estudos de Concorrência, Consumo e Comércio Internacional (IBRAC) [Brazilian Institute of Studies on Competition, Consumer Affairs and International Trade] has grown over the years.

Is IBRAC a professional society?

We describe it as our ABA Section of Antitrust Law, I think it's the equivalent. And how it has grown over the years and how much it contributes to the work of the Agency, I think it's because of that that people from the Agency are now at IBRAC and the people that worked with us when we were there, and the new people rely a lot on and trust in what IBRAC has to say.

Maybe a minute or so on challenges that lie ahead. That is, this has been over twenty years of a real success story, sustained improvement step by step, continuing ascent. How do you keep it going on that path? What's necessary to make that work?

At this point in Brazil CADE's challenges are not that different from other antitrust agencies around the world. I think you have to make sure that the good team stays there, and for that I think you need a good leader, and that good leader will be able to have a strategic plan in place, will be able to prioritize, will be able to continue to excite the team, and keep things going. The structure is already there. I think from now on it is more of the same, which does not mean that it's less important – actually, quite to the contrary, because it's not new anymore. But there is still a lot of work to be done.

The last question I would like to finish with is imagine that you're talking to a successor, someone who's going to come into a senior leadership position, if not the head of CADE itself, and they ask you: "What do you know now that I ought to know on my first day? Suggestions for me about coming in, getting off to a good start, and doing a good job? You're my personal trainer. Tell me what I ought to think about in doing that."

First of all – I think we've gone through this during this conversation – you listen to friends of the agency, inside and outside the agency, and also at international organizations and other foreign authorities. They will help you know when it's time to change and rethink, readjust your strategy. Second, one that is related to it, keep your eye on international best and recommended practices. You're not going to get it wrong if you pay attention to that. You can be creative here and there, but pay attention to that. It will help you with your credibility, too. Third – something that I heard once from John Fingleton – you're not going to be good at everything.

John Fingleton was the head of the Office of Fair Trading, one of the two UK authorities, and a leading figure in antitrust.

And a good friend. You're not going to be good at everything, so you need to have people around you who will excel at things that you don't excel at. For example, I think I am good at communicating ideas as if they were my own, I'm good with implementation. I'm not so creative myself, so I hired and I worked with people who are very creative and who share with me angles that I wouldn't be paying attention to if it weren't for them. So it's about building a team with people who will complement aspects that you don't have.

I think it points to an important consideration that may not be obvious. Part of coming into this role requires a level of self-assessment, to look at your own skills, to look at your own personality, and to develop a sense of what you're good at but what you don't do so well. Or you don't do it at all. Maybe you're a terrific economist but don't know so much of the law; maybe you're a brilliant lawyer but economics hasn't been your formal training; maybe you have great instincts about technical analysis but you aren't by nature the political scientist who understands everything about the country; maybe you've been a star in domestic matters but you don't know that much about things international. It seems as though a key starting point is to know yourself.

Oh yes, that is the key starting point. The second step I would say is to be willing to do homework. You have to be continuously committed to grow. Third – and we've been through that – ask questions.

And in doing your work make the best possible use of your strengths and build and rely on a team that can complement what you do. That is a good way for leaders to think about their work – and I think this is such a key lesson to close on – which is to know yourself in an honest way. You don't have to be a super human being or a perfect human being.

Well, I'm certainly not.

Not too many of us have gotten to that point. I'm sure maybe someday there will be one walking around, but I haven't met them yet. But to have that understanding of yourself – honest assessment; a true appreciation of what you do well and a knowledge of where you have to learn more, as you said, and the dedication to do that; and to surround yourself with a team that can support you by complementing what you do. In many ways that is where you begin that process.

I think these are all the elements. If there is a recipe – it's hard to have a recipe for that – I think it involves all those ingredients. It was a collective effort and I'm very proud of having been part of this great team. It's been a great ride.

Han Li Toh*

Competition and Consumer Commission of Singapore, Assistant Chief Executive (2009-2013) & Chief Executive (2013-2019)

You are the Chief Executive of the Competition Commission of Singapore (CCS) and a Commissioner on that body. Singapore has ascended in a breathtakingly short time to a position of striking influence and preeminence in the global scene. It's a relatively small jurisdiction in terms of population and land mass, a relatively small institution in a sea of larger institutions, larger countries, but if the measure of an agency is its ability to guide, lead others, and provide an example of how things should be done, not simply in the Association of Southeast Asian Nations (ASEAN) region in Asia but globally, Singapore stands out again and again. We're delighted to have you with us today. To begin, can you tell us a bit about the professional path that brought you to where you are in the Competition Commission today?

It has been 10 years. I've been at the agency since 2009. I'm from the Singapore Legal Service, which basically staffs all the legal jobs in the public sector in Singapore. I was seconded, and still am seconded, to the Competition and Consumer Commission of Singapore (CCCS) since 2009. I came in as the Assistant Chief Executive and looked after all the enforcement and the legal matters where I was in charge of the Legal and Enforcement Division. I was there for 4 years, where I also appeared as counsel for the Commission and argued the cases on appeal, so it actually set me up quite well. When I became Chief Executive in 2013, I had already been in the organization for 4 years. I knew the organization, the strengths and weaknesses, and I was able to ease into that role quite a bit easier. Of course, the big difference is that when you become the Chief Executive, you don't just look after the lawyers, you

---

* Interview conducted on 29 May 2019.

also have to look after the economists. I think, over time, you learn to be bilingual, meaning to say legal-speak and economic- speak. I had some formal training in economics. I did a master's degree in public policy at the Lee Kuan Yew School of Public Policy in Singapore, which also includes a stint at Harvard, and we had economics in that module. That was useful. I was a pure lawyer in Cambridge, United Kingdom. Economics only came a lot later, a year before I joined the agency. I took a year off. I was on a scholarship, and I spent a whole year just doing the master's. It was really a great year, just immersing yourself in academia and writing papers.

Of course, it's striking to see what a remarkable investment Singapore makes in human talent and capacity.

I think we always try to keep good people in the public sector. In fact, the accusation is that there are not enough good people in the private sector. Of course, one thing that we do is to try to pay competitively. We can never match the private sector, but we do track what the market rates are. Even if there's a discount, it shouldn't be too steep. That's an important element of retaining talent.

As you say, you can offer psychic compensation in the form of the opportunity to do good work, that makes a difference, but not to have the psychic compensation be 50 percent of the payment for doing the work.

I would assume that this experience you had in government before you came to the CCCS gave you a perspective on government and governance so that you came to the agency with a useful understanding of the public administration framework in the country.

I was pretty much a lawyer before I came in. I was a criminal prosecutor. I had done my fair share of rape and murder cases. I was a district judge. Actually, in the public policy space, I have to say I didn't have that much experience, so that was acquired on the job. I think legally, in terms of evaluation of evidence, evidence gathering, adjudication, that was a strong point. Singapore is an administrative system, like the European Union or the United Kingdom, so we take positions, we impose penalties. When the decisions are drafted, I think that is the easy part. How to make sure they're well drafted, that evidence is carefully considered – That was the strong legal background I came from. But I think the public policy side was really something I had to acquire. Of course, I did a formal degree, but that's just the theory, and I think the practice was acquired on the job, understanding what the sentiment is, how to work with the politicians. That was something new.

How important is that dimension of political awareness? We are told again and again that an agency should be autonomous in the sense that it takes technical decisions on how to use its authority without having an elected official say, "Punish my enemies; reward my friends." But at the same time, as I think you're suggesting, you can't be completely divorced from the larger environment in which national policy, national sentiment, emerges. How important is that to the head of an agency to have that awareness?

I think the first thing is that decisions have to be taken on a principled basis. All our decisions are reasoned, written and published, so that anybody can read and know and understand how we arrive at decisions, and that they're not based on nonlegal and noneconomic considerations. But at the same time, you need to work with the government to understand the priorities of the day in terms of prioritization because you can't take on every kind of case. You need to understand what the concerns of the government are today. So, although we're independent in terms of decision making, we still need to work with the government.

Can you say a bit about the kinds of relationships you develop with government institutions outside your own walls? How, as the Chief Executive, but also with your entire team, do you go about building those relationships that give you that sense of public priorities and, more broadly, public sentiment about what policy should be?

First, we have an advisory role. We advise government agencies on the impact of government policies on the marketplace. It's non-binding, but I think it's useful, and over the years we see more and more agencies coming to us. I think Singapore is always very conscious of the fact that we don't want to be seen to have restrictive policies on the market. We always promote ourselves as an open economy. So we have the competition policy framework and mindset.

We had a policy before we had the law. First, that helps us to build relationships with the government agencies. We have a platform of a committee of practice for economic regulators. We get together and talk about emerging issues. Many times cases are cross-cutting. For example, in airline joint venture cases you have to work with the aviation regulator.

A crucial sector for the success of Singapore.

Yes, that's right. Allegedly the best airport in the world, right? [Laughter] You also need to understand how airline joint ventures improve welfare and benefit consumers as well and benefit Singapore as a whole. So that was one aspect. The other aspect is in transport. We all know about ride hailing, Uber and Lyft. We had a case involving Uber merging with the local ride-hailing company called Grab. We had to work with the transport regulator very closely. It was actually unregulated. They regulated taxis, but they didn't know how to regulate ride hailing. So we kind of became the regulator for ride hailing. The government has decided that they're going to regulate ride hailing from next year onwards. But, in a way, what we have done has become like an experiment for them. I think a lot of the lessons learned are useful to the transport regulator. Every time we issued a media release on the Grab/Uber case, the transport regulator would come out and affirm it because we had discussed this beforehand, and I think that is important.

Was that a relationship that emerged in a fairly smooth way – that is, in part, because of the shared understanding of how important the service sector is, the openness of the economy? Anything you can do to make Singapore seem to be an exciting, enjoyable place to visit, including the local transportation framework? Is that something they saw right away and said, "These are not adversaries, but these are useful partners in making policy"?

We broadly agree on the direction, but of course the devil's in the details. For example, I think you can understand the transport regulator may be uncomfortable with dynamic pricing because at a peak period the fares –

It's great when it goes down.

That's right, that's right. So they may want to have a bit more input on the pricing and all that. At the edges, there are some differences, but I think broadly they say, "We need to encourage this new form of transportation. It's a great augmentation to taxi services. Commuters like it." They have done public surveys that actually people preferred this to taxis until the merger happened, and then people preferred taxis because prices went up. But it was an important new form of transportation, which I think the regulator was keen to promote at the broad principle level, and of course, as I said, in the details there can be some differences.

How much did the development of that and other relationships you have with public agency departments depend on your investment of your time in building relationships with your counterparts in these institutions?

I think the advisory role was good because you end up being like a repeat customer. We have a very close working relationship with the Central Bank because we're seeing in the financial sector, which in Singapore is quite important sector. We're looking at things like payment wallets, or the insurance industry, which frankly can be modernized; I think it's still quite traditional. So, yes, I think we worked on quite a few things together beforehand, so when it comes to the cases, that helps a lot.

Tell me about how important it is for you to make clear to your team inside and to outside audiences what your priorities are, what your plans are. How significant is that as an element of your responsibility and its impact on how well the institution performs?

We have a 5-year strategic plan where we look at the 5-year horizon. In order to derive that plan you need to do scenario planning. I think many people are familiar with the scenario planning methodology. It was devised by Shell, the global energy company, where you look at driving forces and all that. And you need to do that every 5 years. We're just ending a cycle. We're going to start again. The 5-year cycle informs us about what we want and need to look for in the medium term. But every year we have a work plan. The work plan feeds into the 5-year cycle, but it looks more immediately at what are the issues of the day. Digital has been a big thing for a number of years, and I think many agencies look at that, so that has been quite a large bit of our work.

How do you do that inside? How is the plan built?

For the 5-year plan, there is a discussion with all the stakeholders, getting feedback, and then we build a plan [...] It's not openly published, but we just consult all the key stakeholders, and then we derive our 5-year plan.

In turn, those aims are made clear to your whole team inside the agency.

Yes. Then, after that, every year we have the work plan. It will be more detailed, but it could also have new elements, like for example, consumer protection, which was a new role we took on last year which wouldn't have been in the previous 5-year plan because, at that time, we didn't have consumer protection. So, some of the new areas of consumer protection have come up, and that's going to inform us about the work plan for each year. For some issues I have a green light, like digital, but we do look from year to year at what are the things we need to add or amend along the way.

I wanted to ask about the transition that took place as you ascended to the leadership position inside the Commission. Was there a transition when you became the Chief Executive? In a number of basic ways, you become a face of the institution. You are more in the spotlight and onstage all the time. Is that an adjustment?

Let me talk about internal adjustment first. The Chief Executive is also a Commissioner, so you need to manage the discussions at the Commission level as a Commissioner. By the time the matter comes up to the Commission it would have been curated by me, so, in a way, it kind of represents the management position as well. But, of course, I am only one of ten Commissioners, so again I need to manage the discussions. If the other Commissioners have issues, we'll need to stick it back onboard and maybe do further work. That's the first thing you need to manage.

The second is, as the head of the agency, you need to manage the whole agency together with the parent ministry. I should add that the parent ministry doesn't get involved in the decision making because that's the Commission's job, but they get involved in funding. So there's the odd administrative thing about me getting enough budget and making sure our lease is extended, among other things. Last year, when we took over some new consumer protection officers, there was the issue about integrating them into the system, creating more space, and renovation.

And of course, there are external issues, which you touched upon. Not just outside government but within government, there could be an issue that comes up, and you have to represent the agency's view and have a dialogue at a high level. And I think externally, when there's a media conference, which I would generally chair, you have to explain to the journalists the position of the case. Or, if it's a regional international meeting, then yes, again. I think it is important to build up the team, and when it's possible, I would sometimes send some of my deputies or directors to represent the agency, or even the staff. It has to be collective; it can't just be one person, otherwise you'll be flat-out all the time. That is important.

The team gives you a process for having a strong internal debate about individual matters. I assume that's an important method of guidance for you.

Yes. The cases are discussed at the management level with my management team, the directors and assistant chief executives, before they go up to the

Commission. So a single case is looked at by many eyes. I know some agencies delegate. We don't generally do that because we want collective wisdom on methods, and try to incorporate as many views as possible in the final product.

How do you promote a debate that is constructive in the sense that it does involve identifying all potential weaknesses, other points of view, but is also trusted as being for the good of the agency so that individual case handlers, and others, don't feel they're under assault, but they know that the agency has to establish high standards, there are appeals, you have to justify what you do in front of a capable audience? How do you build that culture?

I think you touched on it, because the fact that the matter can be appealed means that you need to be strong on the principles and on the evidence. If it was policymaking, it could be slightly different because that is a different consideration. The fact that matters are appealed means we would always test the robustness of the findings, of the assumptions, of the evidence. Of course, there can be discussions about approaches. Not everything is quantitative. There can be qualitative considerations. But we do try to accommodate all views as far as possible.

Of course, you are a commission. You have a college. Some agencies have a single administrator who makes all decisions. Others have this collective decision-making process. What goes into, in many ways, when you're the Chief Executive of a Board? What is different about it? What are the special considerations that go with being a member of the college and having this decision-making process?

Actually, we always try to go unanimous. There are some agencies that have dissenters, but that's not how we operate. We always try to debate a case. Actually, sometimes it can have various iterations and take several meetings before we agree on a position, but we always try to accommodate all views. We have never had a dissent. Internally, there can be fierce debate –

In theory, could a member of the Board publish a dissent?

Yes, in theory he could. Under the Act a majority would be sufficient. But in practice it hasn't happened. We have had strong views; we do try to take into account the views, and if needed we adjust arguments in the case to take them into account. So, it has to be sorted out internally with fierce debate, but I think at the end of the day the product should be more robust that way.

As the Chief Executive or as a member of the Board, do you play the dual role?

I have a Chairman, so he manages the college of Commissioners. But I'm always sitting by his side and trying to balance off and explain to him why the management and the team have taken a position, and then, we try to see how we can accommodate the Commissioners' views on this.

What goes into that process? That is: you have the Board, you have a number of people, they are capable individuals, they are thoughtful. As the Chief Executive, as a contributor of the view of the staff, as the conduit for that, but also as a colleague, how do you go about working with the Board in a way that brings these two roles together, decision maker and Chief Executive? How do you perform that in a way that increases the confidence of the Board that we're on a good path?

I think the Commission wants assurance that evidence is strong, that we have a good case on appeal. And one thing we do, for complex cases, is always have an external opinion. We could get an opinion from a Queen's Counsel, because our law is based on the UK law. We have a good working relationship with the Queen's Counsel. In fact, I met some of them at the American Bar Association. We send our lawyers for attachment in these chambers. That has been going on for a number of years. So that's one.

For the economic side, we have a good relationship with the economic consultancies. We also send our economists for attachment in these consultancies. We would ask for a report on the case, and I think that would give some assurance to the Commission that there's another set of eyes looking at this. Otherwise, it's just talking to each other all the time, and I think they do want to see the external view, the external consultant's view, the counsel's view or the economist's view, and that is quite important.

Very interesting to bring in this other perspective as a quality control mechanism to give you confidence to do this. Do you meet with the Commissioners individually, too, as the Chief Executive? Do you have a periodic meeting where you say: "In my capacity as Chief Executive, this is what we're doing and I would like to hear your thoughts"? Is that part of your process?

Not really. We meet every 2 months. They complain it's often enough. [Laughter] So, it's not as if you don't see them. You see them 6 times a year, and I think that's really quite enough. For mergers we have a slightly different process. We delegate it to 3 Commissioners rather than the full 9 or 10, and if the 3 of them agree that you can cure at what we call Phase 1, it doesn't go before the full Commission. If they can't issue a green light, then it goes before the full Commission.

Is this a dedicated group of 3, or does that –

It's random. It's equal misery. If you've done your turn the last time, somebody else will look at it. I never sit on these 3 because, as I said, I represent the management view. I don't want to influence. There will be 3 other Commissioners and not myself.

Would you say that, when you look at your whole agency – you're not a huge agency – in your capacity as Chief Executive, you get to know everyone pretty well?

We're all on one floor, yes. [Laughter] We are just a few footsteps away.

How much of your time do you spend in a week doing what might be called "walking the halls," going through the corridors, just dropping in, saying, "I just want to see how you're doing; I want to know how it's going"? Is that part of your routine?

The concept is quite open plan, so it's easy to just meet people. Of course, we have a few platforms. I have a monthly staff meeting with all the staff where we share various HR methods or case updates. So it is really quite easy. We have an open-door policy, they can just walk in anytime to talk to me about things. Sometimes, we would schedule a case handlers' meeting with a case team to discuss a case if there are some issues. It's really quite flexible and open.

So you don't have the difficulties that arise in so many agencies of having an immediate effective communication of policy developments, of your aims?

Yes. That is one of the upsides of being small. Of course, there are the downsides of being small, but this is the upside. But we could always have more manpower.

You could always have more people, especially as this mandate expands.

Yes, exactly.

Was the addition of the consumer dimension to the mandate accompanied by a corresponding increase in resources?

We had about a grand total of 11 head counts. [Laughter]

Congratulations. Don't spend it all in one place.

It has just been exactly 1 year since we have taken on consumer cases. It's always volume, and you need to be clear about what you want to take on and prioritize. That is key.

From the leadership role, expanding the mandate, how do you decide – if I give you another 500,000 Singapore dollars – whether to spend them on a digital market study or on an expanded program to identify fraud in e-commerce transactions? How do you decide where that pool of money is going to have the most benefit for you?

We have a case decision matrix, which I guess other agencies call prioritization principles. It's really like an intersection of a Venn diagram where you look at things like public interest, economic impact, and you look at the strength of the case. In consumer, one of the things certainly is the conduct widespread: is the conduct egregious? If it's a single, one-time infraction, you may not want to take action. We have a nongovernmental organization (NGO) which does the mediation role. They have a call center. They are quite good at getting refunds and so on. You might just be happy to let it, you know. When the conduct is egregious, repeated, preying on vulnerable consumers, then we have to take action. So then, there is a kind of prioritization framework.

One of the distinctive features of your tenure and your colleagues has been engagement with authorities outside of your own boundaries. How significant is that engagement as a part of your leadership responsibility, and how is that seen by Singaporeans, by public officials, as being related to the interests of Singapore itself?

I think the first thing is Singapore as a whole says that we want to learn international best practice – and that is not just for us but for any agency – find out what's going on in the world, take the best bits, and bring it back. I think that has always been our policy, our practice. So no different. We learn from the established agencies what are the best practices. An interesting thing about competition is that you work on the same cases sometimes. Last year we blocked a merger involving marine products and the U.S. FTC also blocked the merger. Funnily enough, we took out the statement of objection. They took out the preliminary injunction. When the judge in the United States granted the injunction the case was withdrawn. So we're thankful to our U.S. counterparts for finishing off the job. [Laughter] So, because of the common cases and common themes it's critical. That's one. Second, best practices.

Then, I think regionally we are very committed to the ASEAN Southeast Asian grouping. We are currently the Chair and are going to hand over to Malaysia shortly. There have been a lot of projects in terms of capacity building. One of the projects was to ensure all 10 countries have competition law. We are 9 out of 10 now, less Cambodia.

A lot of partners are helping us with capacity building, building up the agencies. We have the Germans, the Japanese, Australians, New Zealanders, Canada, the European Union – they have all invested efforts in helping us build up the region, as well as the Organisation for Economic Cooperation and Development (OECD). We're very grateful for those partnerships.

Does it put a bit of a strain on the small agency that you are to have, as I sense many countries have done, a number of countries in the region saying: "You've had a great deal of success. You have a great team. Can we come and visit? Can we have someone spend some time with us?" You're seen as a great resource, and the great resource attracts a good deal of interest. It would seem to me that it's an additional – not drain in a bad sense – demand on your resources and your time.

We are always welcoming people to visit us. We have taken attachment officers from the region, but also from developed agencies like the Australian Competition and Consumer Commission (ACCC), who just like to come to Southeast Asia to spend some time. [Laughter]

Who wouldn't want to be in Singapore especially if they're in Melbourne during their winter? "Okay, let's go to Singapore."

It's really just a subject of physical space, where my HR people tell me, "Look, there are no more tables or chairs." But that's really the only limitation. Otherwise, of course, if we can host, we host. And we do send people as well to not just established agencies. Grace has gone to the Indonesian Competition Authority (KPPU) to learn about communications. So it's a two-way street.

I have a last question to pose to you, and this is the omnibus question that involves giving advice to a potential successor, someone who's going to be the new Chief Executive, for example. Maybe they haven't had the experience that you have of having been inside the Authority, and you reflect on a decade of experience. What do you tell me about what I should be thinking of coming in? What can I do in the short term or the longer term to be an effective Chief Executive, senior official in the agency? What's your advice?

I'm going to assume you already have the technical stuff; otherwise you wouldn't be appointed as my successor. So I'm going to assume you already have the technical ability.

But imagine that, like yourself, I've been a lawyer my whole life; or, surprisingly, I'm an economist, and that's what I've done.

Sure. But even then, I would assume you have the capability to build it up quite quickly, so that one is less of an issue. I suppose the key to all this is stakeholder management. When I say "stakeholder", I'm not just talking about the staff. I'm talking about the parent ministry and the politicians, the lawyers and economists outside, the businesses, and the consumers. How do you manage all these groups of people effectively? You have to invest time. That's really, I think, what the Chief Executive has to do […] You are the face. So they want to know what the position is or what is happening, and you have to be ready to present the agency position. I think that is the key.

I gather that suggests that a very nice-to-have – maybe must-have – element in the appointee's background is that they have some understanding of that larger ecology in which they'll be operating.

The policymaking process, the political process, how business is done, absolutely […] I guess you have to acquire it on the job along the way because it may not be something you immediately have. I certainly, in the last 6 years, have picked up a lot of things along the way. Good lessons learned.

I assume also you build an inner management team that complements your abilities and your strengths. You supplement by bringing in other dimensions.

Yes. Because I think, for technical things, you have your staff, you have your case officers, and they can always update you on the case details. But for some of the other issues, you need to be more sensitized in how to deal with those.

If you look at the whole experience, what might be the biggest surprise you found in doing the job, the aspect of it that you didn't anticipate so much at the front end but that turns out to be significant?

I have practiced many areas of law. I think for competition/antitrust there really is a lot of commonality around the world in terms of some of the issues, a lot more than criminal, which is very domestic. That has really been a pleasant surprise; that you can come to the American Bar Association and listen to some ideas, bring them back and implement them. You would get a lot less of that in other areas of the law, so I think that has really been a surprise, rewarding and nice.

The Institute of Competition Law

The Institute of Competition Law is a publishing company, founded in 2004 by Dr. Nicolas Charbit, based in Paris, London and New York. The Institute cultivates scholarship and discussion about antitrust issues though publications and conferences. Each publication and event is supervised by editorial boards and scientific or steering committees to ensure independence, objectivity, and academic rigor. Thanks to this management, the Institute has become one of the few think tanks in Europe to have significant influence on antitrust policies.

Aim

The Institute focuses government, business and academic attention on a broad range of subjects which concern competition laws, regulations and related economics.

Boards

To maintain its unique focus, the Institute relies upon highly distinguished editors, all leading experts in national or international antitrust: Bill Kovacic, Mario Monti, Eleanor Fox, Laurence Idot, Frédéric Jenny, Ioannis Lianos, Richard Whish, etc.

Authors

4,000 authors, from 85 jurisdictions.

Partners

- Universities: University College London, King's College London, Queen Mary University, Paris Sorbonne Panthéon-Assas, etc.
- Law firms: Allen & Overy, Cleary Gottlieb Steen & Hamilton, Baker McKenzie, Hogan Lovells, Jones Day, Norton Rose Fulbright, Skadden Arps, White & Case, etc.

Events

Brussels, Dusseldorf, Hong Kong, London, Milan, New York, Paris, Singapore, Warsaw and Washington, DC.

Online version

Concurrences website provides all articles published since its inception.

Publications

The Institute publishes Concurrences Review, a print and online quarterly peer-reviewed journal dedicated to EU and national competitions laws. e-Competitions is a bi-monthly antitrust news bulletin covering 85 countries. The e-Competitions database contains over 23,000 case summaries from 4,000 authors.

www.ingramcontent.com/pod-product-compliance
Lightning Source LLC
Chambersburg PA
CBHW071413230926
51846CB00001B/77
9781954750043